INSIGHT GUIDES

The world's largest collection of visual travel guides

TURKISH COAST

Edited by Metin Demirsar

Editorial Director: Brian Bell

APA PUBLICATIONS

Part of the Langenscheidt Publishing Group

The authors of this book examine Aegean and Mediterranean Turkey from a contemporary angle rather than from a nostalgic-historical perspective that most travel books about Turkey are based on. The emphasis is on the modern- day Turkish Coast and its people.

We would like to introduce you to the principal contributors of this book: **Alev Alatlı** wrote many chapters in the history section and co-authored the feature about Turkish people. Alatlı was also one of the main contributors to *Insight City Guide: Istanbul*. Alatlı has won many literary and journalistic awards. In 1987, the Turkish Writers Association named her novelist and short story writer of the year.

Demirsar

Project editor **Metin Demirsar** is a Turkish journalist whose articles have appeared in many foreign newspapers and magazines, including *The Wall Street Journal*. Demirsar also contributed to, and later revised and updated, both *Insight Guide: Turkey* and *Insight City Guide: Istanbul*. He also wrote *Personal Guide to The Turquoise Coast*. Demirsar has an MA from the Graduate School of Journalism of the University of Southern California. His wife, **Tülay Demirsar**, acted as his secretary during the project, completed the index, and helped compile the travel tips and put the text of this book on computer.

A husband-wife team, **William A. Edmonds** and **Anna G. Edmonds**, wrote several sections. The Edmonds are American missionaries who have lived in Turkey for 35 years. William Edmonds, director of the Redhouse Press, an English language publishing house in Istanbul which produces dic-

W. Edmonds

A. Edmonds

tionaries and other special topic books, also wrote an article on Turkish carpets. Anna Edmonds, a Redhouse Press writer and editor, wrote parts of the history section and several key features. She is the co-author of *Biblical Sites in Turkey*. **Sevâ Ülman Erten**, an Ankara-based correspondent for *United Press International*, contributed the features about holiday villages and Yasar Kemal, Turkey's best known novelist. Erten is a Turkish national.

Jay Courtney Fikes, an American anthropologist, wrote the chapter on Ionia with related features about Izmir and Ephesus. He is author of *Step Inside the Sacred Circle*, a collection of American Indian allegorical animal stories. Fikes is married to a Turk and has taught at Marmara University in Istanbul. He works in Washington D.C. as an advocate for American Indians.

Laura Le Cornu, and **Juliette Rossant** contributed several features. Le Cornu and Rossant are reporters for Compass News Features. Both are Americans. They also sub-edited *Pnal Guide to The Turquoise Coast*. Le Cornu has a BA in political science from Goucer College in Baltimore, Maryland. Rossant has a BA in classical archaeology from Dartmouth College and an MA in creative writing from the Johns Hopkins University.

British citizens **Robert Love** and **Brenda Wild**, a husband-wife team, joined project editor Demirsar to write the feature on the 1915 military Gallipoli campaign. Love and Wild both teach physics at Istanbul's Vehbi Koç High School.

Ara Güler, one of the world's great living photojournalists, provided many of the pictures in this book. Güler is

Erten

Fikes

Le Cornu

Rossant

Güler

Güner

correspondent of *Time-Life Books, Magnum Photos* and *Stern Magazine.* Güler's discovery and stunning photography of Aphrodisias in the 1950s has made the ancient Roman city an important destination and paved the way for excavations at the site. Güler's photography also appeared in *Insight Guide: Pakistan* and *Personal Guide to The Turquoise Coast.*

Semsi Güner, the chief photographer of this book, is no newcomer to Apa. His superb photography has also appeared in all three previous Apa titles dealing with Turkey – *Insight Guide: Turkey, Insight City Guide: Istanbul*; and *Personal Guide to The Turquoise Coast.* A former opera baritone and graphic arts designer, Güner has been taking pictures of Turkey and the world for the media for 30 years.

The article on the Blue Voyage was written by **Galip Isen**, who spends his summers taking well-to-do tourists on cruises along the Greek islands and Turkish Aegean and Mediterranean coasts aboard his yacht.

Selma Manizade, a graphic arts designer, compiled the travel tips at the back of the book. Manizade, a Turk who has lived most of her life in the United States, works for Türkiye Emlak Bankası, a bank.

Aliza Marcus and **Yuri Feher** collaborated to write the section about Adana and the East. Marcus, an American freelance journalist who works for *Turquoise* magazine in New York, also wrote the article on the late industrialist Hacı Ömer Sabancı. Marcus, who contributed to *The Book of World City Rankings*, is a graduate of Columbia University's School of Journalism.

Hungarian-born Feher is in the process getting a PhD at New York University in Anthropology.

Enis Özbank, who contributed many pictures to this book, is a *Sipa Press* photojournalist who has had his work featured in *Time Magazine, Newsweek, Paris Match* and *Epocha.* **Patricia Roberts**, a freelance journalist and writer who lives in Paris, wrote the section on Rough and Smooth Cilicia and the features on Turkey's olive oil industry and water sports.

Nergis Yazgan and **Gernant Magnin** teamed up to write about wildlife and environmental issues of the Turkish Coast. Yazgan is Turkey's leading wildlife conservationist. Magnin is a project officer with the International Council for Bird Preservation (ICBP), a Cambridge UK-based ornithological society. His publications for ICBP include: *Bird Killing in Malta; An Account of Illegal Bird Catching in Cyprus during 1987*; and *Falconry and Hunting in Turkey.*

The project editor also wants to thank Kusadası-based **Demir Ünsal**, director of Vmay Tours Travel Agency, for giving him a personal tour of the ancient sites on the Menderes (Maeander) River Valley. He is also grateful to **Artun Altıparmak**, publisher of Istanbul's *ABC Kitabevi A.S.,* without whose constant encouragement and generous support throughout this book could not have possibly been conceived, started and finished.

Material for this edition was organised in Apa's London office by update editor **Dorothy Stannard**. The book was updated by **Canan Silay**, a freelance journalist living in Istanbul who regularly contributes to Insight Guides and other publications on Turkey.

Roberts

CONTENTS

Maps

TRAVEL TIPS

TRAVELLERS' DELIGHT

Stretching from the nation's border with Greece to its frontier with Syria, the Turkish Coast is a coastal strip that has thousands of miles of unspoiled sandy beaches and coves fringed by pine forests, hundreds of pristine fishing villages and market towns, and a wealth of ancient ruins found nowhere else in the world.

The ruins of fabled cities like Troy, Pergamum, Ephesus, Halicarnassus, Xanthus, Side and Karatepe are just a few of the sites of antiquity that dot the coast, waiting to be explored by travellers.

Since the days of Antony and Cleopatra, the southwest corner of Turkey, known today as the Turquoise Coast, has been a playground for yachtsmen cruising to the deserted coves of the Gulf of Gökova, Hisarönü and Sömbeki bays and the Gulf of Fethiye. The so-called Blue Voyage into one of these bays is the ultimate form of relaxation that the harried westerner should experience.

The Turkish Coast begins in Thracian (European) Turkey at the town of Enez, near the Greek border, and the wide Bay of Saros, which has some of the finest beaches of Turkey. It continues south to the desolate Gallipoli Peninsula, scene of a fierce World War I military campaign, and the Dardanelles, the strategic strait where the legendary Leander drowned while swimming to his lover, the Virgin Priestess Hero. Gökçeada, Turkey's largest island, and Bozcaada, an island known for its tasty wines, guard the Aegean mouth of the Dardanelles.

The major part of the Turkish Coast lies in Asia across the Dardanelles. The Asian part of the Turkish Coast begins at the town of Çanakkale and covers a bulging peninsula that in ancient times was known as the Troad. The ruins of Troy, Assos and Alexandria Troas dominate this peninsula. Further south is the Gulf of Edremit, one of Turkey's most picturesque bays. The Gulf is famed for its long stretches of beaches and resort towns of Edremit, Burhaniye and Ayvalık, facing the Greek island of Lesbos. Pergamum, one of the magnificent sites of antiquity, is just south of the area near the modern town of Bergama. The region from the Gulf of Edremit to Izmir, Turkey's third largest city and second biggest port, was known in the past as the Aeolian Coast.

The Izmir area was known as Ionia in the past. The ruins of more than 50 Ionian cities are within a two-hour-drive from Izmir. Ephesus, a Hellenistic city just south of Izmir, is one of the world's most frequented ancient sites.

Surrounded by mountains, the area is rich in wildlife and unusual bird species – a delight to nature lovers. More species of fauna and flora can be seen on the Turkish Coast than in most regions of Continental Europe. It is one of the few areas in the Mediterranean where giant marine turtles wade ashore to lay their eggs, or endangered monk seals frolic on offshore islands.

Preceding pages: Columns of Perge; boat on the lake at Antalya; bejeweled Turkish women; strolling along the beach; the ruins of Aphrodisias; frieze from the Myra theater; windsurfing at Gümbet. Left, the catch of the day.

Old Stone Age 600,000–7000 BC: Cave-dwellings at Karain.

Neolithic Period 7000–5500 BC: First settlement at Hacılar, earliest agriculture; Çatal Höyük, first cultural centre.

Calcholithic Period 5500–3000 BC: Development of Hacılar and Çatal Höyük; new settlements at Canhasan, Beycesultan and Aphrodisias.

The Bronze Age 3000–800 BC

3000–1900 BC: Troy I through Troy IV.

2000–1200 BC: Hittites establish their capital at Hattusa and extend rule over central and western Anatolia; first written history.

1900–1260 BC: Troy V through Troy VII.

circa 1260 BC: Fall of Troy.

circa 1100–1000 BC: Aeolian and Ionian Greek migrants establish settlements along the Aegean Coast.

circa 900 BC: Rise of the Carians, Lycians and Phrygians.

circa 800 BC: Foundation of the Panionic League; rise of Ionian/Aeolian Greek culture in Western Anatolia.

The Dark Ages 700–480 BC

circa 700 BC: Birth of Homer in Smyrna (Izmir); rise of the Lydians.

667 BC: The city of Byzantium (now Istanbul) is founded.

561–546 BC: Reign of King Croesus of Lydia.

546 BC: King Cyrus of Persia defeats Croesus, beginning Persian domination of western Anatolia.

499 BC: Ionian cities revolt against Persian rule. The rebellion is crushed.

490 BC: First Persian invasion of Greece led by Darius defeated at the Plains of Marathon.

circa 484 BC: Herodotus is born in Halicarnassus.

480 BC: Second Persian invasion of Greece by Xerxes ends in defeat at Salamis (480) and Plataea (479).

The Classical Period 479–323 BC

405 BC: Sparta destroys Athenian Navy in Battle of Aegospotami on the Dardanelles.

386 BC: Persia subjugates Ionia again.

334 BC: Alexander the Great invades western Anatolia.

The Hellenistic Period 323–131 BC

323–188 BC: Wars between Alexander's successors.

261–241 BC: Eumenes I reigns in Pergamum.

230 BC: Alliance between Rome and Pergamum; Attalus I defeats the Gauls invading Anatolia.

133 BC: Attalus III bequeaths his kingdom to Rome.

The Roman Period 130 BC–AD 331

88 BC: Mithridates, king of the Pontus, revolts against Romans.

64 BC: Romans win war with Mithridates, securing most of Asia Minor.

41–40 BC: Antony summons Cleopatra to Tarsus and begins love affair.

31 BC: Antony is defeated at the battle of Actium. Antony and Cleopatra commit suicide in Egypt (30 BC).

AD 44–56: St. Paul journeys through Anatolia to spread the teachings of Jesus; followers of Jesus are called Christians for the first time in Antioch.

AD 313: Christianity becomes state religion of the Roman Empire.

The Byzantine Period AD 330–1453

330: Constantine establishes Constantinople as new capital of Roman Empire.

527–565: Reign of Justinian; period of greatest Byzantine power and influence.

677–718: Arab armies sweep across southern and western Anatolia, but fail to conquer Constantinople.

1071: Seljuk Turks defeat Byzantines at the Battle of Manzikert and overrun most of Anatolia.

1071–1238: Seljuks rule Anatolia from Konya; the Sultanate of Rum.

1096: First Crusade of Latin armies invade western and southern Anatolia on their way to Jerusalem.

1204: Latin armies of the Fourth Crusade sack Constantinople.

1240: Ottoman Turks descend on western Anatolia as vassals of the Seljuk Dynasty.

1261: Michael VIII Pelaeologos recaptures Constantinople and restores the Byzantine Empire.

1354: Ottoman armies, led by Ghazi Süleyman Pasha, cross the Dardanelles into Europe.

1402: Mongolian ruler Tamerlane defeats Ottomans under Beyazıt I, setting back Ottoman expansion by a generation.

1453: The Ottomans under Mehmet II capture Constantinople, renaming it Istanbul; the Ottoman capital is established there.

The Ottoman Period 1453–1922

1459–1517: The Ottomans conquer Serbia, Greece, Syria and Egypt. Selim I becomes Caliph (AD 1517).

1520–1566: Reign of Süleyman the Magnificent. Height of Ottoman power; Ottomans conquer Rhodes, Baghdad, Hungary and Libya; the Mediterranean is turned into a Turkish lake.

1571: Turks conquer Cyprus. First Ottoman defeat in the naval Battle of Lepanto by Christian forces.

1669: Crete falls to the Ottomans.

1699: Austria and her allies sign the Treaty of Carlowitz, the first Ottoman admission of defeat; Ottomans lose many central European territories.

1854–1856: Crimean War ends in Russian defeat.

1876–1909: Reign of Abdülhamit II.

1878: Turco-Russian wars ends in Ottoman defeat; Serbia, Montenegro, Bosnia, Bulgaria and Rumania become independent; British govern Cyprus.

1909: Abdülhamit deposed and exiled; Young Turks take power.

1911–1913: Balkan Wars; Turks lose Macedonia and a section of Thrace.

1914: Turkey joins World War I as ally of Germany. Russia, France and Britain declare war on Turkey.

1915: The Turkish forces, led by Mustafa Kemal, repel allied landings at Gallipoli.

1918: Turks are driven out of Palestine and Syria by British forces. Turks surrender to the Allied Powers.

1919: Italian forces occupy Antalya and southwest Turkey. French troops seize Adana and southeast Turkey. The Greek army occupies Izmir and invades western Anatolia.

1919–1922: Turkish War of Independence. Greeks are defeated by the Turks and leave Anatolia.

The Republican Period: from 1923

1923: The Treaty of Lausanne establishes the sovereignty of modern Turkey, determines borders, and organizes the exchange of minorities between Greece and Turkey; Turkish Republic is declared; the Sultanate and the Caliphate are abolished; Mustafa Kemal Atatürk becomes first President.

1925–1938: Westernizing economic and social reforms introduced by Atatürk include abolition of the *fez*, adoption of the western calendar, introduction of the Latin alphabet and women's rights.

1946: Turkey becomes charter member of the United Nations; opposition parties founded. First general elections called.

1952: Turkey becomes full member of NATO.

1960: Cyprus becomes independent state; Military coup in Turkey.

1961: Former Prime Minister Adnan Menderes is condemned to death.

1971: Military topples government of Prime Minister Süleyman Demirel.

1980: Military intervention led by Chief of Staff General Kenan Evren. Evren becomes head of state.

1983: President Evren names Turgut Özal as Prime Minister after General Election.

1989: Turgut Özal is elected President.

1993: Özal dies and Süleyman Demirel becomes President. Turkey's first female Prime Minister, Tansu Çiller of the True Path Party (DYP) takes office.

1996: The islamic Welfare Party (Refah) and DYP form coalition government, with Necmettin Erbakan as Prime Minister and Tansu Çiller as Deputy Prime Minister.

The story of human life in Anatolia is one of peoples who succeeded each other in irregular procession across the land. It is a story of varied and increasingly complicated levels of existence with each group building upon the houses and on the ideas of the previous inhabitants. People added 19 yards (17 meters) to the hill of Troy in the 3,000 years they occupied it. Users of stone tools were followed by users of both stone and metal; metal workers learned to mint standardized coins, the use of which improved their business, and which continues to affect today's economy. Often the groups interacted with civilizations some distance away. The Miletian astronomer Thales was able to predict the eclipse of the sun in 585 BC because he knew about an 18-year periodicity which Babylonian astronomers had observed about eclipses.

lution, meant the difference between savage subsistence and the beginnings of human control of the environment.

More accurately, an important dividing line in the description of human development can be drawn at the time of the Neolithic Revolution, well before the advent of writing. Up until the appearance of the written word, our information is based largely on inference. Before it, we can surmise the general outlines; after, there is a crescendo of known developments, persons and events.

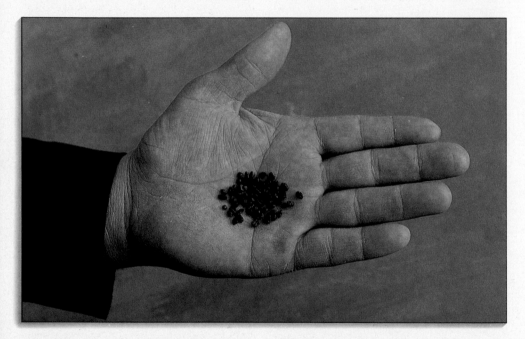

Neolithic Revolution: The records of civilization in the Near East begin with a revolution, a turning point when people changed from being at the mercy of their environment to their becoming herdsmen of wild animals and cultivators of wild grains. This innovation, which is known as the Neolithic Revo-

The division is not a clear-cut one. Nor did it occur evenly everywhere. Perhaps it was stimulated by the warming of the earth's atmosphere after the last Ice Age.

The major areas of this revolution in the Middle East were the drainage basins of the Tigris and the Euphrates rivers, the Fertile Crescent. Much of this lies farther east than the province of this book, but the northwest point of that Crescent extends into the rich farmland of the Cilician Plain (today's Çukurova). Between Antakya and Silifke, on the slopes of the Taurus Mountains,

Above, wheat particles found at Karain Caves.

28

across the flat land to the west, and extending north along the Mediterranean Coast, archaeologists have found evidences of this change. Here fishermen, farmers and herders have left the clues with which scientists are piecing together the story of man's beginnings and his achievements.

Human life in the Middle East appears to go back about a million years. Only in the relatively recent past – perhaps 10,000 BC – did people begin using tools. And it was about 8000 BC before people started shaping their tools for specific purposes and controlling food production.

By 5500 BC people had metal tools; the first metal they used in quantity was copper – the Chalcolithic Period. At the same time, the original groups of people to live in primitive settlements perhaps were those who could harvest and store enough food to carry them through winter.

The next advance came with the discovery of how to make bronze. The Bronze Age, when this metal was shaped into strong tools, commenced around 3200 BC. Copper, lead, nickel and arsenic are abundant in Anatolia, but archaeologists are not sure where the tin, which was needed to combine with copper to make bronze, came from. It may have been mined in the Taurus Mountains or it may have been imported from Mesopotamia.

Social changes: A metalworking industry meant a permanent settlement, some division of labour and some kind of social organization along with trading arrangements. With this advance, village life became more complex; buildings were constructed for purposes other than just habitation.

The Bronze Age lasted about 2,000 years. During that time writing was invented and brought into Anatolia by foreign Assyrians around 1900 BC. The use of iron, with its superior strength, was introduced into the area around 1400 BC and established the Iron Age.

The theory associated with iron is that its abundance meant eventually that cheap weapons were available to the masses who then used them against their neighbours. The invading "Sea Peoples" at the turn of the first millennium destroyed civilizations, causing a major regression to a more primitive type of living in western Anatolia – a period described as the "Dark Ages."

Indo-European invaders: The Middle and late Bronze periods (2000 to 1000 BC) are known largely from the finds in Troy. The beginning of the period was marked by waves of Indo-European invaders, some settling peacefully and taking on many of the customs of the indigenous groups, others causing considerable destruction to the cities in their paths.

The Battle of Kadesh, which was concluded with a treaty of political alignment between the Hittites and Egypt, was fought on the Orontes River south of Antakya in about 1285 BC. This established the Hittites as an internationally dominant kingdom and set a northern limit to Egyptian influence in the Middle East. The Trojan War between the Greeks and the Trojans ended in about 1250 BC, probably opening Anatolia to invasion by another wave of barbaric tribes.

Beginning about 700 BC, more accurate dates can be assigned to recorded events. Cimmerians from the Caucasus sacked Gordium around 690 BC; Tarsus was ravaged by the Assyrian Sennacherib at the same time. Lydians plundered Smyrna (Izmir) a hundred years later, and King Croesus was defeated at Sardis by the Persian King Cyrus in 546 BC, beginning the period of Persian influence. Persian control of the western coast and influence of Persian art lasted until Alexander the Great's conquests between 334 and 323 BC.

The written record of past events in Anatolia started in about 1900 BC when the Assyrian merchants living on the outskirts of the Hittite capital of Kanesh (near Kayseri) sent letters to their business associates in Mesopotamia. These letters were inscribed in cuneiform on clay and then baked in an oven. In them are references to people such as the Ahhiyawans who were living at the time on the coast.

The earliest group of people living in Anatolia for which we have a name is the Hattians. When they came and where they came from are a mystery. They were a non-Semitic, non-Indo-European group who were influential enough to give the name of their land to the next invaders who probably called themselves Nesians.

The Nesians, one of the many ethnic groups who invaded the area apparently from the east, established one of their capitals at Hattusa (Boğazköy) and another at Kanesh (Kültepe). Their ruler styled himself

"King of the Hatti;" they and their Indo-European language are known, with some oversimplification, as Hittite.

Lycians of Xanthus: The invasion of these Nesians, or Hittites, coincided with the arrival on the coast of the Ahhiyawans who seem to have come from the west and with whom the Hittites had commercial relations. They may have been the people whom Homer called the Achaeans; if so, more connections – business, military, cultural – between the Hittites, the Trojans and the Greeks may be uncovered. The Ahhiyawans appear to have been an early Greek colony living around Miliwandas. (Can this be Miletus?) Another Hittite influence on the coast shows in the record that during the reign of King Suppiluliumas the Hittites fought the Lukka nation, presumably the Lycians living around Xanthus.

The Hittites were apparently present on the coast as far north as Izmir, although their settlements up to now are known to be single sites. A stone statue of a Hittite still guards the pass at Karabel east of Izmir; there is a relief of a "Mother of the Gods" on Manisa Dağ. This scattering of remains has made archaeologists wonder what the Hittites were doing so far from Hattusa or Kanesh.

Another, possibly different, pre-Indo-European group was known as the Pelasgians. They were present in northwestern Anatolia before the Trojan War. Their name suggests that they came from the sea; however, that may merely describe them rather than being what they were actually called. According to Homer, who is the earliest source for such information, the Pelasgians were allies of the Trojans. Herodotus locates their capital on the Sea of Marmara.

At least two other peoples living on the Mediterranean coast of Anatolia at the beginning of this period used Indo-European languages: the Assuwans who spoke Luwian and the Hurrians.

Anatolian coastal districts: The names of the districts in Anatolia at one time indicated political identities and dominance. At present they describe the areas in general geographic and cultural terms. Starting in the north, the coastal regions are usually referred to as Thrace, the Troad, Aeolis, Lydia, Caria, Lycia, Pamphylia and Cilicia.

Thrace originally included all of today's European Turkey and stretched into Bulgaria and Greece. Greek mythology says Orpheus, who charmed open the gates of Hell with his playing of the lyre, was born on the shores of the Hermus (Meriç) River, the boundary between Turkey and Greece. Thracian invaders – or Phrygians – are probably the ones responsible for the destruction of Hattusa about 1180 BC.

About 1160 BC the Phrygians, known also as the Mushki, appeared and grew in power on the eastern borders of Ionia and Aeolis. They may have brought about the downfall of the Hittites. Their contribution to life on the coast included their improvement of the trade routes known as the Royal Roads, one of which went east from Izmir through Dorylaeum (Eskişehir), Ankara and Boğazkale; another slightly south led from Sardis through central Anatolia and the Cilician Gates; both eventually ended at Susa, now a ruined city in western Iran.

The golden touch: The Phrygian King Midas was so rich that everything he touched turned to gold, including his beloved daughter. To rid himself of this fatal curse, he bathed in the Pactolus River which flows past Sardis and from which King Croesus got his gold. (Incidentally, British archaeologists are speculating that the ass's ears which Apollo gave Midas when the king preferred Pan's pipes to Apollo's may be a combination of two well-known medical conditions: abnormally long ears, and an excessive growth of hair on the edges of the ears.)

Phrygians are credited with inventing the frieze. They were known for their music; the Phrygian mode was supposed to be stimulating; its cadence may have been preserved through early hymns. (The Lydian mode was considered to be decorous; the Ionian mode, which the western major scale is based on, was called "wanton." The Aeolian harp is one on which the wind performs.)

Phrygian power was interrupted when the Cimmerians from the north invaded Anatolia briefly about 700 BC. The Cimmerians may have gone off with Midas' treasure since no gold was found in his presumed tomb. The Phrygian Empire was absorbed into the Lydian Empire, and then it passed into Persian control. Under the Attalids it was part of the Pergamene Empire.

The Troad: At one time the northwest corner of Anatolia covering what is now the province of Çanakkale was called Lesser

Phrygia. By classical Greek times it was the Troad. The first person to establish a city in the Troad, according to legend was Teucer, a king who came to the mainland from Lesbos. His son-in-law was Dardanus, the hero of the Dardanelles. (Teucer's great grandson was Tros, to whom we owe the name Troy.) The Dardanians were allies of the Hittite King Mutwatallis in the Battle of Kadesh. They fought a few years later on the side of the Trojans.

The habitation of Troy from 3000 BC to AD 300 has given archaeologists a sequence against which to measure other sites. Levels I through V in Troy belong to the early Bronze Period. The buildings were made of

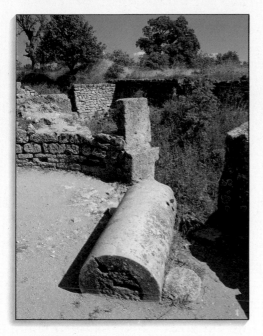

mud brick on top of stone foundations in the shape of a megaron, a long rectangular building with an entry porch.

From the time of Level II on (circa 2400 BC), Trojan potters used a wheel. They must have learned this skill from the people who lived in northern Syria or in Cilicia who had been using it before. Pottery similar to what was found first in Troy II has later been discovered in many places near the coast north of Izmir. Two kinds of jars are common at this level, one of them in a semi-human form, the other with two shapely

Above, scene of the ruins of Troy.

handles. Similar kinds of jars are also found in Tarsus and Yümüktepe (Mersin).

Treasures of Priam: The people living in Troy II were skilled in working with metals to make weapons, saws, jewellery and vases. The influence of their artistry spread over western Anatolia, Crete, Thrace and into the Balkans. It was the objects they valued and tried to save from a fire that archaeologist Heinrich Schliemann believed were the treasures of Priam.

By Troy V potters were using a red or a reddish-brown slip. Sometimes they put a reddish cross on the inside, a mark which has been on pots in Tarsus (and the Hittite city of Kanesh) and which suggests a link between those places. Also, bronze was manufactured from this time on.

The fortified city of Troy VI, lasting from about 1900 to 1300 BC, is similar to Hittite forts: the engineering techniques of offsets (ledges) and columns to add strength to the walls were used in Hittite Alisar and Bogazkale. These Trojans seem to have been newcomers to the area, probably one of the Indo-European invaders. Their pottery was a gray "Minyan" ware, perhaps originally an Anatolian rather than a Greek design as was once thought.

Homer's epics: Troy VIIa, built on top of the earthquake ruins of Troy VI, was destroyed during a huge fire in about 1250 BC. Most archaeologists identify this event with the war between the Trojans and the Achaean invaders from Greece who are remembered in Homer's epics.

Following that war a number of groups of people apparently scattered, founding cities along the Mediterranean Coast. Of these, some Pamphylian cities claimed a Trojan background: Perge, Aspendos and Sillyum (but not Side which is of later date).

The pottery in Troy VIIb is knobby like that which was being made in central Europe around the same time rather than anything made in Anatolia; thus it would seem that people from Europe were travelling south into Anatolia. Troy VIIb also was destroyed by fire – probably in the course of another war brought on by invaders – around the year 1180 BC.

Troy VIII (700-334 BC) was called Ilion; and today very little exists of it. Troy IX was not an important town to anyone, except perhaps, to the pilgrims who came to its

Temple of Athena to pay their homage to Homer and his epic.

Aeolis was settled by the first group of people who were uprooted from their land in Greece by invading Dorians toward the end of the second millennium. Pushed from Thessaly and Boetia, the Aeolian refugees settled first in the area around Old Smyrna (Izmir). They probably moved in on an already-resident group who may have been Hittites, themselves earlier immigrants. Undoubtedly the Aeolians intermarried with those residents. The Aeolian territory extended from the Gulf of Edremit towards the Bay of Izmir.

Its cities included Pitane and Cyme on the coast, but by far its most important city was Pergamum (Bergama), which for a hundred and fifty years under the Attalid kings, rivalled Egypt in political power and cultural brilliance and architecture.

Whoever the natives were, the Aeolians were shortly supplanted by the Ionians who migrated after the collapse of the Achaean kingdom of Mycenae sometime before 900 BC. Their geographic influence reached from a bit north of Izmir south to Miletus. During the eighth and seventh centuries BC they led in the development of civic organization with the Panionic League of 12 cities. They sent out a number of colonies to the shores of the Dardanelles, the Marmara and the Black Sea.

Their cultural influence was even more impressive. The Temple of Diana in Ephesus, an architectural masterpiece, and the Mausoleum in Halicarnassus (today's Bodrum) were two of the Seven Wonders of the Ancient World.

The historians: On the coast, the earliest historians were Ionians. They lived at the time of the Persian dominance, but their works contributed not to Persia, but to the importance of the Greek language and to the growth of Greek/Hellenistic analytical thought. (Even yet their name in Turkish identifies Greece as "*Yunanistan*," the land of the Ionians.) Three of the historians were from Miletus: Cadmus (circa 540 BC), sometimes confused with a Phoenician god and credited with inventing letters; Dionysius, and Hecataeus (circa 500 BC). The latter began his history remarking, "I write as I deem true, for the traditions of the Greeks seem to me manifold and laughable." Xan-

thus of Sardis and Herodotus of Heraclea (Latmus) were precursors of the "Father of History," Herodotus of Halicarnassus (485-425 BC).

Lydia (Is this Lud of the Old Testament?) was a bit inland; its centre was Sardis. Caria was around the Bay of Cos. Lycia is the land south of a line drawn from Antalya across the mountains to Köyceğiz.

The Lycians who around 1400 BC were raiding Cyprus from Crete settled temporarily in Miletus. Then they moved south to the area around Xanthus. During the Battle of Kadesh, Lycians fought on the side of their fellow Anatolians. Later, according to Homer, soldiers fought with their leader

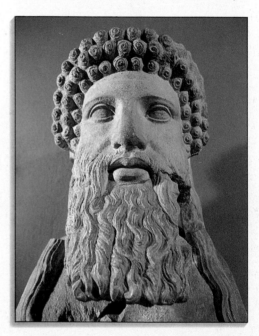

Serpedon on the side of the Trojans in Troy from faraway Lycia and "the whirling waters of Xanthus."

Native stock Anatolians: The Carians and the Lydians asserted that they were native stock Anatolians. They were probably right, but their importance did not develop until they were stimulated from outside Persian and Greek influences.

The Carian and Ionian centres included Miletus, Knidos and Halicarnassus. Up until 500 BC they dominated Greek rational thought. Besides the historians, a remarkable number of philosophers were born in Miletus. Thales, the forecaster of the eclipse, also confounded his critics who claimed that philosophers could not be successful in business. He predicted a bumper crop of olives, cornered the market, and made a killing. Anaximenes and Anaximander searched for the basic principle of the universe; the first said it was air, the other claimed it was limitlessness.

As for Halicarnassus (Bodrum), one of its famous sons was Herodotus. Another man whose name still resounds was the good King Mausolus whose sister-cum-wife built a splendid mausoleum for him when he died about 352 BC. Two queens named Artemisia ruled in Halicarnassus. Both were remarkably adept as captains of their ships in sea

point is known for its treacherous seas; the new residents constructed a causeway joining the point to the hilly island to the west. In this way they created a double harbour, one south and one north, saving some ships from having to round the point in a storm. About the same time of their move, the Knidians acquired the statue of Aphrodite by Praxiteles which attracted many tourists to their city.

The Lydian capital was Sardis. Lydians appear to be associated around 800 BC with the Etruscans who showed up then in Italy, having come from the east perhaps because of a famine. Three Lydian kings, Gyges, Alyattes and Croesus, are particularly well

battles, the first against the Persians in 480 BC, the second (widow of Mausolus) against the Rhodians in 351 BC.

Statue of Aphrodite: Knidos was founded by the Dorians, the group who had pushed the Ionians and Aeolians out of Greece and then were pushed out themselves. As a coastal city, Knidos was troubled by pirates, and when it drove the pirates off it sent offerings of thanks to Delphi. In about 360 BC, the city moved from its first location (near present-day Datça) to the tip of the peninsula. That

Left, bust of Hermes, the messenger of God.
Above, blissful family life in antiquity.

known: Gyges began his career as a prime minister in about 700 BC, but having assassinated his king in order to save the queen's honour, he took the throne and set about expanding his holdings.

Under King Alyattes, the Cimmerians were defeated. They had invaded Anatolia from the northeast and killed Gyges. (Following their defeat they retreated to the Crimea.) By occupying the Phrygian lands left unattended in the Cimmerians' wake, Lydia came in contact with Persia and aroused the greed of its kings.

Minting coins: The Lydians under King Croesus reformed the monetary system. Previously, coins were an alloy, "electrum," made of varying amounts of silver and gold. The Lydians standardized the values of minting their own coins of pure metal, guaranteeing their quality and thus stimulating business. King Croesus was defeated by the Persian King Cyrus in 546 BC.

Within a few years most of Anatolia was under Persian control, directed from Susa through their regional governors or satraps. That control continued for about two centuries. In general, it was a benign rule, the Persians mostly recruiting soldiers and levying taxes. One of their satraps, Pharnabazus, built a palace for himself in 546 BC on the shores of Lake Manyas east of Troy. His

Darius to engage them in a naval battle at Lade off their coast in which they were trounced. Darius went on to fight the Athenians only to be defeated himself at the Plains of Marathon in 490 BC.

In 1982, a particularly exciting discovery of a shipwreck was made off the Turkish mainland at Ulu Burun south of Kas. The contents of the shipwreck, which dated about 1400 BC, has expanded the knowledge about the cargo traded at this period and also of the people who had ties all around the Mediterranean.

The wreck held an amazing variety of objects: tin, glass and ostrich eggshells, for instance. Its cargo in large part was raw

palace garden was distinguished for its "paradise of birds" – a distinction that has lasted into the present times.

South, in Lycia, the many tombs from this period have made the region fascinating. They include pillar tombs (such as the Harpy Tomb in Xanthus with its original frieze now exhibited in the British Museum), house tombs and temple tombs (such as at Myra) and sarcophagi (as in Sidyma, Fethiye and Antiphellus/Kas).

Ionian uprising: A rebellion by Ionians of Miletus led to their sacking the Persian stronghold of Sardis in 495 BC. That in turn immediately provoked the Persian King

materials. Copper ingots – six tons of them – shaped like animal hides may have been molded in Ugarit in Syria just south of the Antakya border. Ivory may have come from Syria or India. Amber – a puzzle about what its commercial use was – seems to have come from the Balkans.

Nubian ebony: Some pottery came from Cyprus. There were vases from Mycenae and Crete, jewellery from Canaan, seals from Egypt, and ebony from Nubia. Some of the items from the wreck were identified from pictures on Egyptian tombs; one Mycenaean kylix-cup helped date the wreck because of its popularity during the 15th century BC. A gold chalice indicated that part of the cargo may have been intended as a royal present. A gold scarab was inscribed with the name Nefertiti. The large amount of copper suggested that an army was to be equipped with bronze helmets and swords, but which war they were to be used in and against whom is not known.

The finds are lodged now in the Museum of Underwater Archaeology in Bodrum while study of the wreck goes on.

Cave man: Some of the early peoples in Anatolia lived in caves for at least parts of the year. These caves, particularly in Beldibi, Karain and Belbaşı in the Antalya region, have preserved evidences of the transforma-

and hand axes have been found from this early period. The stone tools were carefully balanced and shaped to fit neatly in a human hand. Archaeologists have tried harvesting wild wheat with these kinds of tools and have decided that a family working for a month could bring enough to keep them going a year and with some to spare for barter.

Among the evidences of the changes that were taking place are the bones of domesticated animals, the sharp stones fashioned to fit sickle blades, the storage pits for harvested grain, and later the first man-built dwellings.

Elephants and hippopotamuses: The caves near Antalya have revealed, along with less

tion in peoples' lives 8,000 years ago.

Stone arrowheads discovered there are shaped with a tang to fit into a longer handle; they suggest that the people had begun to use both spears and bows. Tiny, sharp stones probably set along the edges of curved blades made sickles. These indicate the harvesting, but not yet the sowing of grain. Some of the blades still retain a patina which shows long time use. In both the Beldibi and Samandağ (west of Antakya) caves, scrapers

Opposite page: left, frieze of a naked man; right, woman with a lyre. Above, a scene of fighting from the Alexander's Sarcophagus.

exotic remains, evidences of species of elephants and hippopotamuses. The Samanda Cave also contained bones of rhinoceroses, red deer, porcupines, oxen and boars. It is also possible that the first hunting and exploring by these people who lived in the caves were done as they sailed and fished along the coast.

Pictures painted on the cave walls and scratched on pebbles left in the caves are usually of hunting scenes. These may well have had a religious significance – a prayer for success in the search for food, or an offering of thanks to the spirits of the dead animals. Some have a timeless aesthetic value: a rock carving of a leaping stag at the entrance of the Beldibi Cave shows the grace of a master artist. The painting of hunting scenes seems not to have continued long after the domestication of plants and animals, which lends strength to the supposition that the act was related to the need to insure a supply of food by making an appeal to the gods.

Some time later cult statues, particularly of the Mother Goddess, appear in rooms that probably were used for religious or funerary purposes. They seem to have a link with similar symbolism in both Neolithic Çatal Höyük south of Konya and in Crete.

Pottery is predated by stone, wood and

Cyme, an Aeolian city just north of Izmir.

Cilicia is today's Çukurova, the fertile plain south of the Taurus Mountains. In Hittite times it was known as Kizzuwatna. Olba (Uzuncaburç) was important in the Hellenistic Period. Among the ruined buildings is a third century BC. Temple of Zeus with columns topped by Corinthian capitals still in place.

Tarsus and Mersin: Excavations at Tarsus and Mersin have unearthed stunning handmade pottery which is like the early pottery found in the Karain Cave. Some of the earliest of these had patterns made by incising the wet clay.

The lowest level excavated at Mersin

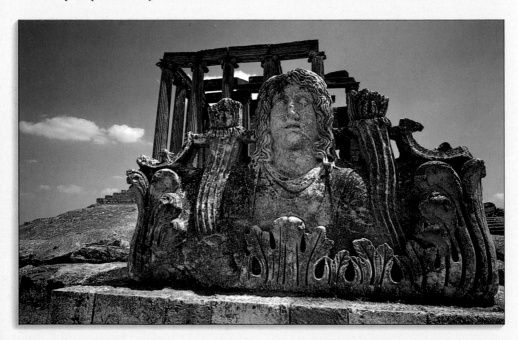

woven baskets and bowls. It appears that around 6500 BC the people living on the coast learned how to make pottery from those who lived on the Anatolian plain. There is a strong similarity between the pots found in Çatal Höyük and the first pots of the Antalya region.

Pamphylia was the coastal country which included the cities of Perge, Aspendos, Side and Alanya. Aspendos appears to have had connections with the Lesser Hittite King Asitawandas of Karatepe; its fifth century BC name was Estweddiya.

The city of Side was founded in the seventh century BC by colonists who came from

(Yümüktepe) revealed items from the Neolithic Period. People had been living there earlier, but those levels have not been explored because they are under water. The walls of the Neolithic city were made of round pebbles perhaps from the stream bed or the sea. No mortar has been used; they were dry walls which have lasted longer than if they had been made of mud mortar which would wash out in a rainstorm.

Yümüktepe overlooked a trade route along the coast that went into central Anatolia through the Cilician Gates. The village was helped by the items, particularly obsidian, of that trade, and it must have loaded its own merchandise onto the caravans to be sold in the interior. Perhaps sea shells found in the palace temple in Hattusa came from here.

The importance of obsidian: Obsidian was probably more valuable than sea shells because of its hardness and its quality of flaking with a sharp edge. Obsidian is valuable to archaeologists now for another reason: it is to be found naturally only in specific places around the volcanoes of Hasan Dağ, Erciyes Dağ and Karaca Dağ which are in the interior of the country. When it appears in the early levels of Mersin and Tarsus, or in the Antalya caves, it indicates both with whom the people were trad-

tains was known in Hittite times as Kizzuwatna. It seems to have been a region of a number of petty kingdoms whose inhabitants used Hittite hieroglyphics for their inscriptions but who themselves did not speak Hittite. Kizzuwatna remained Hittite after the collapse of the central Empire under Phrygian attack.

Lesser Hittite sites: One of these lesser Hittite settlements was at Karatepe on the Ceyhan River north of Adana. Fragments of a Hittite-Luwian and Phoenician bilingual inscription found at the small citadel there have helped to clarify some of the complex relationships among the Assyrians, the Urartians and the Late Hittite kingdoms.

ing and that they had developed some level of commercial skills. Tarsus between 2700 and 2400 BC was a fortified town; its ruler was a minor king. Double-handled pottery produced there is like that found in Troy II and IV. Archaeologists say that probably this shape originated in Cilicia or further east around Islahiye and was carried north from there. A vase from Cilicia was found in the Fourth Dynasty tomb in Egypt, indicating a connection between those two areas too.

The southern slopes of the Tarsus mountains.

Left, the Temple of Zeus at Aizanoi. **Above**, the amphitheater at Pamukkale.

Other evidences of the Hittites exist around Karatepe. South, near the village of Babaoğlan, is a castle (probably Roman in origin), and beside it is a rock carving of a man wearing the hat of a Hittite king. This suggests ties between Syria and the region of Hierapolis Castabala (now the village of Bodrum) a few miles beyond a bend of the Ceyhan River. The spectacular Castabala is distinguished now by a medieval fortress. Castabala was its Roman name; its king Tarcondimotos fought for Mark Antony and was killed at the Battle of Actium. Castabala was a Roman city built on some earlier Greek and Hittite settlements.

When Alexander the Great began his campaign to conquer the Persian Empire and free the Ionian Greek cities of Asia Minor in 334 BC, he fashioned himself in the likeness of Achilles and Heracles, from whom he claimed lineage. In less than one year Alexander, leader of the League of Corinth and the Macedonian army, swept through Asia Minor, liberated the Greek cities, reestablished democracies, and introduced an advanced coinage standard that revolutionized trade and commerce. On his way to conquer the Persian Empire, Alexander paid tribute to his hero, Achilles, at Troy.

After visiting Troy, Alexander confronted his first Persian army at the Granicus River (modern Kocabaş River near the Sea of Marmara). This decisive battle demonstrated his enormous personal valour and the brilliance of his military tactics. The Persians set a trap for Alexander by forcing him to ford the river at a point where the banks were extremely steep so that his troops had difficulty in holding close formations. But Alexander courageously led his cavalry and broke the Persian line. Alexander was wounded badly by a blow through his helmet that reached the bone and while he was left unconscious his troops sorely beat the Persians, massacring most of the Greek soldiers who fought for the Persians. Alexander recovered quickly and sent the 2,000 surviving Greek mercenaries to Macedonia to work as slaves in mines.

Persian panoplies: Alexander sent 300 Persian panoplies (sets of armour) taken at Granicus to Athens as an offering to Athena. The armour bore the inscription: "Alexander, son of Philip and the Greeks (except the Spartans) to the barbarians who inhabit Asia." Not only did this dedication omit Sparta but it also omitted the Macedonians who made up the largest part of Alexander's troops. Alexander chose not to call himself King but simply son of Philip, paying respect to the Greek's love of democracy.

From this victory he continued along the coast of Asia Minor, freeing Greek cities from Persian rule. He fought a long and difficult battle against the Persians at Halicarnassus (Bodrum). At Aspendos, the citizens requested not to be garrisoned. For this privilege, Alexander demanded a large sum of tribute as well as horses for his cavalry, for which Aspendos was famous. The citizens refused. Alexander responded by demanding an even higher tribute, and taking all the horses he needed.

However, many cities such as Ephesus, Side and Phaselis willingly opened their doors and treasuries to him. In the Greek cities Alexander won popularity by establishing Greek-style democracies in place of the oligarchies which had ruled under the

Persians. He left in place the Persian system of satrapies but placed finance in the hands of a separate person – usually a Macedonian or a Greek, but some Persians were included.

Alexander's main achievement was to introduce Hellenistic culture to the east and change the map of the world forever. He left garrisons in many Greek towns along the coast, encouraging intermarriage and an exchange of culture. Along with his army and navy, Alexander also brought with him artists, poets, philosophers and historians to record and commemorate his adventures.

Above, bust and statue of Alexander the Great.

Even though Alexander failed to establish an empire in Asia which would foster a brotherhood of peoples, his expedition successfully laid the framework for the spread of Greek thought and customs throughout Asia. The extraordinary centuries following his death are known as the Hellenistic Age. This era, from 323 BC to 30 BC, was characterized by the demise of the Greek city-states and the establishment of large kingdoms, modelled on the Macedonian monarchy. This period saw the spectacular growth of trade and commerce as well as the development of a common culture made possible by use of the Greek language, and the adoptions of Greek institutions.

After Alexander's death, his newly-established empire dissolved and the successors, the Diadichi, battled among themselves for 20 years.

Finally, three main kingdoms emerged: the Macedonians in Greece; the Seleucids in Syria; and the Ptolemies in Egypt. Control of western Asia Minor, however, fell outside of the three major empires, first ruled by one of Alexander's generals, Antigonus the One-Eyed, and later by another general, Lysimachus.

Monarchies: The new political order of this age was the large monarchical kingdom. These great monarchies, governed by autocratic rulers and vast bureaucracies, were in dramatic conflict with the Greek love of autonomy.

Because the Greeks were a major source for the development and defence of the state, the kings allowed the Greek city-states to assume a degree of independence within the monarchical territories. Some Greek city-states combined to form leagues or federations such as the Ionian League.

The large political units encouraged international trade, fostered urban economies and led to the adoption of common law. The most important cross continental caravan route during the Hellenistic period began in India and stretched across the Persian Gulf to the Tigris, continued to Seleucia, the commercial capital of Asia, and finished at Ephesus. Olives, wine, sheep and grain were the most commonly traded agricultural products from the Aegean Coast. Pergamum maintained a monopoly on parchment and textiles, particularly gold weave cloth. Miletus was the centre for the wool industry.

Sculpture flourished in the Hellenistic Age in Pergamum and along the Aegean Coast. The Gauls who invaded Anatolia in the second century provided material for two innovative schools of art at Pergamum in the first and second centuries BC. Sculptors depicted the Gauls as noble fighters.

Stoics and cynics: Strong interest in philosophy also grew during this period as the old gods of Olympus failed to satisfy intellectual curiosity. Although the Greeks and Hellenized natives continued to follow the old religions there was a concurrent growth of king worship, mystery cults and magic. The Stoics, the Cynics, the Skeptics and the Epicurians evolved reflecting a new growth of individualism and humanism.

The most important instruments facilitating the growth of philosophy in the Hellenistic Era were the new libraries established in Pergamum, Antioch and Alexandria.

Grandiose architecture: There was a trend towards the ornate and the grandiose in architecture during the Hellenistic period in Asia Minor. Due to a declining interest in religion and the city-state there was a significant decrease in the number of temples built. The new emphasis on ornate decoration was reflected in the popularity of the Corinthian order. Hellenized Greeks favoured temples with an increasing number of columns and more elaborate sculpture on the column drums and volutes of the capitals. For example, the Temple of Apollo at Didyma (334 BC) was so immense that the cella was never covered but left open to the sky.

In summary, the Hellenistic Age was a period of much contradiction and complexity. While it represented a period of extensive material gain it was also a time of great poverty among the working classes. The forces of the day nurtured a new spirit of individualism and man believed himself more and more a citizen of the world. On the other hand, the advent of large monarchical kingdoms made possible a much more despotic control of the individual's life.

Although the Roman armies first set foot in Asia Minor in 190 BC for the purpose of defending Greece which was under attack from Antiochus III, this advance laid the stage for Rome's eventual domination of the entire Mediterranean basin. For many years, Rome cultivated strong alliances with kingdoms in Asia Minor, in order to protect its boundaries. In particular, Rome relied on Pergamum to control smaller kingdoms in Asia Minor and to act as a buffer state between Rome and the Seleucid Empire. Demonstrating its strong allegiance to Rome, Eumenes II of Pergamum supported Rome's campaign in Greece and Asia Minor. In the face of a strong enemy army at the final Battle of Magnesia, Eumenes' troops proved essential for the Roman victory. This decisive battle put an end to Seleucid rule in Asia Minor and Rome acquired the vast territory ruled by Antiochus III.

The Romans were reluctant to take on the governing of yet another large province so soon after acquiring Greece. Therefore they handed the province over to Eumenes who agreed to administer the kingdom and strictly adhere to Rome's foreign policy. This relationship insured that western Asia Minor was governed in the interest of Rome but the responsibility of rule lay with the Pergamene kings.

The last Pergamene king, Attalus III, was radically different from his predecessors. He was unpopular as a ruler and pursued his personal interests in botany and pharmaceutical sciences rather than responsibilities as king. He had no heirs. Therefore, to prevent the rise of petty tyrants who would likely take over in the absence of a strong rule, he bequeathed the royal possessions of Pergamum and the supremacy of western Asia Minor to Rome in 133 BC.

Roman province: Rome responded to the bequest by immediately appointing a five-member commission to take control of the new province of Asia. When the commission reached Asia in 132 BC, the country was in a state of civil war. The new government faced resistance from Aristonicus, an illegitimate son of Eumenes, who had the backing of the poor and the landless peasantry. In expectation of greater freedom under the Romans, the free cities refused to support Aristonicus. The cities had fought alone until 131 BC when an army was raised in Rome under the consul Crassus. The support of the city of Ephesus helped turn the war in favour of the Romans. In 129 BC Aristonicus was defeated by the Roman general Aquilius, who put down the final stages of the revolt and set about organizing the new Roman province of Asia.

Rome's political and economic policies for the new province of Asia resulted in hardship for most citizens. Annually appointed governors from Rome were largely uninformed and ignorant of local issues and citizens' needs. Moreover, the people did not feel the same reverence and respect towards the new Roman governors who, unlike their predecessors, were not patrons of art.

Exploiting the masses: While some of the governors including Aquilius made contributions to civil life in the province, a large number used their positions to exploit the citizens with extortionate taxes. For example, following the civil war when local governments were in a state of depression, high taxes were levied by the government in order to meet wartime expenses.

Through direct contacts with the Greeks in Asia Minor, Romans were greatly influenced by Greek religion and culture. Children of upper class Roman families learned to speak and read Greek. The Romans, fascinated by Greek literature and philosophy, translated Homer, and copied its forms in writing Rome's epic histories.

The founding of Constantinople as the new capital in AD 330 by Constantine I resulted in a shift of the imperial centre to the east. The division of the Empire into East and West gradually assimilated Roman Asia Minor into the Greco-Anatolian world. By the time the western Roman Empire collapsed in the fifth century, the assimilation was complete, and the Latin Roman Empire had been replaced by the Greek-dominated Byzantine Empire, which lasted until the Ottoman conquest in the 15th century.

Right, Cleopatra captivated men.

ANTONY AND CLEOPATRA

When Antony summoned Cleopatra to Tarsus in 41 BC to confront her with charges of scheming to support his enemies, the stage was set for one of the greatest love affairs in history, Antony's own tragic downfall, and the transformation of the Roman Republic to the Roman Empire. Antony was seeking to enhance his prestige in Rome, secure the eastern boundaries, as well as avenge Rome's only defeat at the hands of the Parthians. He was in desperate need of troops and money to campaign and conquer the Parthians. Cleopatra's objectives were nothing less than the restoration of the Egyptian Empire as it had existed under Ptolemy II Philadelphus. She was willing to trade the wealth of Egypt to Antony for support of the Roman legions. In his brilliant tragedy, *Antony and Cleopatra*, Shakes-peare describes Cleo-patra's dramatic arrival at Tarsus to meet Antony:

For her own passion,
It beggar'd all description: she did lie
In her pavilion cloth-of-gold of tissue
O'er picturing that
Venus where we see
The fancy outwork
nature: on each side her
Stood pretty dimpled
boys, like smiling
Cupids

Antony captivated: If Antony had not been captivated by Cleopatra the first time he met her in Rome when she was Julius Caesar's mistress, he was taken captive now. Antony delayed his plans to conquer the Parthians. The two returned to Egypt where they spent the winter as lovers.

In 40 BC Antony returned to Rome to reestablish his position in the empire and resolve his differences with Octavian, ruler of the western half of the Roman Provinces. Also during this period he married Octavian's sister Octavia. Beginning with his absence in Egypt, Antony's power slowly declined while Octavian fortified his position within the empire, secured the western boundaries and won popular support. In order to reestablish his power in the east, Antony again waged war against the Parthians.

Four years after their last meeting, Antony summoned Cleopatra, this time to Antioch, in order to marshal support for his campaign. In return for Cleopatra's financial backing, Antony gave the Egyptian Queen part of Phoenicia and northern Judea and promised to wed her and legitimize her children. Antony was severely defeated and returned to Cleopatra who refortified him with money and supplies. Octavia, sent by Octavian, also came to Antony's rescue, but he sent her back precipitating a break between the two leaders.

Xenophobic fervour: Tensions between Antony and Octavian accelerated in 34 BC when Antony, celebrating victory in Armenia, staged a ceremony in which Cleopatra was pronounced Queen of Kings with Roman territories given to her children. Octavian destabilized Antony's position among the Roman legions by rousing xenophobic fervour against Cleopatra. In 32 BC, Octavian declared war against Cleopatra.

Antony assembled a navy at Ephesus to prepare for battle with Octavian. He was once again assisted by Cleopatra, although she was of little help. She had little to gain from his victory against Octavian, for if Antony won the battle he would return to Rome in triumph, out of her influence and back into the arms of Octavia. What followed was the decisive battle at Actium in 31 BC, where Antony realized his absolute defeat. Conquered and with no hope for a reconciliation with Rome, the lovers returned together to Alexandria where first Antony, then Cleopatra, committed suicide.

All along the Turkish Coast are places where the two lovers supposedly romanced. Antony purchased the city of Coracesium (today's Alanya) for Cleopatra to express his love for her. At Cedrae, an ancient island city in the Gulf of Gökova, Antony was purported to have transported the fine silt sand of its beach (known as Cleopatra's Beach) from the Nile to satisfy his lover. Travellers can also visit Cleopatra's Hamam in the Gulf of the Fethiye where the Egyptian sovereign allegedly built baths. These baths are now partly submerged as a result of earthquakes. ∎

By foot over hot, dusty, steep roads, by jouncing horsecart, by rocky sailboat, St. Paul the Apostle journeyed the length of the eastern coast of Anatolia from Antioch-on-the-Orontes (Antakya) to Alexandria Troas (Odun Iskelesi south of Troy) during the middle years of the first century.

"I have been constantly on the road," Paul subsequently wrote. "I have met dangers from rivers, dangers from robbers, dangers from my fellow-countrymen, dangers from foreigners, dangers in towns, dangers in the country, dangers at sea, dangers from false friends. I have toiled and drudged, I have often gone without sleep; hungry and thirsty, I have often gone fasting; and I have suffered from cold and exposure."

Beginning with Antioch about AD 40, Paul's influence and that of the early disciples spread Christianity throughout the eastern Mediterranean. Three centuries later Christianity had become the major religion of Asia Minor.

The tentmaker: Paul was born in Tarsus, which is today a busy city in one of the richest agricultural regions of Turkey. As a boy he learned the trade of tentmaking. While studying in Jerusalem he was an accomplice in the stoning of Stephen, who was the first Christian martyr. But later, after seeing a vision of Jesus, he devoted himself body, mind and spirit to preaching the word of Christ.

Paul's career as a disciple started when a follower of Jesus, Barnabas, called him to work in Antioch (Antakya) in AD 43.

The people whom Paul met in Antioch must have influenced his thinking. Of those attending the synagogue, there were Gentiles who had been attracted to the moral virtues they found in Judaism. Paul held firmly to the prime article of Jewish law: "The lord is our God, one Lord."

While other Jews believed they could be faithful to the law only by keeping to their own community, for Paul, God's very oneness meant that Jesus, who announced God's kingdom, was calling to all the people. Thus Paul's mission came to be focused on the Gentiles.

Paul was not always successful. He re-sented it when his companions, John, Mark and Barnabas, found him overzealous. Even in some of the churches he started there were many who did not like him. He often ran foul of the law and was imprisoned more than once for his beliefs.

It is often thought that Paul's bitter experiences only reinforced his inner certitude that he could understand and communicate across the ages his insight into Christ's teachings as the fulfilment of the law.

Considering that St. John wrote to the Christians in Laodicea (near Pamukkale), Thyatira (Akhisar), Sardis (east of Izmir), and Philadelphia (Alaşehir), which could have been on Paul's route between Galatia, Phrygia and Ephesus, it is quite possible that Paul had visited them in addition to Ephesus where we know he spent a lot of time. It is also possible that he went to the others of John's "Seven Churches of Revelation" (Smyrna or Izmir and Pergamum or Bergama as they are called now).

Places where he definitely stopped off at are exceedingly interesting.

Antioch-on-the-Orontes (Antakya) was an important commercial and educational centre, enriched by handsome public buildings. Known as a sports and recreation centre, celebrations honouring Apollo were held at the Temple to Daphne in a sacred wood southwest of the city.

Among its bustling population of nearly a half million people was an important Jewish segment. Some of these people had fled Jerusalem during the persecutions of people who were friends of Stephen. In Antioch, the movement grew, and soon its members began using a name – Christians, the followers of Christ – to identify themselves.

Expulsion: From this church in Antioch, Paul and his companions set out to broadcast their message abroad. Sailing to Cyprus and then to Perge, Paul preached his first sermon to the congregation at the synagogue in Pisidian Antioch (Yalvaç between Konya and Afyon). The crowd he attracted was largely Gentile, and the Jewish members so resented their intrusion that they had Paul and Barnabas expelled from the district.

The disciples then moved to Iconium

(Konya). Again they preached to a large group of people, and they narrowly escaped a plot to stone them. However, one young woman of Iconium, called Thecla, was so captivated by Paul's preaching that she braved scorn and danger to follow him.

A 2nd-century book, *The Acts of Paul and Thecla*, was written about her exploits and it names her as Christianity's first female martyr. The book also gives a description of Paul: he was short and bald, had hollow eyes and a hooked nose, but was so full of grace that he seemed sometimes like a man and sometimes like an angel. Thecla later lived as a nun and established a hospital at Ayatekla on the peninsula south of Silifke.

In his first journey, Paul concentrated on interior cities. In his subsequent trips he spent longer periods of time in the major ports, hoping to convert people who would carry Christianity around the world.

Paul was twice in Alexandria Troas, a thriving Aegean port just south of today's Odun Iskelesi. The first time he didn't stay long. Church historians date the beginning of the Christianization of Europe to that call, although there already were members of the sect in Rome. Maybe it was not a coinci-

Above, mosaic of Jesus at Hagia Sophia Museum, Istanbul.

dence that Luke, who had a concern for the western movement of Christianity, appeared in the story at this point. (It is unfortunate that the records of the other apostles, who worked in Egypt or in the East, have not been preserved as Luke's account has been.)

When Paul was back in Alexandria Troas on his third journey, he and his friends stayed up talking late into the night. Suddenly a child who had been perched in a window fell out and landed three floors down on the ground. Paul dashed out to find the boy and was able to reassure his family that no harm was done and he was only badly shaken up. The discussions resumed where they had broken off.

Beautiful Ephesus attracted pilgrims from all over the Mediterranean because of its Temple to Diana. Its theatre, its Temple to Serapis, its Celsius library, its odeon, its gymnasiums, are just some of the other grand public buildings that give us today a sense of the wealth of community life when Paul was there.

Performing miracles: For two years Paul stayed in Ephesus teaching the word of Christ, converting people to Christianity, and performing his many apparent miracles of healing. By then many people had joined the Christian community.

However, the silversmiths' trade in cult objects was hurt by Paul's condemnation of idols. The merchants created a serious disturbance during which a crowd collected in the theatre yelling, "Great is Diana of the Ephesians!" The demonstration threatened to turn nasty until the town clerk appeared to warn the crowd that, while Paul was within the law, they were not.

At the end of Paul's third journey he stopped in Miletus to visit the leading members of the church in that region. His farewell speech to his friends was full of wistfulness and affection as he reminded them of their long friendship and of how he had taught them everything he knew.

Paul was a controversial figure in the early church, partly because of the mixture in his teachings of Hebraic and Greek thought. The controversy over his teachings and his contributions to Christian dogma has not ended. But as important as his theology is his quality: a man who was passionately possessed to preach the news of the love of God as embodied in Jesus Christ.

In AD 1070, the advancing Seljuk Turks took Jerusalem from the Arab Fatamids, and in the following year they all but annihilated the Byzantine army at Malazgirt (Manzikert) and captured Emperor Romanus IV Diogenes. Within 20 years, the Seljuk armies had overrun most of Anatolia. Its army towered across the Bosphorus, casting a dark shadow over Constantinople itself (1092). The Byzantine Empire, which for seven centuries had held back Asian hordes, could no longer fulfil its historical mission as the European bulwark against eastern invasions. Constantinople itself was threatened.

Fearing the worst, Emperor Alexius I (1081-1118) joined Simeon, Patriarch of Jerusalem, in urging papal aid to drive back the Turks. The appeal was seconded by several prospering Italian cities: Pisa, Genoa, Venice and Amalfi. These Italian cities wanted to end Arab Moslem domination in the eastern Mediterranean and open the markets of the Near East to European trade.

Pope Urban II, dreaming of a united Christendom, took to the road in 1095, sounding out leaders and ensuring support for a crusade against the Moslem Turks. One cold November morning at Clermont in Auvergne, he made one of the most influential speeches in medieval times:

"O race of Franks! Race beloved and chosen by God!... From the confines of Jerusalem and from Constantinople a grievous report has gone forth that an accursed race, wholly alienated from God, has invaded the lands of these Christians, and has depopulated them...Jerusalem, that royal city, situated at the centre of the earth, implores you to come to her aid.."

The First Crusade: Now, after centuries of argument, the two great faiths, Chistianity and Islam, resorted to war. In the meantime, the Seljuk Turks, "the accursed race," did not speak of Crusades, but of Frankish (French) wars, or of the "Frankish invasions." In July 1096, Kılıç Arslan, whose father, Süleyman, was the first Turk to secure lands from the Byzantines, learned that an enormous number of Franks were en route to Constantinople. Not yet 17, Seljuk Emperor Kılıç Arslan already controlled most of Anatolia.

Now these Occidentals were nothing like the kind of enemy armies to which the Turks were accustomed. There were several hundred knights and a large number of foot soldiers, but there were also children and old people in rags, with strips of cloth in the shapes of crosses sewn onto the backs of their garments. This army looked "more like a wretched tribe evicted from their lands by some invader," thought the Turks.

Walter the Penniless: By the time the Crusaders, who set out from France in 1095

under Peter the Hermit and Walter the Penniless, arrived in Constantinople in 1096, they had been decimated by famine, plague, leprosy, fever and battles on the way. Byzantine Emperor Alexius welcomed them but could not provide enough food, so they broke into the suburbs and plundered churches, houses and palaces. In his haste to free Constantinople from these locusts, Alexius gave them ships to cross the Bosphorus and advance on Iznik where Kılıç

Preceding pages, a caravan passes the remains of the Church of St. John in Pergamum. **Above**, Byzantine icon from the Antalya Museum.

Arslan's bowmen awaited. The Seljuk forces marched out of the city and almost wiped out the First Crusaders. Walter the Penniless was among the slain while Peter the Hermit fled to Constantinople.

In 1097 new Crusader armies crossed the straits and besieged Iznik. Kılıç Arslan retreated only to face them in Şarhöyük (Doryleaum) near Eskişehir. "The Franks cut the Turkish army to pieces. They killed, pillaged and took many prisoners who were sold to slavery," wrote Ibn al-Qalansi, an Arab annalist from Damascus. "When this event, so shameful for Islam became known, there was real panic. Dread and anxiety swelled to enormous proportions."

In October 1097, the Franks were in Antioch, then Syria's largest city. Two years later, they occupied Jerusalem. "Wonderful things were to be seen," reported the eyewitness Raymond Agiles. "Numbers of Saracens were beheaded. Others were shot with arrows, or forced to jump from the towers; others were tortured for several days and then burned alive. In the streets were seen piles of corpses of men and horses." More than 70,000 Moslems were butchered and hundreds of Jews killed by the Crusaders.

Latin Jerusalem: Thus founded, the Latin Kingdom of Jerusalem lasted 44 years (1099-1143). In 1144, Zengi, a young slave-born *atabey*, or Seljuk military leader, recaptured Urfa for Islam. His successor, Nurettin, of equal courage and greater ability, took over. The Moslem resurgence compelled St. Bernard to appeal to the Pope for a new crusade. In 1147, the German Emperor Conrad III set out with his army followed by French King Louis VII. They took the route of the First Crusade. At Şarhöyük, where the First Crusade had defeated Kılıç Arslan, Conrad's army met the Turkish forces commanded by Seljuk Sultan Mesud I, and was so soundly defeated that hardly one Christian in ten survived.

The French army was decimated by starvation and Moslem raids. The collapse of the Second Crusade stunned Europe.

In the 40 years of peace that followed the Second Crusade, Nurettin spread his kingdom from Aleppo to Damascus. When he died, Selahattin Eyyubi (Saladin the Great) brought Egypt and Moslem Syria under one rule (1175). A four-year truce with the Latin Kingdom came to an end in 1188 when Reginald waylaid a Moslem caravan, taking rich booty and a number of prisoners, including Selahattin's sister. Saladin responded by attacking Reginald's army at Hittin. He then turned to Jerusalem, which fell after a siege.

The Third Crusade: Encouraged by the Italian fleet's domination of the Mediterranean, and Christian control of Tyre, Antioch and Tripolis, Emperor Frederick Barbarrosa set out for Jerusalem in the Third Crusade. The Turks quickly harassed his army and cut off his supplies; hundreds of Christian soldiers starved to death and the Emperor drowned (1190) while bathing in the Göksu River near Adana. Richard I (The Lionheart), the newly crowned King of England, took over. Accompanied by Philip Augustus, the King of France, Richard reached and freed Acre (1191). At this time, Philip, ill with fever, returned to France. After a few indecisive battles Richard was able to advance within 12 miles of Jerusalem, but he too fell ill and sued for peace.

The Fourth Crusade (1202-1204) was led by the Venetian Republic, which agreed to the campaign on condition that it took half of the spoils of the conquest. However, the Venetian Doge had no intention of attacking the Holy Lands. Instead he aimed at conquering Christian Constantinople. The prospect of capturing the richest city in Europe was irresistible, and threats of excommunication fell on deaf ears. The Venetian fleet sailed for Constantinople, capturing the Hungarian port of Zara on the way. In the past, the Greek Orthodox Church of the Byzantine monarchy had offered little help, but had profited immensely from the Latin Crusades: it had regained most of Asia from the Turks and had been happily watching the mutual weakening of Moslems and Latins in their struggle for Palestine. But the time had come for them to pay.

The Venetian armada was before Constantinople on June 24, 1204. The Crusaders landed and set the city on fire. The blaze raged for eight days, spread through three square miles and laid a considerable section of the city to ashes. Soldiers looted homes, churches and shops. St. Sophia's great altar was torn to pieces for distribution of its silver and gold. Thousands of art masterpieces were plundered or damaged. The capture of Constantinople by the Latins prepared its occupation by the Turks.

Who, indeed, were these Turks that appeared in the western world, upset its traditions, changed its course and infuriated Pope Urban II into malediction: "that accursed race!"? Ancient historians called them the "scourge of God," and were terrified. Yet, even the most prejudiced admitted that they were not savages. They had a sense of honour and justice, and often proved themselves "more magnanimous than the Romans." They ate and drank moderately, lived and dressed simply, their only ornamentation being the delicate embroidery that attested the skilful fingers of their women.

Steppes people: The Turks originated from the steppes of Central Asia. Geologists tell us that today's arid regions of Central Asia were once much coveted land, nourished with great lakes and rivers. The recession of the last ice age dried up this area and as rainfall was insufficient to support the people, city after city was abandoned as men migrated in search of water.

As late as 1868, some 80,000 inhabitants of western Turkestan, the "Turk country," were forced to leave because their region was being inundated by moving sand. Half buried in sand laid the cities of Bagkara (Bactra) and Anav (Anau) where in 1907 Pumpelly unearthed the remains of a civilization which had cultivated wheat, barley and millet, used copper and domesticated animals. Pumpelly dated his findings to 9000 BC This meant the culture of Turkestan was very advanced by 5000 BC, the year of the Egyptian Pyramids.

Historical records show the proto-Turkish tribes settled somewhere between the Ural and Altay mountains circa 1400-1200 BC, about the time when Jewish tribes appeared in Canaan. They spoke one of the 14 "Turkic" languages, which are neither Semitic nor Indo-Aryan, but agglutinate in structure. Semi-nomadic, the Turks cultivated land, raised animals and worshipped a *Sky Tengrı* (*"tengri"* from "tien," the heavens; *"tanrı"* in contemporary Turkish) and other lesser gods of the sun, the moon, the earth, the ancestors and the fire. Their beliefs differed

sharply from Greco-Roman paganism. Turkish cosmology did not offer a scene where gods fought with man to keep him in his place, but provided a serene and fraternal relationship. In his capacity as the elder brother, *Sky Tengrı* taught them every worldly thing they needed for survival, including how to light fire.

The history of Central Asia is no more than the story of the endless struggle of Turkish tribes for better pastures and water. As the desert expanded, the steppes shrunk, forcing the nomadic tribes to take refuge in oases and adapt to a settled life. Thus the region served as a *"vegina gentium,"* a peoples' womb, which raised kings and sultans to the civilized empires. However, there was another law at work: that the old empires eventually absorbed the invading Turks who settled to become a minority aristocracy. The two oldest civilizations of the world, the Chinese and the Persians, assimilated them so that within 50 years the invaders had become passionate defenders of their adopted civilizations and religions.

Islam: One such clan took its name from its leader, Seljuk. In AD 900, the Seljuk clan, like many Turkish tribes, adopted the Islamic faith and became the "Sword of Islam" against the Crusaders. Its dominions grew from victory to victory, until its descendants ruled Persia, Iraq, Syria and Asia Minor. A kindred clan under Ertuğrul, fleeing Mongol invasions in Central Asia, came and found military employment with the Seljuk Bey (Prince) of Konya, and received a tract of land to pasture its herds.

When Ertuğrul died (1288), he was succeeded by his son Osman (Othman), the eponymous founder of the Ottoman Empire. Seeing the Seljuks were too weak to stop him, Osman declared himself an independent bey of a mini-state in northwestern Anatolia. Between him and the Sea of Marmara lay a number of Byzantine cities. The most important among them, Bursa, surrendered to his son, Orhan, who made it his new capital (1326). Orhan took the title "Sultan of the Ottomans." The Byzantine Emperors made peace with him, gave him their daughters in marriage and allowed, begrudgingly,

Left, a Turkish Zeybek warrior.

his son Süleyman to establish Ottoman strongholds on European soil. When Orhan Bey died in 1359, the Ottomans were well on their way to forming a dynasty.

Murat I (Ameurth) conquered most of the Balkans; Dimetoka fell to him in 1361, Filibe in 1363 and Sophia in 1389. He eased their submission by giving them a more efficient government than they had known under Christian rule, and made Edirne (Adrianopolis) his new capital. Beyazıt I, the "Thunderbolt" inherited his father's crown on the battlefield of Kosova, near Mitrovica, Yugoslavia in 1389. He besieged Constantinople four times. In his grandfather's traditions he married a Christian woman, Lady Despoina, sister of Lazerevitch, the ruler of Serbia.

Tamerlane: A new threat appeared from the East in the form of Tamerlane of Genghis Khan's stock. Tamerlane's army had recently taken Baghdad (1393), forcing its Arab sultan, Ahmed, to seek asylum with Beyazıt I. When Beyazıt refused to extradite Ahmed, Tamerlane entered Asia Minor. In 1402, the two kinsmen joined in battle near Ankara. A year later Beyazıt died a prisoner. Constantinople rejoiced, Christendom was saved from the Moslems by other Moslems for another 50 years to come. As Tamerlane's army marched back to Central Asia, Beyazıt's son, Mehmet I, reorganized the Ottoman state, which was in shambles. Mehmet I left his son Murat II to subdue Hunyadi Janos in the Balkans. When Murat II died after 30 years of rule, Christian historians ranked him among the greatest monarchs of his time.

Sultan Mehmet II, "The Conquerer," spoke five languages, excelled in mathematics and engineering, cultivated the arts, supported colleges and pious foundations. He is said to have equalled his father in culture and conquests, political acumen, and even the length of reign. It was to his cannons that Constantinople fell (1453), changing the course of European and Ottoman history.

In conquering Constantinople, the Ottomans took over a feature peculiar to the Byzantine Empire: one allowed to exist in the capital of colonies established by the European city-states of Genoa, Amalfi, Pisa, Venice, Ancona and Narbonn. Granted trading privileges and tax exemptions, these foreign enclaves were allowed to manage their religious and administrative affairs and to conduct their own legal and judicial business. The conquerer would not allow these foreign elements to retain their military strength. He dismantled their fortifications, but did not concern himself with the manner in which these Franks lived and traded. The capitulations of 1521 confirmed those privileges which the Venetians had enjoyed under the Byzantines. This was followed by those concessions granted to France (1536) and England (1580). In addition to commercial and navigational rights, these treaties allowed the European powers to appoint consuls in the Ottoman dominions and gave them jurisdiction in civil matters over their own nationals. Subsequent French capitulations gave the French kings the right to protect every Roman Catholic of non-Turkish nationality in all parts of the Ottoman Empire.

"Millet" system: Thus arose the most characteristic administrative feature of the Ottoman Empire: the millet system. Millet is the Arabic word for "nation," and in this case it meant the sultans granted varying degrees of autonomy to their non-Moslem subjects. The millet of Rum (Romans), for instance, consisted of those who obeyed the Greek Orthodox Patriarch, and the Armenian millet of those subject to the Gregorian Armenian Patriarch. The development of the system meant that the Turks themselves became members of a millet – millet of Islam, for sure, but a minority amongst Arabs, Kurds and the rest! The name "Turk" came to denote a vulgar brethren back in Turkestan. In 1828, a Scottish traveller, Charles MacFarlane, would say that the Turks "indeed consider our word Turk insulting. I remember seeing a poor Greek well kicked for exclaiming 'Turkikos!' where he thought no Turk would hear him!"

The steppes had supplied the sultans, but the Ottoman melting pot had engulfed the horsemen so fast that of 292 grand viziers of the Ottoman Empire, only 78 could claim Turkish parentage.

Sultan Mehmet the Conquerer died (1481) at the age of 51, just when his army seemed to be on the verge of conquering Italy. A contest among his sons gave the throne to Beyazıt II, a reluctant warrior who nevertheless managed to build an armada of 270 vessels and destroy the Venetian fleet off the coast of Greece. In 1512, he left his throne to his son Selim I.

The Grim: Sultan Selim I, known in the west as Selim The Grim, despised his father's pacifism. He started out by campaigning against Shah Ismail of Iran who had raided the Turkish frontier. Capturing Tabriz, he made northern Mesopotamia an Ottoman province. He then turned his army against Syria, Arabia and Egypt (1517) and carried the caliphate to Istanbul. Thereafter, the Ottoman sultans, as caliphs, also became spiritual leaders of the Moslem world.

Süleyman the Magnificent succeeded his father as sultan at the age of 26. Francis I had been proposing since 1516 to the European

later, Süleyman returned and unsuccessfully besieged Vienna (1539). On the way back to Istanbul, his army ravaged southern Austria. He returned west again (1539), where Venice bore the brunt of his assault, losing its possessions in the Aegean and the Dalmatian Coast (1540). Four years later, at the age of 72, the master of Egypt, North Africa, Asia Minor, Palestine, Syria, the Balkans and Hungary was dead. The Ottomans were the strongest power in Europe and Africa.

Until Süleyman's death, the only limit to Ottoman advance seemed to be determined by their ambitions. Then there set in, at the end of the 16th century, a period of standstill, when the Christian powers began to

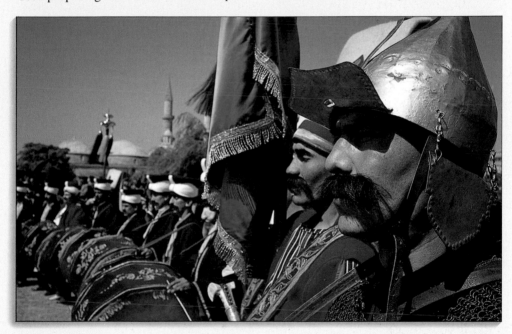

powers that they should utterly destroy the Ottoman state and divide its possessions among themselves as infidel spoils. Süleyman himself supposed that the best defence was offence. In 1521, he captured the Hungarian strongholds of Szabacs and Belgrade. In 1523 Rhodes fell. Hungary joined the Empire in 1526, amidst cheers from Protestants, for Luther had urged the Protestant princes to stay home, "for the Turks were obviously a divine visitation and to resist them would be to resist God." Three years

Above, Ottoman Janissary band plays martial music.

challenge Turkish supremacy. Following a temporary revival, under the vigorous Köprülü family of grand viziers, of military ardour and success which terminated in the second siege of Vienna (1683), stagnation and decline set in. The Peace of Carlowitz (1699) marked the beginning of the end of the Ottomans. The next blow came with the Treaty of Küçük Kaynarca (1774) signed with Russia, now consolidated under the House of Romanov. Soon the Russians opened the Black Sea, which for two centuries had been a Turkish lake, to commerce and navigation. Within a decade, Crimea and Caucasia were under Russian rule.

The decline continued into the 19th century, despite reforms of the armed forces, and establishment of a Council of State, a Penal Code and a State bank, institutions that were to prove abortive in practice.

Iron Fist rule: The 1877-1878 Russian War was a disaster not to be forgotten. The empire lost most of its European possessions. Greece had already gained its independence (1830). With Sultan Abdülhamit, the Ottomans wooed the Moslem nations under their rule and found a new ally in the west: Germany, which helped build the Baghdad Railway, a project that facilitated traffic to the holy cities of Arabia and reinforced the Turkish ruler's position as Caliph. For 30

tafa Kemal Pasha (later named Atatürk), the victorious commander of the Turkish forces at Gallipoli, arrived at the northeast Black Sea port of Samsun and began the three-year national struggle for independence.

Under Kemal, Turkish nationalism was ignited, the Greek army was defeated and the French were pushed back. Italy withdrew its troops. The allied powers signed an armistice in 1922. The Treaty of Lausanne (1923) recognized Turkey's present boundaries, ended the capitulations and allowed for the exchange of minorities between Greece and Turkey.

The Republic: Turkey was proclaimed a republic on October 29, 1923, and Mustafa

Smyrne

Le port et le Mont Pagus

years he ruled with an iron fist, keeping the country out of major foreign wars, but Abdülhamit could not cure the ills of the empire. In 1909, Abdülhamit was toppled. The Committee of Union and Progress, which replaced him with a puppet sultan, convened Parliament. But soon the empire was plunged into one war after another, culminating with its defeat in World War I, in which it had sided with Germany.

Istanbul was occupied by the British, while the Italians seized Antalya and the southwest coast, and the French occupied the Cilician coast. In May 1919 the Greek army invaded Izmir. Three days later Mus-

Kemal was elected its first president with Ankara designated as the capital.

Sweeping reforms were carried out by Kemal to westernize the nation. The Sultanate was abolished and the Caliphate suppressed. Atatürk replaced the Sharia, the Islamic Holy law, with civil, trade and criminal codes adopted from the west. Turks adopted last names.

In 1925, the *fez*, the symbol of Islamic Orthodoxy, was banned, replaced by the *şapka*, the western-style hat with a brim. Atatürk said of the *fez*: "It is a badge of ignorance, indifference, backwardness and hostility to civilization." He urged Turks to dress like westerners because "it would help them think like westerners."

In 1928, the Latin alphabet replaced the Ottoman script, severing Turks' ties with their past. The government in 1934 prohibited the use of the honorary Ottoman titles *ağa, efendi, bey,* and *pasha*, and banned the playing of oriental music on Turkish state radio – a ban that was to be later repealed. It also prohibited the wearing of religious garb in public.

Womens' rights: Isolated from men and treated as second-class citizens during the Ottoman period, women in the republic were now encouraged to mix with men at parties, attend public functions, take jobs in the civil

school who touched neither alcohol nor coffee and kept his palate additionally uncontaminated by abstaining even from tobacco. For drinks at the meal my friend's host provided only water; but the water was of four different kinds, each served in a different carafe: one from the sweet waters of Europe, one from the sweet Waters of Asia, the others respectively from Beykoz and Yeşilköy. He asserted that each of these waters had a special flavour and quality and recommended one for the fish, another for the *pilav*, the third for the sweet and the fourth for the fruit.

This episode took place during the brief Caliphate of Abdülmecit, when Turkey re-

Vue des Quais et la Poste Hellénique
"Αποψις Προκυμαίας, Έλληνικόν Ταχυδρομείον"

service and go to the theatre. Even beauty contests, unthinkable in the past, were encouraged. In 1932, a Turkish woman was crowned "Miss World." Turkish women were granted suffrage in the same year and 18 were elected deputies in 1936.

An English observer summed up the reforms this way: "One evening between the World Wars, a friend of mine, then representing a leading London newspaper in Constantinople, was invited to dinner with a Turkish acquaintance, a gentleman of the old

Left, Izmir in the 19th century. **Above**, "Infidel Izmir" during the Greek occupation.

tained the forms, at all events, of an Islamic state. The host was perhaps exceptional in his connoisseurship of the finer points of water-drinking, but he was still a normal Turk in his abstention from liquor.

A bare quarter of a century later the Turkish government, claiming that in its Anatolian provinces originated some of the earliest wines made by man, was inaugurating the export of Turkish wine of good quality as a permanent national industry. There can be few more striking illustrations of the change in the outlook of the Turkish state brought about by the Revolution of Mustafa Kemal."

Throughout touristic towns along Turkey's Aegean and Mediterranean coasts in the early hours of the morning after the discos and bars have sent their last customers home, another part of Turkish life begins. From the smallest village in the east to the capital of Ankara to the tourist city of Marmaris, *muezzins* ascend to the tops of minarets to call faithful Moslems to morning prayer (*ezan*).

The muezzins wail from the minarets: "Allah [God] is the great. Allah is great. I do testify that there is no god save Allah." It is a potent message.

According to their birth certificates, the Turkish population is 99 percent Moslem, mostly Sunni. Since the 1920s, due to Kemal Atatürk's religious reforms, Turkey has been a secular state. Therefore religious freedom is guaranteed to all non-Moslems.

During the Ottoman Empire a large number of minorities were free to practise various religions. Today, for example, a small community of Sephardic Jews remains in Istanbul and groups of Greek Orthodox, Armenian Orthodox and Catholics are scattered across the country.

Although Islam is the dominant religion in Turkey, it is practised in a wide variety of ways and rituals. It isn't surprising to see an elderly woman in traditional Moslem garb, the *çarşaf*, covered from head to toe in black, with her teenage daughter decked out in blue jeans and a Michael Jackson t-shirt walking side by side.

While the Koran, the Moslem holy book, forbids alcohol consumption, Turks of all ages drink *rakı* and wine in restaurants and bars. In the southern resort towns, discos and restaurants with Turks wearing the same scanty clothes as other Europeans on holiday can be found next to mosques.

Secular Turkey: Atatürk, the architect of modern Turkey, believed firmly in a secular state. He abolished religious law and instituted in its place secular law. Also Islam was removed as state religion and the day of rest was changed from Friday to Sunday like the Christian West. He also created a secular

Left, Moslems gather for Friday prayers at Istanbul's Blue Mosque.

school system. The Roman alphabet replaced the Ottoman script, which was based on Persian and Arabic, further separating Islam from education.

However, since the 1980s there has been an increasing interest in Islam. The 1982 constitution reinstated religious education in primary and secondary schools as a reaction to the growing militancy on university campuses in the late 1970s.

This was followed by a considerable increase in the number of government-controlled religious schools to educate teachers and clergy for the mosques. The strength of Atatürk's belief in secularism as a founding principle of the state is so deeply ingrained in the fibre of the whole country that any dangerous tilt toward Islamic fundamentalism seems highly unlikely, western diplomats say.

There are two major religious holidays on the Islamic lunar calendar. Since the lunar calendar is approximately eleven days shorter than the Gregorian, Moslem holidays begin earlier each year. *Kurban Bayramı* (Sacrifice Festival), the most important religious holiday of the year, is equivalent to Christmas for Christians.

The festival observes God's intervention when Abraham wanted to sacrifice his son Isaac to God. According to Moslem belief, Allah ordered Abraham to slaughter a sheep instead of his son. *Kurban Bayramı* is a four-day religious affair. Several days prior to *Kurban Bayramı* shepherds drive flocks of sheep into the cities to be sold for slaughter. On the first day of the *bayramı* men go to the mosque early in the morning for prayer. After prayer, the head of the family slits the sheep's throat, skins and butchers it.

A simple meal of lightly spiced sauteed meat from the animal, called *kavurma*, is prepared in most homes. One-third of the meat is given to the poor, one-third or less is eaten by the family and one-third is given to relatives and friends.

Rigorous fasting: *Ramazan* (Ramadan) is the month of rigorous fasting where nothing is drunk or eaten between sun up and sunset. The fast is broken with flat round *pide* bread bought hot from bakeries at sundown. This is followed by complex meals of favourite foods, eaten in extra large quantities. Just before dawn drummers go through the streets waking the faithful so that they can eat before sunrise. Many restaurants and shops will be closed for large parts of the day during *Ramazan* but it is still possible to find food. It's best to be discreet although many non-Moslems and moderate Moslems will be eating in public.

The month of *Ramazan* ends in a three-day national holiday, known as the Sweet Holiday, or *Şeker Bayramı*. Sweets such as *baklava* and *lokum* (Turkish Delight) are given as gifts.

Prayers which start at 4am are repeated

those who are rich enough must pay legal alms once a year called *zekat*; fast during the holy month of *Ramazan*; and perform the holy pilgrimage to Mecca at least once in a lifetime if one is in good health and has the financial means.

Whirling dervishes: Whirling men in long white robes, their arms extended, dizzying only to the observer – they are the Mevlevi dervishes, members of an Islamic mystic order who perform the *Sema*, a religious dance accompanied by holy music.

It is a dance of ecstasy during which they reach a union with God. During the dance, the dervishes turn left around their own axis while circling the ceremonial area symboliz-

five times a day, becoming a dominant feature of Islamic life. Yet many Turks only go to pray on *bayrams* (religious holidays) or for some even rarer than that. Moslems do not have to go to the mosque to pray. Often shopkeepers spread out their small prayer mats in the direction of Mecca and pray.

Five pillars: The requirements of Islam, which literally means submission, are few and simple. For a believer to be a perfect Moslem he submits to five principles: the first, and most important, is to bear witness that there is no God except Allah, and Mohammed is his prophet. The others are: to perform the five required daily prayers;

ing the movements of the planets around the sun. The palm of the right hand faces the sky and the left is turned toward the ground, signifying man receiving from God and contributing to the people.

The eerie ceremony is best seen during the week of the Festival of Mevlana in Konya, south central Turkey, in mid-December. In Istanbul, several groups of Mevlevi men and women perform their dance and mystic music to audiences at the Galata Mevlevihane (also known as Divan Edebiyah Museum) on the last Sunday of each month.

Above, modern women also pray.

Mevlana Celaleddin Rumi, the great mystic poet, philosopher and founder of the whirling dervishes, was born in Ballkh in Central Asia in AD 1207. He emigrated to Konya, the capital of the Seljuk Empire, which is still the centre of the mystic order. He preached to his disciples a union with God through music and dance. After his death in 1273, his followers, the Mevlevis, became closely connected with the ruling Ottomans.

Circumcision: Decked out in a fancy white suit, fur trimmed hat, cape and sparkling attachments, a young boy is led smiling by his mother to become a circumcised Moslem. Boys are typically circumcised between the ages of four and six, but it's more common in large towns to perform the operation at birth and celebrate the occasion later.

After the actual operation, which is performed in a hotel, circumcision house, or even hospital, a lavish party with close friends and family is held. The boy receives many gifts and money which is usually placed in an envelope and tucked under the pillow of his circumcision bed.

Sometimes mass circumcision parties are held, especially for orphans or boys of poor families, with one *fenni sünnetçi* (professional circumciser) carrying out as many as 1,000 operations in one session. The best known *sünnetçi* in Turkey, Kemal Özkan of Istanbul, claims he can perform a "bloodless operation."

As varied as religious practices are in Turkey so are marriage traditions. Attending a traditional village wedding is one of the most exhilarating social events one can experience in Turkey. For sure it is one of the longest events, typically lasting three or four days. Marriages are held in the autumn after the crops have been harvested and the families can spare the time and the lost labour of their daughters.

The couple is first married by an *imam* (Moslem priest) who comes to the bride's house and performs a short ceremony that includes prayer and an explanation of the marriage vows. All women in the wedding will have the palms of their hands and finger tips reddened with henna (kına) to bring good luck.

Separate parties: The women in the wedding have a party separate from the men where they dance and eat to celebrate the marriage of their friend. The men also gather on the same or following day. They also dance, sing, as well as imbibe vast quantities of *rakı*. Often guns are brought out and fired into the sky with a few tragic mishaps occurring now and then. The Turkish women wash the bride at the village *hamam* or her home and then she is carefully dressed in wedding clothes that include veils and numerous layers of colourful cloth. The groom's friends go to the bride's house to ask for her hand in marriage and are usually refused until they give a gift to the family.

The groom climbs to the roof and breaks an earthenware jug which scares away evil spirits. Finally the bride is shown to her new bedroom where she waits for her husband. When she enters she again asks for a gift, usually a gold bracelet or chain, and then before they sleep they pray together.

In large towns and cities, many of these traditions have been abandoned and replaced by a party for friends and family given in a restaurant or tea garden. All couples must also have a short civil wedding according to modern Turkish law.

Birth and death: A new baby is named only after the whole extended family has been consulted. Usually a baby is named after a relative. The grandparents promise to give the child a gift that will grow, such as a poplar tree (*kavak*). Babies are always dressed with a piece of blue stone or glass that purportedly wards off the evil eye. This is not part of Islam but of folk belief. Many adult Moslems also wear the blue eye for the same reason.

When a Moslem dies he or she is carefully washed by someone of the same sex and placed on the bedroom floor. The body is then wrapped in a 16-foot-long white burial cloth. First it is taken to the mosque and put on a special stone catafalque in the courtyard designed for coffins. After the regular prayers, the *imam* leads special services for the dead before the coffin is taken to the cemetery, often shouldered the distance by male relatives of the deceased.

It is common to see religious men with hands behind their backs counting a *tespih* (worry beads) in long and endless motions. Worry beads, similar to Catholic rosaries, come in all sizes and colours. They are sold near mosques or in shops that sell Korans and calligraphy.

Visiting Ottoman Turkey in 1893, Lady G. Max Muller, wife of a British MP wrote: "We had expected to see all nations here, and we had indeed! It was as if the Tower of Babel has just fallen, and its inhabitants were pouring down the streets of Shinar. The sharp-featured Semites, the almond-eyed Mongols, the Arayans."

A careful eye will note that the Turks still come in all features! Not surprising, perhaps, when one considers that the country is not only a bridge between Europe and Asia, but also the former nucleus of an empire which extended from Vienna to Tabriz, and from Crimea to the southern tip of the Arabian Peninsula.

Melting pot: When the World War I defeat resulted in the loss of imperial territory for the Ottoman Empire, forcing the Sultan's subjects to take refuge within the present boundaries of the Turkish state, the ancient melting pot enjoyed still more ingredients. The refugees from the Balkans, as well as Russia, the Arab states and the Aegean Islands brought with them their ways of life and further enriched the culture.

One important feature that contributes to that variety is that Turkey is a peninsula which occupies a 300,984-square-mile (781,000-square-km) area, approximately three times the size of Great Britain. The major part of the country consists of high plateaus. The topography and the climatic conditions differ widely from one region to another. Temperatures of way below zero can occur, while days of over 113° F (45° C) are not uncommon. The result is that as the figs and grapes ripen on the Aegean Coast, Erzurum in the northeast may be overwhelmed by a snowstorm! Put it in another way, as the westerners enjoy a good swim, easterners are still wearing their overcoats and rubber boots. No wonder then, that the population (more than 60 million) is heavily concentrated in the west and along the coast where the biggest cities are situated.

When large segments of population from

Preceding pages: women folk dancers; piggy back ride. Left, a village beauty. Right, a city beauty.

the rural areas learn of the pleasures of urban life from television or movies, or from direct observation via cheap public transportation, they decide to live in the cities. But above all, increasing unemployment and ongoing social and political unrest are the major causes of mass migration from eastern provinces.

As urbanization accelerated, especially after World War II, housing shortages became severe, and *gecekondus* (squatter houses, shanty towns or overnight houses) sprang up almost overnight around the sub-

urbs of major Turkish cities like Istanbul, Izmir and Adana.

Turkish shanty: Like all social problems, the Turkish *gecekondu* has some aspects which are universal and some which are distinctively Turkish. Perhaps the most distinct thing about the *gecekondu* is that it appears to occupy an intermediate position between the situation in England and the situation in India. In all three countries migrants from rural areas require housing. In England, the government builds houses for them, administered by the municipalities. In India, they camp in the streets. In Turkey, they build their own houses – ramshackle hovels on the peripheries of cities – without asking the state to pay for any of the construction or building materials or for their labour. Whole gecekondu cities are known to have been built within two or three years at these sites. But these gecekondu towns are built on somebody else's land, most often on state-owned property. "Were it not for the land problem, one can argue that this is the cheapest and most efficient form of low income housing known anywhere in the world," notes Professor C.W.M. Hart of the University of California. These slum houses, however, upset town planning schemes. The frustrated authorities become more and more certain that nothing can be done in these cities unless the newcomers return to their hometowns. Unless a reverse migration can be started, municipal officials in many cities argue, the beautiful maps of new housing and town planning projects of cities will perish even before they are completed.

Unbelievable as it may seem to the upper and middle classes of the major developed cities who pass the gecekondu areas with a shudder, an overwhelming majority of the people who live in these areas firmly believe they are better off than they were in the villages they came from. They are sure they have improved themselves as a family. The parents are satisfied with that advance themselves, but they hope and pray and plan for their children to climb up the next rung of the social ladder, from peasant gecekondu-dweller to university graduate in two generations. It does not appear that putting schools in every village in Turkey and factories in half of them would stem the tide. "Why wait a hundred years for that to happen?" say the gecekondu people. "It's much easier and quicker to move to the city and build a gecekondu. There you will find not only factories for work but decent schools for your younger children."

Nowhere in coastal Turkey is the gecekondu problem as acute as in Adana, the country's fourth largest city and the industrial, agricultural and commercial hub of the south. The city's population has been growing at an alarming annual rate of 6.5 percent because of migrations from the rural areas of eastern Turkey. Expecting its population to double to two million by the year 2000, Adana's municipal authorities are building a new city to the northwest, rehabilitating the slums and moving some of the urban poor to the new neighbourhoods.

The exodus: In Adana, where 85 percent of the housing are substandard structures without proper drinking water, sewers and electricity and where the highest number of malaria cases is reported in Turkey each year, the majority of the gecekondu people are of Kurdish and Arab descent who migrated to the region at one time as seasonal cotton or fruit pickers and decided to stay. They came in waves mainly from the southeast provinces of Diyarbakır, Urfa, Siirt, Mardin, Adiyaman and Van where unemployment figures reach 30 percent of the work age population, employment prospects are grim, and the land is too arid for farming.

The exodus from the rural areas to Adana and other big cities of southern and western Turkey still continues from these and other areas of Anatolia. The migration from that part of Turkey, officials predict, will end only when a series of hydroelectric dam projects on the Euphrates and Tigris rivers, known as GAP, are completed and begin irrigating the arid steppes between the two rivers of southeast Turkey. The first big step in the project, the Atatürk Dam, is already operational.

Travellers to the Çukurova region can see many of these seasonal migrants with their tents pitched along the main highways, always displaced, working for a pittance and exploited by the big landowners, known as the ağa. These seasonal agriculture workers – Turkey's Okies and Arkies – follow the farming season, planting cotton and other crops in the spring, picking fruits and vegetables in the summer and harvesting cotton in October and November. They usually return to their families in the villages during the winter after the crops have been harvested only to come back in spring.

An interesting fact is that on the west coast, though nowhere else in Turkey, perhaps over half of the gecekondu people do not come from Anatolia at all. There are two other sources for the gecekondu population, which when combined at least equal or outnumber the Anatolians.

One of these groups is the göçmen, the immigrant group, whose members were born, or whose families originated, outside Turkey. The other group are the people who were displaced as a result of extensive road building, slum clearance and urban renewal projects, as in Izmir.

Balkan Wars' Refugees: The older *göçmen* groups are grandchildren of Turkish refugees who fled their homes in the Balkans as a result of various wars from 1878 onward, and the contracting boundaries of the Ottoman Empire. One can find residues of every conflict that Turkey ever fought since the Crimean War 1854-1856, living in pockets of *göçmen* settlements scattered throughout the country, not only in the *gecekondu* of cities but in the countryside as well. Most of the inhabitants of smaller towns and farmers of Thrace, European Turkey, are of *göçmen*

properties (homes and land) left by the migrating Greeks.

The relatively new group are Turks from the Balkan countries of Greece, Romania, Bulgaria, Yugoslavia, Albania and the Aegean Islands who arrived after World War II. Most of them were given farming land in Anatolia, which they were required to cultivate for at least ten years. Some of the farm lands given to these immigrants were either sold or abandoned as soon as the ten-year limitation was up and these Balkan Turks too flocked to the cities.

Migration continues: The migration from Greece, Yugoslavia and Bulgaria to Turkey, which is still going on, is perhaps the most

origin. During the Russian-Turkish War of 1878, nearly 1.5 million Turks living in Bulgaria fled to the present boundaries of Turkey and were settled.

A total of nearly 500,000 Turks from Greece were exchanged for Turkey's 1.5 million Greeks in 1923, as part of an agreement struck between Ankara and Athens ending three years of bitter hostilities. These Turks were settled all over the country, but mainly concentrated in the western part of Turkey, including the Aegean and Mediterranean where they were given the

Above, men celebrate at a circumcision.

interesting. Typically, these people are Turks by ethnic origin, Moslem by religion, who find residence in the three countries intolerable whatever their economic conditions in their home country. Rather well-off families from the Greek province of western Thrace, where 150,000 Turks still live, have been known to sell their farms and move to Turkey because of the Greek government's discriminatory policies against ethnic Turks. Often they move to the city and buy a *gecekondu* for which they pay hundreds of million T.L. without a land title deed. The money thus paid represents the life savings of such a family which would be wiped out if their farms were to be demolished by Greek authorities.

The most recent migration was the arrival of nearly 330,000 Turkish refugees from Bulgaria in 1989, in what has been described as the biggest population movement in Europe since World War II. About one million Turks continue to live in Bulgaria. The Bulgarian government expelled these Turks, who had been protesting their forced assimilation into the Slavic society. Most of these Turkish refugees have been distributed throughout the country, but nearly one-third have moved to Bursa, a province in western Turkey. Some of these Turks have returned to Bulgaria since the fall of Bulgarian Communist Party chief Todor Jivkov, hoping that the political reforms sweeping that country and Eastern Europe will also benefit them.

In addition to the immigrants from the Balkans there are also recent arrivals from Central Asia, many of whom escaped communist China by way of Pakistan. These East Turkestan Turks, resembling the primordial Turks who conquered Anatolia in the 11th century, with slanted eyes and oriental features, have moved primarily into the cities of western Turkey, including Istanbul.

The Yörüks: Visitors to the Turkish Coast will often encounter nomadic tribesmen leading their camel caravans along the highways. These are the Yörüks. During the hot summers, the Yörüks camp out in the high mountain plateaus that surround the coast. In winter, they come down into the valleys and the coast. The Yörüks were nomadic Turcoman warrior tribes that ventured into Anatolia after the Seljuk victory over the Byzantine army in 1071 at Malazgirt and settled in the more remote areas of western and southern Turkey. Their name was derived from the Turkish word *"yürümek,"* to walk, which appropriately describes their way of life as wanderers.

They can be seen principally in the coastal foothills of Muğla and Antalya provinces and also farther east in the Mersin and Adana provinces. In spring time, they hold a *panayir*, spring festival that is a continuation of the Greek *panegyria*, or religious holidays. During the *panayir*, the Yörüks pitch tents, sell handicrafts, handmade carpets and food, and play the *davul* and *zurna* (the drum and the oboe) and dance.

The Yörüks are famous for their colourful costumes, tents, delicate embroideries and fancy flat weave wool carpets, the most famous of which are the *kilims*. They also produce fine pillow covers, saddlebags and sacks. The best collection of Yörük artifacts can be seen in the ethnographic section of the Antalya Museum.

Coastal minorities: Travellers to the Turkish Coast will also from time to time come across members of the non-Moslem minorities, the Greeks, the Jews, the Catholics and the Armenians.

A few hundred Greek farmer families, all elderly people now, still inhabit the Turkish Aegean islands of Gökçeada (formerly known as Imroz) and Bozcaada (Tenedos) – their existence, their own schools and religious practices are guaranteed by the 1923 Treaty of Lausanne. Some of these families operate pensions and restaurants in these islands and produce wines.

The region's Jewish population is concentrated in Izmir, Turkey's third largest city, where there are about 2,000 Sephardic Jews, but small clusters of Jewish families exist in Adana and Antakya, near the Syrian border. Jews have lived in Anatolia since Alexander the Great's time. But not until 1492, when Spain expelled Jews during the Inquisition, did large numbers settle in the Ottoman Empire. Welcomed by the sultan partly for their wealth and business acumen, the refugees became influential merchants and diplomats. For centuries, the Jews went to their own schools, the *Yesivot*, and spoke *Ladino*, or Judeo-Spanish, a mixture of medieval Spanish and Hebrew that in time contained words of Turkish, Greek and French origin. Today, older Jews are still fluent in *Ladino* and speak Turkish with a heavy accent. But few young Jews speak *Ladino*, even at home. And many Jewish families send their children to Turkish schools to learn flawless Turkish. Only one course in elementary Hebrew is taught at the *Yesivot*, but no instruction is given in *Ladino*, or Jewish history and literature. Most Turkish Jews are prominent industrialists and businessmen. There are many educators, artists, musicians and distinguished journalists among Turkish Jews.

Esoteric sect: One esoteric sect is the Dönme (which means Apostates in Turkish), a Jewish group that converted to Islam in the 17th century. The Dönmes, who number several hundreds in Izmir, are followers of the "False Messiah" Sabatai Zevi (1626-1676), a mystic Jewish leader who preached the Kabala and claimed he would lead the dispersed Jews back to redeem Israel. Zevi's mystical views about Israeli statehood came 200 years before the birth of Theodor Herzl and Zionism. Over one million Jews from every social class and in every country in Europe, Asia and Africa hailed him as their deliverer, though he was disavowed by conservative Jews as a paranoid personality who had hallucinations. Zevi was born in Izmir in a house that still exists in the Kemeraltı shopping district and is considered holy by Dönme adherents. The Sultan, seeing Zevi's movement a danger to his

exceptions, the Turkish state has never considered Catholics as Turkish citizens, mainly because the Latin Church was confined to Christians from the West and was never strong among natives. With the exception of the Armenian Catholics, they were not incorporated into the "millet" system during the Ottoman period, and had to rely on the protection of France, Italy and England. Many Catholics, such as the Italians, Maltese and French, in fact, maintain their European citizenship, though some have adopted dual citizenship. A great many of the British and French Catholics living in Izmir belong to the class known as the Levantines. Nearly all have been born in Tur-

empire, imprisoned him and ordered him to abandon his faith or face death with his followers. Zevi, to the dismay of his supporters, converted to Islam. His hard core backers followed suit and became Moslems. Dönmes are outwardly Moslem, but in secret observe certain Jewish rites and customs, but in no way do they associate with the Jews, whom they describe as *kafirs* (infidels). The rejection is mutual.

An estimated 2,500 Roman rite Catholics who live on the Turkish Coast are concentrated in Izmir and Adana. With one or two

Left, a camel trainer and **right**, a peasant girl.

key and in many cases their families have lived in the country for several generations. Their retention of European citizenship is often the only connection with the nation from which they originated.

A final Christian group that lives on the Turkish Coast are the Armenians who number about 5,000. The Armenians, who are Gregorian Orthodox Christians, live mainly in Adana, Iskenderun and Antakya and in other scattered communities in the Hatay province.

Ethnic jokes: The joke that goes around these days in Turkey about the Turks is that they are made up of two essential elements:

the leek-eaters and the zucchini-eaters. The leek-eaters are those who come from the wrong, that is the western, side of the Meriç (Maritsa) River, which separates Turkey from Greece. The zucchini-eaters are the Anatolians who are further divided into two: the lovers of *lahmacun*, a pizza-like pastry, and those who claim they would eat anything caught from the sea, even if it were their own fathers! Put in these terms, the coastal line starting from Istanbul all the way down to Antalya, to the point where the hot *kebabs* of southeast Turkey begin to take over, is occupied by the leek eaters. The connotation is that these people are all but vegetarians who consume "any thorn or weed" that comes

tion business of Turkey, building the make-shift apartments replacing the *gece-kondu* in the cities and the hotels and holiday villages of the Turkish Coast. They also con-trol the bakeries of Turkey. Other Turks say the Laz have the ability to smell where money can be made. Making up affectionate jokes about the mercurial Laz, designed to disprove their claims to be geniuses, is a national pastime. One popular Laz joke is: What did one Laz say to the other Laz who was hammering at the wrong end of a nail? He said, "That nail belongs to the opposite wall, you fool." However, the Laz don't take that lying down. It is said that upon watching a Zeybek, a national folk hero from Muğla, dance the

their way. The thorn is of course the arti-choke, and the weed is the endive, cooked in olive oil, which eastern Turks would not touch! (Try the delicious *istifne salad* in the Isle of Cunda off Ayvalık, on the Aegean, and see for yourself!) Cold food is unthink-able in the east where the diet is based essentially on cereals and *kebabs*.

Consumers of *hamsi* (anchovy) in the east-ern Black Sea Coast look down upon both. As far as they are concerned they owe their superior intelligence and agility to that pro-tein rich seafood! Immediately recognized by their fair skin, red hair, blue eyes, and large noses, the Laz dominate the construc-

slow rhythm of the *aksak*, a popular dance, a Laz was heard to comment "Given so much time to decide where to place his foot next, even my old father could do this dance, for heaven's sake!"

Turkish women: Contrary to popular belief, the ordinary Turk did not keep a harem of women. Nor was the Islamic license to take more than one wife a rule. That a woman's place was, and to a large extent still is, at home, should not be understood as the patri-archal system of, for example, Rome, where the man, as indisputable head of the family, had the right to be the judge, jury and execu-tioner of members of his family. Latife

Tekin, a prominent Turkish woman novelist, explains the Turkish case this way:

"In our society, a woman's place is at home. This means she reigns at home. Man belongs to the streets; he rules in the world outside. Men are alienated, lonely and tense at home. Women feel the same outside. That's why they never leave the house unless fully armoured, that is, dressed to their teeth.

That the men are seen as extra elements in the house, and that they are shooed to coffee houses are the overt manifestations of this fact. The men's and women's realms compete fiercely, wildly. I remember my mother kissing the door when my father left. My mother, our mothers, may be rightly called

outside the home, tilling the fields and harvesting crops. The reward is a closely knit family, with children who leave home only upon marriage, and grandparents who do not know what an old peoples' home is.

The young enjoy the loving umbrella provided by their family and so they should, for in this day and age it is often the case that those above the age of 21 are still being taken care of by their families! While the practice is the main deterrent against the current ills of drugs and alcoholism that strike the young in the western countries, it demands upholding of the old values and rules of behaviour. More often than not, you will find that men who have raised children of their own will

radical feminists as they never forfeited their territory in favour of men's. Anatolian women refuse to buy their final garment, the funeral shroud, with their husbands' money. They bring it with them as part of their dowry, bought for them by their mothers or grandmothers."

Very much like the ancient Anatolian mother goddess Cybele, the Turkish woman mothers her son and husband. If that means having to provide for them as well, she works

Left to right: a Turkish girl carries her sister; old woman embroiders new designs; a farmer with gold teeth smiles; a Yörük with his camel.

not, as a sign of respect, smoke (certainly not drink) in the presence of their fathers.

Yet, industrialization does not permit niceties and is breaking down the traditional family system. Once out of their realm, women should not expect to be pampered. At the end of a hard day's work, riding at the back of an overcrowded city bus, the young are too tired to give their seats to the elderly who should not be out on the streets at that time of the evening anyway. Urbanization, which in final analysis alienates people, helps to hide the wavering from communal sanctions and codes of behaviour. The result is pollution in both senses of the word.

Adana kebab, *Mevlana candy*, *Izmir köfte* and Bodrum's *mantı* are some of the unique regional specialities from Turkey's Aegean and Mediterranean coasts. Today's Turkish cuisine reflects the extent of the Ottoman Empire which spanned from North Africa, through parts of the Middle East, the Balkans, and in Europe to the gates of Vienna. The legacies of the Ottoman and Seljuk courts include a rich selection of appetizers, soups, meat dishes, vegetable dishes, elaborate desserts and, of course, Turkish coffee.

During the Ottoman Empire, Istanbul, Izmir and Bursa were centres of sophisticated court cuisine due to the influence of European foods and the cosmopolitan lifestyle of the people. Even though soldiers and administrators from the major cities, particularly the janissaries, travelled and worked throughout the country they did not facilitate an exchange of cuisine with the rural areas. Until the establishment of the Turkish Republic in 1923, cuisine in the rural areas reflected the nomadic lifestyle and meat-eating traditions of the Turkish people who originated from the Asiatic steppes.

After the collapse of the Ottoman Empire in the early 1900s Turkish cuisine underwent a metamorphosis. With the establishment of the young republic, flocks of Anatolian villagers migrated to the major cities and regions along the coast, and brought their regional produce, cooking and eating habits. Also a flood of Turks living overseas returned to Turkey with food needs. Turks from Crete and Greece brought cooking techniques for seafood to the Aegean Coast. Middle Eastern spices and condiments were introduced to the eastern Mediterranean Coast by Turks from Syria.

Fresh ingredients: Turkey is one of the few countries in the world which produces enough food for its own needs. From the major cities in western Turkey to the smallest village near the Russian border, travellers can find open-air markets selling an abundance of fresh produce, homemade yogurt, honeys and jams. The market atmosphere is frantic, jubilant and festive – shoppers give the impression of visiting the market for the first time, greeting each other warmly, enthusiastically selecting their products, and bargaining furiously over every melon and fresh fruit. The crowd is easily moved by the aggressive salesman, whose marketing techniques include tempting the exhausted customers with wedges of juicy watermelon, chunks of soft creamy cheese, and handfuls of shiny, salty black olives.

Dining out in Turkey is an epicurean's delight. The palate is privilege to a most unique combination – the great tradition of the Turkish kitchen and flavour of fresh ingredients. In the early morning hours along almost any coast you can find fishermen gathered on the wharves munching on hot *simit* (a roll of bread shaped like a lifesaver and covered with sesame seeds) and drinking their first tea, guarding the catch of the previous night and exchanging adventure stories like their ancestors did a millennia ago as they wait for seafood restaurants to buy fresh fish directly from them.

Mornings in Turkey begin best on a sunlit balcony with a sumptuous Mediterranean breakfast. A typical breakfast both at hotels and in restaurants is a fairly substantial meal consisting of *beyaz peynir* (feta), honey or jam, black olives, boiled eggs and piles of fresh Turkish bread which resemble Italian loaves. In Antalya, the traveller will be lucky if he is served a local speciality known as *patlıcan reçeli* (eggplant jam), miniature eggplants preserved in sweet syrup, which is spread on bread or mixed in yogurt.

Eggs menemen: You can easily have a light breakfast of coffee and cheese toast at any cafe. For a more substantial breakfast, visit a *Süt Iş* (milk shop). These small restaurants, catering to the morning crowd, specialize in various kinds of milk and egg dishes. One popular breakfast dish is *menemen*, a delicious concoction of eggs, peppers, tomatoes and cheese, served in a pan and accompanied by small buttery buns called *poğaça* and various kinds of cheese *börek* (layered pastry leaves cooked in the oven). *Süt Iş* shops also create a variety of smooth milk-based puddings and sweet desserts, such as *sütlaç*

Preceding pages: grand buffet lunch at a Turkish resort. **Left,** fish and *shish kebab*.

(rice pudding), *tavuk göğsü* (breast of chicken pudding) and *aşure* (Noah's pudding) with allegedly 99 ingredients.

Turkish black tea, brewed until intensely strong and bitter and then diluted with water, is drunk with plenty of sugar throughout the day from small tulip-shaped glasses. Many foreigners find that Turkish tea helps counteract some of the oily Turkish dishes. Tourists will be offered tea wherever they have to wait, from carpet shops to the bus station. It's considered an affront to the host if a guest refuses refreshments. For something lighter, try apple tea, the best of which is made from dried apples and petals already sweetened, or *ıhlamur*, a linden tea highly touted as a remedy for upset stomachs.

Turkish coffee, with its peculiar muddy grinds at the bottom of the cup and strong taste, is famous around the world for its use in forecasting the future. However, it is not as readily available as tea. When ordering coffee, the visitor should specify *sade* (unsweetened coffee), *orta* (medium sugar) or *şekerli* (extra sweet). The *çayevi* (tea shops), the social nerve centre of every village and town, are generally frequented by men who leisurely linger over glasses of tea and play backgammon with lightning speed.

Lunch: Lunch is eaten between noon and two in various kinds of street side restaurants and *büfes* (sandwich stands). The most popular noon meal in Turkey is the *döner kebab*, layered lamb, ground beef and spices roasted on a vertical spit, and served thinly sliced over rice or in a roll with tomatoes, hot peppers and french fries. Generally, lunchtime restaurants in Turkey specialize in one kind of dish or cooking technique. For example, *kebab* houses (*kebapçı*) serve all sorts of grilled or baked meat dishes. The *pideci*, which is another speciality restaurant, serve freshly baked thick flat bread piled high with delicious toppings such as cheese and eggs, *sucuk* (a spicy salami) or a mixture of the day's offerings.

Another favourite noontime snack is *lahmacun* (Turkish pizza), a thin crisp dough topped with ground lamb, onions, spices and served with ice cold frothy *ayran*, a fortifying drink of beaten yogurt, spring water and a dash of salt. *Lahmacuns* are sold on street corners but the best ones are usually found in *pide* shops – served crisp and hot out of the wood burning oven. Hot *lahmacuns* from Adana and along the southeast coast are especially tasty.

For those with a hearty appetite and more time to spend for lunch, a stop off at a *hazır yemek lokantası* (prepared food restaurant) will guarantee a substantial meal. These restaurants, offering a wide variety of hot traditional Turkish meat and vegetable dishes, don't need to advertise for they are easily found. From the street, the day's selections, unpretentiously displayed, can be viewed. A beaming *garçon* and other staff members will beckon the guest to dine inside as he strolls by. First the tourist should carefully examine the dishes, an array of meats, vegetables, *pilâvs*, bubbling, roasting, and steaming in large steel containers over the stove and steam tables. Usually menus and price lists are unavailable, so selection must be made by pointing to the desired dish.

The kebabs: With great pride and flourish, the chef will serve generous portions, saying repeatedly *afiyet olsun* (bon appetit) and then stand firmly behind the customer waiting for verdict on his food. The meat dishes include several kinds called *kebabs*, such as *tas kebabı* (mutton with tomatoes and onions), *bahçıvan kebabı* (a gardener's stew), or *köfte* (meatballs) such as *terbiyeli köfte* (meatballs in an egg and lemon sauce). Add to this *pilâv* (rice), or spinach puree with a poached egg, or a dish of homemade yogurt and the meal will get the visitor through hours of sightseeing.

Dinner is eaten anytime between 7 pm and 10 pm although many meals last until midnight. Restaurants are classified into two main categories, those serving meat dishes, and those serving seafood. Some, however, will have a combination of both. If you are feeling energetic, visit a *gazino* (a traditional nightclub) where you will be treated to a full night of food and drinks followed by entertaining belly dancers, singing and traditional Turkish music.

When eating at a restaurant, don't bother asking for the menu because usually there is none available and besides, the Turkish method of ordering is much more appetizing. It's best to follow the waiter to the kitchen where he will give a special viewing of the evening's choices. All the hungry tourist needs to do is indicate his choice by pointing at the dish.

A traditional dinner begins with *meze*

dishes (appetizers), a dazzling variety of cold and hot treasures, ranging from salads to savoury pastry to melons. Many Turks make a meal out of these appetizers. The traveller may choose too because he may feel stuffed after consuming these rich tidbits. *Meze* dishes are typically consumed with the milky-looking drink called *rakı* –the national alcoholic beverage flavoured with anise–served with water and ice. Turkey boasts four locally brewed beers as well, *Efes, Marmara, Tuborg* and *Venüs*.

Appetizers: At a meat restaurant the *meze* usually include only vegetable and meat dishes. Cold *meze* dishes are brought to the table by a waiter as soon as the guest has been

selling peeled fresh almonds and walnuts mounted on a bed of ice, peanuts caked in salt, and of course, lottery sellers plying their wares among the tables or on stands.

One of the best *meze* dishes to look for anywhere along the coast is *çiğ köfte* (raw meatballs) – they are Turkey's answer to steak tartare. Raw lamb, bulgur wheat and parsley pounded together create a tender, very spicy small meatball that is tempting even to those who don't usually eat raw meat. *Zeytin yağlı* vegetables cooked in olive oil and served cold make up a large category of *meze* dishes, such as stuffed green peppers, tomatoes, grapevine leaves and mussels. The vegetables or shells come

seated. The waiter arrives with a tray or trolley piled high with small dishes which he proceeds to put on the table. You should stop him there and choose what you want and send back the rest. Behind him another waiter is carrying a large green salad – the customer should send this back if he doesn't think he can eat it. Other salads will be available that are more interesting, like shepherd's salad (*çoban*), white bean salad (*piyaz*), and *karışık turşu* (mixed pickles). If the restaurant is outside near a harbour, the tourist shouldn't be surprised to find vendors

bursting with a mixture of rice, pine nuts, currants and spices. Small lamb's brain served cold with lemon on lettuce are greatly sought after by Turks. There is also a variety of spreads for bread including *ezme* (a fiery hot tomato and onion *salça*, or paste), *haydari* (a thick garlicky yogurt dip), and *cacık*, a thinner version with slices of cucumber, olive oil and parsley, often served like a soup. Turks make amazing pickles out of every kind of vegetable and even some fruits. *Erik*, small green plums, are transformed into tart-sweet pickles that go well with olive oil-laden food. Turks also drink pickle juice. Southerners from Adana are

Above, the chef slices *a döner kebab*.

especially fond of a dark red turnip juice, *şalgam suyu*.

Out of the more than 40 ways to cook the humble eggplant most of the best recipes are *meze* dishes. The simple *patlıcan salatası*: coarsely chopped peppers, tomatoes, onions, and of course eggplant, must be tried. Diners at traditional Turkish food restaurants should sample the more complicated *imam bayıldı* (literally "the priest fainted"), a whole eggplant stuffed with onions, tomatoes and a sweetish olive oil dressing, often eaten as a main dish. Simple eggplant puree is rendered sublime with bits of smoky eggplant skin. Eggplant slices also come fried topped with yogurt or green peppers.

There are also triangle-shaped pastry stuffed with spinach, *pastırma* (cured beef); the most exceptional are stuffed with fish and mushrooms. One unusual hot *meze* is the *kadın budu köfte* (lady's thigh), an appropriately named meatball shaped like large Italian sausage made from lamb and rice and deep fried eggs. *Rakı* drinkers often eat a great deal of *Arnavut ciğeri*, Albanian-style lamb's liver served cubed and sauteed in olive oil and onions.

After the *meze* dishes, or as an alternative, the diner may order from a variety of traditional Turkish soups, usually thickened with flour or bulgur wheat and garnished with a fresh squeeze of lemon juice. Year round

Böreks: Like many foreign diners in Turkey, you may confuse the arrival of another massive tray of dishes, this time piping hot, with the main course. But these are just the appetizers. Among the most traditional are the *böreks*. Similarly named cheese and spinach pastries are served at breakfast or lunch in *börekçi* cafes and from street carts. At dinner you should try *sigara böreği*, tightly rolled cigarette-shaped layered pastries stuffed with cheese, deep fried and served piping hot. A version called *Avcı* (hunter's) *börek* are Chinese-style spring rolls with a filled with a combination of crisp vegetables or minced meat.

Turks try several varieties of lentil soups made with bulgur wheat, rice and vegetables. *Adana çorbası* is a vegetable soup with meatballs and chickpeas. In the summer it's best to try tomato soup, created from the ripe juicy tomatoes of the southern coast, or *balık çorbası*, fish soup. In winter, Turks across the country savour *tarhana çorbası,* made from yogurt curds and flour that is mixed with broth, very popular in Denizli. Special restaurants serve an unusual soup called *işkembe çorbası*, made from lamb's tripe and served with plenty of garlic and vinegar. This dish is also highly recommended by the locals as a remedy for a *rakı* hangover.

Meat dishes: If the traveller can resist consuming too many appetizers, the waiter will eagerly take orders for meat. In addition to a large number of *köfte* appetizers, a variety of grilled meatballs of various sizes and spiciness is available, including *kaşarlı* (with cheese) and *sebzeli* (with vegetables). Customers should save some of their cold appetizer dips to use as a good sauce for the main course. Also they can order a mix grill including *pirzola* (lamb chops), *böbrek* (kidneys) and *ciğer* (liver).

An *ocakbaşı* is a restaurant specializing in grilled meat. Similar to a Japanese sushi bar, guests are invited to sit and watch the food being barbecued over coal. The most popular grilled *kebab* is *cöp şiş*, tiny pieces of skewered meat grilled and served with flat thin bread, onions and tomatoes. *Şiş kebab* (shish kebab), famous around the world, is made from chunks of lamb or beef – but tourists should look for the unusual and delicious regional *kebabs* often found at each *ocakbaşı* and meat restaurants. In Adana, the fiery hot mixture of ground meat grilled on a skewer called *Adana kebab* is a must. If a less spicy version is desired, choose *Urfa kebab*. *Iskender kebab*, named after its creator, the Iskenderoğlu family in Bursa, is another Turkish speciality of layered *pide* bread, slices of *döner*, spicy tomato sauce, yogurt and burnt butter.

Many *kebab* dishes are cooked in the oven (*fırın*) such as lamb *tandır*, leg of lamb cooked slowly until it falls apart and *kağıt kebab*, lamb meat cooked inside a paper package fragrant with thyme, onions and garlic. *Güveç* is the name for various stews which are roasted in a slow oven and served in individual earthenware pots, such as layered lamb *güveç* made with onions and eggplant, chicken *güveç* served with baby okra, tomatoes and peppers, and shrimp *güveç* baked in a light tomato sauce and covered in

melted cheese. Circassian chicken is a creamy dish made with shredded chicken in a walnut sauce that is reminiscent of the creamy white skin of the sultan's highly prized Circassian harem women.

Seafood: Fish restaurants along the coasts are replete with their own unusual *meze* specialities that have developed from the stock of seafood recipes brought back by Turks returning from Greece and innovative chefs enlarging their repertoire of dishes. Visitors to the region will find many of the cold *meze* dishes common in meat restaurants as well as an array of seafood salads, such as octopus salad marinated in lemon

Left, fish, cheese and *rakı*. **Above**, stuffed grape leaves and radishes.

juice especially good in Bodrum. In Marmaris, pickled sea bream, and shrimp salads are highly recommended.

Two popular hot seafood *meze* specialities are golden fried *kalamar* (squid) rings and *midye tava* (mussels) served with a special sauce. In tourist areas various kinds of seafood *börek*, a mixture of the local catch wrapped in leaves of tender pastry, have been added to the menu. Sardines wrapped in grapevine leaves and grilled is an unusual dish eaten primarily in August when sardines are plentiful.

As a rule, Turkish chefs grill and bake only large firm fleshed fish. The best season for eating fish is from early autumn to late spring

the coast near Mersin, is *balık doldurması*, a stuffed pike with rice, pistachios, and spices bursting from the fish. Along the Mediterranean jumbo shrimp, meaty and tender, are grilled with garlic and butter – these are highly prized by the locals for their unusual size and taste. The Turks also enjoy eating spiny lobsters which they grill and serve with butter and lemon.

Vegetables find their way into Turkish cooking in *mezeler*, pickles, salads and stews of meat and vegetables. They are also eaten separately in side dishes, such as pureed spinach, broad beans marinated in olive oil and white beans in light tomato sauce. Turks only eat vegetables that are in season, grown

but fish is fairly expensive in Turkey, so the price quoted by the waiter will probably be a per kilo price and not a portion price.

Flatfish: Along the Aegean Coast tasty *ton balığı* (small tuna) are best simply grilled and served with lemon. Sword fish caught in deep water are often grilled on skewers with tomatoes, green peppers and onions, while smaller *dil* (sole or flatfish) are grilled whole. One of the best fish from Izmir is the *trança* (halibut) which is cooked in the oven (*buğulama*) with tomatoes, peppers, onions and *kaşar* cheese and served in the pan. This dish is usually shared by several diners. Another unusual dish, found further down

locally and of high quality. Wandering through any village market you will witness Turkish women selecting with care fruits and vegetables that have just been picked. After a tour of the market you will know what to order for a vegetable dish at a restaurant in the evening. If sweet peas are in season as in early summer or baby okra or the sweet pimento peppers of the south in the autumn, order these and you will be highly satisfied. Unusual twists added to the stock of Mediterranean recipes include the Turkish version of Greek *mousaka* made with layers of cauliflower instead of eggplant, stuffed marrow that are spiced with dill and mushroom caps stuffed with *pastırma* and cheese. Marrow is also used to stuff *börek* in Afyon and Denizli, and eggplant *börek* is common in Mersin.

Turkish cooking knows no limits when it comes to preparing rice, and other grains in *pilâvs*. *Pilâv* is the quintessential Turkish food. *Pilâv*, originating in China, made its way along the ancient silk road west through Turkestan to Anatolia. There are over one hundred recipes for hot rice, bulgur wheat and *kuskus* (egg dough in small pellets). Dishes are cooked with butter or olive oil and the simplest is plain rice served with chickpeas called *düğün pilâvı* (wedding rice), popular all over Turkey. If you like liver try

season – figs, water melons, peaches and apricots - sliced and arranged artfully on a plate, or one of the more elaborate and tempting Turkish desserts. Many restaurants do not make their own dessert and instead the diner can finish his meal over Turkish coffee while a waiter races to the local *pastane* (pastry shop) to buy you something fresh. Most meat restaurants have a selection of milk-based puddings and sweet desserts. Ice cream is popular along the south coast – favourite flavours include regional ripe fruits and nuts. The Bamyacı Ice Cream Parlour in Alanya is perhaps the most well-known ice cream maker in Turkey. The parlour serves two dozen flavours, includ-

iç pilâv, rice cooked with currants, nuts, bits of liver and flavoured with cinnamon. *Mantı*, often called Turkish ravioli, are tiny lamb filled dumplings cooked in broth and served with a garlicky yogurt sauce and butter steeped in red peppers. These small packages, popular when the weather turns cool, should be enjoyed by all travelling companions together because of their intense garlic content and taste.

Dessert anyone? After a rich Turkish meal the only room left may be for the fruits in

ing *Kahramanmaraş* ice cream. This is made by pounding milk for hours with a long metal peg. In Antalya look for cinnamon cones filled with ice cream and dipped in chocolate. Antalya also hosts some of the best pastry shops specializing in *baklava* with pistachio and *kaymak* (clotted cream) baked inside layers of flaky pastry.

Bodrum boasts golden morsels called *lokma*, which are fried doughnuts drizzled with syrup sold from stands which line the white streets. With Turkish coffee, the weary traveller can try one of the sweet, heavily flavoured Turkish liquors or the local brandy and cognac for a pick-me up.

<u>Left</u>, *Adana kebab*. <u>Above</u>, *baklava*, a Turkish pastry.

TURKISH CARPETS

The words, "Wanna buy a Turkish carpet? Come into my shop, it won't cost you anything. Just have a look," may be the first words that a tourist hears in the bazaars or on the streets of Turkey. Whether the salesman knows much English or not, these sentences are spoken eloquently and persuade the sometimes unwary customer into a purchase even when there was no intention of buying.

Handwoven carpets and flatweaves are perhaps the most available and widespread sale items in Turkey. Admired worldwide, Turkish handwoven coverings – for walls, floors, even tables are the best known of Turkish export items.

Turkish rugs are most easily found in tourist areas – sold in large commercial shops, small boutiques and even on the street. Carpet salesmen can be the most aggressive and, at the same time, the most hospitable of all salesmen in Turkey.

Tea – either regular or apple – or coffee almost always forms part of the ceremony involved in the purchase of a carpet. The salesmen pull down from the numerous orderly piles literally hundreds of carpets which they throw at the feet of potential customers, one by one, with studied aplomb. And as the traveller soon learns, every salesman is an "expert."

Historical background: Oriental carpets have for centuries been considered works of art. Great speculation over the origin of knotted carpet weaving and the earliest dates of flatweaves is an interesting intellectual exercise. Suffice it to say that in Central Asia the Turkic nomads were most influential in the origin and spread of this art and they are maintaining that position of prominence even today. Along with the fame and exciting designs of the oriental carpet is the newly discovered and recognized fame of the less classical flatweaves or *kilims,* as they are generally called.

Unlike its competitors for the tourist market – ceramics, copperware and recently, leather goods – a woven item lives and grows

with association. Purchasing a woven item is akin to buying a friend for life.

Each woven piece can be seen as the unique expression of the weaver which becomes the unique expression of the buyer and user. Quality carpets and rugs, like good bottles of wine, age gracefully if they are taken care of; the colour and gloss become heightened in the carpet, the motifs and colour harmony of the flatweaves mellow and gain a subtle warmth. Beautiful muted colours often result from the aging process, a

quality that many carpet sellers feel enhance the value.

Learning where to find carpets and *kilims,* and how to judge their authenticity and quality does not require volumes of research or a special knowledge of history, although the more one learns about Turkish carpets the more one will undoubtedly want to know. Here are a few basics about Turkish carpets. These handmade articles which can be classified as textiles from the weaving and knotting process are basically of two kinds, the knotted carpet and the woven flatweave. They are highly decorative, both are used as covers, and are produced on a loom with a

Preceding pages: at the carpet farm in Milâs. Left, weaving a *kilim*. Right, nimble fingers work on a rug.

warp (the continuous threads through the fabric) and a weft (the filler).

Knot power: The knotted carpet is made with the double Turkish or *Gördes* knot, a strong, durable knot which is tied around the warps with its ends clipped to make the resulting pile. Checking whether a carpet has been tied with this knot is very difficult once the carpet has been woven so one can only take it on faith. The *Sina* knot, common in Persian carpets, is an alternative and does produce a finer carpet since the knot is tied around a single warp rather than the double warp as in the Turkish knot.

The number of knots per square centimetre is a guide to the fineness of the carpet; the between the different coloured areas of the rug. In the *kilim* technique, motifs and patterns are produced as the weaver winds coloured weft yarn around pairs of warps. *Cicims*, *zilis* and some types of *sumak* are woven using three elements, the warp and weft and coloured extra-weft wrapping or "float" yarns. In the weaving of a *cicim* usually two women work together, one at the back of the rug and one at the front. They pass the weft yarn through the warp threads working simultaneously on both sides in a "semi-wrapping" technique. The *zili* displays a "weft-float" brocading technique.

Expressing culture: Flatweaves and knotted carpets are expressions of the indigenous

more knots the finer the carpet. The more knots the finer the weave, and generally speaking, the stiffer the carpet backing. A silk carpet may have 100 knots per square centimetre and can go up to 900 knots in a square centimetre. Wool carpets will have fewer with a standard of 36 knots per square centimetre.

Flatweaves or flatwoven rugs are generally called *kilims* because of the common weaving technique, but these can be further classified as true *kilims*, *cicims*, *sumaks* or *zilis* depending on the type of weave. A true *kilim* is made with a *kilim* "slit-tapestry" weave. The end result is a slit produced culture of Turkey. They are woven throughout Anatolia and the coastal regions by women and girls. They are a traditional expression of a people and their way of life and still part of the economy of many Anatolians. The environments out of which flatweaves and knotted-pile carpets come are different. To understand this is to appreciate the richness of each of the traditions which developed independently side by side. Those who weave one do not weave the other.

Flatweaves are traditionally woven in the home for domestic use and result from the

Above, carpet weaving amongst ruins.

cultural need for coverings and containers for the nomadic tribal groups. They are lighter and more flexible compared to knotted carpets and besides being useful as wall hangings and floor coverings they appear as numerous other articles: *heybes* (saddle bags), *yastıks* (pillow covers), clothing or grain sacks, seat covers, horse trappings, cradle covers, etc. Unlike the knotted carpet which has always been a sales item to the West, or to the Turk as an investment, flatweaves have only recently begun to be produced as a sales item.

Flatweaves in general carry a great deal of symbolism and can reflect a historical context that experts now claim goes back as far as the Neolithic Period in Anatolia. The implications are social, ethnic and cultural. Some of the finest examples of these are still being woven by the Yörüks and the Avşar Turkmen of the Oğuz clan which came to Anatolia with the Seljuks in the 14th century. These groups, originally nomadic, migrated through the ages throughout Anatolia and in some places still maintain their identity and old customs. To them must be attributed the honour of having preserved some of the finest examples of flatweave art.

Symbols of life: Thus we can see that flatweaves were functional to the way of life of the Turkic nomads who migrated from Central Asia to Anatolia. They were produced to meet the needs of their living conditions – portable, functional for a tent life, practical. The women used the products easily available in their handicraft – wool and animal hair, which they made themselves. In the matter of the decoration and composition, traditionally the end product had to bespeak the very existence from which they had emerged. The motifs are a reflection of their life, and their understanding of it. This meant that a young girl may record in her weaving her concerns about finding a husband, marrying, having a family and living a long life with an assured peaceful death. The motifs traditional on the flatweaves record a story and symbolize a heritage not in writing but in weaving.

Güran Erbek, a Turkish art historian, has put it this way: "According to the Anatolian beliefs, the prayer cloth woven by a young maiden to be used by her future husband has a special meaning. The motifs produced by winding the threads around the warp present an expression of her expectations for the future: happiness, reproduction and a long life. Motifs comprise a language for the women and young maidens. Their happiness, sorrow and desires are expressed through those motifs. It is through those motifs that they display the thoughts which they cannot transform into words, which are considered inappropriate when uttered. A tomb stone on a *kilim*, generally perceived as death, is a way of saying 'I'd die if I ever have to part from my beloved.'"

Times have changed but *kilim* motifs and patterns are still personal – individually and tribally, and have changed little through the ages. As mentioned, originally they were an expression of the spiritual and religious elements in the lives of the tribal groups. The very names which continue to be used to identify them are an indication of this heritage. The meaning may not have the original significance now but as they have been passed from grandmother to grandchild they become an expression of what the weaver is. This is not as true of carpet weavers who have traditionally woven for middlemen and are given cartoons (patterns on squared paper) to weave from.

Traditional motifs: Some of the common traditional nomadic motifs still being used on flatweaves today bear out this fact: *elibelinde* (hands on hips) symbol of motherhood and fertility probably derived from the Anatolian mother goddess figure; *koçboynuzu* (ram's horn), a sign reflecting fertility, heroism, power and masculinity; *aşk ve birleşim* (love and union), an emblem related to the oriental ying-yang symbol for the harmony between male and female; *el/parmak/tarak* (hand/finger/comb), symbols to ward off the evil eye or to insure protection in birth and marriage; *nazarlık* (evil eye), a representation against the effect of an evil glance; *çengel* (hook), another symbol against the evil eye; *yılan* (snake), *ejder* (dragon), *akrep* (scorpion) all symbols indicate a desire for protection from nature, also they are signs of happiness and fertility; *kurt ağzı, kurt izi* (wolf's mouth, wolf track) protection against the wolves, the predator of sheep; *hayat ağacı* (tree of life), these stylized trees and plants stand for the desire for immortality and life after death; *çiçek* (flower) stylized motifs of roses, carnations, tulips and hyacinths reminiscent of the Garden of Eden; and *kuş* (bird) motifs evoke many things – women, love, joy, happiness, power and strength. These and many others are related to the everyday life of rural villagers or nomads and speak of their condition. No wonder they have continued to be used.

It is interesting to note that the word used by village women for motif is *"gelenek,"* which actually translates as "tradition;" a word which evokes considerably more meaning and emotion.

In knotted carpet weaving many of the same themes are used but they do not carry the same symbolic intensity of meaning. Those designs most suited to the knotting technique are used. Also, carpet designs have been more formal, emphasizing floral and complicated geometric patterns and all of these have been influenced by changing market tastes. Thus they have transformed through the ages.

The dyes: Traditionally, weavers of both the knotted carpet and flatweaves spun their own yarn from the wool of their own sheep, and also dyed it. These dyes were natural dyes from leaves, bark, roots and fruit. Often the processes were family secrets. This practice in time has given way to use of chemical dyes. Distinguishing whether the dye used is natural or artificial in a given piece can be determined over a period of time and exposure to sunlight. Natural dyes are more highly treasured by carpet buyers as more authentic and as they don't fade easily. Carpets dyed with artificial colours fade fast. One should ask a salesman if the dyes in the piece are natural or artificial, but only a real expert can dare challenge the answer and prove it.

Some experts suggest that when buying a carpet the customer should lick the corner of a handkerchief and rub it over a spot on the backside of the carpet. If it comes off coloured, the dye, whatever its source, is probably not fast. This certainly is an indication that the piece will mellow with age!

The content of the warp and weft is important in the value of a handmade article. Wool – machine or hand spun – cotton, natural silk and artificial (floss) silk, camel or goat hair, can all be used. The inclusion of animal hair is infrequent but is characteristic of the flatweaves of certain tribal groups' products and the mixture of elements is more common and is used to give strength and texture rather than artistic effect. Yörük weavers use a great deal of goat hair. Some authorities claim that pure, long haired lamb's wool makes the best woven pieces. Yörük weavers prefer this. The wool from the sheep which graze on the high plateau is softer, stronger and more lustrous because of the climate and food in a grazing area.

Types and sizes: The types and sizes of knotted carpets are not strictly uniform although there are general categories. The following dimensions can help serve as a general guide: *yastık* (cushion cover) 40 x 25 centimetres (small) or 100 x 60 cm (large); *çeyrek* (medium size) 135 x 60 cm; *seccade* (prayer rug) 180 x 120 cm to 200 x 130 cm. A group of larger carpets include *karyola* (bed size) 220 x 150 cm or *kelle*, 300 x 200 cm; *taban*, which is larger than six square metres; and *yolluk* (runners), come in various widths and lengths.

Flatweaves vary greatly in size and shape depending on the type. Often the shapes are defined because of the maximum width of the horizontal loom which is portable and particularly suited to the nomadic weaver.

Most carpets and flatweaves have been traditionally related to a geographic area. Sometimes they also carry the name of the group which produces them. Thus names were and continue to be carried with this nomenclature. This is changing both in interpretation by experts and also in the actual production within a given geographic area. Given motifs and styles in various carpets (especially the flatweaves) can now be produced in different sites quite independent of a geographic location. This is more true of the flatweaves.

Individual expression: Actually the original designation was probably incorrect since specific motifs, patterns and colour combinations were more likely to be the expression of an individual tribal group and moved with this group as it migrated. There are of course exceptions to this. As commercialism begins to get the upper hand the conglomerate of varieties will be more evident.

The beauty of Turkish weaving design in both carpets and flatweaves is a function of colour, motifs and overall composition. Its common characteristic is the repetition of geometric units. A central theme may dominate, surrounded by complimentary motifs. A favourite composition of carpets is a central diamond or medallion or two or three fringed by other motifs. On the carpets the central unit is usually contained in a border or borders. In flatweaves motifs generally are arranged on either a diagonal or vertical/horizontal axes and the composition is confined within parallel stripes extending the length of the piece.

Some nomadic groups known as Yörüks, such as the Karakeçili, Saçkarali, Sarıkeçili and Honamlı, still weave their own types. The Karakeçili in the Balıkesir-Kütahya region weave their typical group designs as do the Yüncü Yörüks. The latter group mainly winters in the south on the skirts of the Taurus Mountains but spends their summers

areas continue south to Denizli, Isparta down to Antalya. Some *parmaklı* (finger) *kilims* common in Eskişehir, Afyon and Kütahya continue as far as Isparta and Burdur, but don't go further south. The *elibelinde* motif, widespread in central Anatolia appears quite uniquely in a typical theme of the Antalya region. The *gülbudak* rose motif on the other hand is unchanged throughout the country.

Hereke silk: In Hereke, just east of Istanbul on the Sea of Marmara, the finest woven carpets in Anatolia are produced. That is, they are made with quality control and have the most knots per square centimetre. Hereke carpets are of two types, wool and

in the pasturelands between Eğridir and Lake Burdur. The groups originally moved or were moved from their lands in central and eastern Anatolia during various upheavals in the Ottoman period. Thus the designs have migrated with them.

The effect of these migrations, the heritage of earlier periods – perhaps Neolithic, Phrygian – and those earlier motifs brought in from the western islands can be seen on western flatweaves. The snow-tooth-edged diamond designs common in Eskişehir, Afyon, Kütahya, Nevşehir and surrounding

Above, giving the sales pitch at a carpet shop.

pure silk. The wool carpets generally have 36 knots per square centimetre while the silk range from 100 to 196. Their designs are mainly copies of classical floral Turkish or Persian carpets or new creations by contemporary designers. At one end of each carpet the name Hereke is woven in. In earlier times this was in Arabic script.

Carpets from the Çanakkale region near the Dardanelles are generally woven in the villages of Ezine or Ayvacık. Many still have traditional designs dating to the 16th and 17th century famous *"Holbein"* carpets, so called because the rugs were depicted in several of Hans Holbein's paintings. A typical composition consists of one to three rectangular medallions surrounded by geometric motifs usually on a red field or, rarely, on a yellow field.

Bergama carpets have geometric compositions similar to the Çanakkale ones, but the colours are darker shades of red and blue. Kozak carpets are also related but are smaller in size. They may have *mihrap* (prayer) niches, single or mirrored in the middle field. In structure the knots are thick and visible and give the carpets a soft texture.

Brighter colours: Yuntdağ carpets, though similar in composition, have brighter colours such as strong green and even sometimes purple. The most familiar design is two

dominate not only the prayer niches but also in the borders. Present production, though good, does not match the earlier masterpieces. The weave is always fine, 16 to 36 knots in a square centimetre. Sometimes these carpets have a cotton warp.

Yatak carpets: Çal (Denizli) is famous for its traditional large-sized Yatak carpets. Using strong yellow, black, blue and some red on a cotton warp, they exhibit a long, shiny pile. The field of the carpet is plain with scattered rosettes and squarish forms. The traditional carpets are rare and hard to find.

Karakeçeli carpets do not belong to any specific region but are woven in western Anatolia in the Manisa, Kütahya, Balıkesir

by three or four squares of different colours formed by intersecting bands.

Yağcıbedir carpets are woven in the Balıkesir region mainly in the settlements of Yörük tribal groups, the Yağcıbedir. They are easily recognizable because the main colours are dark red, dark blue and ivory. The single or mirrored prayer niches are filled with stylized leaves, flowers and stars. These all have both a wool warp and weft.

The towns of Kula and Gördes were particularly famous in the 18th and 19th centuries. Even today they are known for their finely woven and elaborately designed prayer rugs *(seccade)*. Floral forms pre-

and Eskişehir regions by tribal segments of the Karakeçeli. The characteristic features of their carpets are a lustrous long and soft pile in red, blue and white and a composition of multi-hooked diamond shapes. Closely related to these are the Yüncü carpets formerly woven by nomad Yörük or Yüncü tribal segments in the Balıkesir region. Generally they are of finer weaves and have double multi-hooked diamond motifs.

Usually Milâs carpets have either a single prayer niche or two or three narrow mirror image niches with stylized floral forms. The

Left, an ancient rug. **Right**, a modern silk carpet.

older carpets were bright red, blue, green and yellow but today the common colours are soft brown, beige, yellow and pastel shades. The warp can either be wool or cotton.

Döşemealtı carpets: The most important carpets of the Antalya region come from the villages of Kovacık and Şağıoba in the Döşemealtı region, the latter being the common name for the whole group. The yarn for both the weft and warp is of plateau wool and the predominant colours are red and blue, the dyes being produced from the local plants.

The Dobağ Project of the University of the Marmara which is trying to introduce natural vegetable dyes in the area around Balıkesir has been most successful in encouraging the women to continue their home production with better dye stuffs. An example of the new interest in the preservation and recreation of carpets and *kilims* is TEH, Turkish Handwoven Carpets. This project under the supervision and guidance of the Ministry of Culture and Tourism specializes in the production and sales of Turkish handwoven knotted-carpets and flatweaves.

With the aid of computers, historic woven pieces have been collected in photographs, coded, classified and catalogued and in some cases reconstructed from museum fragments or even paintings and are being handwoven by expert weavers using natural dyed yarns of Shetland and merino sheep's wool and silk.

Güran Erbek, the author of the beautiful sales catalogue of flatweaves for this project, mentions that the research on specimens and motifs – in particular their meaning, took the research team to 9,000 villages where they interviewed 110,000 weavers. The collecting and bringing to light of the thoughts of these village women in itself is indicative of the high regard now being shown for this unique Anatolian art form.

The Net group: The setting up of commercial centres for the production and sales of carpets and rugs is a way to meet the economic challenge. One such is the Tavas Centre built by the Net Group of Companies, one of the world's largest producers and exporters of carpets, just 14 miles (24 km) from Denizli. The centre, besides its vast sales area, includes dyeing, designing and weaving workshops where local village girls presently weave on 80 looms. Net, which operates the Bazaar 54 chain of gift shops and carpet sellers, also has a commercial carpet production centre in Sultanköy, near Kuşadası. Net also produces quality pure silk carpets at a workshop in suburban Istanbul. These kinds of centres are not unusual in urban settings, and are now becoming part of the scene at touristic crossroads.

The most unique carpet display centre in the world is undoubtedly the Ildız Carpet Farm, near Bodrum, six miles (10 km) from Milâs. Set up by the Ildız Company, a large producer and carpet exporter, it is probably the world's only carpet farm. Ildız opened the farm in 1984 to revive carpet making in Milâs, a traditional weaving centre. It is located in a dry, almost rain-free region.

At the farm, experts wash and dry under the sun tens of thousands of handmade wool carpets manufactured or bought by the Ildız Company, an Istanbul-based concern which owns the Tribal Art Carpet Shops chain. Ildız, which operates 3,000 looms throughout Turkey, specializes in the manufacture of pastel-coloured Milâs wool carpets, using natural root dyes. The 17-acre farm is capable of drying as many as 20,000 carpets at one time. The best time to visit the farm is in the early summer when thousands of carpets are spread out on the ground, like a huge colourful mosaic.

The carpets are brought there from the different villages of Milâs, Bodrum and other Turkish cities. Their backsides are burned until they become charcoal black. The carpets then are washed with a special shampoo and vinegar, dried in a gigantic centrifuge, and spread out under the sun for as long as three months. The colours of natural dyed carpets don't fade, but some of the artificial coloured ones do so quickly. The carpets are classified into five categories according to the degree of colour fading and then priced. Carpets whose colours have faded sell at lower prices.

A recent survey of changing village social patterns has revealed that instead of a decrease in the number of village women weaving, there is an increase. With greater mechanisation of the agricultural processes and an increase in demand as well as better labour reimbursement standards, the women are turning to weaving in order to supplement their village income. This helps them gain a sense of individual worth and personal income in a highly inflationary economy.

Since the days of Henrich Schliemann and his discovery of Troy, Turkey's antiquities have been plundered by treasure hunters, adventurers, crooks and smugglers, all out to make a fast buck. Visitors to such places ranging from the Metropolitan Museum in New York City and the Dumberton Oaks Museum in Washington D.C. to the British Museum in London, the Pergamum Museum in Berlin and the Louvre Museum in Paris will find thousands of ancient artifacts that were illegally exported from Turkey.

Turkey has been the home of 38 civilizations, ranging from the Hittites to the Turks and the Trojans to the Greeks. With an estimated 20,000 monuments and sites of archaeological importance in Turkey registered with the Ministry of Culture, the country has the world's richest deposits of subterranean and submarine antiquities. Many ancient sites are located in uninhabited, isolated areas. They have not yet been excavated or protected, leaving them open to treasure hunters and smugglers. Turkish officials say that the smuggling of Anatolian antiquities will continue as long as there is a demand for old art objects.

Illicit exports: In some cases in the 19th century, the rape of Turkey's archaeological wealth was tacitly approved by weak Ottoman sultans, kowtowing to western European governments. European diplomats, abetted by their governments, removed statuary, entire buildings and city walls from ancient sites along the Turkish Coast.

Charles Fellows, who served as the British Consul in Asia Minor in the 1840s, with the support of the British Navy, carried off many exquisite pieces of sculpture and entire friezes to the British Museum in London, from ancient ruins on the Turkish Coast. Two of the most magnificent items he stripped and removed that are now exhibited at the British Museum are the Nereid Monument, a magnificent Lycian tomb, and the original reliefs of the Harpies Tomb, both from Xanthus in southwest Turkey.

The Mausoleum: Another collection from Turkey that found its way to the British Museum through government-sanctioned trafficking of antiquities is the remains of the Mausoleum of Halicarnassus, one of the Seven Wonders of the Ancient World, including 17 slabs of the Amazonamachy (a battle between the Greeks and the Amazons) and the statues of King Mausolus and his wife Artemesia the Younger. Modern day Turks deplore the Ottoman government's giveaways and demand that all relics stolen from Turkey should be returned.

The Turkish mafia: Authorities believe that the Turkish mafia, with its international drug and gun running connections, is involved in

smuggling antiquities from Anatolia, using peasant farmers and treasure hunters and bribing officials for illegal digs. The Culture Ministry says there are more than 100 treasure hunters in Turkey, of which only a few are officially sanctioned to excavate in designated plots of land. Most treasure hunters use metal detectors to locate old coins. Once the objects are out of the country they are sold to major art dealers and then sold to private collectors or museums.

Fake statues, coins and busts abound, and

Above, removing amphoras from the sea bottom is considered an act of smuggling.

even experts have difficulty in distinguishing forged objects. These fakes can be found anywhere in Turkey from the Covered Bazaar in Istanbul to various sites along the coast and the Anatolian hinterland.

Retaliatory steps: The Turkish government has begun to take retaliatory steps to get many of the antiquities back, including taking foreign museums to court and threatening to suspend current excavations by American and European archaeologists. It has tightened regulations governing private treasure hunting and severely increased the penalties for individuals convicted of smuggling antiquities. A person convicted of antiquities smuggling could face a prison sentence of from five to ten years.

It has also restricted scuba diving in the Aegean and the Mediterranean to reduce the smuggling of treasures from shipwrecks. Diving, for instance, is strictly forbidden where ancient shipwrecks exist. The Institute of Nautical Archaeology, an affiliate of Texas A.M. University, has mapped out more than 125 ancient shipwrecks along the Turkish Coast.

Using diplomatic pressure, the government succeeded, for instance, in getting East Germany to agree to return 7,400 Hittite cuneiform tablets that had been taken out of the country by German archaeologists at the turn of the century from the Hittite city of Boğazköy, near the central Anatolian provincial capital of Yozgat, for cleaning and coding. During 1940, Germany returned 3,000 of the tablets, but after World War II, the remaining tablets stayed in what then became East Germany.

The Kharun treasures: Another blow against antiques smuggling was accomplished when Turkey, after suing the Metropolitan Museum for seven years for the return of a 2,600 year old collection of gold and silver, known as the "Kharun (or Croesus) Treasures", finally retrieved them in 1993.

Allegedly the richest man of the ancient world, the 6th century BC Lydian King Croesus' treasure was dug up by villagers near Uşak town in western Turkey; and some 260 gold and silver pieces were smuggled westbound in 1966. The Met paid $1.7 million for what are now valued at $20 million, but denied their possession for nearly two decades. Before the New York Federal Court had reached a verdict, the Met decided to return the collection to Turkey in the summer of 1993. The Kharun Treasure is now on display at the Uşak Museum. Ankara is also trying to get art collectors in the United States to return 1,900 silver coins, known as the "Elmalı Treasures", that were removed from a village near Antalya.

Turkish authorities, however, have not been able, and don't seem likely, to recover the "Gold Treasures of Troy" removed by H. Schliemann. The famous (and infamous) German archaeologist excavated and smuggled the invaluable antique jewellery to Berlin in the late 19th century. During World War II, the Soviet Army carried the collection, deposited at the Berlin Museum, as war booty to Moscow. It was kept in the depths of the Pushkin Museum's store room until the end of the 1980s. Soon after the Berlin Wall was pulled down, the whereabouts of the treasure was revealed. The Troy Treasures were brought to light and were put on public display (temporarily) at the museum in 1996.

Today, three ambitious parties – Germany, Turkey and Greece – ardently claim possession of it. A different approach is held by a group of Russian scholars who advocate that the treasure belongs to no single country, but should travel the globe on perpetual display. Nor has the Turkish government been able to persuade the German authorities to return the relics stripped from Pergamum in the 19th century and now exhibited in the Pergamum Museum in Berlin. One of the most important buildings that was removed stone by stone and rebuilt at the museum is the so-called Altar of Zeus, a magnificent temple of the Hellenistic period.

The Dorak affair: The most spectacular artifacts smuggling in recent years took place in the late 1950s and was known as the Dorak Affair – so named since the unusual gold jewellery were from the village of Dorak near Bursa. The incident tarnished the reputation of James Melaart, a controversial British archaeologist, who claimed that a Greek woman showed him the treasures in Izmir. The treasures were never found, the woman disappeared, and the authorities, suspecting Melaart's involvement, permanently suspended his excavations at Neolithic sites in Turkey. Melaart was suspected of smuggling the artifacts out of the country.

"A sense of freedom in the heart of nature" has come to be the motto of a number of holiday villages which have sprouted along the Aegean and Mediterranean shores of Turkey. Not long ago for most Turks vacationing meant visiting friends and relatives in some other city. With the start of the tourism development, the concept of vacationing began to change. In the summers, Turks started going to seaside resorts in the wake of the construction of hundreds of hotels and pensions on the Turkish Coast.

France, Italy's Valtur Tourism Organization and the Turkish state tourism concern, Turban, were the first to open sprawling, vacation village resorts in what were then little known, rarely visited romantic settings in Turkey, such as Foça, (north of Izmir) and Kemer (south of Antalya), Kuşadası (south of Izmir) and Marmaris. Today these sites are bustling resorts offering dozens of five-star accommodations.

The pioneers: Since the mid 1980s, sparked by Turkey's tourism boom, dozens of holi-

The four S's: The development of holiday villages started in the 1970s and 80s and continued throughout the 90s. In Turkey, as in other countries, the idea of holiday villages was born out of people's longings not only to enjoy the sea but increasingly to get away from the noise, pollution and the humdrum of big cities. Holiday villages are characterised by their remoteness and vacationers enjoy the opportunity to get away from the stress and return to nature. Europeans tend to go to the Turkish vacation resorts in search of the basic four S's: sun, sea, sand and sex.

In the early 1970s, Club Méditerranée of

day villages have gone up along the Turkish Coast, mostly Turkish-owned, modelled after Club Med, and no less sophisticated than the pioneers. In 1997, the bed capacity of the almost 80 officially-rated holiday clubs reached more than 32,000. Construction is continuing on a myriad of resorts that will double Turkey's vacation village capacity by the end of the century. Most of the villages are rated first class, such as Club Letoonia, in Fethiye, now operated by Club Med, but there are several "second class" resorts that provide fewer sporting activities and less hedonistic living and pleasures. Even the big name, luxury international hotel concerns are getting into the act. The Ramada Renaissance Antalya is one example of a hotel which is now holiday village.

Most of the vacation villages have been built around Antalya at Kemer to the west and Belek to the east, and the lower Aegean coastal strip, which is famous for its stunning surroundings and favourable climate with an average 300 days of sunshine a year. A Tourism Ministry licence is needed to set up a holiday village. Official regulations state holiday villages must be set up "in a suitable touristic area or close to archaeological sites while providing various sporting and recreational activities next to comfortable accommodations and satisfying food."

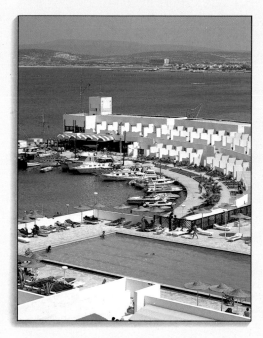

Horses and donkeys: With competition growing every day, the villages try to outdo one another with an array of sporting activities, including tennis, windsurfing, rowing, waterskiing, bicycling and sailing. Sometimes organizers have horse and donkey riding expeditions and hiking tours into the nearby mountains. Antalya now has an 18-hole championship golf course open to international tournaments. Set in **Belek Tourism Centre**, 18.5 miles (30km) east of Antalya

Left, lights flicker at a coastal holiday village. **Above**, the Golden Dolphin (Altın Yunus) Hotel in Çeşme.

town, the National Golf Club of Turkey seems to have become another golf paradise, with its idyllic setting amongst pine and eucalyptus trees, and year-round facilities. Several luxury hotels in the area offer reduced rates for their guests, including Adora, Altis, Attaleia, Iberotel, Paradise Tatbeach and Sirene. One holiday village, Klassis Resort in Silivri, 40 miles (65km) west of downtown Istanbul, has an 18-hole golf course open to international tournaments, and a riding club. Outdoor recreational activities are aimed at the guests making the most of their stay, while spending money at the same time.

Children's heaven: A blessing in most of the Turkish-run holiday villages is that, unlike their foreign counterparts where sometimes children below the age of seven are not accepted, they are heaven for little children. The Tourism Ministry requires the Turkish villages to have special play areas and safe, shallow swimming pools for kids.

To protect the guests and maintain a clubbish atmosphere, holiday villages don't allow outsiders to enter the premises and security is strict. Food at holiday villages is usually a mixture of fresh salad, vegetables and local dishes, served buffet-style.

The Marmaris Holiday Village is considered the best in the Turban chain, which operates 22 villages, hotels and marinas, all of which are up for privatization. It is located near the resort town of Marmaris at the confluence of the Mediterranean and Aegean. With 230 bungalows scattered among pine trees and pink and white oleander shrubs, the Marmaris Holiday Village is a favourite haunt for upper class Turks.

Flamboyant businessman: The luxurious Martı Holiday Village nearby is owned and operated by Halit Narin, a flamboyant textiles magnate and former president of the Turkish Employers Association, and generally serves an upper class clientele. Resembling a medieval château from the sea, the Martı has 289 spacious bedrooms with minibars, colourful curtains on windows with matching bed covers. Along the beautiful stretch of beach from Kemer to Antalya are dozens of villages, including Club Salima, the Ramada Renaissance, Club Alda, and further down on the eastern coast, Club Robinson and the famous Club Med – the first in Turkey.

Surf's up in Turkey and there are a dozen ways to make a splash along its coastline as this aquatic playground aspires to be *"California gibi"* (like California, like wow), offering a plethora of hydra-hype. Choose your weapon: catamarans, lasers and windsurfers skim in between waterski boats and sea cycles, which dodge bobbing snorkellers who float in fear of careering banana boats, forever on a collision course with noisy jet skis, the bane of the beach.

If the water gets too crowded, rise above it all, strapped onto a parachute and yanked to the sky by speedboat, for a gull's-eye view of the bikinis and local sand sharks below.

Beach Blanket Bingo: It was only a matter of time before Turkey created its own version of Beach Blanket Bingo. The arrival of acid colour surfer shorts in every corner shop from Ayvalık to Iskenderun was a hint that the arrival of day-glo Body Glove suits were just a tidal wave away.

In general, watersports have become the domain of the holiday villages which line Turkey's coast and which offer a wide range of sports activities and instruction patterned after the Club Med concept. Available sports activities include waterskiing, windsurfing, sailing, snorkelling, canoeing and usually one gimmick – the conspicuous rubber water weenie, ridiculous sea tractor or geriatric paddleboat. Some clubs offer scuba diving, like Club Alda in Beldibi, Kemer, which offers PADI diving instruction taught by PADI certified teachers.

Where the clubs do differ, unfortunately, is in their attention to safety. In their haste to attract package tours, many resorts use inadequate sports equipment and untrained staff. Club Alda maintains safety is its number one rule and is a member of Club Intersport, a Swiss sports organization which presides over Club Alda's activities and staff. Club Alda prohibits parasailing on its rocky beach but adventurers can set sail next door at Club Salima or the Ramada Renaissance Resort.

Sea life abounds: Scuba diving is gaining popularity in Turkey, especially off the coast of Marmaris at the confluence of the Mediterranean and Aegean sea. Foreigners must always be accompanied by a Turkish dive guide and diving must be within posted legal boundaries.

Much of the country's coast is off-limits to underwater activity in order to preserve its rich history, as priceless antiquities and shipwrecks dot the shoreline. To dive within the law, ask the local tourism office for the government's diving *"harita."* Don't push your luck: if you are seen even wearing diving equipment in restricted areas, chances are you'll spend the night in jail.

Dive centres are located along the coastline in major tourism centres but not all are recommended by professional divers. Centres that received the thumbs-up include Companie and Barracuda in Bodrum, the dive centre at the Turban Resort in Marmaris, and Heinz and Gabi's centre at the Akman Hotel in Çamyuva, Kemer.

The Scuba Shop in Istanbul is a good place to start if planning a dive in Turkey. The PADI certified staff run all levels of instruction and can arrange your dive excursion or put you in touch with a recommended centre along the Aegean or Mediterranean. Before making a dive with your guide, ask to see credentials: either a PADI or CMAS card and an updated Turkish diving licence (*Rehber Balık Adam Lisansı*). Turkey has three decompression chambers, should the unfortunate need arise: in Bodrum, Çeşme and at the naval complex in Çubuklu, Istanbul. But, like many other things, they are only as good as the people who operate them.

River rafting has become increasingly popular as an organized sport in Turkey, and three rivers have excellent potential for white-water fun. Köprülü Çay and Göksu River on the Mediterranean coast are ideal for beginners and intermediates; and the Çoruh River in the Black Sea region offers challenging rapids for the more daring. Club

local children and kayaks. Two sports clubs, Alraft which operates from Alanya, and Medraft in Antalya, organize trips and rent rafting gear, but if you have your own equipment, contact Silifke's Tourism Office for assistance in planning a river trip. Find out if a permit is required and take a local guide along who knows the river well. Don't forget Barbarossa's fate – wear a life jacket. (The German Emperor drowned while bathing in the Göksu.)

Windsurfing has become an art form along Turkey's beaches as carnival-coloured sails cut graceful arcs across the bays. The Gümbet area of Bodrum is ideal, with a number of sheltered bays that channel steady

Robinson in Side offers one-day "float trips" down scenic Köprü Çayı (Bridge River) near Selge. Guests float down the river in small rubber boats, passing under the shadows of vertical canyons and cliffs and stopping periodically for picnics and water games.

Barbarossa's fate: The Göksu River flows from the Taurus Mountains to Silifke through one of the most beautiful valleys in Turkey. The river is ideal for rafting excursions but tour agencies have been slow to capitalize on its currents, leaving the fun to

<u>Left</u>, marine life as seen by scuba divers. <u>Above</u>, champion windsurfer takes time out.

winds. The area is full of shops that specialize in the seemingly impossible sport.

Bird watching: Perhaps the most favoured of all sports is "bird watching," a seasonal, predominately male recreation which reaches its hormonal zenith at Kadınlar Plajı (Women's Beach) in Kuşadası. During summer, hundreds of Speedo-clad hopefuls jam the beach, cheek to cheek, on a less-than-respectful sightseeing mission. (*Topless tourist var mı?*) The few unfortunate women who end up on this stretch of sand become the centre of undesirable attentions as the boys leer, lurk and lunge while vying for viewing position.

Be it to enjoy the flowers, the birds, the insects, the landscape, or just the silence of a stretch of untouched beach, visitors travelling along the Turkish Coast will surely get their share of the best of Turkey. Although many areas, especially on the Aegean Coast, have been recently converted into modern tourist resorts, a score of deserted and mostly clean bays, beaches and real Mediterranean maquis (shrub lands) can be discovered by individuals who leave the better known and trodden pathways. Hundreds of books the size of this guide would not be enough to describe all the beautiful natural sites and abundant wildlife found on the Turkish Coast. But here are highlights of places where nature, rare birds and wildlife can easily be observed.

Bird watchers' paradise: Starting off in northwestern Thracian Turkey is Lake Gala, near Enez, on the Meriç (Maritsa) delta, separating Turkey and Greece. The area is rich in rare birds, including the Shag *Phalacrocorax aristelis*, the Bittern *Bautaurus stellaris*, the Glossy Ibis *Plegadis falcinellu*s, and the Greyling Goose *Anser anser*. Bird watchers from all over the world come to this area to observe these endangered species.

Foreigners must get permission from the kaymakamlık, the county commissioner's office in Enez, to go on a bird watching expedition in the border area. The Turkish-Greek border is one of the most heavily guarded regions in the country. Trekkers should also avoid taking cameras and remember the fate of two eccentric British bird watchers who were detained in Enez for two months in 1983 on charges of espionage, after they were caught taking pictures of rare birds in a military zone. (The two men were later freed.)

Bird migration route: The Dardanelles is one of the world's main routes for bird migrations. Together with the Bosphorus, it is the only place in Turkey where Europe and Asia are separated by a narrow stretch of open water. This is important for the large migratory birds which, in order to save energy, use uprising warm air – the so-called thermals – to soar to high altitudes and then to glide downwards, thus travelling many miles without beating their wings once. These thermals only occur above narrow straits and this explains why large, soaring migratory birds like storks and birds of prey converge at those bottlenecks. During August, September and October, large numbers of birds may be seen flying over the Dardanelles on their way from northern Europe to warmer climates for the winter. A good strong pair of binoculars will help the bird watcher observe the seasonal migration.

When you cross the Dardanelles by ferryboat, you might notice small groups of flying birds which follow the bends of the strait, flying so close to the water's surface that their wings seem to touch the waves. These are Shearwaters, until recently called Manx Shearwater but now generally referred to as Yelkouan Shearwater *Puffinus yelkouan*. Although for probably thousands of years these amazing birds have been flying every day from the Black Sea to the Aegean and vice versa, their exact breeding places are still unknown. Ornithologists (bird scientists) assume that the Yelkouan Shearwaters breed on the cliffs of the Black Sea and that their main feeding grounds are in the Aegean, necessitating hundreds of miles of travel each day.

Environment endangered: Travelling further south brings the nature observer to large stretches of maquis, the more original type of Mediterranean vegetation, which covers an area that begins at the Bay of Edremit and continues south as far as Izmir Bay.

Maquis is in fact a low shrub community, consisting of small trees and bushes two to four yards (two to four meters) high, ideal for nesting of some bird species, such as the Little Bustard *Tetrax tetrax*. Some typical plant species found in this region are Cistus species, tree heather, rosemary, thyme and juniper. Maquis is used extensively by the local inhabitants as a source of fuel wood, animal fodder and dye for clothing.

Unfortunately, in many places this vegetation has been replaced by more stony areas with low rounded bushes, caused by irresponsible cutting of the original shrubs and subsequent overgrazing by sheep and goats that stunts the recovery of most plants and trees. If the cycle of degeneration intensifies further, environmentalists argue that most of the shrub will disappear, turning the region into true steppe country. If water were to flush down the top soil quickly, it would create a land that is of no use for humans and wildlife; but fortunately, this stage is encountered only sporadically on the Turkish Coast. Meanwhile, the Association for the Preservation of Nature (Doğal Hayatı Koruma Derneği) and TEMA (the Foundation for Fighting against Erosion) vigilantly work and campaign for the conservation of the natural life of Turkey.

Swampy marshland: One of the least known but richest bird sanctuaries of Turkey is the

grating from the vast tundra lands in Northern Europe.

Other birds that nest in Çamaltı Tuzlası are the Black-winged Stilt *Himantopus himantopus*, unmistakable with long pale red legs and thin, straight bill, and the Avocet *Recurvirostra avosetta*, known for its long legs and upturned bill. Izmir municipal authorities have given priority to the clean up of the Bay of Izmir and have instituted a project which includes a new sewage system and dredging the bottom of the bay.

One of the most endangered wetlands on the Turkish Coast is the Küçük Menderes (the Little Maeander) River delta between Izmir and Ephesus, around the district

Çamaltı Tuzlası, a big swampy marshland along the northwestern part of Izmir Bay. Heavy industrial pollution in Izmir Bay is threatening the 182 bird species known to live, breed or winter in Çamaltı Tuzlası. This marshland is a wintering ground for the graceful Flamingo *Phoenicopterus ruber* – as many as 3,000 flamingos were counted in the area recently by Turkish ornithologists, and the Dunlin *Calidris alpina*, large flocks of which come down to the area while migrating.

Preceding pages: white pelicans in the Göksu delta. **Above,** the kingfisher, commonly encountered on the coast.

known as Pamucak. The region is a breeding ground for the Squocco Heron *Ardeola ralloides*, a brownish bird that spends its days perched on tree tops. A dozen hotels have already gone up and others are under construction – activity that is likely to scare away many of the rare bird species that breed in the area.

Anatolian leopard: South of Izmir, after Kuşadası is the Dilek National Park on the Dilek Peninsula. The area consists of high peaks, deep canyons, and has a rocky coastline. This area was one of the last known habitats of the Anatolian Leopard *Panthera pardus tulliana* that still lived in the 1970s but that has become virtually extinct due to human pressure. The Booted Eagle *Hieraaetus pennatus* is a breeding bird found in the national park's pine forests, and there are several breeding pairs of the Peregrine Hawk *Falco Peregrinus*. Outside the breeding season Eleonora's Falcons *Falco eleonorae* can be seen nesting on the rocky islands off Dilek Peninsula. Part of the National Park is managed for tourism.

A little further to the south is the Büyük Menderes (Maeander) River delta. A large part of the delta has been cultivated with cotton as the principal crop. The Menderes River has attractive vegetation, including the characteristic tamarix, trees or shrubs with

north of Bodrum, is Bafa Gölü, a lake region at the foot of ancient Mount Latmus, known today as the Beş Parmak Dağı (The Five Finger Mountain). The Short-toed Eagle *Circaetius gallicus*, the White Stork *Ciconia ciconia* and the Little Egret are some of the birds that breed and winter along Bafa Gölü, famous for the ruins of Heraclea and the Sanctuary of Endymion. Villagers who inhabit the eastern shores of Bafa Gölü are known to hunt birds on the lake as well as in the mountains, threatening bird populations in the area.

The Bodrum region is a renowned resort that, regrettably, now suffers from uncontrolled building development. The coastline

slender branches and feathery flower clusters, common near salt water and often grown as a windbreak. The Menderes River delta is the breeding place of, amongst others, the Dalmatian Pelican *Pelicanus crispus*, an endangered species with a world population of less than 2,000. In winter, the delta holds large numbers of wintering waterfowl, including many species of duck, geese and Great White Egrets *Egretta alba*. The delta is a famous hunting area, and the subsequent disturbance of all wildlife has been noted by national and international environmentalists as immense.

South of the Büyük Menderes River, but

is covered with houses and hotels, some of which drain off their sewage untreated into the Aegean.

Marine turtles: The complex wetland system comprising Köyceğiz Lake, the reed beds and marshes between Dalyan and the beach at Iztuzu, form a unique combination of different habitats encountered nowhere else in the Mediterranean. Apart from its ecological importance, the area is certainly one of the most attractive places on the Turkish Coast. The Iztuzu Beach is a major breeding ground for the Loggerhead Sea Turtle *Caretta caretta*, and in 1986 and 1987 the national and international conservation movement succeeded in stopping the construction of a 3,000-bed hotel on the beach. Noise and lights from the hotel, environmentalists argued, would endanger the newly-hatched turtles, which would get lost and head inland instead of seeking the safety of the sea.

In 1988, the area was declared a Specially Protected Zone by the Turkish government. During 1989, the state Environmental Affairs Office, in cooperation with a German conservation organization (AGA) and the Turkish Society for the Protection of Nature (DHKD), took additional measures to protect the magnificent Loggerhead Sea Turtles. A demarcation line on the beach protects the

markably high, and the Dalyan story can be considered a big victory for conservation that serves now as a model for other areas and countries with important nesting beaches for marine turtles.

A walk along the 2.8-mile (4.5-km) long Iztuzu Beach is rewarding, starting off on the eastern tip and ending in the west where one can get a lift from a fishing boat to Dalyan village. During the high season, volunteers from DHKD show videos on the life of the sea turtles in an information centre in Dalyan, and leaflets and posters are handed out in the village and on the beach.

More turtles: The Dalaman Beach area, further southeast holds even more turtles

nests with the eggs, buried about 20 inches (50 centimetres) under the surface, and no-one is allowed at night on the beach during the July-September breeding season. The adult female loggerhead may weigh 300 to 400 pounds (136 to 181 kg.) The female nests three or four times in a single season.

Any kind of housing or hotel development that would drive away the female turtles and upset the hatchlings is prohibited. In 1989, the breeding success of the turtles was re-

Left, pegs show bathers where marine turtles' eggs are incubating and mark the no-entry zone. **Above**, a marine turtle wades ashore.

than the Dalyan area. It is completely unprotected, according to a report prepared by the World Wide Fund for Nature. The only tourist development on this long beach is in the Sarıgerme region. But Dalaman River, which empties into the beach area, is being severely polluted by wastes from the state Seka paper plant. The pollution, the report says, threatens the health of both turtles and humans, requiring immediate solution.

Just south of Antalya is the Olympus National Park, a large scenic area covered with pine and cedar forests, which is good for trekking and mountain climbing. Until recently, the National Park extended all the way down to the sea to protect one of the last breeding sites of the Monk Seal *Monachus monachus*, a 10-foot-long marine mammal that has become extinct in most Mediterranean countries in recent years. The Monk Seal needs coastal caves with an underwater entrance, and is extremely sensitive to human disturbances like fishing and dynamiting.

The Turkish population of Monk Seals is estimated at a mere 30-60 animals, yet Turkey ranks as the second most important country in the Mediterranean for the *Monachus monachus*. Objectionably, the coastal strip within the National Park has been given away to touristic development, and undoubtedly the Monk Seal won't be able to withstand the increased human presence. This will be another site lost for the Monk Seal, and one step further towards its extinction in Turkey.

The Bey Mountains southwest of Antalya also contain an abundance of the European Ibex *Capra ibex ibex*, an agile wild mountain goat with long, upturned horns. The European Ibex population, however, is being depleted because of hunting, environmentalists say.

Göksu delta: Near Silifke is the Göksu River delta, one of the most prominent wetlands on the Turkish south coast and undoubtedly one of the most important wildlife areas in the entire Middle East. The delta is situated on a peninsula and the beaches are of great importance for two Mediterranean species of sea turtles, the Loggerhead Sea Turtle and the Green Turtle *Chelonia mydas*. It is also here that the Purple Gallinule *Porhyrio porhyrio* has its sole breeding ground. Other rare birds that breed in the delta include the Marbled Teal *Marionetta augustirostris*, the Graceful Warbler *Prinia gracilis* and the White-breasted Kingfisher *Halcyon smyrnensis*.

For wintering waterfowl the area is of international importance. Two main lakes, Akgöl and Paradeniz Gölü, and adjacent steppe and sand dunes are the main features in the western part of the delta, while large portions of the northern and eastern parts of the delta are under cultivation. Recently the Göksu delta has been threatened by uncontrolled housing projects, mainly holiday villages, and the construction of shrimp and fish farms. Conservation organizations try to stop most of these undesirable developments that will certainly disrupt wildlife. In the long run "wildlife tourism" will prove to benefit the local people more than the standard hotel development.

People who want to visit the Göksu delta must follow the main road from Antalya to Adana that passes Taşucu and Silifke. Just after Taşucu, beyond the paper mill, turn right and follow the road along the sea. After about 1.6 miles (two km), you will see a holiday village on the left, located between Akgöl and the sea. All you need to do is hop over the sand dunes to search for Akgöl and its bird life amongst the reed beds. From the east, Paradeniz Gölü can be reached from the village called Kurtuluş.

The Çukurova delta: The Çukurova delta, south of Adana, was formed centuries ago by sediments brought by the rivers Seyhan, Ceyhan and Berden. Originally the delta was a wild area of which large parts were inundated with water annually after winter, and every time a thin layer of fertile sediment was deposited. During the 1950s, most of the river banks were embanked, and large marshes and lakes drained to fight malaria and to obtain farmland.

Now the Çukurova delta is Turkey's primary agricultural breadbasket, with cotton the chief crop. Extensive irrigation networks and other agricultural measures, such as intensive use of pesticides, have converted the Çukurova delta largely into an artificial area. Fortunately, the Çukurova delta still provides large stretches of unspoiled salt and freshwater marshes, dunes, beaches and lagoons. The main lagoons, with beautiful scenery, are Tuzla Gölü, Akyatan Gölü (easily accessible from Karataş) and the Yumurtalık Oil Terminal Complex (only to be reached from the village by that name, in the east). Total beach length is 69 miles (110 km), and many beaches serve as breeding sites for the Loggerhead Sea Turtle and the Green Turtle.

From an ornithological point of view, the Çukurova delta is of immense importance. It is home to large populations of Marbled teal, Black Francolin *Francolinus francolinus*, and one of the largest populations in the Mediterranean of the Kentish Plover *Charadrius alexandrinus* with about 3,000 breeding pairs. During April and May the region is extremely good for the observation of the migration of White Pelicans *Pelicanus ono-crotalus*. In spring, no less than 7,000 pelicans can be seen on their way to breeding grounds in Europe. In winter, more than a staggering 100,000 waterfowl can be present on the main lakes. Amongst the mammals that make the delta their habitat is the Egyptian Mongoose *Herpestes ichneumon*.

The natural parts of the Çukurova delta are threatened by the ever-advancing agriculture. The enormous accumulation of chemical fertilizers, herbicides and pesticides used in an uncontrolled way in the farmlands will certainly be detrimental to the environment in the long run. A greater potential threat may come from the oil refineries and

directly or indirectly threatened by uncontrolled building development, pollution (untreated sewage and industrial wastes), overhunting (mainly in the coastal wetlands) and the increased number and mobility of tourists. Rapid touristic development of the coast is often glossed over by pointing to the needs of local people, but counter arguments to this are that in many cases the big money in newly explored regions is earned by investors from far away cities, and inquiries show that tourists come to Turkey to enjoy its historical and natural richness.

So for healthy development in the long term, there is the need to be extremely careful with what's left on the Turkish Coastline.

transshipment ports in the Gulf of Iskenderun, east of the delta, and leaks from oil tankers plying the Mediterranean. The sea current is westerly, parallel to the coast. One major accidental oil spill might well devastate all natural life in the Yumurtalık lagoons, the largest and most original part of the region. The establishment of an action plan in case of environmental emergencies is urgently needed.

As can be gathered, there are considerable environmental problems on the Turkish Coast. The natural beauty and wildlife are

Above, griffon vulture flies overhead.

The example of Spain's Costa Brava, where the tourist boom went wild and local people are left with expensive hotels on a coast that has been destroyed forever, should certainly not be allowed to be repeated. Environmentalists feel strongly that lessons should be learned and careful tourism planning is needed to protect the environment, develop the tourism industry and maintain the strength of the economy.

One way to control development is through proper legislation. It is hoped the Turkish government will soon establish a general management plan for the entire Turkish Coast.

Few coastlines in the world can boast the range of natural beauty, history, sporting and cultural resources, industry, and health facilities that the Turkish Coast does. You can enjoy the thermal baths of Kestanbol, try hang-gliding around the Assos cliffs, drink the wine of Bozcaada, study the displays in the Çanakkale and Bergama museums, watch the yacht races at Ayvalık, taste spicy *kebabs* in Adana, explore the pits of Heaven and Hell or visit ancient sites like Pergamum, Ephesus and Karatepe. For serene vacations, visit the deluxe holiday villages in Kemer, Bodrum, and Kuşadası, noted for its Genoese castle. From the large petrochemical industry at Aliağa to the boy carrying tea on his swinging tray, the Turkish Coast offers variety, colour and entertainment, as well as many opportunities for business and relaxation.

The region includes modern cities like Izmir, Antalya and Adana, and bustling resorts like Kuşadası, Bodrum and Marmaris. The Turkish Coast, a cradle for many early civilizations, is one of the world's most fertile areas. Nurtured by a dozen rivers, it produces an abundance of sunflower seeds, grains, figs, cotton, olives, melons, citrus fruits and fresh vegetables for local consumption and export markets, making Turkey one of only seven countries in the world that are self-sufficient in food supplies.

Many resorts along the Aegean and Mediterranean Turkey offer all forms of water sports, from windsurfing and waterskiing to parasailing and banana boat riding. Scuba diving is particularly popular around Çeşme and Bodrum, which are famous for their sponge fishers and underwater archaeologists. Turkey's main windsurfing centre is at Gümbet, where world champion windsurfers often compete. Visitors to Ölüdeniz (the Dead Sea), a lagoon-like inlet on the Mediterranean near Fethiye, can paraglide from the 6,400-foot summit of rocky Babadağ, to the beach below.

Since the days of Antony and Cleopatra, the southwest corner of Turkey, known today as the Turquoise Coast, has been a playground for yachtsmen cruising to the deserted coves of the Gulf of Gökova, Hisarönü and Sömbeki bays and the Gulf of Fethiye. The so-called Blue Voyage into one of these bays is the ultimate form of relaxation that the harried westerner should experience.

Sail down the gulfs of Gökova and Fethiye, two of the most magnificent bays in the Mediterranean or explore Bodrum's unique Museum of Underwater Archaeology. Located in a Crusaders' castle, it has the world's oldest known shipwrecks. Go scuba diving in waters that have sunken cities and rich marine life, and swim along a coast where Antony and Cleopatra once roamed together as lovers. In Milâs, south of Izmir, tour the unique carpet farm, where tens of thousands of carpets are washed and dried under the blazing sun to test their quality. In Demre, visit the Church of Saint Nicholas, where the original Santa Claus delivered sermons.

The Turkish Coast is highly indented with many deep bays, rocky promontories and miles of sandy beaches, ideal for sailing, swimming and windsurfing. It is also one of the most fertile regions in the world. The inhabitants make their living by growing and selling sunflowers, potatoes, olives, cotton, citrus fruit, figs and daily exporting flowers.

The coast is also a hunter's paradise, rich in wild boar, game birds and mountain goats. Travellers come from as far as Japan to hunt for the ibex, a wild goat with long backward-curved horns which inhabits Turkey's southern mountains. Visitors also fish for *alabalık*, or trout, on the Manavgat River.

The Turkish Coast begins at the sleepy market town of Enez on the Turkish-Greek border and ends in Antakya, ancient Antioch, near the Syrian frontier. European Turkey includes the wide Saros Bay with its fine beaches and the Gallipoli Peninsula, scene of a World War I military campaign, and the Dardanelles, which separates the European and Asian shores of Turkey's Aegean.

The towns on the Çanakkale Peninsula, such as modern Çanakkale, are located on ancient Troad. The sites of Troy, Alexandria Troas and Assos of antiquity are found in this region. Further south is the Aeolian Coast with the resort towns of Edremit, Ayvalık and Foça, with its many hotels and holiday villages.

Izmir, which stands about halfway down Turkey's Aegean Coast, is the nation's third largest city and second biggest port. The metropolis is also the gateway to Ionian cities like Claros, Ephesus, Priene, Miletus, and the remains of the monumental Temple of Apollo at Didyma. The resorts of Çeşme and Kuşadası are just a two-hour drive from Izmir.

From Kuşadası, travel inland along the fertile Menderes (Maeander) River Valley to the flourishing market towns of Aydın and Denizli.

Beyond the Menderes River to the south lies the province of Muğla, which in ancient times was called Caria. The resort towns of Bodrum, Datça, Marmaris and Fethiye lie in this region.

An imaginary line east of Marmaris brings you to Turkey's Mediterranean Coast with its touristic hub in Antalya. The ancient cities of Perge, Side and Aspendos, with its stupendous Roman theatre, beckon the traveller. After Alanya, the coast was known as Rough Cilicia because of its jagged, inhospitable shoreline. The town of Anamur with its magnificent Castle dominates the central Mediterranean. Rough Cilicia finally gives way to the fertile plain known as the Çukurova with its bustling cities of Mersin, Adana, Iskenderun and Antakya, ending the Turkish Coast.

Foreign tourists visiting Aegean and Mediterranean Turkey travel mainly to the Turquoise Coast, the southwest corner of Anatolia, or focus their attention on famous sites such as Ephesus, or resorts such as Çeşme and Kuşadası. Very few of these travellers have ventured east of Alanya, on the Mediterranean, or regions north of Izmir, on the Aegean, except for Troy and Pergamum, mainly because of the lack of information about these areas and the absence of sufficient hotels and pensions.

This book partly fills this gap with information about the lesser known sites as well as with insight to better known destinations such as Izmir, Bodrum and Marmaris.

Preceding pages: beach at the Dead Sea; windmills in Bodrum; the Aegean sunset; Bodrum's streets; an afternoon nap. **Right,** *rakı*-drinking fife players perform at a camel fight.

THE NORTHERN AEGEAN

The Turkish Northern Aegean stands on two continents, Europe and Asia, and is divided by the Dardanelles, the ancient Hellespont. Due to the lack of information about this region, it is one of the least known and less developed touristic areas of Turkey. But since the early 1990s, the famous ruins of Troy near Çanakkale and the ancient sights of Assos have been attracting more visitors from all over the world. The Northern Aegean is an enchanting region.

The European part lies on the southwestern edge of the landmass known as Trakya or Thrace. It includes the areas around the Bay of Saros, the Gallipoli Peninsula, the Dardanelles and Gökçeada, Turkey's largest island. This area stretches from the farming community of Enez on the Turkish-Greek border to the charming village of Seddülbahir at the tip of the Gallipoli Peninsula – the scene of intense fighting during the 1915 Gallipoli campaign. Gökçeada is one of Turkey's few Aegean islands. The 3,000 Aegean Sea islands, many of which hug the Turkish mainland, are mainly Greek territories.

Inland, Thrace is an agricultural breadbasket with gentle rolling hills and fields of sunflowers, potatoes, mulberry bushes, fresh fruit, vegetables and tobacco. Wine is made from grapes produced in the region. The population is homogeneous. Most of the inhabitants are farmers and fishermen. There are also descendants of Turkish refugees who fled from the Balkans during various wars fought between the Ottoman Empire and Czarist Russia; a great many are children and grandchildren of Turks who came from Greece during the population exchanges between Greece and Turkey starting in 1923.

Sardalya (sardines), *ton balığı* (Turkish tuna) and *kefal* (gray mullet) are caught in abundance along the Dardanelles and the Bay of Saros, canned at the town of Gelibolu, and then exported. The Dardanelles is a strategic body of water that connects the Aegean with the Sea of Marmara, the Bosphorus and the Black Sea. Shaped like an S, the 42-mile (68-km) long waterway is known for its swift, erratic currents that make navigation hazardous. Sometimes dense, impenetrable fog descends on the Straits without warning, endangering shipping and the coastal villages. The Dardanelles, which is less than a mile (1.2 km) wide at the narrows, is the only warm water outlet for the Russian Federation and other Black Sea nations.

The Asian part of the Turkish Northern Aegean is the region that is immediately south and southeast of the Dardanelles, an area that lies within the boundaries of the province of Çanakkale. This bulging landmass, known to the ancients as the Troad, is the northwest corner of Anatolia. Çanakkale, the provincial capital, is the biggest city in the region.

The Troad includes many famous sites from Homer's *Iliad*, including the ruins of Troy, the burial mound of Achilles, which was honoured by Alexander the Great before his invasion of Asia Minor, and Bozcaada (Tenedos), where the Greeks withdrew to induce the Trojans to receive the wooden gift horse. The highest mountain in the area at an elevation of 5,810 feet (1774 metres) is the legendary Kaz Dağı (Mt. Ida), where Paris gave the golden apple to Aphrodite, thus precipitating the ten-year Trojan War.

Many other fascinating sites dot this area, including the ruins of Sestus and Abydos on the Dardanelles. The legendary Leander swam the Hellespont nightly to visit his lover, the priestess Hero, in Sestus, guided by a torch she put on the shore. He drowned one night in a storm when the winds extinguished the torch. Hero, in her sorrow, plunged into the water and committed suicide. Aristotle, the father of logic, taught for three years at Assos, near the quaint and charming village of Behramkale, facing the gorgeous bay known as Edremit Körfezi and the Greek island of Lesbos. In the west is Alexandria Troas, a once bustling city with a population of several hundred thousand, now in ruins.

THRACE

Turkey's Aegean Coast begins at **Enez**, a farming community on the Meriç (Maritza) River along the Turkish-Greek border. In classical times, Enez, or Ainos as it was called, was a flourishing port city. Due to the silting of the Meriç, Enez is now two miles (three km) from the Aegean. In 481 BC on his way to Thermopylae and Salamis, the Persian King Xerxes visited Enez. Alexander the Great and his army also marched through Enez in 334 BC.

Enez, an important commercial centre during Roman times, was linked to the *Via Egnatia*, the overland route that connected Rome to Byzantium. With the fall of the Roman Empire, Enez was plundered by various barbarian tribes. In 1384, the town came under the rule of Genoese merchants. The Ottoman Turks conquered the city in 1456.

Medieval fortress: The ancient city lies beneath the modern settlement, a town of 3,000 people with a small square and court house. There is virtually no remains of the ancient period save for an imposing medieval fortress.

The walls and a column of a cathedral remain standing to the left of the town's gate. The presence of a minaret base and a stone *minber* (an Islamic prayer pulpit) indicates that the structure was used as a mosque during Turkish rule.

Near the ramparts, travellers can see a deep depression that was once a chapel. Afif Erzen, an Istanbul University archaeologist who has excavated the site, discovered two graves beneath the chapel. About 200 yards (180 metres) outside the main gate are the remains of an underground church, and nearby is the **Türbe of Has Yunus**, the tomb of the Turkish naval admiral who conquered Enez.

The **Meriç River** delta with its neighbouring **Lake Gala** is a breeding ground for many unusual and endangered bird species. Its marshlands are favoured grounds for Turkish duck hunters. The area, however, is in a mili-

124

tary zone. Photography by members of the public is strictly forbidden.

Enez has no adequate hotels, and therefore travellers who want to spend the night in the region are advised to stay in **Keşan**, a pleasant town 39 miles (62 km) east.

Enez is best reached by driving from Istanbul, a distance of 163 miles (260 km). The trip takes about four and a half hours. There are regular bus services also from Istanbul. Motorists follow the Sea of Marmara on E5/100 highway past the town of Silivri, turning left on the E25/110. The road continues inland after Tekirdağ along rolling farmlands. They then would turn left on route 550 to Keşan and take the secondary road to Enez. Travellers arriving in Turkey from Greece and Bulgaria at Ipsala or Edirne can take route 550 to Keşan to travel to Enez.

NATO war games: A dirt road which follows the **Bay of Saros** back to Keşan has some of the finest beaches of Turkey. The whole region is the setting for annual North Atlantic Treaty Organization (NATO) war games, beginning the last week of September and lasting usually one month. The manoeuvres include amphibious landings along the Bay of Saros, parachute drops near Keşan and mock inland tank battles.

From Keşan, route 550 continues to the narrow, rocky **Gelibolu** (Gallipoli) **Peninsula**. The first town that one comes to is **Bolayır**, which dominates the narrowest point of the isthmus from the top of a hill just off route 550. The Aegean, the Sea of Marmara and the Dardanelles can be seen from Bolayır. A public park with cypress trees off the main square contains the **Tomb of Gazi Süleyman Pasha**, the warrior son of Ottoman Sultan Orhan who led the Ottoman forces across the Dardanelles in 1354, giving the Turks a permanent foothold in Europe. Süleyman Pasha, who died in 1389, is buried with his horse. Nearby is the **Tomb of Namık Kemal** (1840-1888), a nationalist poet, playwright and journalist who spent much of his time in prison and forced exile because of his patriotic views.

In the fertile fields of Thrace.

The hill is honeycombed with concrete pillboxes which were used as gun emplacements during World War I. A farm road continues along the top of the hill to **Çimpe Kalesi**, a Byzantine fortification which eventually became Süleyman Pasha's stronghold. Further southwest is the promontory known as **Namaztepe** (Prayer Hill), just above the cove where the Ottoman troops first crossed the Dardanelles from Anatolia under Süleyman Pasha's leadership. When the Ottoman soldiers reached Europe, they held a mass prayer at this point, which is now commemorated with a simple monument.

Piri Reis: The road continues for about 10 miles (16 km) to **Gelibolu**, a picturesque town famous for its sardine canneries and numerous Ottoman monuments. A regular ferryboat service takes passengers and cars across to Lapseki on the Asian side of the Dardanelles. The waterfront has a protected wharf, lined with small fishing boats, and the remains of an eighth-century Byzantine castle. In the main square on the waterfront is the **Bust of Piri Reis** (1465-1554), the great Ottoman admiral and mariner from Gelibolu whose map of the coast of the Americas produced in 1513 confounds even today's cartographers because it was drawn only a few years after Columbus discovered the American continent. Piri Reis drew the map, which is now in the Topkapı Museum in Istanbul, in colour on a gazelle hide.

Other sites to visit in Gelibolu are the 15th-century open air mosque known as the **Namazgah**, located on the lighthouse point. Nearby is the **Tomb of Karaca Bey**, the standard bearer of the Turks as they liberated the town in the 14th century. Near the grave is the **Cenotaph of Hallacı Mansu**, a famous Moslem dervish whose real grave is in Baghdad. Another landmark is the **French Cemetery**, where French soldiers killed during the Crimean War (1853-1856) are buried.

If you plan to cross to the Asian-side Lapseki town by ferry from Gelibolu, a delicious fish lunch at one of the wharf-

The town square at Eceabat.

front restaurants can be a pleasant pastime while waiting for the next ferry.

The road continues along the Dardanelles past **Cumalı Çayı**, a stream formerly known as **Aegospotami**, where the Spartan navy under Lysander defeated the Athenian Fleet in 405 BC, ending the Peloponnesian War in one of the greatest naval battles in history.

Battle sites: Before the road reaches Eceabat, a road forking to the right goes to **Gallipoli Campaign Battle Sites** around the broken Sarı Bayır mountain range and Suvla Bay, and includes numerous Australian, New Zealand, British and Turkish war graves, such as those at **Anzac Cove** and **Lone Pine**, **Conk Bayır** (**Chunuk Bair**) and **Kabatepe** (**Gabatepe**). On a slope by the point known today as Akbaş Limanı is the ancient settlement of **Sestus**.

The town of **Eceabat** has several pleasant outdoor fish restaurants and a stunning view of the Dardanelles. A regular ferryboat takes passengers and vehicles across to Çanakkale. The village of **Kilitbahir**, with its heart-shaped fortress, is directly across from Çanakkale, and small ferries take cars and commuters across the Straits.

The road continues along the Dardanelles and then inland to **Alçıtepe** (Krithia), a village which has a privately-owned war museum with a collection of mementos of the Gallipoli Campaign. The magnificent **Mehmetçik Anıtı**, the Turkish War Memorial commemorating the 100,000 Turkish soldiers killed during the Dardanelles campaign stands on a hill at Morto Bay. Underneath the memorial is a small war museum. Nearby is the lonely **French War Cemetery**.

The **Tumulus of Protesilaus**, who was the first Greek soldier to have fallen in the Trojan War, is believed to have been located nearby. But it is believed to have been destroyed during the 1915 fighting. The Commonwealth **Cape Helles War Memorial** overlooks the village of Seddülbahir and its castle at the tip of the Gallipoli Peninsula. Several British war cemeteries are located in the Cape Helles region.

Scene from Kilitbahir village.

THE GALLIPOLI CAMPAIGN

The calm blue sea was "absolutely red with blood" for a distance of 50 yards from the shore. It was "a horrible sight to see." Red ripples washed upon the beach and everywhere the calm surface of the water was whipped up into a ghastly discoloured foam by thousands of falling bullets. The sun was shining.

–from Alan Moorehead's *Gallipoli*

Such was the description of the massacre that took place at the Cape Helles Allied landing site known as V Beach, on April 25, 1915. It was given by British Commodore C. R. Samson as he flew in a reconnaissance plane over the battle site where the Turks held up units of the British 29th Division.

Nearly 50,000 Allied troops went ashore that day at seven different beaches along the Gallipoli Peninsula in Europe, and Kumkale, on the Asian shore of the Dardanelles, beginning an eight-month military campaign aimed at defeating the Ottoman Turks in the Great War.

At V Beach, three heavily-armed and well-trenched Turkish companies, led by a courageous sergeant called Yahya Çavuş, held back overwhelming numbers of British forces for more than 24 hours, slaughtering the first waves of soldiers as they hit the beach. Entire battalions, including the Royal Dublin Fusiliers and the Royal Irish Rifles, were almost annihilated, losing over 60 percent of their men in the first day of fighting. Yahya Çavuş and all of his men were also killed.

Turkey enters war: Shortly after the outbreak of World War I, Ottoman Turkey sided with Germany and Austria. The Allied powers, Britain, France and Russia, felt that Turkey, weakened by successive Balkan wars, could be forced to accept peace by a decisive show of strength launched against it. The Allies believed that a peace with Turkey would free the stranglehold

against Russia and influence the neutral Balkan states to join Serbia in assaulting Austria. The action chosen was to dispatch an Allied fleet to the Dardanelles. The objective was to destroy the Turkish defensive lines and force a passage into the Sea of Marmara and threaten Constantinople.

On February 19, 1915, the fleet took up position and began its bombardment of the outer defences. The attack caused panic in and around Constantinople, the Turkish capital.

Bombardment resumes: On February 25, the fleet resumed its bombardment of the forts with a lot more precision and effect. By March 4, the outer and intermediate forts had been demolished and the way was open for a major assault on the inner forts.

At the beginning of March the fleet began its attack on the inner defences. At first the shelling caused confusion amongst the defenders but, in fact, little damage was done to the permanent defences. However, by March 12 the situation looked very grim indeed for the

Left, Mustafa Kemal observes enemy positions during the Gallipoli Campaign. **Right**, the Turkish War Memorial at Morto Bay.

Turks and the German High Command considered defeat imminent. A quote from Admiral von Tripitz summed up the German feelings, "It is a dangerous situation. The capsizing of one little state may affect fatally the whole course of the war."

On the morning of March 18 the British fleet, reinforced by a French squadron, reopened its attack on the inner forts with the intention of forcing a passage through the Narrows. To the Turkish defenders, the sight must have been awesome as it was the largest armada ever assembled. At first, the Turkish defenders retaliated valiantly but were gradually silenced and by mid-afternoon the situation had become very critical.

Disaster strikes: With victory in sight, the battleships moved in for the kill, and it was then that disaster struck. First the *Bouvet*, a French battleship, exploded and disappeared with most of her crew. Within minutes, three major British warships had either joined her at the bottom of the sea or had been disabled.

At this point, the fleet withdrew in the belief that it was being attacked by either mobile shore batteries or land launched torpedoes. Later, it became known that a small Turkish minelayer, the *Nusret*, had penetrated the British screen and had laid mines which had gone undetected. These were responsible for the damage done to the fleet.

Fortunately for the Turks, the Allies were more concerned with their naval losses than with resuming the attack, and did not appreciate how close they were to victory. The assault was abandoned and a new campaign was planned involving a joint operation between the navy and the army. The latter was to land on the peninsula, to overcome the Turkish defenders and then occupy and control the Dardanelles.

Anzac landing: The first landings by Allied troops took place at 5 am on April 25, 1915, as the Anzacs (Australian and New Zealand Army Corps) set foot in what proved to be the wrong place. Even so, the troops advanced steadily against light opposition up the ridges of

Scene from Turkish trenches.

the Sarı Bayır Mountain Range. Turkish coastal troops were fleeing in terror. Fortunately for the Turks, at this point, a young Turkish Colonel, Mustafa Kemal, later known as Atatürk, appeared on the scene. Kemal, commanding the Turkish Army 19th Division, arrived ahead of his troops, stopped the fleeing soldiers and asked why they were running away. They replied that the "*Ingiliz*" (British) were coming and they had no ammunition. Kemal's answer was, "You can't run away from the enemy." He quickly ordered them to fix their bayonets and lie down. Seeing this action the Australians also began entrenching. "This was the moment of time that we gained," Kemal was to write in his memoirs.

The Turkish officer was the first commander to recognize the importance of the heights of the Sarı Bayır Mountains as holding the key to the entire Gallipoli Peninsula. He quickly ordered his troops to occupy the heights and then mounted a counterattack with his two best regiments.

The fighting raged on for many days as both sides attacked and counterattacked on the slopes. Although it cost many lives, no progress was made by either side. The Turks held the higher ground and the Anzacs were confined to a small perimeter around the beach, precariously clinging to the sides of the mountain.

Johnnie Turks: Gradually, both sides developed a great respect for each other which bordered on affection, as typified by the Anzac's description of the enemy as "Johnnie Turks" and their refusal to use gas masks, saying that, "The Turks won't use gas. They are clean fighters." And neither side did.

The landings by the British and the French at Cape Helles had mixed results. On some beaches, such as V Beach, the Turkish opposition was murderous, but on others it was nonexistent. Overall, the landings were successful but the leadership was poor and the advance was uncoordinated. In general no advantage was taken of opportunities offered. Over a period of months, and after many frontal assaults against

enemy trenches defended by machine guns, the Allied line was pushed forward at great cost. However, the Turkish position grew stronger while the Allied attacks gradually weakened until both sides were exhausted and stalemate resulted.

Basically the campaign, like many others in World War I, was marred by unimaginative leadership, culminating in a series of costly mistakes and lost opportunities.

Suvla landings: In August the Allies endeavoured to break the impasse by landing troops at Suvla Bay, just north of the Anzac positions. The landings were a complete surprise and were virtually unopposed. Again, bad leadership ruled the day and the advantage was not seized and, after heavy losses, the position was deadlocked.

By late 1915 the Allied General Command had concluded that further military operations on Gallipoli had very little chance of success and that the army should be withdrawn. The evacuation was probably the most imagina-

Turkish troops prepare to depart for Gallipoli from Istanbul.

tive and successful operation of the whole campaign. Between December 1915 and January 1916, the whole army was evacuated from the peninsula with few casualties, although tons of equipment were abandoned.

So ended a passage in military history that still captures the imagination. It was the baptism of fire for the new nations of Australia and New Zealand, and it demonstrated the courage of the Turkish soldiers. It also created a Turkish hero, Mustafa Kemal, who had a higher destiny to fulfil. For the Allies, Gallipoli was a calamity and saw the fall from favour of many high-ranking officers and politicians. Some reputations were made, but many were lost. The Dardanelles venture was to serve as the model for the evacuation of Dunkirk and the invasion of Normandy during World War II.

The peninsula and its close environs mark the graves of approximately 110,000 men. Of these 34,000 were British or Commonwealth troops, 9,000 French and 66,000 Turkish. (According to another source, the number of dead is much higher.)

Gallipoli today: In 1918, after the armistice, British troops occupied the peninsula and controlled the Dardanelles until forced by the Turks to leave in 1922. The battlefields of 1915 were, where possible, made safe and the allied dead laid to rest in carefully prepared cemeteries where they fell. Memorials to the Allied dead were raised at Cape Helles, Lone Pine, Conk Bayır and Morto Bay. There are Turkish monuments all over the peninsula but the largest now dominates the headland at Morto Bay.

The main World War I battlefields are all situated towards the south of the peninsula, Anzac and Suvla Bay on the Aegean shore and Cape Helles on the southern tip. There are several companies in Çanakkale, Eceabat and Gelibolu offering tours of the area but, for the individualist, the best way to see the sites is to obtain a map and, using the yellow Commonwealth Graves Commission signs as a guide, locate the cemeteries which mark the main areas of fighting.

Suvla Bay is situated in a natural horseshoe of hills extending south of Anzac Cove. The dominating feature of these hills is Conk Bayır, which overlooks both Anzac and Suvla. On a clear day the **New Zealand Memorial**, which sits on top of this hill, can be seen from long distances.

Lonely beach: Suvla is best approached from the coast road heading north past Anzac Cove and Arı Burnu (the Cape of Bees). Lala Baba, the southernmost extremity of the battlefield is signposted to the left. Further on is another left turn that skirts the salt lake and leads to **Green Hill**, **Azmak**, **Hill 10**, and **Anafarta**, the major foci of the battle in this area. The lonely beach at Suvla is very welcoming with fine, yellow sand and a clear, blue sea. It is an excellent setting for pitching a tent and spear fishing.

The best approach to Anzac is to take the road that leaves the main coastal highway just north of Eceabat. It goes west and is signposted Anzac Koyu, Gökçeada or Kemalyeri. In the distance

Anzac Beach Cemetery.

is the tree-covered ridge marking the site of the Anzac battlefield. On the right hand side of the ridge is the Kabatepe War Museum, which has a good collection of war artifacts and old battle photographs.

Travelling from the museum toward the sea one soon sees the Commonwealth War Graves Commission signposts indicating the various cemeteries. One can follow the high ground which was, in general, held by the Turkish defenders, or go down towards the sea. The former route gradually climbs to Lone Pine and the **Australian Memorial**. Still climbing, the road passes through what was no man's land and the remains of trenches and tunnels can be seen on either side, the Turkish to the right, Anzac to the left.

A short distance farther on is the **Nek** with its Turkish Memorial. In the distance and higher up is Conk Bayır and the New Zealand Memorial. Beside the memorial is stacked a pyramid of cannon balls and Turkish trenches which marks the spot where Mustafa Kemal supposedly gave his legendary order: "I don't order you to attack, I order you to die. In the time it takes us to die other troops and commanders can come and take our places."

Below the brow of the hill is a large Turkish memorial, shaped like an open hand. From Conk Bayır, one has a complete view of both Suvla Bay and the Dardanelles. It was here that Kemal led the Turkish defence. The tours tend to return back to Anzac Cove. A new Turkish Memorial stands with the following words spoken by Atatürk in 1934 inscribed on its façade:

"*Those heroes that shed their blood and lost their lives..*

You are now lying in the soil of a friendly country.

Therefore rest in peace.

There is no difference between the Johnnies and the Mehmets to us where they lie side by side here in this country of ours..

You, the mothers,

who sent their sons from far away countries wipe away your tears;

Your sons are now lying in our bosom and are in peace.

After having lost their lives on this land they have become our sons as well."

Cape Helles is best reached from Kilitbahir and Alçıtepe, where there is a private war museum. South of Alçıtepe the British and Turkish War memorials dominate the horizon. The Commonwealth War Graves Commission signposts are up everywhere. The road to the memorial passes the French Memorial.

Westward from Alçıtepe is a track leading to the **Nuri Yamut Turkish Memorial** at Zihindere, or Gurkha Bluff. The centre of intense fighting in 1915, this area claimed 10,000 Turkish soldiers. There is still evidence of the tragedy and it is not unusual to find bones and other relics in the fields.

The Cape Helles Memorial overlooks the village of Seddülbahir and its fortress and V Beach. Nearby is an unpretentious cemetery for the valiant Yahya Çavuş and his men.

The Lone Pine Memorial commemorates the Australian dead.

THE TROAD

The Troad is the ancient designation for what today is called the Biga or the **Çanakkale Peninsula**. It did not have a firm boundary, but extended inland along the Dardanelles covering about the same area as the present-day province of Çanakkale.

Çanakkale, located on the Asiatic side of the Dardanelles, is the centre of the province of the same name. By car it's now about five hours from Istanbul by TEM (Trans-European Motorway). There is a marina for yachtsmen who want to tie up here.

Çanakkale sets the pattern for the area with its ties to ancient, Ottoman and modern history. First Xerxes and Alexander the Great built bridges of boats as they moved their armies across the Straits (the Hellespont). Probably those bridges reached between the narrowest point of Abydos (Nağra Burnu north of Çanakkale) and Sestus (Akbaş north of Eceabat). The Straits has challenged such swimmers as Leander and Lord Byron to conquer their waters.

The Çimenlik Fortress Museum (formerly the Sultaniye Fortress) which one sees just west of the ferry landing at Çanakkale was built in 1452 by Ottoman Sultan Mehmet the Conqueror. Süleyman the Magnificent repaired it. Later the Queen Mother Hatice Türkhan (who later completed Yeni Cami in Istanbul) restored it and the heart-shaped **Kilitbahir Fortress** directly across in Europe. With these two castles the Turks controlled the passage through the Straits when the Allied Fleet tried unsuccessfully to force its way through in the World War I Çanakkale Naval Battle on March 18, 1915, a prelude to the Gallipoli landings. Reminders of that day are visible in the damaged walls and the several cannons placed around the park. A replica of the minelayer, **the Nusret**, is firmly docked on the terrace wall.

On a hill, on the European side of the Dardanelles, facing Çanakkale, is a figure of a giant Turkish soldier with the inscriptions taken from a poem by Necmettin Onan entitled *"Dur Yolcu"* or *"Stop O Passenger"*, commemorating the Gallipoli Campaign. Roughly translated it reads:

"The earth you thus tread unawares is where an age sank. Bow and listen.

This quiet mound is where the heart of a nation throbs."

Fresh seafood: Near the ferry landing are restaurants where you can savour the fresh seafood specialities in a leisurely meal. A daily ferryboat service takes travellers to **Gökçeada**, the island of **Imroz**, from Çanakkale, as well as from Kabatepe, on the Gallipoli Peninsula. Gökçeada has a military base for commando training but the general atmosphere is relaxed and welcoming for Turkish and foreign visitors. The smaller, sleepy Bozcaada (Tenedos) offers a prettier and more friendly environment and excellent fish and meze restaurants. Both Gökçeada and Bozcaada still have a tiny Greek population, the original inhabitants of these

Left, relaxing after a hard day's work. **Right**, a Hellenistic vase.

islands which are known for their beautiful beaches, fortresses and slow, bucolic existence. Boats to Bozcaada leave from Geyikli, near Ezine town further south from Çanakkale. Regular ferryboats also operate between Çanakkale and the village of Kilitbahir; and Eceabat, across the Dardanelles from the boat landing.

In the main square, the clock in the tower sounds the hours. A tree-shaded promenade extends northeast along the sea front. Stately houses on the hill to the north date from the 19th century when Çanakkale was a busy international commercial centre. The exports of those years (valonia oak [tannin], cereals, lumber, wine and pottery) are still important to the city's economy. The name by which it is now known comes from the quantities of ceramics and terracotta (Çanak in Turkish) which continue to be made in the region.

Travellers to Çanakkale should visit its old **Aynalı Çarşı**, or Bazaar with Mirrors, near the town's centre, for souvenir hunting.

Just south of the main part of the city near the E24/500 road to Izmir is the **Archaeological Museum** (open 9 am to noon and from 1:30 pm to 5 pm every day except Monday). Here are displayed finds from sites around the Troad: graceful, decorated vases from Troy, coins, gold wreaths, small statues from various sites, goddesses with ornate headdresses.

The Dardanus Tumulus: Leaving Çanakkale and travelling south, the first site that you come to is that of the **Dardanus Tumulus**, indicated by a yellow sign showing a turn off the main highway. (Or it can be approached from the road to Güzelyalı.) After following a dirt road for about a mile one finds the walled entrance to the family tomb in the midst of a pleasant pine grove.

Dardanus, the mythical hero after whom the Straits was named, came from Samothrace where he had been caught in a flood. By good fortune he was able to float across to the mainland on a skin bag. His luck continued and he married the daughter of Teucer, the first person to found a city in the region.

Dardanus' grandson was Tros; when Tros became king the people and the land took his name. Or so they say.

The beach of Dardanus continues on to **Güzelyalı**; the whole area makes a pleasant summer vacation centre. Hotels, camping spots, pensions and restaurants are varied, good and plentiful, and the swimming and surfing are excellent. In Güzelyalı, the **Tusan Hotel** is an excellent place to spend the night. The **Emre Family Pension**, owned by the *muhtar* (village headman), provides inexpensive accommodations with friendly service.

From Çanakkale or Güzelyalı one can make day excursions to various sites; here you can relax on the beach, paint the changing colours of the sea and the mountains, or enjoy the hospitality and stories of the families who have chosen to live here year-round.

Trojan war heroes: A tour west of Troy around the plain begins with the side road which forks off to the right to **Kumkale** just south of Intepe. If one keeps to the shoreline one sees – at least in the distance – several tumuli considered to be monuments of the heroes of the Trojan War. Some of them are in a military zone and therefore not open to tourists; some of them have revealed graves or identities of actual or legendary heroes, and each has enough Hellenistic shards scattered about to keep the legends alive.

The **Tomb of Ajax** is near the village of Yeni Kumkale on the east side of the Küçük Menderes River. Emperor Hadrian believed, when he found the bones of a very large man near here, that he was seeing the mortal remains of Ajax. He picked them up reverently and had a new tumulus cast up over them.

Shortly beyond Yeni Kumkale, and over the dikes that line the river, is the **Castle of Kumkale**. It is presently a military post. A fierce battle during the Dardanelles campaign in 1915 concentrated on the Kumkale Fortress located on the point where the Dardanelles begins. Soldiers who died fighting are remembered with a monument.

Mound of Achilles: The road turns south at Kumkale and at once the two tumuli attributed to Achilles and to his friend Patroclus are visible on the coast. Again the area is in a military zone. South of them is **Cape Sigeon**, and then the **Tumulus of Antilochus**, the one who carried the news of Patroclus' death to Achilles. On the sea west of Yenişehir is **Beşiğe Tepe**, perhaps the Tumulus of Penelaus, one of the Greek warriors. Items from here in the Çanakkale Museum date from the same time as Troy I – about 2500 BC. They include a necklace of gold and semiprecious stones, some loom weights and a curious four-handled pot.

Not far from **Üveycik** is a prominent dark hump of a much later date than the five Trojan War heroes; it is known locally as **Sivri Tepe** and may be the tumulus of the Emperor Caracalla's friend, Festus.

The port of Odun Iskelesi was the former jumping-off spot for Bozcaada, the island of Tenedos. Ferries carrying passengers, trucks and passenger cars now leave from Geyikli, about 2km (1.2 miles) north of Odun Iskelesi and take a bit less than an hour for the twice-daily (three in the summer) crossing.

Bozcaada is the island behind which Agamemnon hid his ships while the Trojans tore their city gate down so they could tug the clumsy horse inside.

Venetian crusaders: The main harbour of the island in bygone years was guarded by a handsome fortress built perhaps first by Venetian Crusaders. Genoese and Byzantine architects had a hand in it before Mehmet the Conqueror and Süleyman the Magnificent added to it. Besides the towers and curtain walls, it encloses the remains of a mosque, an infirmary, barracks and an arsenal.

The island is 26 square miles (42 square km) with long stretches of golden sandy beaches. Bozcaada wines are famous throughout Turkey, and much of the sunny island is planted in vineyards. Bozcaada is said to be the most windy part of Turkey. Strong winds start blowing across the island towards the end of August.

For a completely relaxing vacation, the island offers plenty of comfortable, not-too-expensive hotels and pensions with many restaurants serving fresh fish, excellent meze dishes on a par with the best restaurants in Istanbul, and good local wine. Bicyclists should enjoy the roads here.

Alexandria Troas: Somewhat less than three miles (five km) south of Odun Iskelesi on the mainland are the scanty ruins of **Alexandria Troas**. The city's founding is recent relative to most of the coastal towns. Started at Alexander the Great's orders around 330 BC, it had its heyday under the Roman Empire. Its ancient baths can still be seen today.

St Paul's Journeys: To those who want to trace the missionary journeys of St Paul, Alexandria Troas is of interest because he visited it twice. His first stay was short: here he had a vision of a Macedonian calling to him to come and preach to people across the Aegean. The second time St Paul was in Alexandria Troas was towards the end of his third journey when he stayed there for a week with some of his friends. From Alexandria Troas St Paul continued his journey by land to Assos.

Selling wool handbags and carpets in the Northern Aegean.

The thermal springs of **Kestanbol** next to Alexandria Troas have been a centre of healing for as long as people have lived in this area. The 150-bed capacity establishment attracts those from the Çanakkale region who are seeking relief from problems like rheumatism, gout, skin and bone diseases, heart and nervous disorders, and metabolism imbalance.

Neandria's ruins lie between Alexandria Troas and Ezine on Mt. Çığrı. The city walls, built probably in the fifth century BC, can be traced. Capitals of its seventh-century BC temple are in the Istanbul Museum. They are much like the capitals from Larisa. Neandria lost its residents to Alexandria Troas when the latter was founded.

Between Kestanbol and **Gülpınar** the road goes past several seaside camping spots and another hot spring with colourfully stained rocks at Tuzla. The lack of development there contrasts to that at Kestanbol.

Many yellow signs point to **Apollo Smintheon** (Chryse) where there is a 2nd century BC temple in the town of Gülpınar. Smintheus is one of Apollo's several names. It means "the killer of mice," and refers to the legend that Teucer (Dardanus' father-in-law) built his first city here where mice gnawed his men's bowstrings.

At the far southwest point of the Çanakkale peninsula stands the dark fortress of **Babakale** (Lefton). An inscription at the entrance to the castle reports that early in the 18th century this was a place where hated and evil pirates dwelt. It adds thankfully that Mustafa Pasha got rid of them. Mustafa Pasha went on to build a mosque, a Turkish bath and a fountain in Babakale. Fishing and mining are the main activities of the village now.

One can approach **Assos** (Behramkale) by sea (there is a yacht marina in the harbour at the foot of the hill) or by road from Gülpınar, Ayvacık or Küçükkuyu.

The most dramatic way leads from Ayvacık through the pretty pine forest near Paşaköy from where there is a view

Playing backgammon at Behramkale.

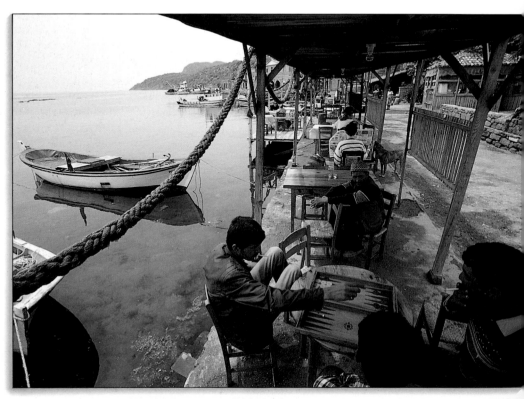

of the acropolis in the distance. Near Behramkale is a 14th-century Turkish bridge arching over the stream to the side of the road.

Aristotle and Assos: Assos was established about 1000 BC by Aeolians from nearby Mitylene. It was ruled successively by Lydians, Persians, Pergamenes, Romans, Byzantines and Crusaders until Sultan Orhan took it over for the Ottomans in 1330. During the fourth century BC its ruler was the eunuch Hermias, who was trying to be the philosopher king of his teacher, Plato. Aristotle taught here for three years and finally married Hermias' adopted daughter.

The craggy peak of Assos was surrounded by a wall; the care with which it was built is evident in the sections that stand today. The theatre, council chamber, gymnasium and agora are marked with signs. Archaeologists are busy with some reconstruction of the Temple of Athena, built about 530 BC. This temple is interesting to art historians because of its combination of Doric capitals and an Ionic frieze. Much of the organization of Assos resembles that of Pergamum: the main temple was on the acropolis, the gymnasium and the agora with its arcades and the theatre built into the side of the hill were below the temple area.

The wide view from the acropolis is more dramatic than that of Pergamum because you can look out across the deep blue sea to the Greek island of **Lesbos** or **Mitylene** (Midilli in Turkish) about six miles (10 km) away.

A fledgling Bodrum: The atmosphere in the restaurants and hotels at the harbour of Assos is that of a fledgling Bodrum. Some of the same elements are present: a historic site, a harbour, an artist colony, good swimming and lots of sun. An international theatre festival is now organized in Assos in late September. An increasing number of aspiring young theatre groups come from different parts of the world to perform in the streets, temple and bridge of the village and the villagers enthusiastically take part in the plays.

The bridge to Assos.

TROY AND THE TROJAN WAR

A beauty contest, a big war with lots of heroes on both sides, the best publicity ever written, and then a treasure hunt to find the hidden gold – what a perfect combination Troy makes for a place to stir one's blood!!

To see Troy is to share for a moment in the excitement of soldiers clashing swords and shields, of the dust beneath their horses' hooves whitening their faces, of the smell of their sweat at the end of a day of hard fighting.

Schliemann's world: **Troy**, an ancient city in northwestern Turkey, was excavated by a German businessman, Henrich Schliemann, who revolutionized scholars' ideas about classical history. The city is a series of levels, some on top of each other – most levels difficult to distinguish – that go back 5,000 years to the Early Bronze Period. It is where the story of the Trojan War took place. Most significantly, it is remembered as the setting for much of the greatest poetry ever composed, Homer's *Iliad* and *Odyssey*.

Ancient ruins, excavators, Greek myths, epic poetry – there is much to Troy. Each of the parts is fascinating, but none by itself makes full sense.

To see Troy (or Truva in Turkish), it is easiest to start from is Çanakkale, a port on the Dardanelles 20 miles (30 km) northeast of the site. You need to take the E24/500 highway toward Izmir. After passing Intepe, you should take the country road that forks to the right with the yellow sign pointing toward Truva.

In ancient times, the low hill of Troy overlooked a plain close to the fork of two rivers, the Scamander (Küçük Menderes) and the Simosis (Dümbrek). Since then the bed of the Scamander has moved slightly west and the hill has risen due to the accumulation of debris over the centuries.

Wooden horse: The approach to the site is protected by a fence, along with gift shops, soft drink bars and the museum ticket window. Your imagination is immediately teased by the wooden horse at the entrance. You can climb into the horse, pretend that it is about to be tugged inside the walls of Troy and shout as you come to capture the sleeping Trojans. But would anyone now fall for that trick?

Many of the items found in the excavations are presently displayed in the Archaeological Museum in Çanakkale. These include a terracotta sieve from Troy II, graceful stemmed goblets from Troy VI, and a black-glaze vase decorated with an owl from Troy VIII. The last often reminds visitors of Schliemann's complaints in his book *Ilios* about "innumerable owls, which built their nests in the holes of my trenches; their shrieks had a weird and horrible sound, and were especially intolerable at night."

The general tour around Troy leads first to the massive tower in the strong wall of Troy VI, up through the east gate, and past the carefully constructed houses from Troy VI to those more carelessly made in Troy VII.

The treacherous Trojan Horse, now a symbol of peace.

Wine-dark sea: From the top of the hill you can look out to the Plain of Troy and beyond to Homer's "wine-dark sea," the Aegean. The next thing that comes in sight is Schliemann's great north-south trench. Northwest of a paved ramp and against the wall of Troy II is the place where Schliemann found gold. The part of the treasure that he sent to Berlin disappeared during World War II (after the Berlin Wall was demolished, it was discovered to have been carried off to Moscow's Pushkin Museum) but a few pieces which the Turkish government placed in the Istanbul Archaeological Museum, remain. Some speculate that the west gate, beyond where the treasure was found, is the gate that was enlarged so that the wooden horse could be hauled into the city.

The Roman theatre was built on top of the Troy VI walls. The main city gate next to it, the Dardania Gate, was guarded by a tower. This tower, or the one by the east gate, could be where Andromache fainted seeing Achilles drag her husband by his heels in the dust.

Schliemann's biography: Henrich Schliemann was one of the first people in history to ask where Troy had been and what was still there. From early childhood, Schliemann was inspired by Homer's epics and determined to prove that Troy was a real city. Poverty, disease, shipwreck, fire and the loss of his sweetheart didn't deter him from his goal. Starting as a grocer's helper, Schliemann taught himself several langauages including English, French, Russian, Arabic, Latin and Greek.

He memorized the whole of the *Iliad* and the *Odyssey*, and a number of books in other languages, too. He worked hard as an importer of indigo. Then he went to California and struck gold. He happened to be there when the state joined the Union, so he became a citizen of the United States. At last he was an independently wealthy man. In 1871 he began the excavations for which he is most famous.

To see Troy is to exult with Schliemann at his moment of truth when he found the city, and pried out of the dirt what he believed was Priam's glistening goblets and earrings. To see Troy is also to see old stones and dry weeds, to be disappointed that Schliemann left so much rubble and so little order. People are often tempted to ask what all the fuss has been about. To begin to make sense of the site it helps to have a map of the many layers and a good guide.

Nine levels: Schliemann thought that there were seven levels of city in the tumulus which he dug. He recognized two more levels later, and archaeologists have sorted out many more distinct periods; nine levels are still used for reference. However, so much has been built on top of and using bits of previous cities that one can excuse Schliemann for being confused.

The people who occupied the bottom layer (Troy I) lived in the city around 2500 BC. They left implements of copper, lead, stone, terracotta and bone, enabling archaeologists to determine that they made their pots by hand. Not much else is known about them except that they lost their homes in a huge fire which swept the city.

The residents of the second level (Troy II) who built their city a few years after the fire, enjoyed several improvements. They seem to have been the same people or relatives of those who lived in Troy I, although there were important differences. Could the disaster have inspired an international emergency relief project that brought in new ideas? Among these were the potter's wheel and the kiln. The artisans of Troy II were skilled in the working of gold, silver, copper and tin – none of which existed in the neighbourhood. Thus they must have been engaged in commerce with other countries.

Treasures of Troy: This is also the level which Schliemann believed was Priam's Troy. His excitement upon seeing the first glimmerings of gold reverberates through his description. Schliemann instructed his workmen to take a break to prevent them from seeing his treasure. He cut into the dirt and rocks with his knife at the risk of the wall collapsing above him. With the help of his wife he packed the treasure they had found into her shawl. Together they smuggled it into their house and later out of the country.

At first Schliemann claimed that someone had collected the hoard in a box and had tried to escape with it. Trapped, perhaps by fire or an enemy, the Trojan abandoned it at the city wall just as the fire brought the adjacent royal house down on top of it, he said. Later, having found four more caches of treasure near by, Schliemann decided that the gold had fallen from the upper story of the palace and been hidden there for centuries.

Schliemann's discovery drew worldwide attention and fired the imagination of archaeologists. People accepted the idea that, however fictional the ancient gods and goddesses may have been, Homer had told the story of a real event and people.

Schliemann's work opened up the productive field of archaeology. Thenceforth, the search was on to uncover more and more of the treasures hinted at in classical literature.

The obsession: A quotation printed on the title page of Schliemann's book, *Ilios*, hints at how often he recited to himself Homer's *Iliad*, mulling over it for any clues that would lead him to the right place. In Andrew Lang's translation the lines read, "yet will we twain, even I and Sthenelos, fight till we attain the goal of Ilios; for in God's name are we come."

With later, more skilful excavation, archaeologists were able to conclude that Troy II predated Homer's city. It is still not known for certain what destroyed the city Homer wrote about, but one explanation offered is that warriors (perhaps from Central Europe) invaded and conquered it.

The archaeologists have likewise felt that with Schliemann's huge trench Troy suffered another catastrophe. He was the first to dig there; scientists have profited by what he uncovered. But he destroyed too much in his singleminded purpose of finding only the city. Or was he merely looking for gold?

After Troy II, waves of migrations continued for 400 years while the less prosperous cities of Troy III, IV and V came and went.

Genetic change: Archaeologists have not determined what happened between Troy V and Troy VI that caused the later city to flourish. Did some genetic change occur because of the marriage of the two peoples – the native inhabitants and the invaders?

Troy VI (about 1300 BC) was the height of Troy's splendour. Perhaps a balance had been reached among the different residents in their skills of government and commerce. It was in the city-states which developed then that each man learned to exercise his responsibility for the political, ethical and aesthetic life of the community. This was an improvement in the history of human relations that apparently came out of nowhere.

Stately city: Troy VI was a stately city for its time. It was bigger than the cities it covered up. Its houses were well built and arranged in an orderly fashion. Its walls are sturdy and placed with a keen eye for defence. Its citizens did a lot of trading with Crete and Cyprus: they must have been good sailors.

Professor Ekrem Akurgal thinks that Troy VI was the home of Priam of the *Iliad*. He and American archaeologist Carl Blegen think the city came to an abrupt end in 1275 BC due to an earthquake rather than a war.

About a generation later the city of Troy VII (which was less well built) was sacked and gutted, probably by Achaean invaders. Smoke from the fire can be traced on the stones of Troy VII. The late George Bean, who taught classical history and archaeology at Istanbul University for 25 years, and Professor Blegen put Priam's city at this level. Was this time lapse between the earthquake and the fire the reason why Homer thought it was a long war? Akurgal suggests that it was Troy's power and her threat to mainland Greece that brought the war upon her. He also suggests that without the earthquake which weakened her defences the city could not have been taken.

In the two events – the earthquake and the fire – are found several more puzzles about the story of the Trojan War.

Was the *Iliad* about Troy VII? That epic makes no reference to the final capture of the city. Did Homer not know who won the war? Had the earthquake been forgotten?

The Odyssey: Then there was the *Odyssey*, which does not include the wooden horse and the capture, and Troy VII. Does this mean that Homer did not compose both epics? Or did Homer compose several works – now lost – which covered the whole story?

Was the fall of Troy the critical event which opened the remainder of the Mediterranean to attack by the Sea Peoples and which brought on the Dark Ages, beginning about 1200 BC when civilizations of Anatolia, including the Hittites, were lost? What happened to the well-organized people who had built Troy VI? Was their leader an enlightened despot who ruled them with such harsh discipline that the survivors of the earthquake end up hating him? Did they assign the guilt for their misfortune (translated into the gods' displeasure) to him and thus do everything in their power to revert to former, less sophisticated behaviour?

Myth and reality: Why the wooden horse? Was there a connection between the belief that Poseidon created the first horse and the opinion that the Trojans were famous for taming horses? A connection between the belief that Poseidon caused earthquakes and the story of the downfall of Troy? Would the passage of time have so mixed myth and reality that history reported that the impregnable city (Troy VI) could only be destroyed (Troy VII) by a divinely-related horse (read Poseidon's earthquake)? Or was this simply Homer's poetic license?

The cities of the next level, Troy VIII, lasted about 500 years, and the most important building during that time was the Temple of Athena.

Troy IX, the city enlarged by the Romans who thought that they were going back to their roots, was inhabited until about AD 400. Its importance decreased when Constantine located his

Troy's tiny amphitheatre.

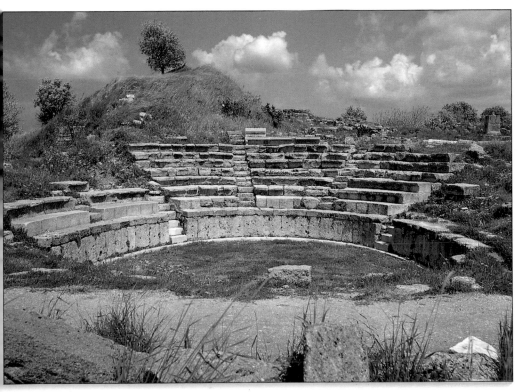

capital city on the Bosphorus rather than on the Dardanelles.

The story: For a romantic, to see Troy is to imagine the most beautiful woman of all time, her bright robes blowing about her, with Paris, hot from battle, leading her to his perfumed bed.

The legendary background of the Trojan War was the curse on the family Atreus (whose sons were Agamemnon and Menelaus) for cannibalism. The more immediate mythical instigator was the goddess Eris (Discord) who did not get invited to a wedding that she wanted to attend on Mt. Olympus. Piqued, she tossed a golden apple among the guests inscribed with the words, "for the fairest." By rank and prestige, Zeus should have decided who got the apple, but he did not relish handling all the jealous women who would lose. Rather, he turned the honour over to Paris, the handsome son of King Priam of Troy.

Paris had been spending his days on Mt Ida, south of Troy. The three goddesses who most wanted the apple went to the bother of finding him there. Here, Zeus's wife tried to bribe him to give it to her by offering wealth and power. Athena, one of Zeus's daughters, promised glory and fame in war.

Judgment of Paris: But in the beauty contest Paris decided that the goddess of love, Aphrodite who was also Zeus's daughter, was "the fairest." Her reward for the prize was that, instead of being stuck with sweet, innocent Oenone to whom he was pledged, Paris won Helen, the sultry, sophisticated and experienced wife of Menelaus, King of Sparta. Considering the criterion he had to use, and that he was a mere mortal (the most intelligent of animals – and the most silly, according to his fellow Anatolian, Diogenes), Paris made the best of a difficult situation. The story does not say whether or not he knew what his choice would mean.

However, Menelaus must have had some premonition of the trouble he was getting into by marrying a much-sought-after beauty. Helen had her pick of all the eligible men in Greece, and

An embankment in Troy.

144

had settled on Menelaus, perhaps because she thought she preferred an older man. At their nuptials Helen's father had all her suitors swear to stand by her husband if anything happened to her.

Paris sailed to Sparta and was welcomed by Menelaus. In Euripides' *Trojan Women*, Helen called him a "Seed of Fire" and exclaimed, "O, a Goddess great walked with him then." As soon as Menelaus had turned his back, Paris ran off with Helen, "bearing unto Troy destruction for a dower," according to the play *Agamemnon* by Aeschylus.

When Menelaus discovered that he had lost his wife, he called on his friends to fulfil their promise. Not all of them were eager to help him at the outset. Odysseus, king of Ithaca, did not want to leave his wife Penelope and their son so he pretended he was insane. Achilles' mother knew that her son would be killed if he went to Troy so she put him in a dress and made him play with a bunch of girls.

The war begins: It took a couple of years for the Greeks to get themselves organized and outfit all their ships – a thousand by poetic count. As soon as the Greeks reached Troy the war began. Almost at once Hector (the son of Priam and the brother of Paris) killed the Greek Protesilaus. According to an oracle, that death determined the outcome of the war, for the side to lose the first man was destined to be the ultimate winner of the conflict.

The war dragged on for many years turning at times in favour of the Trojans, at times in favour of the Greeks. Homer's *Iliad* takes up the story towards the end of the tenth year. The beginning introduces the brilliant, swift-footed Achilles who is angry at Agamemnon, an anger that was to lead to the deaths of many heroes. Their quarrel was over a slave girl.

On the Trojans' side Hector has often been seen as the most sympathetic of Homer's characters. He embodied courage, integrity, tenderness and sorrow as he fought a war which had been thrust on him.

Family bliss: Hector's – and Homer's – kindness is illustrated in a scene between him, his wife Andromache, and their son. As Hector was leaving for the day's battle, Andromache accosted him, to remind him that he faced dangers and he had responsibilities to their family, as demanding as those of the defence of Troy. Hector replied that honour in war (he would have chosen Athena in the beauty contest!) was more lasting than personal comfort. Then – in a very human touch – he reached down for his son. But the boy cried at seeing his father's battle gear. So Hector took off his gleaming helmet with its horsehair crest and, laughing, kissed his son and tossed him in the air.

The end of the war came when the Trojans were so successful that they started to burn the Greek ships. Achilles, who was still sulking about the slave girl and threatening to pull out, finally let his best friend Patroclus wear his set of armour in battle. The sight of Achilles' shield was enough to frighten the Trojans away, but Patroclus was killed by Hector.

Achilles' wrath: Stung, Achilles forgot his anger at Agamemnon. He resumed his soldier's role to revenge his friend's death by killing Hector. Gloating furiously, he tied Hector's feet to his chariot and dragged him around and around Patroclus' tomb.

The *Iliad* ends with the funeral rites for Hector after Priam managed to get through the Greek lines and ransom his son's body. Helen joined Andromache in the dirge, lamenting her involvement in the war and mourning for Hector's gentleness of heart, calling him "of all my brethren of Troy far dearest to my heart!"

Homer picked up parts of the story in the *Odyssey*, reporting that shortly thereafter Achilles himself was shot in the heel – the only vulnerable spot on his body – and killed by Paris.

Paris too was mortally wounded by Philoctetes. He died when Oenone, a nymph whom he had abandoned for Helen refused to heal his wound.

Horse gift: The death of such a hero appeared to the Trojans reason enough for the Greeks to give up. They had folded up their tents and taken their ships off. As a parting gesture, the Greeks left a toy on the beach for the Trojans to play with: a wooden horse.

Laocoon tried to warn his friends about Greek gifts, but he and his son were mysteriously swallowed up by a sea monster, so no-one believed him. The Trojans pulled the horse inside the city for safekeeping and spent the night celebrating their easy victory. In the dark the Greek soldiers slipped out of the horse, the Greek fleet returned and Troy fell in flames. The Greek leaders took many of the Trojan women prisoners. Odysseus, for instance, took Queen Hecuba. Cassandra went to Agamemnon. Polyxena, the daughter of Priam, was taken by the ghost of Achilles and was slain on his tomb. Andromache was claimed by Neoptolemus.

The Greeks scattered to their homes. Menelaus took Helen back with him. Helen, the declared reason for the war, remained uncriticised and as desirable as ever. One explanation of this seeming impossibility was that Helen had really spent the war untouched in Egypt, but it took a lot of convincing even for Menelaus to buy that one. In Euripides' play *Helen*, she greets him effusively on his arrival in Egypt:

Hail to thy wife's restored at last!
upon which Menelaus responds,
Wife indeed! lay not a finger on my robe.

Euripides' more generous portrayal of Helen is in the *Trojan Women* in which she points out to Menelaus that had Paris chosen Athena in the beauty contest, Greece would have fallen to the Trojans:

...thus my love
Hath holpen Hellas. No fierce eastern crown
Is o'er your lands, no spear has cast them down.

Odysseus sailed around for ten years barely escaping many dangerous obstructions as he tried to reach Ithaca. Homer related the events at the end of his journey when he overcame the suitors who had been pestering his clever, patient Penelope to marry again so that one of them could become king.

Homer's life: From ancient times everyone who has spoken Greek or who has been acquainted with the culture of the northeastern Mediterranean has known Homer. It is generally accepted that he was a poet who lived in 850 BC (about four hundred years after Troy VII) and breathed art into the epics of the *Iliad* and the *Odyssey*. He was a resident of Asiatic Turkey, born in Izmir. His native tongue was Greek. Tradition says that he was blind.

Homer worked with material that was so well known that he had only to refer to Helen or to Hector for his hearers to fill in the rest of the story. Thus there had to be a large body of lore already existing on which he drew. Homer did not use the complete story of the Trojan War; instead he selected what would suit his subject, using the common myth as his framework.

Homer probably intended both the *Iliad* and the *Odyssey* to be recited or sung, not read. Perhaps the occasions for their performances were festivals at court; perhaps they were recited on the presumed anniversaries of Hector's death, or of Odysseus' homecoming; perhaps there were contests for the best recitations. The earliest known written texts existed about 550 BC which means that for maybe three hundred years they were passed by memory from one person to the next. One wonders how much the original was changed during that time.

Early tourists: Among the early tourist visitors to Troy was Xerxes who made a big sacrifice at the Temple of Athena, but who was then defeated at Salamis. Alexander the Great followed him. He believed that one of his ancestors was Achilles. Alexander, just before beginning his Asiatic campaign, offered a sacrifice at the Tomb of Protesilaus, near Cape Helles, to ensure that he had better luck than the first Greek Prince who fell in the Trojan War. He also picked up a piece of armour in Troy which he thought had been at the Temple of Athena since the Trojan War.

At the time of Julius Caesar – about 800 years after Homer – Virgil took up the story of the Trojan War. In his *Aeneid*, he followed the hero until Aeneas, a Trojan prince, founded Rome. One of Virgil's last desires was to see the place he had written about.

The Crusaders left Troy alone, but Dante, who was their contemporary, chose Virgil to guide him through the Inferno and into Purgatory. With the Renaissance, no European gentleman was considered educated who did not know the classics. Even more than Dante, Goethe in the 18th century drew on Homer and Virgil. His works, *Iphigenie auf Tauris* and *Achilleis*, and his heroine Helen in Faust, were created out of their influences.

The inspiration: The story of Troy presents a number of puzzles. For one, after fighting so hard for so long, why did the Greeks go meekly home? Even the archaeologists see no evidence that they made any use of their conquest. That raises the question of what the war was all about. Was it over the control of the Dardanelles? Theirs was not the last army to fight over the Straits. Was it because the Trojans were so rich from the commerce that passed through their land that others wanted to rob them? Or was it just over the beautiful Helen – as the story seems to say.

There may be some things about Troy that were easier for ancient Greeks to accept than they are for us. They were closer to the time of the Trojan war. They did not have to be persuaded that Achilles and Hector really lived. They knew exactly where Troy was and where their heroes were buried. They did not have to study hard in school to learn a language that no-one spoke anymore. They could go to a temple-museum and marvel at the trophies from the war: shields, swords, perhaps even Achilles' heel.

The image: That image – perhaps to see Troy at its deepest level is to remember Homer's *Iliad* and *Odyssey*, the epic poetry the ancient world considered so great that it was sacred. On these two works the Greeks based their judgment of human behaviour. On these two great books is great Western Literature still judged. No European literature is known to be dated earlier than Homer; few Western writers have come close enough to the richness of his language, the breadth and glory of his humanity, the tenderness and detail of his observations of the world.

Turning point: However overgrown with myth, Troy is a real place. It can be visited today; the stones which were scarred with smoke of fire from the devastation can be seen and touched. No matter how interpreted, one or several battles took place here which marked a turning point in Western history and thought.

Of all writers who have been touched by what happened here, Homer most perfectly preserved these conflicts between freedom and responsibility; the weakness and nobility of humanity; evil pride and heroic striving. His portrayals of people, of their emotions and their appetites, grandeur and frailties, above all of his own humanity, have illumined the lives of people throughout the ages.

A path cuts through Troy's walls.

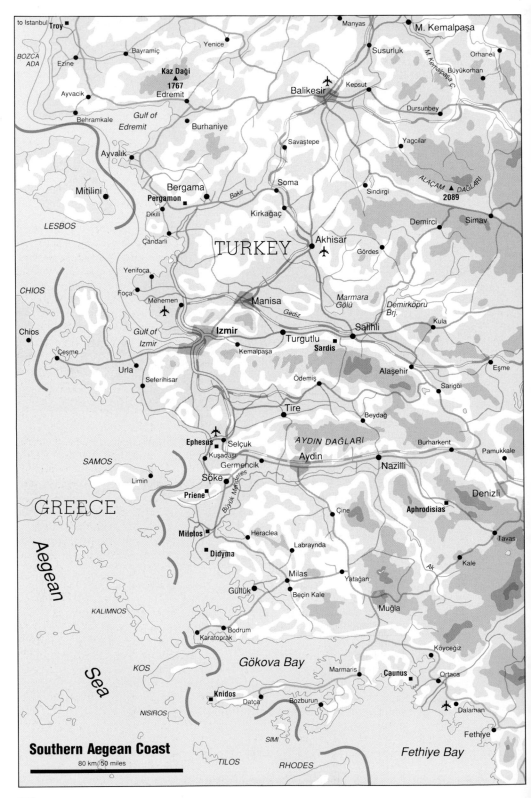

Southern Aegean Coast

80 km/50 miles

150

THE SOUTHERN AEGEAN

The southern Aegean Coast of Turkey begins at the southern slopes of Kaz Daği (Mt Ida) of the Trojan legend and ends at the beautiful Bay of Marmaris. The region has miles of unspoiled beaches, ruins of hundreds of classical sites unmatched anywhere in the world, pristine fishing villages and empty coves ringed by pine forests. It also includes exciting resort boom towns such as Çeşme, Kuşadası, Bodrum and Marmaris. Turkey's third largest city, Izmir, is situated about halfway down the coast.

The northern part of the region was known as Aeolia with its capital at Pergamum, which was the regional capital of the Roman Empire.

Famous citizen: Special information is also provided about the towns of Ayvalık, Foça and Çandarlı (Pitane), whose most famous citizen was Arcesilaus, disciple of Plato and founder of the New Academy.

Ayvalık's name would appear to mean a stand of quinces (*ayva*), more probably, the source is the name of a local mussel, *ayvada*. The Greek word for the same mussel, *kydonia*, was once the name of the city. This is in keeping with the seafoods which have made Ayvalık a great attraction.

Today Aeolia has become a playground for foreign travellers seeking sun, sand and relaxation. Hundreds of hotels, holiday villages and resorts have opened along the coast, stretching from Edremit (the ancient port of Adramyttium Thebe) to Izmir.

While there are citrus fruit orchards, cotton fields and large stock piles of lumber around Edremit and Burhaniye, the major crop of the region is olives. Magnificent groves, some with gnarled trees several hundred years old, stretch for miles along the highway and disappear over the distant hills.

Izmir, Turkey's second largest port, is the gateway to the ancient province of Ionia, which has 55 historical sites, including the ruins of Ephesus, which was a magnificent city during the Hellenistic Period.

In 1952, Dame Freya Stark, a distinguished British travel writer, visited all 55 sites, and came across only one other foreign tourist. Today as many as two million foreign tourists visit Ephesus every year.

Villagers along the southern Aegean Coast raise fighting camels. Camel wrestling is a favourite spectator sport of the region. The Super Bowl of camel wrestling takes place in January when Turkey's top fighting camels slug it out.

The region southeast of Ephesus is the winding Menderes (Maeander) River Valley with many significant archaeological sites, including Priene, Miletus, Didyma. One of the world's geographic wonders is located at Pamukkale, which is famous for its white calcified water cascades and hot baths. Aphrodisias, which lies in the heart of the cotton-growing fertile Menderes River Valley, is becoming another Ephesus as archaeologists, funded by the National Geographic Society, make new discoveries at the site that was known as the "Florence of the Roman world."

Native people: The southernmost region of the Turkish Aegean lies within the boundaries of the province of Muğla. In antiquity the region was known as Caria and was inhabited by the Carians, an independent and indigenous people known for their skills as mariners. The Carians fought the invading Persians and Greeks and were conquered by both.

The most important remains of the Carian civilizations are the Mausoleum of Halicarnassus in Bodrum (one of the Seven Wonders of the Ancient World), the Gümüşkesen Mausoleum in Milas and the holy shrine of Labraynda in the hills of Mt Latmus, today's Beş Parmak Dağı. Bodrum, considered by many to be the St Tropez of Turkey, is an exciting town with hundreds of nightclubs and discotheques that will appeal to younger visitors.

The southern Aegean offers boating cruises in the Gulf of Gökova. The area is also known for sponge fishing.

Preceding pages: Ayvalık, a serene town.

AEOLIA

Somewhere between Assos and Edremit the region of the Troad stops and that of Aeolia begins. **Mt Ida** (Kaz Dağı), the home of the nymph Oenone and her childhood sweetheart Paris, has associations with Troy; Mt Ida slopes gently into Aeolian ports of Küçükkuyu and Akçay.

The Thunder God: Near Küçükkuyu a yellow sign points to a **Temple of Zeus** about three miles (five km) off the highway and just before the village of Adatepe. A bumpy dirt road leads up the mountain to an outlook on the crest of the hill. There, half hidden in pine trees and fluttering talismanic rags, is the tomb of a locally revered holy man. Behind it is an old altar. Zeus the Thunder God would have had a grand view of the entire Bay of Edremit and Lesbos (Greek island) from this perch.

The Edremit coastline, including **Altınoluk**, **Akçay** and **Ören** has become a summer recreation area with vacation centres scattered among tourist attractions. **Edremit**, a city of more than 30,000 people, is near the ancient port of the Adramttium Thebe. Edremit is a sister city with Germany's Piding.

Ayvalık, about 31 miles (50 km) south of Edremit, is a major centre for processing the region's olive oil and its related products. Ayvalık is renowned for its natural beauty and narrow Greek-style streets. While the date for the city's founding is unknown, shards from the Hellenistic, Roman and Byzantine periods found there indicate the existence of a city in ancient times.

Some historians estimate the founding of modern Ayvalık to the 14th and 15th centuries. One of the first references to the island of Alibey (Cunda), was by a 16th-century Ottoman Admiral, Piri Reis, in his book *Kitab-ı Bahriye*. Under the 1923 Lausanne Treaty, Turks from Macedonia, Crete and Lesbos traded places with Greek residents there.

On its beautiful coastline is an archipelago of 23 small islands around **Ayvalık Bay**. Of them, **Alibey Adası** (Cunda), a picturesque island known in Greek as Moshonis (the fragrant one), is tied to the mainland by a breakwater. Regular bus and ferryboat services run between Ayvalık and Alibey Adası.

Another long beach is **Sarmısaklı** south of Ayvalık, where you can find every kind of popular recreation associated with sand, sun and water, including windsurfing and waterskiing.

Satan's table: Beyond the two-star Murat Reis Hotel a road leads up to **Şeytan Sofrası** (Satan's Table), an area with a delightful panoramic view of Ayvalık, its islands and the bay. The outlook was supposedly named Şeytan Sofrası because of its spellbinding sun rises and sunsets and the belief that devils gathered to dine together every evening at this spot. A giant footprint near the hilltop restaurant is said to belong to Satan.

South of Ayvalık is **Çandarlı**, formerly known as Pitane, a city on a thumb of land located about six miles (10 km) west of the main road. Pitane

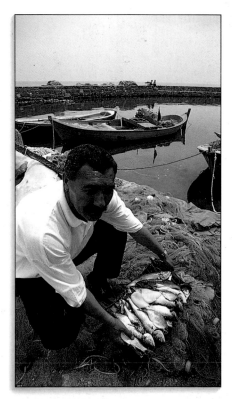

Left, a blue wagon stands in the street. **Right**, selling the day's catch.

was the northernmost city in the Aeolian League. Little of its history is known beyond the broad outlines of the area. Pottery remains discovered in the excavations at Patane are in museums in Istanbul, Izmir and Bergama.

In Ottoman times the city was the home of the grand Vizier, Çandarlı Halil Pasha, who opposed Mehmet II's goal to conquer Constantinople. When the city fell, Mehmet executed the Grand Vizier for treason.

On the southwest side of the narrow peninsula a well-preserved Crusader castle built by the Genoese in the 13th or 14th century occupies what may have been part of the ancient Greek wall.

Pergamum's port: Continuing south on the highway you first go past **Elaea**, the port of Pergamum, indicated only by a small yellow sign pointing down a dirt road to Iskele. The city wall parallels the highway. The next Aeolian city is **Gryneum**, identified on some maps as Çıfıt Kalesi. This low promontory has no marking. It can be found between Yenişakran and Çaltıdere. The presumed ruins of a Temple of Apollo are not much to see, but they are far enough off the road from Gryneum to be a pleasant picnic spot.

Myrina is on the north bank of the Güzelhisar rivermouth; its double hill is visible from the highway. Hellenistic terracotta statues discovered there are in the Istanbul Archaeological Museum and in the Louvre.

Aliaga (south of Myrina) was once a small village whose inhabitants had used stones of Myrna and Cyme to build their houses. Now its residents number more than 20,000, and it is the location of Tüpras Crude Oil Refinery, the PETKIM Petrochemical Complex, the Izmir Iron and Steel Works and the nearby Industrial Free Zone.

The ancient port of **Cyme** (Namurt Koy) is off the highway about three miles (five km) off Aliaga towards the village of Çakmaklı.

Amazon legend: Cyme (sometimes spelled Kyme), an important city in Hellenistic and Roman times, derived its name from a legend about an Amazon. Its rulers contributed to fleets of

Darius and Xerxes when the Persians ruled the land. It also paid more taxes than Ephesus or Miletus – a sure sign of prosperity – when it belonged to the Delian League. Excavations by Italian archaeologists have uncovered some old buildings. Parts of the harbour mole and imprint of a theatre are visible.

A scenic, winding road goes past **Yeni Foça** and **Eski Foça**, 24 miles (38 km) off the main road from Aliağa (or more directly from the turn north of Menemen off the main highway). **Phocaea** (Eski Foça) is near the north end of the broad Izmir Bay.

The ancient residents were well-known as navigators. Their ships were powerful, swift 50-oared vessels capable of carrying 500 passengers. Merchants of Phocaea had business with Egypt, with Amiscus (Samsun) on the Black Sea, and with the colonies of Phocaea, which by the sixth century BC were established in the Mediterranean, among them Marseilles and Nice. Two associations with the French continue: the figurehead on the prow of Phocaean

Sunset at Seytan Şofrası.

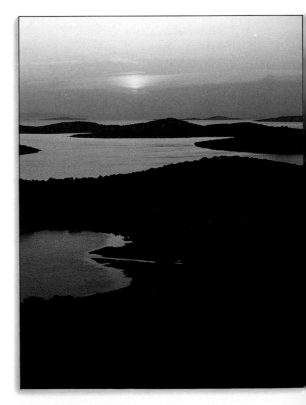

ships was a rooster, supposedly related to the French *coq galois*. Club Méditerranée has a resort village a short distance north of the city.

Seals and Phocaea: Different explanations have been offered for the name of Phocaea which means seal in Greek. One theory is that seals were common in the areas around Phocaea. Others suggest that the outline of one or several of the small offshore islands resembled the marine mammal.

The Genoese who ruled Phocaea in the 13th century built a fortress. In the 14th century the Genoese began alum mining operations at a site about 13 miles (20 km) away and moved therefore to Yeni Foça (New Foça). The Ottoman Turks conquered Phocaea in 1455 and built the **Fatih Mosque**.

Eski Foça, a peaceful little town not much exploited by mass tourism, hosts a music, folklore and a water sports festival in June and has a touch of Old World charm.

Four miles (seven km) east of Eski Foça on the Izmir road next to a stream is a massive, stepped pyramid-like fifth or fourth century BC rock tomb called **Taş Kule**.

On a hill behind the town of **Burumcuk** are the ruins of a fifth century BC city, identified by some as **Larisa**. (It may actually be Cyllene, and the true Larisa may be at Yeniköy on the hill north of Burumcuk.) The site includes city walls, a palace, wells and tombs.

Menemen, population 24,000, is a county capital and market town situated on the Gediz (Hermus) River. There is an old han in the centre of town, an old Ulu Cami (great Mosque) and a monument to Kubilay, a soldier who died in a religious uprising in 1930. Menemen is in the midst of a tobacco and cotton growing region, and its many shops sell harnesses, handles for spades, wooden churn and hemp rope. The pots and baskets found in abundance on the highway are well known Menemen products. Menemen also gives its name to a very tasty local dish made up from a mixture of tomatoes, green peppers and scrambled eggs.

The olive-producing town of Ayvalık.

THE OLIVE
OIL INDUSTRY

An olive grove is one of those magical places where it seems you are never alone, as if your footsteps caught woodland spirits at play, sending them hiding among the twisted trunks of nearby every tree.

The olive tree stands firmly rooted in history, with references dating to the sixth millennium BC, and throughout time, ancient cultures tapped the power of this special evergreen and its perfect fruit to produce light, medicine, food, cosmetics and sacred oils.

A staple of the Turkish diet for many centuries, the olive is revered even today for its important role in the country's economy, as Turkey is the world's fourth largest producer of *zeytin yağı* – olive oil.

Nearly 86 million olive trees thrive in Turkey; 75 percent of these blanket the rolling hills along the Aegean Coast, while the remainder grow in pockets on the Mediterranean Coast, Sea of Marmara and southeastern Anatolia.

Big business: Turkey is home to five major olive oil producers, including the generations-old Komili, now partly owned by Unilever, and Tariş, a government cooperative, and nearly 4,000 independent producers who operate from neighbourhood factories using old-world methods and machinery. In towns like Ayvalık, Muğla, Izmir, Edremit and Çanakkale, olive cultivation is a big business requiring serious commitment as farmers wait nearly two to five years for a new tree to bear fruit and almost 20 years before it reaches maturity. Orchards are a long-term investment and regarded as a measure of wealth, with groves handed down through generations.

Turkey's olive producers and farmers are eager to set tourists straight on the subject of authentic Turkish cooking, good naturedly accusing "big city cuisine" of false advertising by using cheaper vegetable oils instead of the real thing – virgin olive oil.

Annually, Turkey produces more than 120,000 tons of olives, adding $180 million to its coffers. Export revenues total around $45 million. Libya and the Soviet Union are the country's number one and two export markets respectively.

Harvest time: In early spring, Turkey's orchards ignite with green flowers which in May bear tiny fruit that is nurtured by sun and *imbat*, the steady warm west wind. In autumn, when the fruit changes colour from green to reddish-orange to black, the harvest begins. The harvest season is heralded by the arrival of workers and their families who travel from inland villages and set up temporary camps on olive farms.

The workers "milk" the fruit off the trees, handpicking and dropping it into straw olive baskets. Handpicking is slow, labour-intensive and very costly, but few alternatives exist due to the delicate nature of the olive; even the slightest bruising can result in spoiled fruit and bitter oil.

Upon delivery to the factories, olives are hand-graded to remove debris and damaged fruit. Next a washing and crushing cycle separates the stems and the pits, leaving a thick olive pulp which is made into a paste and squeezed through a press. The resulting oil and water mixture is then decanted to capture the pure virgin oil. It takes five kilos of olives to produce one kilo of oil.

Oil tasters: Before being placed in underground storage, the oil must pass the final trial: the taste test. No scientific techniques are needed, just a good nose and sharp taste buds determine the oil's fate. Professional tasters are employed by producers just for this purpose. To one oil connoisseur, whose culinary expertise has been called upon for 40 years, olive oil is simple: it's either very good or it's very bad, and it's a smile or a grimace which indicates the thumbs up or down.

Olive oil is sold in two ways in the Turkish consumer market-place. Virgin olive oil, the finest oil from the first pressing, is labelled *Sızma Zeytin Yağı*. This chemical-free oil has an acidity of less than 1 percent. A less expensive oil, labelled Pure Olive Oil, or Riviera

Type, is widely distributed in the Turkish market and despite its name, is actually a mixture made up of chemically-refined crude olive oil (from later pressings) and a smaller amount of virgin olive oil.

All is not golden in Turkey's olive oil industry these days, as coastal areas are faced with a pollution problem caused by the indiscriminate dumping of *karasu* (black water), the high nitrogen by-product of olive oil production. Illegal disposal of sewage has residents in a panic. Ayvalık is one resort town which is seeking to remedy the situation to protect its tourism business. Present plans call for the relocation of Ayvalık's many small olive oil factories from the city to another site where new plants and a modern treatment facility will be built.

Science is now proving what the ancients knew long ago: olive oil promotes healthy bodies and minds. Olives are an indispensable part of Turkish breakfast and olive oil is the most popular cooking agent in Turkish homes.

Olives for sale.

Consumption decline: Olive oil has been facing tough competition from lesser oils. Industry officials attribute a ten-year decline in domestic consumption to competition from newer vegetable oils, such as corn and sunflower, which entered the Turkish market with ambitious promotions. Turkey's producers are hard pressed to reverse the trend and have been working closely with the International Olive Council, in an effort to launch an advertsing campaign, pitting the high qualities of olive oil against vegetable oils. Olive oil has a clear case as it's the only oil which can be consumed in its natural state, and is medically-proven to help fight cholesterol, as well as aid digestion, bone formation and brain function.

The ancients didn't need science to explain what magic they had contained in their silvery green groves. Sophocles knew what he was talking about when he referred poetically to the olive tree as "the tree that stands unequalled, that can not be surpassed, that bursts forth again and again."

PERGAMUM

As the capital of a fast-growing empire, as a centre of art and religion, as a Mecca of healing, Pergamum in the Hellenistic Period was most impressive. That which remains of it now – ruined buildings, history, legends – attracts visitors by the hundreds of thousands. As a walled city on a peak it had a commanding location when it was ruled by Philetaerus and his successors in the third and second centuries BC; as the citadel today, people look up to it from afar wondering at its power; they gaze down from its heights with awe. It was and is a magnificent site.

History: Pergamene kings claimed descent from a certain Telephus who, according to myth, ruled the area at the time of the Trojan War (1250 BC). Archaeological information, including the discovery of shards, shows that the earliest settlement occurred some time later, around 800 BC. The whole area

came under Persian control after Cyrus defeated Croesus in 546 BC.

Pergamum's real importance began after Alexander the Great's death in 323 when Lysimachus, one of his generals, left a large amount of money there under the stewardship of his officer, Philetaerus. Lysimachus was soon killed in battle, and Philetaerus claimed the treasure as his to use for the good of the city. He also constructed many magnificent temples and new buildings in the city.

Philetaerus' successor, his adopted son Eumenes I (263-241 BC), was able to maintain his position only by buying off the Gauls. They had come from Europe to Anatolia in 279 as mercenary soldiers for the King of Bithynia and had acquired a reputation for being unbeatable, unruly, fierce and warlike. The sculptors of Pergamum were to use the Gauls as models for their many works of art.

Attalus defeats Gauls: Eumenes' adopted son, Attalus I (241-197 BC) decided to take care of his troublesome neighbours, the Gauls. Before the battle, he used a bit of psychology on his own men. In the usual religious service the surprised priests discovered the words, "Victory for the King," written on the sacrificial animal's liver. Only after Attalus' emboldened soldiers had defeated the Gauls did he confess that he had written the words backwards on his hand and stamped them on the liver as he was helping the priest.

It might not be sheer coincidence that the idea and the know-how of writing on skin – parchment – is attributed to a Pergamene ruler at about his time. When Alexandria put an embargo on papyrus to stunt the growth of the rival Pergamum library, scribes found they could use both sides of the parchment sheets and that pages were easier to handle than long rolls.

During Attalus' reign the influence of Rome began to be felt in the area when he gave Rome a sacred black stone from Pessinus that was worshipped as the Mother of the Gods.

Ties with Rome: Attalus' successor was Eumenes II (197-159 BC). He

A statuette of a Pergamene Goddess.

brought Pergamum to its height of power and cultural attainments. To his credit are the Temple of Zeus, the library and gymnasium and the lower agora. Eumenes continued to cultivate good political relations with Rome and reap the benefits. When the Romans defeated Antiochus the Great, the king of Syria, in the Battle of Magnesia in 190 BC, they turned over most of the Syrian lands to Eumenes. Thus in less than 100 years the Pergamene Empire had expanded from a tiny city-state to take in the Aegean Coast of Anatolia as far south as the Maeander River and as far east as present-day Konya.

Eumenes was succeeded by his brother, Attalus II (159-138 BC). Attalus further cemented Pergamum's ties with Rome, consulting with its rulers on major political and economic decisions, regional problems and conflicts.

Attalus spent most of his years warring with his neighbours, including the Kingdom of Bithynia, to the northeast of Pergamum. When Attalus II died at the age of 81, his nephew Attalus III succeeded to the throne of the Pergamene Empire.

Attalus III reigned only for five years (138-133 BC). He was more interested in botany than in politics, writing a book on agriculture which became a reference for the Romans. His specialities were medicinal herbs and poisons which he tried out on condemned prisoners. He ensured his place in the history books by giving his whole kingdom to Rome, shocking the Pergamenes and effectively ending the Attalid dynasty.

Rebellion: The bastard son of Eumenes II, Aristonicus, led an uprising against Rome, organizing disenchanted elements, mercenaries and slaves. At first Aristonicus was successful, defeating a Roman army led by a consul. But within three years the Romans had put down the rebellion.

Pergamum's last attempt at independence took place in 88 BC when it served briefly as the headquarters of Mithridates, King of the Pontus and an avowed enemy of Roman expansion in Asia, who invaded the Aegean Coast of

Modern Bergama as seen from the ruins.

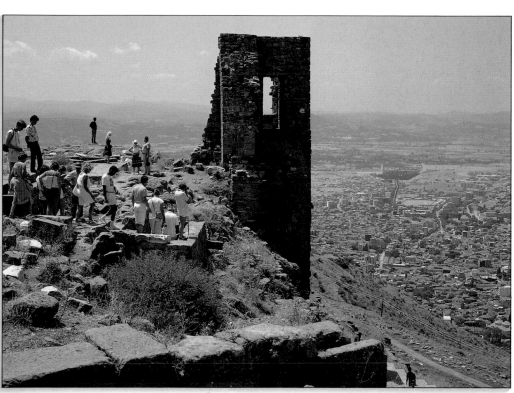

Asia Minor to liberate the Greek-speaking cities. Hundreds of Latins were murdered in the streets. But Roman legions, led by Pompey the Great eventually expelled Mithridates and repossessed Pergamum.

Province of Asia: The Republic of Rome organized the larger part of the Pergamene kingdom into the Province of Asia. However, Rome was not experienced in administering overseas territories, and made a bad job of it at first. Troubled by the insensibility to art in the capital, many of its sculptors moved to Aphrodisias, which became the art centre of the ancient world.

When Rome became an empire, the provinces in Anatolia in general were better administered. The emperors took a more personal interest, and many visited Anatolia, starting with Augustus. Trajan's father had been governor of the province of Asia (which included Pergamum). Caracalla received medical treatment at the Asclepieum after a bad accident at Gallipoli (AD 214). In gratitude he had the Temple of Dionysus covered with marble, and had himself proclaimed the "New Dionysus." In time, the inhabitants of Pergamum moved down from the hilltop fortress to the plain below. The fortress walls were left in a derelict condition and pillaged for stones.

People moved down from the hilltop fortress such as that at Pergamum, leaving the walls untended. In time they picked up the squared stones to build their own houses.

Church of Revelation: Members of the Christian church in Pergamum were criticized by St. John at the end of the first century for various heresies and were told that they lived where Satan's throne was found. Pergamum's reputation, however, grew over the years because one of the Seven Churches of Revelation existed here. Under the Byzantine Empire, Pergamum was a bishopric. Its importance diminished after the centre of power moved from the Aegean coastline to Constantinople in AD 330.

Pergamum was ravaged during the seventh-century Arab invasions. The Crusader Henry of Hainut who was Latin Emperor of Constantinople (1205-1216) took Pergamum in 1212 from the Byzantine Emperor, Theodore Lascaris, who was trying to rule from Nicaea (Iznik).

Early in the 14th century it became a part of the Seljuk Empire and then the Ottoman Empire, at which time Pergamum took its current Turkish name, Bergama. The new city was rebuilt below the acropolis hill after Tamerlane's army destroyed Bergama in 1402 during its brief, bloody rampage through Anatolia. Ottoman control resumed until the town was occupied in 1919 by the invading Greek army for three years.

Since 1923, Bergama has been under the control of the Turkish Republic. Bergama, with a population of some 50,000 today, is the capital of the county of the same name in Izmir Province. Nowadays, the denizens of Pergamum are waging a different kind of battle; one against an international gold mining company. The whole town unanimously campaigns against this new "in-

A Roman statue at Pergamum Museum.

160

vader" because it would use cyanide to exploit the gold-rich soil of Bergama, thus destroying agricultural life (once the operation is underway, nobody would buy the peasants' produce for fear of possible poison leakage) and threatening human and animal life.

Archaeology: The historic buildings from the Hellenistic and Roman periods of Pergamum, which are of interest to tourists, are located in three separate areas: the acropolis, the present town and the Asclepicum or medical centre. It is common to start one's visit with the acropolis because from that height one has a panoramic view of the old city and the relationships of the various parts, and also because the oldest buildings are there.

The highest point of the acropolis in the Hellenistic Period was controlled by the army. Here were placed the barracks and the arsenal, giving the guards the maximum survey of all sides. The Palaces of the Kings sheltered just below. Those buildings today have not even their bare walls standing.

The **Temple of Trajan** is in striking contrast to the palaces because of restorations being directed by German archaeologists. The white marble columns and flooring of the surrounding enclosure help create a sense of majesty of the people who lived in this part of the ancient city.

It is the only building in this area that does not date back to the Hellenistic times. It was begun during Trajan's reign (AD 98-117) and completed by Hadrian (117-138). Contemporary practice deified the Emperor; statues of Trajan and Hadrian found there are now displayed in the Pergamum Museum in East Berlin.

Slightly below the Temple of Trajan is the **Temple of Athena**. Its courtyard acted as a kind of museum where works of art and curiosities were displayed, many of which were offerings to the goddess. The Doric temple has six columns on the ends and ten on the flanks. The Temple of Athena, as of those in other western Anatolian cities – Izmir, Miletus and Erythrae – was the most important shrine in the city. In Per-gamum, it was related to the Parthenon, according to archaeologist Ekrem Akurgal. Among the bronze statues probably located there were two commemorating the Pergamene battle with the Gauls. Marble copies now in Rome show the "Dying Gaul" and the soldier stabbing himself after having killed his wife to escape capture. Both statues are of the noble foe, the enemy whose courage and devotion raised the struggle above savagery.

Rich library: The entrance to the Library of Pergamum was through the upper entrance of the Temple of Athena, an appropriate association with the goddess of wisdom. Pergamum was one of the centres of ancient learning, and its library once rivalled the great Library of Alexandria, according to ancient chronicles. The library is supposed to have contained 200,000 volumes, but there is a question of where they were all stored since the ruined building seems to have been big enough for only one-tenth of that amount. The library is famous for its rich collection as well as its destruction. Its demise, caused partly by a fire and partly by reactionary Moslem clerics, deprived later generations of much Hellenistic culture. The library continued in its importance as a depository of learning until a love-struck Mark Antony gave most of the volumes away to Cleopatra to take to Alexandria.

In the seventh century, the Moslem Caliph Omar, reasoning that the books were either inconsistent with the Koran and impious, or, if consistent then unnecessary, ordered them all destroyed in Alexandria, according to the late historian George Bean.

The Palaces of the Kings stood east of the Temple of Athena and served as the residences of the various Pergamene kings including Eumenes. It was surrounded by the barracks for the kings' guard of honour and soldiers working in his office.

Just 30 feet (10 metres) below the palaces were arsenals, five feet-long buildings constructed parallel to each other, which played a pivotal role in the defence of the ancient city. The barracks and the Command Tower, built during the reign of Attalus I, stood just above the arsenals. Little or nothing remains of these sites.

The Temple of Zeus, the biggest temple in Pergamum, was protected from a fate similar to that which struck the library. Germans in the 19th century took it out of the country stone by stone and reconstructed it in the Pergamum Museum, now in East Berlin, saving some of it from being destroyed for construction materials. Turks, however, argue that the temple and other Pergamene relics were smuggled out of the country and should be returned. Nevertheless, German archaeologists are planning to rebuild the Temple of Zeus in Pergamum using casts taken from the original temple in the East Berlin Museum.

The two friezes, that of the mythical adventures of Telephus and that representing the Battle of the Gods and the Giants, were sculpted at the summit of artistic excellence in the Hellenistic Period. The Telephus Frieze interests art students because it is an early attempt to give a realistic perspective and physical setting to the figures. The technical skill exercised in carving the marble with such finesse, the knowledge of anatomy, and the sense of drama vividly conveyed in the scenes place these marbles among the world's most fascinating masterpieces.

The Temple of Zeus is the largest of the buildings on the acropolis. Since it was dedicated to both Zeus and Athena (and perhaps to the rest of the Greek pantheon), it would more correctly be known as the Great Temple. Popular ascription of this as "Satan's Throne" (admittedly a dramatic site at which to point) probably lessens St. John's more general condemnation of the Roman government.

Located next to the Temple of Zeus is the upper agora which was surrounded originally by two – and three – storey colonnaded porticoes.

The **Pergamum Theatre,** impressive now in its size and acoustics, stretches up the side of the hill for 80 rows of seats and could hold 10,000 spectators. When there was a performance a wooden stage and backdrop were erected above the orchestra; these were dismantled at the end of the performance or at the end of the season. Above the centre of the lower landing stood the king's box, made entirely of marble. The Temple of Dionysus associated with the Pergamum Theatre (immediately north of the stage) was dedicated to Dionysus, the god of wine and entertainment who was believed to have inspired the first drama. Sacrifices for the actors and their performances were held there before the plays began. The building was impressive and pedestrians walking by could gaze with amazement and admiration.

A long promenade runs south of the stage where people walked, conversed, made business arrangements, and enjoyed the view.

City of temples: Below the acropolis in the south side of the hill are less official buildings, among them the **Temple of Hera**, the **Temple of Demeter**, the **Temple of Asclepius**, the lower agora, and the gymnasium on three levels. Perhaps most of the worshippers at the Temple of Demeter were women who held special celebrations at night with torchlight parades.

In the gymnasium the upper building was for young men, the middle building was for adolescent boys, and the lowest was for young boys. As with other gymnasiums, this was a place for both athletics and academic studies. The complex included an auditorium which seated around 1,000 people and a number of baths. It was in use into the fourth century. There was a ceremonial hall in the eastern part of the gymnasium for receptions, prize givings and other official functions. Next to it was a kind of prayer room where the emperors were worshipped. Water to the gymnasium was pumped from the northern mountains. The middle terrace includes the foundations of a temple dedicated to the patron gods of the gymnasium, Heracles and Hermes.

Pause to look at the construction of the vaulted stairway as you walk down from the gymnasium to the Hellenistic

House of Attalus and the lower agora.

Water supply: Consul Attalus was a man of means. The water from the cistern in his house supplied the fountain in the agora below him. Among the official records found in this agora is one that announces the rules concerning the use and maintenance of the water supply – a matter of supreme importance in the defence of a city on a hill, particularly one which can be blistering hot in summer. (The new **Kestrel Dam** northwest of the acropolis is evidence of that continuing importance. Pipes from a water supply in the mountains follow much the same path as the Hellenistic aqueduct.) A hint of the personality of this Attalus can be found in the inscription on the wall of his living room inviting his friends to come and enjoy life with   him.

The ancient buildings of the lower city date from the Roman Period. The biggest is the **Kızıl Avlu**, or Red Court, built over the channel of the Bergama Çayı (Selinus River) during the reign of Hadrian. The red colour one sees now is of the bricks which originally were faced with patterned marble rather than all pure white stone.

Even without the brick colour and the heavy walls, the building has a completely different feel to it from the temples on the hill. The many places for ritual ablutions and the paired male-female caryatids which held up the roofs of the porticoes indicate that the religious practices observed here may have been to honour the Egyptian gods who were popular in Roman and early Byzantine times, such as Osiris, the god of the underworld and the dead and husband of the fertility goddess Isis. Osiris was related to the Greek gods of the underworld, Pluto and Hades. The Kızıl Avlu was constructed in the second century. During the Byzantine Period the basilica was used as a church dedicated to St. John. One of the towers is now a mosque.

Battles among crocodiles: The Roman amphitheatre, which straddles a tributary of the Bergama Çayı, is one of the very few such structures existing in

Olive trees burst through the Great Altar at Pergamum.

Anatolia. When realistic sea battles among crocodiles were to be staged, the river was dammed.

Also in the valley of the Bergama Çayı was a stadium and a theatre, both having been constructed during the Roman period. Neither the amphitheatre, the theatre nor the stadium have been excavated by archaeologists. These places are best approached on foot. From one of the gates of the theatre a road began that led southwest about half a mile (one km) to the **Asclepieum** or medical centre. (The present road starts in the centre of Bergama.)

As you approach the grounds of the Asclepieum, you will notice the old road and columns (the columns were added during Hadrian's reign), the central courtyard with the small theatre to the far right behind more columns, and on the left the stone and brick ruins of some other buildings. Almost immediately in front of one of the buildings is a rather short broken marble column decorated with snakes twining around a laurel branch – the caduceus, the symbol of the medical profession during ancient times.

Psychotherapy: Treatment at the Pergamene Asclepieum consisted of a combination of herbal medicines, physical therapy, psychotherapy, diet, baths, massage, music, sports and intellectual stimulation. A lively account of some of the practices is found in the writings of the hypochondriac, Aelius Aristides, who was a patient in Pergamum for 13 years at the time of the institution's most famous physician, Galen. Patients at the Asclepieum slept for brief periods on the ground in the sanctuary: this was termed "incubation"; the dreams which they had were interpreted by the doctor-priests who then prescribed a treatment. Among the cures were mud baths followed by running naked around the temples. The theatre and a library housed in the northeast corner of the courtyard helped the patients to while away their recuperation time.

During one bitterly cold night, the staff had Aristides smear himself with mud and run three laps around the temples. He finished by washing off the mud in the sacred fountain.

The institution was so popular that even many Roman senators and merchants came to the Asclepieum for treatment and to see Galen for a check-up or for just plain relaxation. Women who could not bear children would visit the place, hoping medical treatment would result in miracles. One woman, according to a dubious ancient account, was pregnant for five years but could not deliver her child. But after she slept one night at the Asclepieum, and had a vision of the God of Medicine, she at once gave birth to a strapping five-year-old son.

Anatomical procedure: Galen, whose great 16-volume medical treatise, *On Anatomical Procedure*, parts of which have survived to these times, was a specialist in anatomy, human dissection and internal medicine. The bulk of the first nine volumes of his work has survived in Greek and Arabic and constitutes our main knowledge of ancient medical practices. Although he was a

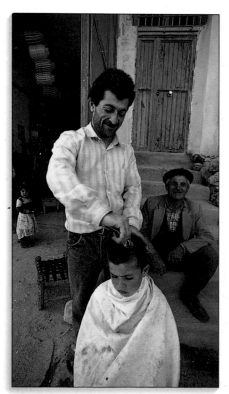

Haircut for a young lad.

highly scientific man, Galen worshipped heathen gods like Asclepius, believed in dreams and portents and even subscribed to absurd folk medicines that bordered on quackery.

The circular building to the immediate left of the entrance to the courtyard was the **Temple of Asclepius**, the Roman god of medicine and healing and son of Apollo, the god of music, youth and poetry exemplifying manly youth. It was built as a small replica of the Pantheon which had been built about 20 years earlier.

South of it and slightly outside the line of the south portico was the round two-storey treatment building with a number of separate rooms. It was linked to the sacred pool near the theatre by an underground passage. Probably people stretched out on its roof (now collapsed) to sunbathe.

The Bergama Museum was built in 1936 to house the finds in the area uncovered since then. It contains a small reproduction of the Temple of Zeus as one would see it in Berlin. A number of pieces of the Hellenistic, Roman and Byzantine periods collected here merit close attention. The items include statues, friezes, ceramics and coins. The museum also includes an ethnographic section of regional costumes, handwork and armaments.

The modern city of Bergama is remarkably unspoiled by its illustrious past and the large numbers of foreigners who spend their time and money only on its history. While the residents are conscious of this concern, many are engaged in the ordinary businesses which support a city and in the agricultural industry of the area. There is a long-standing International Bergama Fete every May and June. Good restaurants, hotels, and camping facilities (one in connection with a hot spring) are available. Shops display onyx items; some offer the famous hand-woven *Yağcıbedir* Bergama carpets, produced in the nearby mountain villages. The dominant colours of these carpets are dark blue and red. The deep blue of the Aegean gives the basic colour.

Snapshots anyone?

IZMIR

With over two million inhabitants Izmir is Turkey's third largest city and second largest port (after Istanbul). It is a cosmopolitan city created by Turkey's most European-thinking citizens directing an influx of rural Turks seeking a better life. In addition to its European ambience, fostered by fine shops, modern hotels, high-rise apartment buildings, and facilities integral to shipping, Izmir offers pleasant surprises to its more independent visitors.

Walking through its less affluent streets you may chance upon a colourful folk dance performed by transplanted villagers or a man prompting his rabbit to select the piece of paper with your fortune written on it. Although Izmir's commercial stature resembles a European town, it remains Turkish in spirit and hospitality.

Izmir's position as Turkey's leading exporter has deep historical roots. Ancient Izmir's commercial development was facilitated by its location, on a deep-water harbour at the end of the Golden Road, a trade route which passed through Lydia, Phrygia, the Hittite capital of Hattusa, and then Mesopotamia. Izmir became a centre for shipping in Ottoman times, after the port of Ephesus was abandoned. During the past 500 years, minority groups such as the Greeks, Sephardic Jews and Levantines have been indispensable in expanding Izmir's trade in figs, cotton, olive oil, steel and textiles.

Infidel Izmir: Moslem Turks liked to describe the city as *"Infidel Izmir,"* because the city's inhabitants before the 1923 population exchanges were overwhelmingly Christian Greeks. No Greeks remain there today. With a population educated above the country average in modern, secular Turkey, Izmir is now praised, at least by the local inhabitants, as Turkey's most cosmopolitan and western-oriented city.

Izmir's prominence as an eastern Mediterranean emporium is illustrated by the annual **Izmir International Fair**, which is held each August 26 at **Kültürpark**.

Izmir is home to NATO's Allied Land Forces Southeastern Europe and Sixth Allied Tactical Air Force headquarters, which guard western Europe's southern flank. The city is obviously patriotic, as indicated by the prominent location given to **Cumhuriyet Meydanı** (Republic Square). Located only a block from Izmir Bay and near Izmir's best hotels, this square features a **Monument of Atatürk** riding a horse and pointing toward the sea. This monument epitomizes the end of an era, for Izmir was the last large Turkish city to be liberated from Greek occupation forces. Izmir celebrates the anniversary of its liberation on September 9.

Two hundred yards (183 metres) east of Atatürk's statue, on the Gazi Osman Bulvarı, is the entrance to the luxurious **Büyük Efes Hotel** with the city's main Turkish Airlines Office located in the arcade below. This showpiece of modern Izmir is rivalled by the nearby Hilton Hotel, opened in the early 1990s.

Left, Mosaic at Ildırı. Right, strolling at Kuşadasi Camp.

Izmir

500 m/ 0,3 miles

Izmir Bay

ALSANCAK

1481
1475
1456
1464

Atatürk Caddesi

Şehitler Caddesi

St. Jean
(Cathedral)

Şehitler C.

Alsancak
Istasyonu
(Alşancak Station)

Atatürk Müzesi
(Atatürk Museum)

Kıbrıs

1449
1456

KARŞIYAKA

IMBATLI

7213 1660
7014

Anadolu Caddesi

1831
1848 1851/10
SOĞUKKUYU
1851/5

1838 1830
1873 1869
1849
Atatürk B.
1729
1875
1672
1743 1728
1742
1696

Zübeyde Hanım Caddesi
M.Kemalpaşa Cad.

Cemal Gürsel

Ferry

Ali Talatpaşa Bulvari

Çetinkaya
1392 Bulvari
Eşref Eşref
1393
1486
1420/2
Ziya Gökalp Bulvari

Atatürk

Cumhuriyet

Pilevne Caddesi

Şair Eşref

MIMAR
SINAN

Dr. M.Ender Cad.
Mimar Sinan C.

1405
1428
1395

Vasif Çinar Bulvari
1378
1382
1379
I. KÜLTÜR

Cumhuriyet
Meydani

Atatürk
Monument

Kültürpark

Pasaport Iskelesi
(Ferry Boat Pier)

Se Nevresbey Bul.
1378

Dr. Refik Saydam Bulvari

Açikhava
Tityatrosu
(Open Air Theatre)

PTT THY
City Terminal

Büyük
Efes

II. KÜLTÜR

1396
1412

Izmir Bay

Turizm
Danişma
Bürosu

ISMET
KAPTAN

**Botanical
Gardens**

Zoo

Gazi Bulvari

Fethibey B.
Halitziya B.
Şair Eşref Bulvari
Necatbey Bul.
Osmanpaşa

1365
1362

Müselpaşa Bulvari
Bozkurt Cad.

BASMANE

Atatürk Caddesi

Kemalettin Cad.

PTT Fevzipaşa
Bulvari

Basmane Istasyonau
(Basmane Station)

Mirkelam
Kervansarayi
(Caravan-
sary)
1313
1308

Gaziler Caddesi
257
1272
1281

Corakkapi
Camii
(Mosque)

1282

Atatürk M
(Atatürk Mu

Belediye
Saray
(City Hall)

Hisar Camii
(Hisar Mosque)

Anafartalar Caddesi
943 945
967
1054
1041

Cumhuriyet
Şehit Fethibey Bul.

Konak Camii
(Konak Mosque)

GÜZELYURT

NAMAZGAH

SEHITLIK
PARKI

Atatürk Heykeli
(Atatürk Monument)

Pasaport Iskelesi
(Ferry Boat Pier)

PTT

Kemeralti
Bazaar
920
816

Agora

952
953
1033
1023
1045

Atatürk
Cumhu

Konak
Saat
Kulesi
(Konak Clock Tower)

Hasan
Tahsin
Monument

Anafartalar
Cad.

922

Salepcioğlu Camii
(Salepcioğlu Mosque)

SAKARYA

982 971

1023
1031

Balikuyu

1041

Gazi Bul

to Istanbul

Fevzipaşa

Belediye Saray
(City Hall)

Ferry

Konak
Camii
(Konak
Mosque)

Hisar Ca
(Hisar Mos

Konak Saat Kulesi
(Konak ClockTower)

KONAK

Kemeralti
Bazaar

Tityatrosu
(State Theater)

E. Ü. Atatürk Kültür Merkezi
(E. Ü. Atatürk Cultural Centre)

Devlet Opera ve Balesi
(State Opera and Ballet)

TURGUTREIS
PARKI

CICI PARK

742 74
Iki Çeşm
Camii
(Iki Çeşme
Mosque)

Yolu
Caddesi

MECIDIYE

628

Sahil
Mihatpaşa

PARKI

TURGUTREIS

Asansör
278 322
302
249

Archaeology
Museum

Rakim Caddesi

KOCATEPE

574

142
177

200
MURAT
REIS
200
240

Caddesi
490
464

Halide Edip Adivar Caddesi

Esrefpaşa Caddesi

558
607
600
541
541

Kemal
98
100
141
155
101
106

Inönü
177

501

Yesilik Caddesi

555

Mustafa

GÖZTEPE PARKI

Caddesi
96
146

BAHÇELIEVLER
BAHAR

502

Mihatpaşa

Gazi Alec HasanTahsin Cad.
79
77

Filiz Ordu C.
Polat Caddesi

Uluönder Caddesi

Ordu Caddesi

9105
2935
2970
2989
2981

Eski Izmir Caddesi

3237

Izmir

1300 m/ 0.8 miles

Inönü

ESENDERE

9088

9090

9087 Yildiz

DOGANAY

Near the Atatürk Statue, facing the main Post Office, is the five-star **Grand Hotel Mercure** (the ex-Pullman Hotel), considered to be the second best in Izmir. Of the many hotels along Fevzi Paşa Bulvarı, the two-star **Kâtipoğlu Hotel** near the Basmane Train Station and the 9 Eylül (9 September) entrance to the Kültürpark, is among the best and most reasonably priced.

A walk along **Atatrk Caddesi** north of Cumhuriyet Meydanı is especially interesting at dusk. Along this bayside promenade, known also as Kordonboyu, lined with palm trees are numerous souvenir shops, hotels, restaurants and government buildings.

Near the French Consulate and NATO Regional Headquarters are the outstanding seafood restaurants, **Orfoz** (at no. 192) and **Imbat** (at no. 278). The former is an ideal place to watch the sun setting over Izmir bay and the lowering of the flags of the 16 NATO countries. The latter is named after the *imbat* or ocean breeze which cools down sultry summer afternoons. At night this street is closed to traffic in order to permit pedestrians and seafood lovers fully to enjoy their respective pleasures.

Jewish quarter: Continuing along the promenade (Atatürk Caddesi) one soon reaches the prestigious **Alsancak** district of Izmir. Many of Izmir's most elegant shops and boutiques are concentrated in the area northeast of the Atatürk Museum and the Alsancak Iskelesi, a ferryboat landing. Gold, leather, and almost anything else can be purchased in the old **Jewish Quarter** at the western end of the **Kemeraltı Bazaar** near the Hisar Mosque.

Izmir also offers plenty of public and religious structures worth visiting. Chief among the public monuments is the **Konak Square** with its lavishly decorated Moorish **Clock Tower** and its **Monument of Hasan Tahsin**, a Turkish journalist who was the first casualty in the fight against the Greeks who invaded Izmir in 1919. The monument, showing the patriotic Tahsin firing a gun at the Greeks, is also referred to as the Ilk Kurşun Anıtı (**The Monument of the First Gun Shot**). Just north of this statue are the buildings of the **Belediye** (Municipal government) where Turkish art is displayed. Across the street is the **Vilayet Binası** (Provincial Governor's office) where elaborate flag lowering ceremonies occur daily, snarling downtown traffic badly for half an hour. From the nearby docks, ferryboats take 15 minutes to cross the bay to Karşıyaka, a suburb which offers seafood restaurants and views of Izmir's shimmering city lights.

City mosques: Perhaps the two most interesting of Izmir's many old mosques are the **Kemeraltı Mosque** and the **Hisar Mosque**. Built in 1672, the Kemeraltı Mosque, also known as the **Hacı Mehmet Ağa Camii**, is a modest but attractive building located on Anafartalar Caddesi in the heart of the Kemeraltı Bazaar. The narrow street leaving this mosque is crowded with shoppers looking for all manner of merchandise. Built in 1598, Hisar Mosque is the oldest and largest Moslem shrine in Izmir.

Located just outside the courtyard in front of the mosque are two nurseries and a small tea garden under an old sycamore tree. Locals believe that young women were sold as slaves in the **Kızlarağası Hanı**, a caravansary and market building behind (southwest of) the tea garden. The most delicious ice cream in Izmir is served at **Mennau**, two blocks toward Fevzi Paşa Boulevard from the Hisar Mosque (899 Sokak 30/A, Hisaronü).

Of the seven original Christian churches (communities) of Asia Minor mentioned in Revelations, only Izmir's still flourishes. The church dedicated to Saint Polycarp, martyr and fourth bishop of Izmir, is located at the corner of Necatibey and Kâzım Bey boulevards. The nine-day ritual honouring St Polycarp begins each February 14. The original church at this site dates back to 1625. Today's exquisitely decorated **Church of Saint Polycarp** dates to 1929. Visitors will find the contrast between its humble exterior and opulent interior is unforgettable.

Just 165 yards (150 metres) southwest is the **Santa Maria Church** built in 1667. Franciscans administer this modest church located at **Halit Ziya Bulvarı**, Number 67, a block south of the **Tourism Information Bureau**.

The Archaeology Museum: Located on a hill southeast of the Government Theatre and Conservatory (opera) and next to the Devlet Hastanesi, or state hospital, the three-storey **Archaeology Museum** contains numerous statues, artifacts, ceramics and frescoes from Greek and Roman sites throughout the region (including Claros, Belevi, Erythrae, ancient Izmir, Sardis and Ephesus). It is advisable to visit the museum before touring such archaeological sites for better appreciation. The exhibit describing Bayraklı, or ancient Izmir, explains the cuneiform tablets excavated at the Hittite site of Kültepe. These indicate that the original name of Izmir was *Tismurna*. Sometime after 1800 BC, the prefix was dropped so that the place-name Smurna remained. Izmir is the Turkish pronunciation of *Smurna* or Smyrna.

Next door is the **Ethnographic Museum**. A two-storey structure which opened in 1985, the museum contains a wealth of old Ottoman and Turkish artifacts, including coins dating to 1389, weapons, carpets, household furnishings, embroidery, jewellery, and exhibits describing production of wood printing, pottery and evil eyes (*boncuk*) made of glass. The exhibits on camel wrestling and military commanders typical of western Anatolia (e.g. *Efe* and *Zeybek*) are fascinating.

The Velvet Castle: Those accustomed to exercise may begin climbing the slopes of **Mount Pagus** from the area near the Basmane Train Station. As one approaches the summit, the winding streets seem to get narrower and the houses smaller. Friendly children and quaint houses make the climb to the **Velvet Castle**, Kadifekale, pleasant. Concealed inside the western walls of Kadifekale are three acres of pine trees, a children's playground, a soccer field and botanical gardens. Doves singing early in the morning make this centre of ancient Izmir especially idyllic. A Byzantine cistern is nestled amid pine trees.

From the western ramparts of the ancient fortress there is a splendid view of downtown Izmir and the harbour. At night the tea garden has live music. Just east of the tea garden several women busily weave brilliantly coloured yarn bags on black-strap looms.

Many of the houses you see around Kadifekale and in the hills surrounding the city are illegal squatter houses, known as *gecekondus* (night landings). A vast majority of these houses were built by waves of peasants arriving from the countryside.

A Hellenistic settlement around Mount Pagus (at the summit of which is Kadifekale) began after 334 EC, as a result of Alexander the Great's command. Kadifekale was connected to the agora by a Roman road. From its northeastern gate the road south lead to Ephesus. The western ramparts, with Byzantine watchtowers on a Hellenistic foundation, have been fortified by successive conquerors (Greeks, Romans, Byzantines, and Ottomans). These walls are wonderful places for strolling, watching sunsets over the wide bay, and contemplating ancient Izmir.

Construction of the Hellenistic city on top of Mount Pagus was allegedly commanded by the Goddess of Vengeance (Nemesis) in a dream of Alexander the Great in 334 BC Alexander, however, didn't apply the goddess' mandate to resettle the Smyrnaeans in the new city. The project began under Antigonus in 300 BC, but it was Lysimachus, conqueror of Ephesus, who completed Smyrna's resettlement by 288 BC. After relocation around Mount Pagus was accomplished, Izmir became the 13th member in a confederation of Ionian cities (the Panionic League). Izmir's population then exceeded 100,000 and the historian Strabo praised it as the "most beautiful city in Ionia."

Agora: The remains of the agora are located on a tract of land in downtown Izmir, one mile (1.6 km) southwest of Kadifekale and half a mile north of Konak Square. The original state agora also dates to shortly after Alexander the Great's dream. The agora included a temple, a marketplace and an indoor meeting place where business and politics were discussed. From an altar to Zeus in the centre of the agora fragments of statues of Demeter, Poseidon and Artemis (hardly recognizable) have been reassembled. The statues of these three nature deities are now displayed in the Izmir Archaeology Museum.

An unusually severe earthquake in AD 178 forced the Romans to rebuild the Hellenistic agora. In the middle of the agora was a marble square. Along the northern gallery 17 columns of what was once a 540-foot (165-metre storey) long, three-storey marble edifice remain. Daily business was conducted inside this basilica-style structure. In the centre gallery was the entrance. On the ground floor were arched galleries and 26 shops. The agora itself was on the first floor. The section with columns standing on steps was the second floor. The third floor was destroyed, except for fragments of beams connecting two columns. At the northwest corner, a marble staircase takes you underground to an impressive vaulted basement where piped water runs continuously.

Nearby are the remains of the aqueduct built 2,000 years ago. Commercial activity today is especially brisk only 330 yards (300 metres) south of here in the picturesque Kemeraltı Bazaar, which begins in the courtyard of the Kemeraltı Mosque.

Success in exporting and rapid industrialisation have obliterated or transformed the rest of Izmir's legendary sites. The **Baths of Agamemnon**, where the king and his soldiers may have recovered after the Trojan War 2,500 years ago, are still used in treating various ailments. The baths are now administered by the **Balçova Hot Springs**, 8 miles (13 km) west of Izmir, near Inciraltı. Those expecting to visit Homer's birthplace near the banks of the sacred Meles River will find that **Diana's Baths** are now enclosed by Izmir's waterworks, east of the Sümerbank factory off the Altın Yol (Golden Road). Homer is said to have written the *Iliad* and *Odyssey* in a cave near Diana's Baths (**Halkapınar Suyu**) where a statue of Artemis was discovered.

172

Izmir's history: Archaeological evidence from Tepekule suggests that Izmir was inhabited by 3000 BC. Now concealed in the industrial zone at the northeast edge of Izmir Bay, the oldest level at Tepekule (Hill Tower) at Bayraklı is contemporary with Troy I. This site was inhabited for 2,000 years by Hittites or Lelegians before Aeolians from the Aegean islands began colonization about 1000 BC. In 800 BC Ionian Greeks displaced Aeolian Greeks. By 600 BC Tantalos, the tyrant who ruled ancient Izmir, was buried in a round tomb almost 100 feet (30 metres) in diameter and a magnificent Temple of Athena had been built. Following two invasions launched by Lydians before 500 BC, Ionian Izmir lay dormant for 200 years, until Alexander the Great and his successors relocated it.

After 129 BC Izmir was ruled by Rome and it continued to flourish. Christianity was introduced to Izmir by St John, or by St Paul after AD 53. The fourth Christian bishop of Izmir, Saint Polycarp, was a direct disciple of St John. Polycarp, who wrote "the love of money is the root of all evil," was burned at the stake in the Izmir Stadium, in AD 153 by order of a Roman administrator. Nevertheless, Izmir's Christian community has persisted until today.

Seljuk Turks controlled Byzantine Izmir from 1078 to 1097, the year Crusaders captured it. In 1261 the Genoese were granted control over Izmir. But, for the next 200 years Izmir was hotly contested by various factions of Christians and Moslems.

Izmir remained under Ottoman rule from the time of Sultan Mehmet I until it was occupied by Greeks in 1919 as part of World War I spoils. The Turkish Republican Army, led by Atatürk, forced Greek evacuation and liberated Izmir on September 9, 1922. The evacuation culminated in a fire that destroyed the city. Historians recently discovered documentary evidence indicating that it was Armenian insurgents living in Izmir who set the city ablaze. For nearly 70 years, Turks and Greeks had accused each other of starting the fire.

Life on the Kordonboyu Avenue.

THE IZMIR INTERNATIONAL FAIR

Izmir's International Fair is an annual extravaganza which tastefully showcases the latest technological and commercial achievements to stimulate export of Turkish products and import of essential items. Moreover, numerous artistic and cultural activities promote international understanding and appreciation of human diversity. By attracting visitors from Turkey's rural areas and from urban centres around the world, the fair provides for an international exchange of ideas as well as goods. It strengthens Izmir's reputation as Turkey's most cosmopolitan city and Turkey's commitment to rapid development and entry into the European Community.

Beginning in 1936, with the sixth Izmir International Fair, the fairgrounds, or Kültürpark, has hosted the colossal trade fair and various smaller fairs. The fairgrounds occupy half a square mile (one square km) in the heart of downtown Izmir and are surprisingly uncrowded in the mornings. They provide an oasis with abundant shade beneath numerous trees, an amusement park for children, tennis courts, jogging trails and cycling lanes, two outdoor theatres, a zoo and plenty of inexpensive restaurants. The fairgrounds also house the regional offices of Turkish Radio and Television.

Visitors to Izmir can reach the fairgrounds most easily by returning to the Basmane Train Station and walking along Anafartalar Caddesi past 9 Eylül Meydanı (9 September Square) and entering the fairground through the 9 Eylül Gate, which faces the square. There are four other gates: the **Lozan** (Lausanne) **Gate**, which faces the Lozan Meydanı (Square) three blocks away from the 9 Eylül University, the region's main institution of higher learning; the **Montrö** (Montreux) **Gate**, facing the Montrö Meydanı which is connected to Cumhuriyet Meydanı by Şehit Nevresbey Bulvarı;

The Izmir International Fairgrounds.

174

the **26 Ağustos** (August) **Gate** in the north and the **Cumhuriyet Gate** in the east, both of which face Dr. Mustafa Ender Caddesi.

The fair's queen: From August 26 to September 10, exhibits from Turkey and more than 25 countries, are open to the public between 3 pm to 11 pm daily. Turkish exhibits are open an additional ten days, until September 20. Evenings are boisterous with excitement and crowds. Many rustics with their peasant wives and children mill about the exhibits wondering with amazement at the new technology. Locals and tourists alike enjoy the best in Turkish entertainment, with belly dancing, floor shows and solo music performances available nightly, and watch Izmir's most talented and gorgeous women competing for the honour of being crowned "Queen of the Fair."

Some of Turkey's leading female and male vocalists have performed at the Izmir Fair, including the lusty blond Sibel Can, a belly dancer turned vocalist; the shapely Güngör Bayrak, an actress famed for wearing see-through dresses; and Bülent Ersoy, a controversial male singer of classical Turkish tunes who once underwent a sex change operation; and Ibrahim Tatlıses, the Elvis Presley of Turkey and the "King of Arabesque" music.

In addition to shopping and being entertained, visitors to the fair can meet people from countries throughout the world. The non-Turkish exhibitors in the annual fair include the United States, Germany, Belgium, Czech and Slovac republics, Palestine, France, South Korea, Netherlands, Iraq, Iran, Sweden, Switzerland, Turkish Republic of Northern Cyprus, Libya, Hungary, Pakistan, Poland, Rumania, the Russian Federation and the new Asian republics, Sri Lanka, Syria, Tunisia, Yugoslavia, the Philippines, United Kingdom, Thailand and Italy, as well as international organizations such as NATO and UNICEF.

Each country or organization has its own pavilion. Countries may include exhibits from 20 or more different private companies or state-owned enter-prises. Within the pavilion space allocated to a particular country the exhibits may change from year to year. More than 1,100 non-Turkish companies, including well-known corporations such as BMW, Bosch, International Business Machines Corp. (IBM), Coca Cola Corp., KLM Royal Dutch Airlines, Air France, Samsung Electronics and Renault participate regularly.

Turkish products: Turkey's exhibitors include about 250 privately owned companies displaying furniture, clothing and textiles, banking services, books and magazines, fruit and vegetables, dairy products and hundreds of industrial products. Among the best known domestic exhibitors are Arçelik, a manufacturer of home appliances, television sets and refrigerators; the Turkish subsidiary of Chrysler, which produces trucks and diesel engines in Turkey; Kent, a producer of confectionery; Kütahya Porcelain with its exquisite ceramics and porcelain; and Tuborg, an Izmir beer and malt producer.

Also represented are about 80 companies affiliated with the Turkish Chambers of Industry, commerce and stock exchanges, 40 companies affiliated with the Development Bank of Turkey, and 35 official enterprises and cooperatives, including the Izmir-based Tariş, one of the world's largest agricultural cooperatives. Tariş produces everything from cotton and yarn to Smyrna figs, sultana raisins and olive oil.

Turkish trade increases: Every year, nearly three million visitors tour more than 2,000 exhibits. In addition to the exhibits, 21 covered pavilions house hundreds of informative and visually attractive displays. Walking through the exhibits convinces you that commerce really has made the world a small place, and that Turkey's share in global trade is steadily increasing.

Tourists who plan to visit Izmir during the International Fair should book their hotels way in advance. It is very difficult, sometimes impossible, to find accommodation in the city during that period as tens of thousands of Turks from other parts of the country visit Izmir for the fair.

IZMIR'S MINORITIES

Izmir's affluent ethnic minorities have played an important role in the development of industry, banking and commerce in the city. What follows is a rundown on who these minorities are and their history.

Sephardic Jews: The Jewish community in Izmir may be 2,000 years old. In response to King Ferdinand's order expelling all Jews from Spain in 1492, Sultan Beyazıt II confided to his courtiers that the Spanish King had foolishly "impoverished his own land and enriched ours." Sultan Beyazıt's invitation to settle in the Ottoman Empire was accepted by thousands of Jews exiled from Spain and Portugal. By 1575 most commerce in the Ottoman Empire was controlled by Jews, and Spanish was the trade language of the Mediterranean.

Today the majority of Izmir's 2,500 Jews are still involved in commerce although it is estimated that less than half of them speak fluently the Spanish of Cervantes' era.

There have been two eras of exodus for Izmir's Jewry. During World War I, some 10,000 left Izmir for Latin American countries. Still, in 1927, 17,000 Jews remained in Izmir. After World War II most of them went to Israel.

Beth Israel: There are seven principal synagogues in Izmir. The oldest and best preserved is the **Beth Israel** on Mithat Paşa Caddesi, number 265. Two of Izmir's older synagogues are on **Havra Sokak** (called the street of the synagogues).

A synagogue built in 1821 is located near the gold merchant's quarter of the Kemeraltı. Its amazingly unobtrusive exterior conceals a splendid interior. The monumental synagogue in the suburb of Karataş was built by the famous Rothschild family.

Most scholars of this period agree that Ottoman Jews were better treated than their European counterparts. The Jewish community of Turkey commemorated the 500th anniversary of their residence in 1992 with elaborate festivities held in Izmir and Istanbul.

The Dönme: Sabatai Zevi, born in Izmir in 1626, triggered a scandal of international proportions. Izmir's Orthodox Jews were outraged when Sabatai proclaimed himself the Messiah in 1665. He attracted such an immense international following that the Sultan ordered him to convert to Islam or die. He duly renounced Judaism.

Believers still exist. Sabatai's followers, called the Dönme (turncoats), live secretively in Izmir and Istanbul. Izmir's Jews condemn Sabatai as a "False Messiah" or charlatan who misled the gullible. "His name is cursed among us," one Jewish businessman said. Nevertheless John Freely, an American educator and travel writer who lives and works in Turkey, reported observing a few elderly Dönme worshipping in a house in Izmir which they regarded as Sabatai's birthplace in his *The Western Shores of Turkey*. The house was for years the home of Osman Kibar, the late conservative Mayor of Izmir who was himself a Dönme.

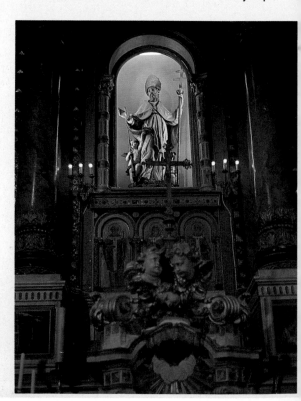

The Latin Church of St Polycarp.

The Levantines: In 1581 an agreement between Sultan Murat III and Queen Elizabeth I granted a seven-year franchise to a group of English merchants known as the Levent Company. These original Levantines were responsible for introducing Europeans to coffee. They also exported figs, currants, dates, lemons, oranges, sultana raisins, carpets, textiles, jewellery and copperware. They and their descendants have contributed enormously to Izmir's commercial development.

Today there are 1,500 British residents in Izmir, most of whom are still exporting items such as dried fruits, tobacco, cotton, grapes and motor engines. They meet frequently and many of them worship together at the Church of St John the Evangelist at the northern entrance to **Talat Paşa Bulvarı** in Alsancak. Two other Anglican churches, one at **Buca** and the other at **Bornova**, are still in use.

Italians of Izmir: The term Levantine has been rather loosely applied to all families of European origin, including French and Italian. Italians have long been active as traders throughout the region surrounding Izmir. In 1261 the Byzantine Emperor granted Italians from Genoa full control of Izmir. Although they lost political control of Izmir after 1320, their descendants still survive in the region. Although they are a closed community not conventionally making marital bonds with Muslim Turks, the younger generation of Levantines are more open-minded. One Caroline Giraud, of a wealthy Izmir family, married Mustafa Koç of the biggest industrial conglomerate in Turkey. Money has no religion.

Today only 1,300 Catholics live in Izmir, primarily of Italian descent. Izmir's chief Catholic churches include **Santa Maria**, the **Rosary Church** near Alsancak Iskelesi, **Santa Elena** in Karşıyaka, **Saint Anthony** in Bayraklı, and **Our Lady of Lourdes** in Göztepe. Mass is increasingly said in Turkish. About 100 children attend the private Italian Primary School and receive instruction in Italian.

Jews pray in a synagogue.

THE IONIAN COAST

Heading west from Izmir on the highway to Çeşme one reaches Urla about 22 miles (35 km), after passing Inciraltı and Güzelbahçe. **Urla Iskelesi** is a small picturesque town half a mile (one km) right off the main highway. Along its tranquil beach are a few hotels and the ruins of the Ionian port of **Clazomenae**. Greek colonists from Peloponnesus settled on the mainland, just 1.2 miles (two km) southwest of where an indigenous population had lived. After the Ionian revolt, around 500 BC, these Greeks moved out to the island in the bay for fear of the Persians. By order of Alexander a causeway connected the mainland to the island. Today a paved road links the mainland to the **Urla Hospital**. Because of their proximity to the hospital, the ruins of Clazomenae aren't open to the public.

Çeşme, once a quaint fishing village and now a bustling summer town, and neighbouring **Ilıca**, famed for its thermal baths, are booming. Their beautiful white sand beaches entice more visitors every year. During the summer season international travellers and residents of Izmir enjoy its daytime sun and nighttime fun. In early July, the Çeşme Sea Festival features art, music and sports activities. Çeşme is uncrowded and enchanting between the end of September and early June.

Çeşme is windy and picturesque, cooler and less crowded than Izmir. It offers plenty of shopping and sightseeing, with a bit of history to provide a break from boating, beaches, water sports and discos.

Stone castle: A tour of the **Genoese Fortress** overlooking the bay affords spectacular views of Çeşme, its harbour, and the Greek island of Chios. This impressive stone castle was built to protect traders originally from Genoa. Inside the 14th-century castle, a small museum displays Hellenistic and Roman artifacts.

Near the fortress are the ruins of an 18th-century inn or caravansary. In

Çeşme as seen from the Castle.

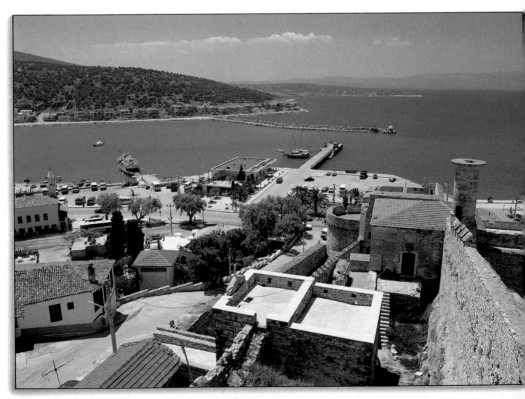

front of the fortress is a **Statue of Cezayirli Gazi Hasan Pasha** and a lion. For Turks the lion symbolizes bravery, and this monument commemorates Hasan Pasha's victory over the Russian navy which attacked the Ottoman fleet in the Bay of Çeşme in 1770. Across the street at the harbour, ferryboats carry passengers about nine miles (14 km) to **Chios**.

Numerous restaurants are located along the promenade at the edge of the harbour and others are situated along **Inkilap Caddesi**, the main street. At night, after this street is closed to traffic, restaurants like the **Imren** are especially enjoyable.

Turkish ambience: Those seeking more Turkish ambience will find it 1.6 miles (3 km) north at the town of **Dalyan**. This little lovely village sits on a little bay where yachts come in to anchor. Seafood connoisseurs congregate to enjoy the food at several fine restaurants such as the **Liman** and the **Körfez Hotel and Restaurant**.

The ruins of **Erythrae** can be found near Ildır, a sleepy seaside village northeast of Çeşme. Erythrae is one of 12 Ionian cities mentioned by the historian Herodotus. Principal attractions include the ruins of **Athena's Temple** and a 10,000-seat theatre. Between the temple and Ildır are ruins of a Roman villa, a mausoleum, and a wall belonging to the agora. On top of the hill are ruins of a 150-year-old Greek church and Athena's Temple.

Fishing villages: On the way from Çeşme, Kuşadası and Selçuk, there are numerous worthwhile but less publicized sites which can easily be reached by private transport or taxi. Leaving Çeşme and Ildır, travelling east toward Izmir, you reach a junction just before Güzelbahçe.

A right turn here (onto route 505) will take you south to **Seferihisar**.

At Seferihisar another right takes one to **Sığacık**, a pleasant little fishing village with an imposing Genoese fortress. Continuing southwest 1.2 miles (two km) one passes the white sandy beach of **Akkum**. The road forks left

Housing development at Erythrae.

toward Teos, about half a mile (1 km) away.

Teos, a prosperous Ionian port, was situated near one large and one small harbour. By 600 BC its wealth and location at the centre of the Ionian region prompted Thales to propose that it be Ionia's capital city. His suggestion was never carried out. The inability of Ionian cities, Teos included, to unite politically left them vulnerable to Persian conquest. After the Persians were expelled from Ionia, Izmir lay dormant for 200 years, between 500 and 300 BC, while Teos regained its prominence as a thriving port.

Teos declined after Romans gained control of Asia Minor, beginning with their naval victory over the Seleucid king, Antiochus III. This decisive battle was fought in 190 BC in the southern harbour of Teos.

The best preserved part of Teos is the **Temple of Dionysus**, located in an olive grove just off the paved road.

Other visible ruins include traces of the Hellenistic-era city wall, a Roman Period odeon and parts of a theatre.

The prototype for Dionysus, the wine god, may have been Bacchus, of Lydian origin. The Lydians representing satyrs in processions of Bacchus dressed in goat skins and sang "goat songs" which may have inspired Greek tragedy. Since Dionysus was their patron, the Artists of Dionysus resided at Teos between 300 and 150 BC. From Teos these professional actors and musicians performed at theatres and musical festivals throughout the Greek world.

Myonneus, Mouse Island, is nine miles (15 km) south of Sığacık. This landmark, known in Turkish as **Çifit Kalesi** (the Jew's Castle) is just north of Cape Doğanbey.

Traces of ancient walls remain on top of this steep and rocky fortress which once protected pirates from the Romans who attacked Teos. There is a causeway, visible only underwater, connecting the mainland to the citadel.

Lebedos was one of the poorest of the Ionian cities primarily because Ephesus and Teos had better harbours. The ruins are located just south of **Ürkmez**, on a knoll overlooking an attractive sandy cove with a restaurant and camping facilities. There are hotels nearby at Ürkmez and Gümüldür.

From Gümüldür there are 11 miles (17 km) of scenic coastline before reaching the cliffs with the partially excavated ruins of Notium. Its ruins include a **Temple of Athena**, an agora, a theatre and an extensive city wall.

Claros: Homer's hymn to Apollo indicates that the **Temple of Apollo** at Claros, 1.2 miles (2 km) inland from Notium, was a famous sanctuary by the seventh-century BC. At the southern entrance to the sanctuary six marble columns have been unearthed in a small canyon. The road entering this sanctuary was 30 feet (10 meters) wide and may have been connected to a harbour at one time.

A short distance north of the entrance is a large altar dedicated to Apollo, and a smaller altar to Artemis, his twin sister. Fragments of statues of Apollo, Artemis, and their mother, Leto, have been recovered.

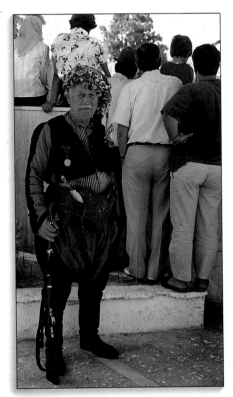

An Efe, a veteran of the Turkish War of Independence

West of the altars numerous columns, including their Doric-style decorated capitals, are plainly visible.

Colophon: Eight miles (12 km) north of Claros is the affluent Ionian city of **Colophon**, built on the mountain behind the quaint Turkish village of Değirmendere.

Colophon's strong navy, maritime trade and abundant farmland made it a prosperous member of the Ionian League. Yet even its ferocious warrior-dogs and famous cavalry could not protect it from Lydian and Persian conquerors. It was ruled continuously by Persians until Alexander the Great. Although Colophon was rebuilt in 281 BC, it was, even with its coastal ally Notium, unable to compete with the emporium of Ephesus. Its disappearance from history is so complete that even the ruins are insignificant.

The territory controlled by Colophonians extended east to the fertile plain of **Cumaovası**. From Colophon north to Menderes (formerly Cumaovası) it is 10 miles (17 km). About halfway between them, to the right of the highway, is the central bottling plant of **Şaşal** drinking water, famous throughout Turkey. **Menderes** is a small town located on a plain where olives, figs, and grapes are grown. From Menderes it is only a few miles to the highway leading north to Izmir or south toward Torbalı and Selçuk.

Twenty-five miles (40 km) south of Izmir, in the middle of a rich agricultural region, is the town of **Torbalı**, where two small castles are open to the public. Another nine miles (15 km) south, on top of a hill to the right of the highway, looms **Keçi Kalesi** (the Goat's Castle). This Byzantine fortress was built around AD 1200.

Selçuk is a small but thriving tourist centre located near the church of St. John, the Isa Bey Mosque, the Artemision and the ruins of Ephesus. Its main attractions are the museum – one of the richest and most interesting in Turkey, the remains of an aqueduct near the train station (where steam-engine trains arrive), a partially restored Ottoman bath

The ruins of Claros.

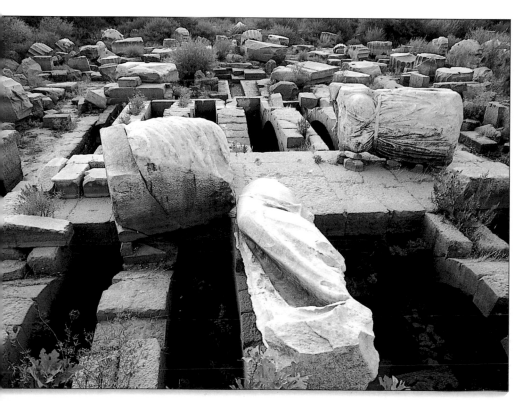

from the 1370s and shops with onyx, carpets, leather and souvenirs.

Before visiting the ruins a trip to the museum (open daily from 8:30 am to 6:30 pm) is highly recommended. In addition to the two famous statues of Artemis, there are numerous examples of funeral relics including Mycenaean bowls dated to 1400 BC, a fresco and marble head of Socrates, a marble head of Eros, a bronze statuette of Eros riding a dolphin.

Tours of Ephesus and Meryem Ana, the purported last House of the Virgin Mary, can be arranged from Selçuk.

A short drive east of Selçuk is the quaint village of **Şirince**. It is still unspoiled by tourists. This small village, founded by Christians who left Ephesus around .D 600, is surrounded by pine-covered hills and orchards of olive and peach trees. Homemade wine can be purchased directly from enterprising villagers. There are three restaurants, plenty of old Greek houses, and two abandoned Greek churches to see.

Only 11 miles (18 km) from Selçuk is the chic coastal playground **Kuşadası**. From here organized tours of Ephesus can also be arranged. Tourist development at Kuşadası has focused on several long sandy beaches and lovely bays located at the centre of a 16-mile (25-km) stretch of coastline.

Belly dancing: Kuşadası's most unusual lodging is at the **Kervansaray,** situated in the heart of town in what was formerly the Öküz Mehmet Paşa Caravansary. This historic landmark has been lovingly restored and converted into a fine hotel. On the ground floor there are several shops, and a beautiful fountain in the middle of a courtyard. The buffet dinners served here nightly are animated by belly dancing and other forms of lavish entertainment.

From mid-April through October the water is warm enough to make swimming a delightful experience. The most pristine beaches are to be found away from the downtown area, extending from Kadınlar Plajı (Womens' Beach) south to Güzelçamlı, and from the Tusan Hotel north to Pamucak.

Trees in full bloom with Selçuk Castle in background.

Visitors can hire yachts or sailboats at **Kuşadası Marina**. Daily boat tours around the coast are also available. Ferryboats leave daily for the Greek island of **Samos**, only one mile (two km) away. Windsurfing facilities and lessons are also available.

Except for Ephesus, archaeological sites are scarce. The village of **Pygela**, formerly situated a few miles north of downtown Kuşadası was founded, according to Strabo, by Lelegians and colonized by Agamemnon. The annual meeting place of the 13 Ionian cities comprising the Panionic League was 16 miles (25 km) south of Kuşadası, near the village of Güzelçamlı and the entrance to the **Dilek Peninsula National Park**. After the Byzantines granted trading rights to Italians from Venice and Genoa these merchants shipped silk, saffron and other goods to Europe from Kuşadası. Under Ottoman control Kuşadası continued to flourish.

In addition to the Genoese castle on the island, there are two interesting Ottoman era structures built by the architect for whom they are named. The **Öküz Mehmet Paşa Mosque** is near the Town Hall, east of the Öküz Mehmet Paşa Caravansary, which was built in 1613. This impressive stone inn provided safety and hospitality to travellers on the trade route culminating here. The open courtyard housed the animals serving the travellers who were lodged in second-storey rooms.

Connected to the mainland by a causeway 1320 feet (400 metres) in length is **Kuşadası**, Bird Island, from which this town took its name. This small island offers visitors a restored fortress, several fine restaurants, a disco, a tea garden serving snacks and beverages, and magnificent views of the ocean and bay.

The Genoese Fortress at Kuşadası may have been built by AD 1500. Later it became the home of Hayrettin Barbaros, an Algerian pirate appointed grand Admiral by the illustrious Ottoman Sultan, Süleyman the Magnificent. In 1546 Hayrettin died rich and famous at the age of 70.

Left, Isa Bey Mosque at Selçuk. **Right**, Kusadası.

CAMEL WRESTLING

Every year in mid-January, the market town of Selçuk is host to the Super Bowl of camel wrestling. For the two days of the Selçuk Camel Wrestling Festival, an atmosphere of gaiety and carnival prevails in the town as the top male fighting camels of Turkey vie for honours, prize money and trophies.

Camel wrestling, or *deve güreşi* in Turkish, is the most popular spectator sport in the southern Turkish Aegean Coast after football.

Desert ship: Before the advent of automobiles, long-distance lorries, trains and jetliners, camels were the principal means of transportation in the Ottoman Empire and the Middle East. Camel caravans carried people and goods from one city to another across miles of deserts and wastelands. Because of its ability to withstand extreme heat and cold, survive long periods of thirst and hunger and stride in a swaying motion, the camel was affectionately described as the "ship of the desert."

Only Yörük Turks, an old-fashioned nomadic people inhabiting the mountain plateaus of coastal Turkey, still prefer camels to cars for public transportation. Travellers to the coast will frequently come across Yörük camel caravans.

Village herdsmen now basically train the beasts as fighters. These herdsmen don't race camels, a popular pastime in some Middle Eastern countries including Saudi Arabia, Kuwait and Yemen.

Camel wrestling is supposed to have started when herdsmen noticed male camels fighting over their females during mating season and turned the affair into a sport.

Weekend tournaments: Camel wrestling meets are held every weekend in many small towns in the provinces of Izmir, Aydin, Denizli and Muğla from January through March. During a weekend tournament, thousands of peasants from nearby villages descend on the towns to bet on their favourite camels and also to sell their produce and display carpets and other handicrafts.

Male camels wrestle as many as 30 times in one winter season, a time when the females are in heat. During the rest of the year they just munch on fodder, ruminate and require special handling. The upkeep of a beast costs an enormous amount of money, but ownership of a camel often brings prestige to peasant herdsmen – the same kind of prestige owning a flashy new sports car would bring to a young city Turk.

Not all camels can be trained as wrestlers. "Great wrestlers are born not made," says Hulusi Kanat, a camel trainer for 30 years and a professional announcer at camel fights. The best camels are those from Iranian mother camels, he says. Camels generally begin wrestling at the age of six, but it is not before the age of 15 that they become big and strong enough to be champions. Some old war horses continue wrestling to the age of 25.

The bulldozer: Turkey's 250 best fighting camels are known as *tülüs*. These camels can earn up to $1,200 and much more on side bets for their owners during each bout, when one camel is pitted against another. Each *tülü* is an awesome sight, weighing over a ton and standing six feet (two metres) at the shoulders and seven feet (2.3 metres) at the top of its hump. Each beast is recognized as a superstar in his own right and has a ferocious name, such as the Bulldozer, the Killer, the Quiltmaker, Deli Tülü (the Mad Camel), the Warrior, the Commando, the Conqueror, Kara "Black" Kemal, Kolombo, Felek (Fate), and Sulfur.

It is at Selçuk, two hours out of Izmir, where the top camels slug it out. Often, more than 120 camels participate in this extravaganza. Before the tournament begins, the Selçuk-Bodrum Highway, a major thoroughfare, is closed to traffic for about one hour as the owners parade their camels, decked out in colourful blankets, pompons, gold bangles and jewellery, through the main street. The camels also wear large cow bells that jingle as they stride through town.

The camels, frothing at the mouth at

the height of the mating season, are muzzled to prevent them from biting jealous rivals or human admirers.

After the opening ceremony in Selçuk, which includes speeches by the provincial governor, the mayor and vote-seeking politicians, the camels are marched to the nearby ancient city of Ephesus for the big meet.

Gladiators of antiquity?: The fights take place on the grounds of a ruined stadium, used during Roman times to feed Christians to the lions and for fights among gladiators. One writer has, in fact, likened the fighting camels to the "gladiators of antiquity."

Thousands of spectators, including women, jam the stadium and sit on the stone seats to watch the matches amidst the playing of drums, fife and folklore performances. Vendors sell popcorn, potato chips, nuts and *simit*, a Turkish sesame seed roll shaped like a doughnut, during the eight-hour program.

Two snorting, bellowing male *tülüs* are brought in. They stand at opposite ends of the stadium. The match begins only after a female camel struts between the two rivals to arouse their excitement and ire. Suddenly the two camels charge at one another like angry bulls, butting heads, bumping sides and kicking with their feet. Often the camels go into a dangerous neck lock or leg lock. The stronger animal tries to crush his opponent with his weight.

Each bout lasts about ten minutes after which two nine-men teams, each wearing red or blue colour leather coverings, pull the animals apart with rope in a tug-of-war fashion. No animals are seriously hurt. The only injuries are bruises and bloody noses. The most exciting matches are among the top heavyweights.

Victory: To win, one wrestler has to knock the other down on his side, chase him out of the stadium or cause him to squeal a camel's version of "uncle." Otherwise the match is a draw.

In addition to prize money and earnings from bets, the animal owners get a camel trophy, a plaque and special handmade carpets.

Camels fight it out at Germencik.

EPHESUS

In the sixth century BC, when **Ephesus** was an affluent Aegean port, Heraclitus, the son of an Ephesian priest, dedicated his philosophical treatise called *Nature* to the Temple of Artemis (Nature Goddess or Mother Goddess). For this famous native son the eternal flux or constant change he recognized as fundamental in nature was best symbolized by water and rivers. The gradual transformation wrought by the **Kaystros River** (Küçük Menderes in Turkish), which flows into the Aegean, epitomizes Heraclitus' theory and explains the demise of Ephesus.

The prosperity Ephesus enjoyed as a port of trade connecting Europe, Asia and Africa was dependent on its having a functional harbour. Ephesus began to decline when its harbour was ruined by the centuries of silt accumulation that occur at the mouth of the Kaystros River. Today the city lies three miles

(five km) from the sea. The region lay nearly dormant from 1450 to 1950.

In its heyday, Ephesus was the most important commercial centre in western Anatolia and had a population of more than a quarter of a million people. Inscriptions found by archaeologists described Ephesus as the "first and greatest metropolis of Asia."

British and Austrian archaeologists excavated the site in the 19th century. The Austrians smuggled out most of the relics found there, but returned the artifacts when the Ottoman government threatened to ban all future Austrian excavations in the Near East.

In recent decades its ruins have attracted tourists from all over the world. Ephesus is, in a sense, an international city again. Nearly two million foreign tourists visit the ancient city every year. The informed visitor to Ephesus may, with a bit of imagination, relive a moment of world history, if he can go there early in the morning to avoid hordes of uninitiated tourists and relearn a lesson about our species' abiding dependence upon Mother Nature.

This Aegean port turned Asian metropolis has been home to various cultures and religions. Little is known about the earliest inhabitants of Ephesus. The Carians, whose most important city was Halicarnassus (Bodrum), evidently considered themselves natives of the region. Sometime later Smyrnaians may have colonized Ephesus and Izmir.

Mycenaean pottery: The earliest archaeological evidence of human occupation of Ephesus is painted pottery of Mycenaean origin dating to 1400 BC, which are on display at the Selçuk Ephesus Museum. These elegantly crafted Mycenaean bowls were widely traded, and appear at sites from Troy to Bodrum. It is unclear whether Mycenaeans settled in Ephesus or simply traded with a local population.

The Ionian region of Asia Minor in which Ephesus is located was definitely colonized by 1000 BC. A political struggle for control of Athens prompted the Athenian colonists, led by Androklos, the son of Kodros, king of

Athens, to establish Ephesus at the northern end of Mt Pilon. Legend has it that Androklos built a temple dedicated to Athena at the place where a wild boar was killed, in compliance with cryptic instructions received from the Oracle of Apollo, which he consulted. The remains of this temple may be on the small hill just west of the Roman stadium. An effigy of the boar stood on the street in front of the temple for centuries in thanksgiving for the fulfilment of the oracular prophesy.

The Carians fought a losing battle against these Greek invaders but managed to kill Androklos. A shrine to him was built near the **Magnesian** (Manisa) **Gate**. His descendants ruled Ephesus for the next four centuries.

Rapacious king: The prosperity of Ionian Ephesus caught the eye of the rapacious King Croesus of Sardis. In 560 BC this Lydian king captured Ephesus and relocated its inhabitants in the area around the Temple of Artemis. Statues of golden calves and beautiful column capitals, one of which bears his name,

were Croesus' chief contribution to the Artemision (Temple of Artemis). He also had a fortification wall built around the city.

After the Persian King Cyrus defeated Croesus in 546 BC, Ephesus was ruled by Persians as a satrapy. Although the citizens of Ephesus continued to trade and practice their religion freely they were obliged to pay extortionist tribute to their Persian masters. From 546 BC until 334 BC, the Ionian region was in turmoil as Greeks and Persians fought each other. When Alexander the Great defeated the Persians on the southern shores of the Sea of Marmara at the Battle of the Granicus in 334 BC, Ephesus was liberated and it became a quasi-democratic city. It was briefly dominated by the Ptolemites of Egypt before being annexed by the Attalid kings of Pergamum.

Roman Ephesus: Roman control of Ephesus began after 133 BC. Although Ephesians joined in a successful revolt against Rome in 88 BC, Roman rule was quickly reestablished. In 27 BC the **The amphitheater at Ephesus.**

Roman Emperor Augustus proclaimed Ephesus capital of the Asian province. It was during this period that Ephesus became one of the largest cities in the Roman Empire; one of only three cities to have street lighting.

Roman Ephesus was a free city governed by two assemblies: one for ordinary citizens (*Demos*), the other for the *Boule,* a 300-member elite. Rich Ephesians could attain prestige by sponsoring public works and ceremonies. The most prestigious ceremonial duties, those of the *prytanis*, could be assumed by both sexes. The *prytanis* paid all expenses incurred in carrying out daily animal sacrifices, supervising all cults and insuring that the eternal fire honouring Hestia, goddess of the hearth, always burned in the Prytaneion.

When Emperor Hadrian visited Ephesus in AD 123, it was still a booming emporium and residence of the Roman governor of Asia. Most of the buildings visible today date from the Roman era when Ephesus had nearly 250,000 inhabitants. The buildings, fountains and monuments commemorate Roman administrators and Ephesians wealthy enough to sponsor public works. Following a devastating attack by a large Gothic fleet in AD 262, the grandeur that characterized ancient Ephesus began to wane.

Christians persecuted: During this era of decadence, Christians were persecuted for refusing to sacrifice animals and to worship pagan deities. The struggle between the pagan Roman religion and the monotheistic Christianity resulted in Christians being killed by lions in the same stadium where gladiators and wild animals entertained Roman audiences. It is believed that after Christianity was endorsed as the official religion of Rome, all the seats in Ephesus Stadium were destroyed. Today the stadium is the scene for the popular camel wrestling festival and the annual Izmir International Music Festival.

The legend explaining the **Grotto of the Seven Sleepers** illustrates the growth of Christianity. Around AD 250, seven Christian boys took refuge in

Modern folk dancing in the ancient theater.

a cave, located about 1,650 feet (500 metres) east of the **Vedius Gymnasium**. When they awoke, after 200 years of slumber, Rip van Winkle-style, Christianity had become the official religion and Emperor Theodosius II proclaimed that they had been resurrected. Several hundred graves dating to the fifth century, including those of the seven sleepers, and a church, were excavated in this cave.

Many biblical scholars believe that St Paul's version of Christianity differed significantly from that of St John and his followers. Paul of Tarsus was a Roman citizen and a Benjamite Jew who did not know Jesus in Jerusalem. The fact that Paul persecuted Christians until his blinding vision on the road to Damascus (Acts 9:1-9) distinguishes him from St John.

Flight from Jerusalem: There is evidence to suggest St John and Mary left Jerusalem to escape the persecution that threatened them. If Professor Brownlee is correct in identifying John as Lazarus of Bethany, then the chief priests' decision to kill both Jesus and Lazarus (John 12: 9-11) would make the flight from Jerusalem a necessity. With its commitment to religious freedom and its already thriving Jewish community, Ephesus must have seemed a safe haven. At any rate, both Mary and John are believed to have lived and died here.

Paul's famous confrontation with Ephesians loyal to Artemis is one of a series of conflicts which culminated in his being decapitated on the outskirts of Rome in AD 64. It was then that St. John became leader of the **Church of Ephesus**. It is believed that John is buried under the church which now bears his name. By the fourth century, when a modest basilica was built over his grave, the glory of Roman Ephesus was gone. The harbour had silted up. Much of the marble used to build the towers and fortification walls surrounding the **Church of St John** (completed around AD 550), located in the town of Selçuk, was brought from the stadium where Christians were once tortured to entertain up to 70,000 spectators.

Library of Celsus.

It is widely believed that the worship of Artemis was a continuation of the veneration of the Mother Goddess and fertility cult suggested by the statues of Cybele scattered throughout Turkey. Statues excavated at the farming community of Çatal Höyük in southcentral Anatolia are 9,000 years old. Yet if Artemis was indeed the mother of all animals, her prototype is likely to have its origins in hunting and gathering cultures. Perhaps the prototype is represented by the Venus figurines and human females depicted in magnificent cave art appearing at numerous sites in Europe and Asia more than 13,000 years ago. The oldest evidence of Cybele-Artemis worship at Ephesus is a plain wooden statue.

Artemis cult: The three well-preserved statues of Artemis on display at the Selçuk Ephesus Museum graphically illustrate the meaning this great mother once had. From the hips down to the toes on both statues, flowers and bees are visible. The belt of the **Great Artemis** (the one wearing the tall crown displayed at the western end of the hall) shows bees and flowers. Next to the **Beautiful Artemis** (displayed at the eastern end of the hall) is a headless statue of Artemis with bees and flowers on her chest. These icons of Artemis imply that the survival of plants and animals requires mutual dependence or symbiosis. Artemis was evidently the chief guardian and personification of harmony in nature. In worshipping Artemis, Ephesians proclaimed that living in harmony with nature was their central concern.

It is frequently asserted that the social structure of bees provided the model for the religious hierarchy entrusted with the worship of Artemis. The Queen Bee which reproduces the species is served by all others. At Ephesus there were hundreds of priests, priestesses and guards devoted to Artemis. The chief priest or Megaysos was in charge of receiving donations to and loaning money from the temple treasury. He and the other priests had their reproductive organs removed to become permanent

Temple of Hadrian.

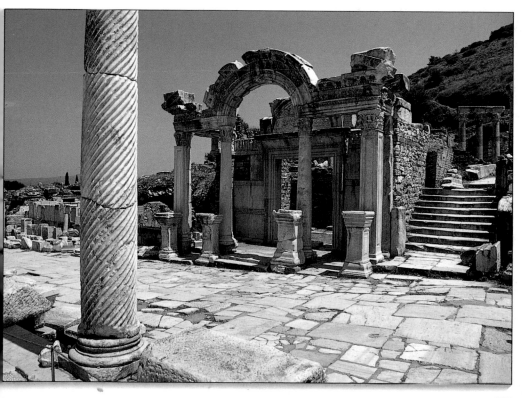

celibates before assuming office. The priestess who assisted the Megaysosin his duties were virgins consecrated to Artemis (reminiscent of the six Vestal Virgins serving the Roman goddess of fire, Vesta).

Testes of bulls: Chastity, fertility and reproduction are key attributes of Artemis. Depicted on the breasts of both statues of Artemis are the testes of bulls which were sacrificed to her. Long misidentified as eggs, these testes symbolize fertility as well.

The necklace which adorns the Beautiful Artemis is comprised of the 12 signs of the zodiac, indicating that she incarnated life and influenced the cosmos. Her association with life was also manifested in the right of asylum granted to criminals who came and sought refuge within the boundaries of the temple.

Although such unconditional love of criminals upset many Ephesians, their request in AD 22 for an end of asylum was not granted by Emperor Tiberius. Evidently the great mother was ex-pected to demonstrate love for all her children.

The first Temple of Artemis was evidently destroyed by the Cimmerians who attacked Ephesus in the seventh century BC. The oldest artifacts associated with this temple date to the eighth century BC and are on exhibition in the British Museum.

The Great Temple: Built between 550 and 460 BC, the first major temple honouring this queen of heaven and earth was magnificent. It was the largest marble structure ever built. A total of 127 Ionic columns, each 20 yards (19 metres) high, supported a roof enclosing a courtyard 163 yards (155 metres) long by 58 yards (55 metres) wide.

On all four sides of the temple are two rows of columns. This **Temple of Artemis**, first located in 1869 by British engineer John Wood was even more impressive than the rival Temple of Hera in Samos and four times larger than the Parthenon in Athens. It was considered to be one of the Seven Wonders of the Ancient World.

Details from a sarcophagus.

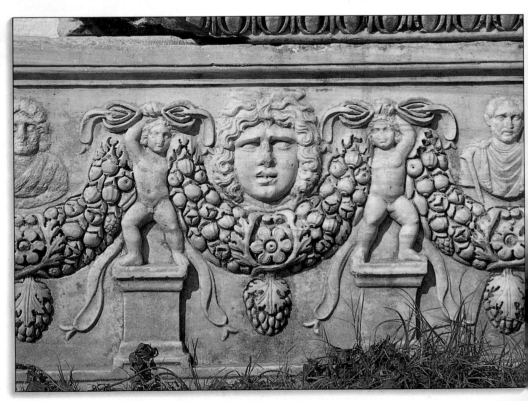

Besides the Temple of Artemis, the Seven Wonders included the Pyramids of Egypt; the Colossus of Rhodes; the Statue of Zeus at Olympia; the Hanging Gardens of Babylon, the Lighthouse at Alexandria and the Mausoleum at Halicarnassus.

The temple was rebuilt after it was burned down, allegedly on the very night Alexander was born in 356 BC, by an Ephesian desperate for publicity. The second major Artemision, built between 350 and 250 BC, was essentially identical to the first except that it was elevated on a base 3.3 yards (three metres) high with 13 steps.

The temple had to be reconstructed again after it was destroyed by Goths who attacked Ephesus in AD 125 and again in AD 262. With the growth of Christianity the cult of Artemis declined to be replaced perhaps by the adoration of the Virgin Mary. Marble from the Artemision was used in the construction of **Haghia Sophia** (the grand **Aya Sofya** basilica in Istanbul) and the Church of St John on the hill in Selçuk. Today a single column rising out of a muddy pool is the only reminder one of what was once one of the Seven Wonders of the Ancient World.

The **Fortification wall** and the original Magnesian Gate were built in the third century BC by Lysimachus. To appreciate the excellent Hellenistic workmanship on the wall, it's best to climb to the top of the mountain where the city wall is better preserved. After entering via the Magnesian Gate a north turn will bring the tourist to the remains of the **Eastern Gymnasium**, built in the second century. Just east of the Odeon stands the mostly unexcavated **Varius Baths**. Just south of the Odeon are the remains of the **State Agora** and the **Basilica**.

A rectangular temple built around 25 BC was located at the centre of the State Agora. The pediment of this **Temple of Emperor Augustus** is now on display in the courtyard at the Ephesus Museum in Selçuk. The pediment illustrates a legend described by Homer. Three allies of Odysseus are preparing to blind

Relief of a flying goddess.

the Cyclops Polyphemus after Odysseus got him drunk with wine. The long 160-metre (170-yard) but narrow Basilica contained the statues of Augustus and his wife now seen at the Ephesus Museum. Located to the west of the Basilica is the **Prytaneion** where the eternal flame of Ephesus burned and where the two famous statues of Artemis were found.

Modern performances: The small theatre or **Odeon** seated 1,400 and was built by a couple of rich Ephesians in AD 150. Although it was used for concerts, it was the political meeting place for the *Boule*. The people's assembly or *Demos* was convened in the well-preserved 24,000-seat Theatre, where today modern folklore shows and plays are frequently performed.

Continuing west toward Curetes Street, to the north of Domitian Square, is the **Memmius Monument** built in the first century BC to honour Roman military commanders. The temple dedicated to Domitian (AD 81-96) is largely unrestored. To the east of the steps at the entrance to the **Temple of Domitian** stands a two-tiered column with reliefs. Just behind it is the cool **Inscription Gallery** where numerous documents pertaining to the history of Ephesus have been found.

About 111 yards (100 metres) west past the **Hercules Gate**, which marks the beginning of Curetes Street, between the Trajan Fountain and the Temple of Hadrian, are the remains of the **Scholasticia Baths**. These heated baths were built in the first century and were repaired frequently thereafter until about AD 400. The last citizen to restore the baths, Christian Scholasticia, is commemorated by a statue. As in all Roman baths, hot, tepid and cold water was available in different rooms. Hot air circulated through baked clay pipes under the floors of the room. The taps provided hot and tepid water.

Next to the baths is a peristyle house that was the Brothel, indicating that prostitution was institutionalized in Ephesus. The upper story of the house has been destroyed and only traces of frescoes remain. A mosaic in the dining **Mosaic in Ephesus.**

room depicts the four seasons while a simple mosaic in the adjacent pool shows three maidens, a servant, a cat and a mouse eating crumbs. A tiny bronze **Figure of Priape**, a god with an overgrown phallus, was found in the brothel and now can be seen as an exhibit in the Ephesus Museum.

Public toilets: To the west of the baths is the Latrina or public toilets. Across the street from the entrance to the Latrina is the western entrance to the baths. Hidden to the right of this entrance is a 20-inch (50-cm) tall relief of Artemis. She is depicted there with an animal head facing right and holding a staff in her right hand.

The **Temple of Hadrian**, completed in honour of Emperor Hadrian by AD 138, is a visual feast. Behind the bases of four columns which once held statues of four Roman emperors rise four Corinthian columns. A richly-decorated arch featuring the face of Tyche, the goddess of chance equivalent to the Roman Fortuna, crowns the two central columns. Above the door behind the central chamber stands a semicircular frontal depicting a bare-breasted maiden surrounded by beautiful flowers and leaves.

On the south side of Curetes Street, several elegant houses built on the slopes of **Bülbül Dağı** (Nightingale Mountain) have been excavated. These three-story structures had courtyards, running water, heating, mosaic floors and walls adorned with frescoes. Originally constructed during the reign of Augustus, these houses were frequently altered until the end of the seventh century. Two of these houses on the slopes are restored and may be entered by climbing the steps just across the street from Hadrian's Temple.

Celsus library: At the end of Curetes Street is the impressive two-story **Celsus Library**. Because it had to be built between the two older edifices, this structure was cleverly designed to look wider than it really is. When Tiberius Julius Celsus, a famous Roman administrator, died in AD 114 his son had this library built as a monument and

Inscriptions at Ephesus.

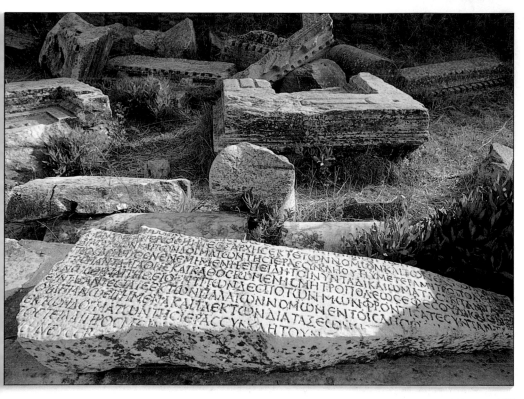

mausoleum. Celsus was buried inside an elaborately decorated marble sarcophagus found under a library wall. The interior of the library was spacious and housed 12,000 scrolls kept in niches designed to minimize damage from humidity. Eight Corinthian columns placed on a podium support elaborately-adorned frontals.

At the north side of the Celsus Library is the **Mazeus Mithridates Gate** which leads into the Agora. Its three passages are reminiscent of a Roman victory arch. The elegantly decorated frieze above the arch has three sections. Upon emancipation, two slaves, Mazeus and Mithridates, built this ornate gate to honour their former master, Emperor Augustus and his family.

Beside the inscriptions in bronze to their master and his family is written the stern warning: "Whoever urinates here will be tried in court." This admonishment reminded Ephesians that the agora or forum was to be entered reverently and not to be sullied.

The **Agora** or shopping centre at Ephesus was a semi-sacred square where various stores were located. Merchandise displayed included locally-produced perfume, Arabic herbs, Anatolian wine, jewellery, foods, ceramics, and artifacts of bronze and copper. Women reputed to be the most beautiful in the East were sold here as slaves.

Today only numerous columns standing at the perimeter of this large square meeting and marketplace remind one of the exchange of goods and ideas from three continents that once transpired here. Excavations currently underway will undoubtedly explain more about the original agora built in the third century BC.

The Temple of Serapis is located at the end of a marble road which begins at the southwestern corner of the agora. This temple, under construction in the second century, was dedicated to Serapis, the Egyptian god of the underworld and judge of the dead. Eight massive marble columns, each weighing 57 tons, lie in front of the temple ruins. After 547 BC, when Ephesus was con-

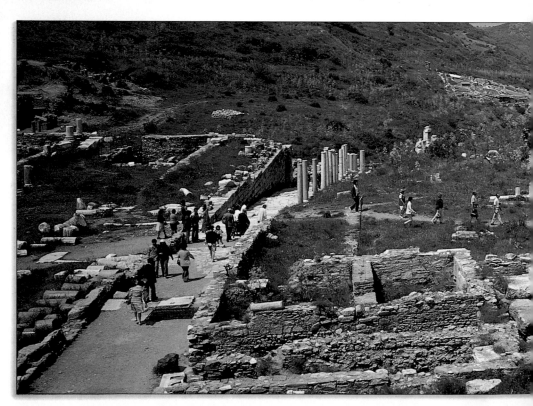

quered by Persians, maritime trade between Alexandria and Ephesus must have been brisk. Numerous Egyptian statues and a peace treaty written on marble also confirm the connection between Egypt and Ephesus. In 299 BC the alliance between Egypt and Ephesus was cemented by the royal marriage between Lysimachus and Arsinos, an Egyptian princess.

From the Celsus Library the sacred or Marble Road goes toward the theatre. Built into the western slope of Mt Pion during the reign of Lysimachus, this impressive, well-preserved theatre seats 24,000 people. Hellenistic plays were quasi-religious, dedicated to Dionysus, the god of wine and entertainment. Prayers and animal sacrifices preceded performances given by masked male actors.

During the Roman era, when St Paul's provocative sermon to Ephesians was delivered here, the theatre was enlarged. St Paul's challenge to Artemis worshippers, and Ephesian silversmiths whose livelihood depended on manufacturing and selling statues of Artemis and her temple, resulted in a riot in this very theatre (Acts 19:24-41). The superb acoustics and star performers, among them the likes of Ray Charles and Joan Baez thrill modern audiences each summer at the Izmir Festival. The top tier of the theatre provides a panoramic view of the **Arcadian Way** leading westwards towards the ancient harbour.

The wide **Harbour Street** testifies to the grandeur that was Ephesus in the first century BC. After docking at the harbour, dignitaries marched 1,650 feet (500 metres) along this marble-paved, arcaded road lined with statues, porticoes and public buildings. A recently-excavated inscription confirms that 50 lamps hung from columned porticoes on both sides of this street at a time when lighted cities included only Ephesus, Antioch and Rome. Between the theatre and the ancient harbour, statues of the four evangelists were, in the fifth century, placed on columns whose shafts are still visible. At the north side of this

Visitors explore streets of Ephesus.

street are the ruins of the Theatre Gymnasium, the Verlanus Sports Arena and Paleistra, the Harbour Baths and the Church of the Virgin Mary.

Nestorian heresy: Located to the north of the Harbour Baths, near the **Church of the Virgin Mary**, the first church ever dedicated to the Virgin Mary, is a long extensive ruin where the Third Ecumenical Council proclaimed in AD 431 that Mary was the mother of Jesus, the son of God. This council recorded that Mary lived and died near Ephesus, and branded Nestor, Patriarch of Constantinople, a heretic for his denial of the virgin birth.

The church was converted from a school of higher education to a basilica in the fourth century. Because this basilica underwent two additional alterations, this narrow, elongated edifice now seems confusing. Near the northern apse is the large baptismal pool where the faithful were immersed and baptized inside what was once a circular baptistery covered by a domed roof.

After being expelled from Jerusalem, St John and the Virgin Mary came to Ephesus. It is believed John's grave lies underneath the church erected by Emperor Justinian, who reigned from AD 527 to 565. Even before the construction of the **Church of St John**, which stands near the Citadel of Selçuk, there was a Baptistery in use there. The circular pool where baptisms were performed had a marble floor and was originally covered by a dome with a glass mosaic.

Toward the eastern end of the church, at the end of the central nave just west of the apse, is the **Tomb of St John**. The burial platform, two steps below the floor, used to be covered by a small dome. The marble mosaics adorning the platform have been restored. For several centuries this church was a shrine visited by pilgrims and by the sick and ailing who hoped the dust from the burial chamber would perform miracles and heal them.

The fortification wall which surrounds the church was built in the seventh and eighth centuries to protect

Praying at the House of the Virgin Mary.

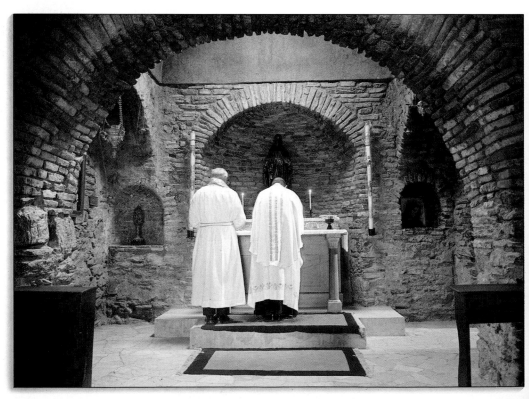

Ephesus against Arab attacks. At the main entrance to the church, the **Pursuit Gate** and its adjoining courtyard were built according to an ancient Hellenistic strategy for defence. If the enemy penetrated beyond the gate they were trapped inside the courtyard which has no exit. In that position they could be killed by men positioned above the courtyard walls.

Turkish conquest: When the Turks arrived in 1304 all that remained of Ephesus was a small Byzantine village which was easily conquered. The **Isa Bey Mosque** is remarkably uncrowded and occupies a huge area at the western base of the hill where the Church of St John stands. It was built in 1375 for the Seljuk sultan Isa Bey by the architect Ali Damessene.

The mosque was subsequently toppled by an earthquake. Sometime soon after the Ottomans took over in 1426 Ephesus was utterly deserted. This double-domed mosque has been restored and has three chambers.

Above the main entrance the last of three original minarets still stands. Surrounding the large inner courtyard are unusually high walls which were partially constructed with marble transported from Ephesus.

Magnificent views highlight the five-mile (7.5-km) ascent from the Magnesian Gate to the souvenir shops and restaurant located on the path leading toward the haven to which St John brought the Virgin Mary after the day of the Crucifixion.

The visionary dream of a German nun, Catherine Emmerich, eventually inspired the search for the **House of the Virgin Mary** (Meryem Ana in Turkish), where Mary lived from AD 37 to 48. In 1891, a search party led by the Father Superior of the Lazarists discovered the House of the Blessed Virgin in a pine forest just before an *ayazma*, a sacred spring. Since its restoration in 1951, this house, which is used as a chapel, has been visited by two popes and millions of pilgrims, both Christian and Moslem.

The building is officially recognized by the Vatican and the Eastern Orthodox churches as the last residence of the Virgin Mary and is considered a holy shrine. Virgin Mary is also considered a Moslem saint. Pope John Paul, the Polish pontiff, held mass in the chapel when he visited Turkey in 1979 for theological unification talks between the Vatican and Orthodox Church Patriarchate in Istanbul.

Each year several hundred thousand pilgrims enter the chapel where Mary's icon stands. After drinking the healing spring water, devout pilgrims attach their prayers to a nearby wall. Chronicles have recorded many miracles, such as the curing of invalids, who entered the chapel on crutches and left discarding them.

In accordance with local tradition, as adopted by Pope Benedict XIV, each August 15 the mass commemorating the Assumption of Mary is celebrated in the surprisingly modest stone chapel. The 30-minute visit that most Selçuk taxi drivers allow is certainly not sufficient to appreciate fully the serenity this shrine offers.

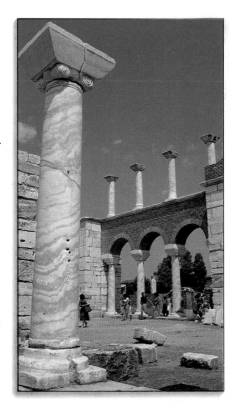

The Basilica of St John.

THE MAEANDER RIVER VALLEY

The **Büyük Menderes Valley**, the site of many cities of antiquity including Miletus, Aphrodisias and Hicrapolis, is one of the most fertile regions in the world. In summers, this broad, long valley, nurtured by the winding 365-mile (584-km) **Büyük Menderes** (the Maeander River of ancient times), is relatively dry. In winter, torrents of streams irrigate the valley, allowing peasant farmers to grow cotton, olives, citrus fruits and vegetables, graze cattle and sheep and raise poultry. In recent years, Söke, Aydın, Nazilli and Denizli, the main cities in the valley, have become cotton boom towns with high standards of living. Many farmers in this region own tractors, trucks and automobiles, sure signs of prosperity in this agricultural breadbasket. From the many twists and turns in the Büyük Menderes River, we get the verb "to meander" in the English language. According to ancient belief, the river's winding channel inscribed the entire Greek alphabet.

The quickest way to reach the Büyük Menderes Valley from Kuşadası is to take one of two minor asphalt roads through the verdant, undulating hills to **Çamlık**, a village and railroad switch-yard station, on the E24/550 Izmir-Denizli highway. By turning right on the Izmir-Denizli highway motorists can drive to the valley below.

Carpets and cuisine: Near Çamlık is the commercial carpet weaving centre of **Sultanköy**, operated by the Net group, Turkey's biggest producer and exporter of handmade Turkish carpets. At **Ortaklar**, the first town in the Büyük Menderes River Valley, turn left, take the E24/320 highway at the junction toward Aydın and Denizli. The junction is noted for its many one-man *kebab* stands, where you can enjoy a delicious *çöp şiş* lunch or dinner. *Çöp şiş* are tiny morsels of lamb meat roasted on coal barbecues along with tomatoes, peppers and onions.

Aydın, a sprawling provincial capital of over 100,000 people, is 14 miles (22 km) from Ortaklar. Founded originally by an odd group of barbarian tribes from Thrace and the Peloponnesus, Aydın was known in ancient times as Tralles. It came under Carian and Persian domination in the sixth century BC. Tralles passed into the hands of Alexander the Great in 334 BC, and was later acquired by the Kingdom of Pergamum. In 129 BC it became a part of the Roman Empire. The Seljuk Turks ruled the city from AD 1186 to 1300. The Aydınoğulları princes controlled the city for the next 126 years before it was conquered by the Ottoman Turks in 1426. The city was held by the Greek army from 1919-1922, until its liberation by Turkish nationalist forces.

Ottoman monuments: Traces of ancient Tralles, which can be seen about a mile north of the present town, include scant remains of a gymnasium, agora and theatre. The city itself has many Ottoman monuments, the oldest of which is the **Alihan Kümbeti**, a 14th-century tomb with the cemeteries of four

Aydınoğlu notables, including Prince Ali Han. This structure is located in the **Üveys Paşa Mahallesi**.

Several 16th-, 17th- and 18th-century mosques are scattered about the town, including the **Ağaçarası Mosque**, the **Süleyman Bey Mosque**, the **Üveys Paşa Mosque**, the **Eski-Yeni Mosque** and the **Ramazan Paşa Mosque**. The 18th-century **Nuh Paşa Medresesi**, a u-shaped Islamic school of theology, can be seen in the city's **Köprülü Mahallesi**. Aydın's main street, **Adnan Menderes Bulvarı**, is named after the Turkish prime minister who was toppled in the 1960 military coup and executed in 1961.

Two towns on the E24/320 highway are **Nazilli** and **Kuyucak**. A country road forks to the right after Kuyucak toward **Karacasu** and Aphrodisias, passing though gentle rolling hills where shepherds graze their sheep.

The ruins of the fabulous Roman city of **Aphrodisias** are located near the village of Geyre, off the right hand side of the road. **Geyre** was once located amidst the ruins, and the villagers used many of the city's stones and statues to construct their houses. The village was relocated in the 1960s as a result of expanded excavations carried out by New York University archaeologists, led by the late Professor Kenan Erim and financed by the National Geographic Society.

School of sculpture: Tourism authorities say that Aphrodisias is likely to surpass Ephesus in size and splendour eventually as a result of Professor Erim's discoveries and excavations. The settlement dates to well before 3000 BC. A Carian city, Aphrodisias made its mark in history during the Roman Period, when it was sponsored by the emperors as a centre of art, sculpture and religion.

The city's School of Sculpture, where many of the Roman Empire's greatest sculptors conducted classes, turned out fine masterpieces from marble quarried in the foothills of the **Babadağ**, a snow-capped 7,000-foot (2,102-metre) mountain northeast of Aphrodisias.

Left, a statue of a god in Aphrodisias. **Right**, a frieze from Roman times.

The **Aphrodisias Museum** houses many of the statues found during excavations by Professor Erim and his team. The most astonishing statue in the museum is of Aphrodite, the patron goddess of the city. Aphrodite's statue bears a striking resemblance to the giant statues of Artemis found in Ephesus, showing a close connection between the two deities.

Aphrodisias was the main centre of the cult of the Carian Aphrodite, from which the town got its name. Pilgrims from all over the Greco-Roman world visited the **Temple of Aphrodite**, parts of which still stand. The temple was transformed into a church after the Roman Empire adopted Christianity as a state religion.

The stadium: The magnificent **Stadium**, built during the early period of the Roman Empire, is perhaps the best preserved in the ancient world. The long, narrow stadium is rounded at both ends and has a seating capacity for nearly 25,000 people. A royal box is on the northern side of the stadium for visiting dignitaries from Rome. The stadium was the site of many athletic events including foot races. A semi circular ring on the eastern part was where gladiators fought.

Other buildings of note in Aphrodisias are a small odeon, where theatrical performances and public debates were held, a well preserved theatre, an agora and a street with columns on each side, and the Baths of Hadrian. Two mounds at the acropolis hill were merely levels of earlier inhabitation. Pottery shards found here showed that Aphrodisias was one of the earliest settlements in the Maeander River Valley, and in western Anatolia.

During the early Christian era, the name of the city was changed to Stavrapolis, or City of the Cross, to wipe out its affiliation with the pagan goddess Aphrodite. A series of earthquakes and invading armies sacked and destroyed the prosperous city. All that remained of Aphrodisias after the seventh-century Arab conquests of Anatolia was a village that took the

Donkeyback riding through Aphrodisias.

name Caria from the ancient Roman province where it was located. In the Turkish period, the name Caria was corrupted and changed to Geyre.

Falcon crest: The country road climbs a mountain and then descends to Denizli, a provincial capital in the Büyük Menderes Valley. Just before Denizli is the village of **Tekkeköy**, famous for its roadside **Şahin Tepesi** (Falcon Crest) **Restaurant** on the top of a cliff overlooking a gorge. The restaurant serves a delicious lamb stew dish called *saç kavurma*.

With a population of 170,000, **Denizli** is an important carpet weaving, mining and agricultural centre. Specially bred Denizli roosters are world famous. Denizli was founded in the third century BC by Seleucid kings of Syria but it only developed during the Roman period. In 1094, the Seljuk Turks conquered the city, later incorporating it into the Germiyanoğlu Principality. The Ottoman Turks took over in 1428. Denizli ("sea" in Turkish) gets its name from an abundance of streams that wind through the countryside.

The ruins of **Laodiceia**, ancient Denizli, are located four miles (six km) from Denizli. Laodiceia was founded by Antiochus I, king of Syria, and named after his wife, Laodice. The ruins include a stadium, gymnasium, aqueducts and a theatre. The city was the centre for one of the Seven Churches mentioned in the Book of Revelation. About five miles (eight km) from Denizli is the 13th-century **Akhan Caravansary**, a kind of motel that was located on the main caravan route in the Middle Ages and that served travellers visiting the areas.

The Cotton Castle: **Pamukkale**, which means Cotton Castle in Turkish, is one of the most spectacular natural wonders of Turkey. Located 14 miles (22 km) north of Denizli, Pamukkale is a cliff of white limestone cascades, tiers of stalactites and natural swimming pools formed over thousands of years by the deposits of mineral and calcium-rich hot streams which run down the hill. The cliffs resemble a fluffy cotton cas-

Late afternoon in Pamukkale.

tle from a distance, especially if you are approaching the site from Denizli.

Pamukkale, situated next to the ruins of the ancient Roman city of **Hierapolis**, has always been known for its thermal springs. A profusion of tasteless hotels and pensions, which operate *hamams* (Turkish baths), have been built in recent years in the surroundings of Pamukkale. But the most popular spa continues to be the old **Pamukkale Motel** with its natural outdoor 35 degree Celsius spring pool where bathers swim throughout the year among toppled columns and marble blocks of the main street of Hierapolis.

The natural springs are believed to be therapeutic for persons suffering from coronary, respiratory and kidney ailments and rheumatism.

The Devil's Hole: The source of the springs is believed to be in a cave-like opening known as the **Plutoneum** or the **Cin Deliği** – the Devil's Hole – behind the hotel in the middle of the terrace of Hierapolis. In ancient times, this cave was believed to be the entrance to Hades, the underworld. Entrance to this cave is forbidden today because of its noxious gases and fumes. Death comes instantaneously to animals, such as birds, dogs and cats, lowered into this cave in baskets. The cave was linked by a passage to the nearby **Temple of Apollo**. In the past, soothsayers and priests were able to operate in this passage by holding their breaths.

The entire Büyük Menderes River Valley lies on the Anatolian fault, an earthquake-bound belt. Several of the towns in the region, including Denizli and Aydın, have been levelled in the past by land tremors. Many towns in the region have thermal and steam baths to benefit from the volcanic nature of the earth's crust below.

Hierapolis was established by the Pergamene kings in the third century BC, but Attalus II, the King of Pergamum, bequeathed the city to Rome in 133 BC. The city prospered during Roman times and three emperors visited Hierapolis during this period. But the city never fully recovered from three devastating earthquakes that rocked the site in the first century and the many wars fought nearby.

St Philip's Martyrium: Other interesting sites in Hierapolis include two theatres, Roman Baths and the Martyrium of St Philip, one of Christ's 12 disciples who lived and was martyred there. The necropolis of Hierapolis is one of the most extensive anywhere in Turkey, with hundreds of tombs in the hillside on both sides of the road west of the town. On most days peasant shepherds graze their sheep among tumbled masonry of the tombs.

About three miles (five km) west of Hierapolis is the **Karahayit Thermal Resort** with its *Kızıl Su*, a reddish mineral water geyser that gushes out of the side of the hill forming red and sulphurous deposits.

The return trip from Denizli to Ortaklar along route E24/320 is a four-hour drive. Halfway to Ortaklar is the unusual geothermal springs at **Çubukdağı** (also known as **Buharkent**, the Steam City). Hot steam gushes out of crevasses on both sides of the highway at Buharkent for several hundred yards, reducing visibility. Neither steam bath spas nor stations producing geothermal energy have been built at Buharkent.

To see the other sites of antiquity in the Maeander River Valley, motorists must turn left at Ortaklar on route 525 toward Söke, Milas and Bodrum.

Magnesia on the Maeander: The ruins of Magnesia-ad-Maeandrum (Magnesia on the Maeander) lie two miles (three km) from Ortaklar to the right of the highway. Aeolian soldiers from the original Magnesia in Greece who fought in Agamemnon's army during the Trojan War are believed to have founded the city around 1260 BC. The descendants of the early founders claimed that Magnesia on the Maeander was the first city in Asia Minor to be colonized by the Greeks.

The city was always prosperous because of its closeness to the Maeander River and its nearness to the major trade routes. Because of its wealth, the city incurred the jealousy and wrath of its stronger neighbours. It was sacked twice in the seventh century BC, first by the Lydian King Gyges and then by the Cimmerians.

Magnesia became part of the Persian Empire during the sixth century BC, and Xerxes spent some time there preparing for his invasion of Greece. The city capitulated to Alexander the Great without a fight in 334 BC.

Finally it came under the domination of the Pergamene kings and Rome. It isn't known why the city was eventually abandoned during the Byzantine period, but it may have had something to do with the Arab invasions in the seventh century.

Themistocles: The most important historical figure associated with Magnesia was Themistocles, the Athenian statesman responsible for the big Greek naval victory over the Persians, led by Xerxes, at the Battle of Salamis in 480 BC. Themistocles spent the last years of his life in Magnesia, having fallen from favour in Athens as a result of a political scandal and branded a traitor. Rather than serve Persian interests against his native Greece, the 65-year-old Themistocles committed suicide in Magnesia by drinking the poisonous blood of a bull. All that remains of the city are walls of some buildings, including traces of the Temple of Artemis and a theatre and odeon.

Söke, a lively market town with a population of over 50,000, is off the road. Prosperity has come to the town as a result of a boom in cotton production. The only historical monument of any significance in Söke is the **Ilyas Ağa Camii**, an old Turkish mosque that was restored in 1821. South of Söke, a country road turns right after the town of **Yenidoğan** in the direction of Priene, one of the most outstanding sites of the classical period.

Priene, one of the best preserved Hellenistic cities in the world, is perched on the side of a mountain off the road. The first thing that strikes visitors is the neat grid pattern layout of the city. Everything has been done on a small scale, compared to its neighbours Ephesus in the north and Miletus in the south, which emphasized bigness in

Grazing among ruins.

their architecture. Lord Kinross, a distinguished British diplomat, biographer and travel writer, who visited the site in the early 1950s, had this to say about the city: "Hellenistic in style, unpretentious in scale, Priene has a simplicity which few cities of Greece can equal."

While Miletus, its chief rival, grew fat on commerce and increased its influence with military might, Priene remained modest and unpretentious, devoting most of its time to the worshipping of the gods, sponsoring of sports events and cultural activities. Its population never exceeded 5,000 people at any one time.

Athenian colonists founded the small city-state during the Greek invasions in the 12th century BC. Although a member of the 12-city Ionian League, Priene always felt a particular closeness to Athens, the mother city.

Seven sages: Priene's golden age was in the sixth century BC when the city produced one of the Seven Sages of Antiquity, Bias, from whom we get the English verb "to be biased." Bias was instrumental in codifying the laws of the city. Priene suffered severely during the Persian invasion of western Asia Minor. In 545 BC the army of Cyrus sacked the city, burning it down to the ground and enslaving most of its people. Priene joined the Ionian revolt against Persian rule in 499 BC by contributing 12 galleys. Alas the Persians soundly defeated the Ionian fleet off Lade, an small island near Miletus and Priene, in 495 BC, and sacked the city one more time.

During his military campaigns in western Asia Minor, Alexander the Great stayed in Priene for some time and financed construction of the grand Temple of Athena.

After Priene came under Roman domination, the city lost its importance and was finally abandoned in the Byzantine period.

Sacrificial victims: Among the buildings in Priene visitors should see are the small **Greek theatre** with five stone thrones in the orchestra for priests, and a special water clock to time speeches at public assembly meetings; the massive

The ruins of Priene.

Temple of Athena with many of its tumbled elephantine columns sprawled about; the **Council House** resembling a tiny theatre; the **Temple of Demeter**, which had a sacrificial pit, where the blood of the sacrificial victims, often humans, were poured down as offerings to the gods of the underworld; and the **Stadium**, where foot races, boxing, the pentathlon and the pancratium, a competition resembling a combination of today's American-style Big Time Wrestling and Thai Boxing, were regularly held.

For a city that was once a grand maritime power and which had a harbour that could hold 200 warships at one time, **Miletus** is a big disappointment to travellers visiting the site. The city was once located at the tip of a headland overlooking the Latmian Gulf. Today it is five miles (8 km) from the sea due to the silting of the Maeander River. The city isn't as impressive as either Aphrodisias or Priene.

A Mycenaean settlement existed there between 1400 and 1200 BC. Later

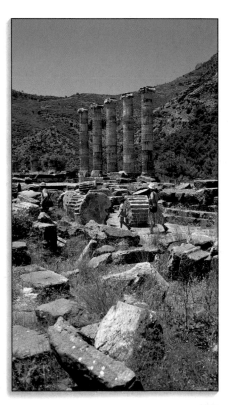

it was occupied by a mixture of Cretans and native Carians and was colonized by the Ionians. The historian Herodotus wrote that the Ionians, having brought no women with them, slaughtered all the male inhabitants and married their wives. The women of Miletus vowed never to sit at the tables of their husbands. It was ruled in succession by the Persians, Alexander the Great, the Romans, the Byzantines and the Turks.

By the eighth century BC, Miletus had set up as many as 90 colonies in the Mediterranean, the Dardanelles, the Sea of Marmara and the Black Sea, and traded goods with Egypt, Lebanon, Africa and Greece.

Solar eclipse: Miletus was also a centre for learning and intellectual enlightenment. It was the home of many learned men, philosophers and scientists, including Thales, Anaximenes and Anaximander. Thales, considered by many to be one of the Seven Sages of Antiquity, predicted the solar eclipse of 585 BC. He also managed to calculate the height of the Egyptian Pyramids by measuring their shadows at the time of day when a man's shadow is equal to his height.

Miletus' steady decline began with the Ionian revolt of 500 BC against Persian rule which ended in defeat. The continuous silting up of the Maeander announced the city's death knell, and it was eventually abandoned. The most significant sites in Miletus are the grand theatre and the Faustina Baths, the Byzantine Citadel, the Heroon (a monumental tomb), the Agora, the Byzantine Church, the Temple of Athena, and the Turkish Caravansary.

Labour strike: The world's first recorded labour strike took place in Miletus during the construction of the theatre about AD 100. The construction workers, dissatisfied with the terms and conditions of their contracts, stopped working. The strike was settled when the sides sought the arbitration of the Oracle of Didyma.

The **Faustina Baths** are indeed splendid, consisting of a dressing room, cold room (*Frigidarium*), warm room

(*Tepidarium*), hot room (*Calidarium*), steam room (*Sudatarium*), boiler room and exercise areas (*Palaestra*). A reclining statue of the River God Maeandros and a statue of a lion can be seen in the *Frigidarium*.

The most remarkable and popular building in Miletus is the 14th-century **Ilyas Bey Mosque Complex**, built by Ilyas Bey, a prince of the Turkish Menteşeoğulları Dynasty that ruled the area before the Ottoman Turks. It includes a single-domed mosque, an attractive courtyard with cemeteries, an *imaret* (a place where poor people were fed), a convent for dervish mystics, and a public bath.

Didyma: The **Temple of Apollo** at **Didim** (**Didyma**), 11 miles (18 km) south of Miletus, is one of the most outstanding buildings of the ancient Greek world, not only in size but in architectural style as well.

The oracle dates back to the seventh century BC, long before Ionian settlers arrived in the region. Control of the cult was in the hands of the Branchidae family, who claimed to originate from Delphi, site of the great oracle.

The temple was destroyed by the Persians in the sixth century BC and by Alexander the Great in the fourth century BC. The vast structure seen there today dates from about 300 BC, built by Seleucus, king of Syria.

Its decline coincided with the rise in popularity of Christianity. Christians finally took control of the pagan building and constructed a big church in its most sacred part.

In ancient times, emperors consulted the oracle for advice. Croesus, the king of Lydia, who once consulted the oracle, was told that a great empire would be destroyed if he were to launch an attack against Persia. In fact, it was Croesus' empire that was destroyed.

Across from the ruins of the temple is the **Kamacı Restaurant**, which serves delicious seafood, including sea bass. The area has many five-star hotels, holiday villages and pensions and a fine beach area known as **Altın Kum**, the golden sand.

The sprawling Temple of Didyma.

CARIA

The region known as **Caria** of the Greco-Roman world corresponds roughly to the boundaries of the present-day province of **Muğla**, in southwest Turkey. The Carians, the earliest-known inhabitants of this region, were a native stock Anatolian people famed for their skills as mariners. Ancient chronicles say Carian sailors served in the navies of the Egyptian pharaohs and of Persian ruler Xerxes. Homer mentions the Carians in his *Iliad* as being "barbarous of speech." (Coincidentally, linguists have noted, the Turkish dialect spoken in this part of the country is the harshest in western Turkey.)

The region is one of the most popular travel destinations in Turkey for foreigners and Turks alike. It is rich in archaeological sites and its shores are among the world's best for yachting, sailing, scuba diving and other water sports. The local inhabitants earn their livelihood from tourism, carpet weaving and farming. Cotton, olives and citrus fruits are grown in abundance.

To reach the Carian hills from Didyma, motorists should drive along the attractive Akbük Bay to highway 525 and turn right. Lake Bafa, on the edge of the Beşparmak Dağı (Mt Latmus of antiquity), is the beginning of Caria. **Beşparmak** means five fingers in Turkish and indeed the top of the rocky 4,557-foot (1,367-metre) mountain resembles the stubs of five fingers. **Lake Bafa** was once a part of the Aegean Sea. But the silting of the Maeander River has left it landlocked and a good 12.5 miles (20 km) from the sea.

The romantic ruins of **Heracleia under Latmus**, one of the least visited ancient sites of Aegean Turkey, cling to slopes of Beşparmak Dağı on the eastern side of Lake Bafa, running down to the village of Kapıkırı. The ruins can be reached by the road that forks to the left after Lake Bafa. A yellow sign points in the direction of the ancient city.

Endymion and Selene: Heracleia is associated with the legend of Endymion and Selene. It has a **Sanctuary of Endymion**, a horseshoe-shaped temple honouring the shepherd demigod. When the Moon Goddess Selene fell in love with the handsome Endymion, a jealous Zeus put him to sleep. Selene then went to sleep with Endymion and bore 50 children, according to the legend. The sanctuary is located near the lake at the lower part of the village, facing a large trailer camp.

Heracleia also has a partly-submerged necropolis of tombs by the lake, an ancient market, a Byzantine church, the Temple of Athena and several miles of well-preserved defensive walls with towers that curve part of the way up Beşparmak Dağı. Monasteries are located on the mountain. Boats can also be hired in the village to visit the Byzantine churches and monasteries on the islands in the middle of Lake Bafa.

The next fascinating site on highway 525 are the ruins of **Euromos**, a Carian settlement just off the road, and its spectacular **Temple of Zeus** with its 16 columns still proudly standing.

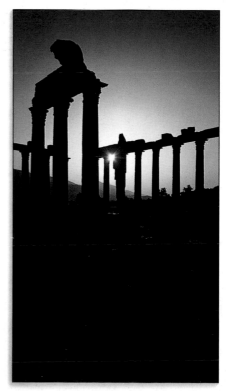

Left, resting at the Gümüşkesen Mausoleum. Right, sunset at Euromos.

Labraynda: Before you enter Milâs, a dirt village road forks left into the rolling hills to the Carian sanctuary of **Labraynda**, a splendid site. The six-mile (10-km) drive up to the holy shrine is bumpy. The village, built on terraces, dates from the fourth century BC. The hamlet is 2,300 feet (700 metres) above sea level.

The most important site at Labraynda is the **Temple of Zeus Labrayndus**, the god of the double axe, the patron deity of Caria. Located on an upper terrace, the temple is in ruins with columns and pillars strewn about the site. Behind the temple is the **First An-dron**, a well-preserved building with a seven-foot (two-metre)-thick wall. The **Androns** – there are several at the site – were men's clubs, where the priests of the shrine gathered for social purposes. Next to it is a **residence** of the clergy.

Fortune-telling fish: The site also has a large tomb, with three sarcophagi inside, on the slope overlooking the temple. Mausolus and other Carian kings maintained at Labraynda a **Summer Palace**, which has not yet been excavated, but is believed to lie near the temple. The holy community also had a **Sacred Pool of Oracle Fish**, which were adorned with earrings and necklaces. According to early chronicles, the gold fish in the pool were capable of making yes and no prophecies by accepting or rejecting food offered after a question. The pool was located in what is now the **Ablution Hall**, along a wall at the lower terrace. Traces of the **Sacred Way**, an eight-mile (13-km) road linking Labraynda to ancient Milâs can still be seen. A man from a nearby village operates a roadside teahouse at Labraynda and serves refreshments, sandwiches and *menemen*, a delicious rural-style scrambled eggs with peppers and tomatoes.

Milâs, one of Turkey's leading producers of handmade wool carpets, is built on the side of a hill, right of the highway. The market town, known to the ancients as Mylasa, was once the capital of the Carian state, but was ruled successively by the Persians, Alexan-

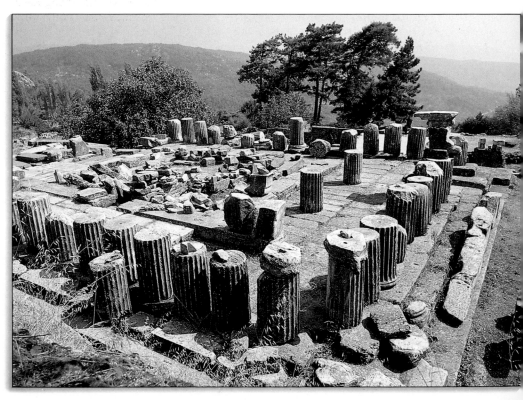

The Temple of Zeus Labrayndus.

der the Great, the Romans, the Byzantines and now the Turks.

The most impressive monument in Milâs is the Roman mausoleum known as **Gümüşkesen**, or the "silver purse," visible from every point in town. Located in a public park overlooking Milâs, the monument is a smaller replica of the Mausoleum of Halicarnassus, with a pyramid roof supported by columns. It was built in the first century, and gets its Turkish name from alleged treasures hidden inside its crypt, which was long ago broken into but is now locked. A strange hole exists on the floor of the funerary monument surmounting the sepulchral chamber below. This hole, according to Richard Chandler, an 18th-century traveller, was used by family members of the deceased to pour libations of milk, honey and wine into the chamber to satisfy the spirit of their beloved one.

The ruins of a Roman temple can be seen near the **Belediye Binası**, the town hall, but all that remains standing is a fluted column standing on an elevated marble floor.

The double axe: One other fascinating site in Milâs is the **Baltalı Kapı**, or the "Gate of the Axe," located on the main street, just off the state hospital (**Devlet Hastanesi**). Baltalı Kapı derives its name from the frieze of a double axe on its façade, symbolizing the divine Kingdom of Caria. The arched gate was in ancient times the beginning of the "Sacred Way" connecting Milâs with the holy shrine Labraynda.

After leaving Milâs the road reaches a junction. Highway 525 continues to head east toward the coal mining town of Yatağan and the provincial capital of Muğla. The other road heads towards the resort of Bodrum. A dirt road near the junction leads to **Beçin Kale**, an old Turkish fortification that has a stunning view of Mils and the valley. Beçin Kale is a 14th-century stronghold of the Menteşeoğlu Beylik, a Turkish dynasty that ruled this area before the Ottoman conquest in 1390. Beçin Kale is situated on a flat, rocky hilltop. The fortress, which is in a state of ruins, can be toured in 20 minutes. Just inside the gates of the citadel, on the right, is a flight of solid marble steps, believed to be part of an ancient temple.

Nearby is the interesting **Medrese of Gazi Ahmet Pasha**, an Islamic religious school named after a Menteşeoğlu statesman. The statesman, Ahmet Pasha, and his wife are buried next to each other in an open part of the *medrese*, and today they are considered to be saints by the local inhabitants. Behind the *medrese* are the ruins of a mosque. This is an excellent picnic spot. A one-man beverage stand near the *medrese* provides refreshments.

Probably the world's only carpet farm, the **Ildız Carpet Farm**, is located on the Bodrum-Milâs Highway, six miles (10 km) out of Milâs. At the farm, experts wash and sun tens of thousands of handmade wool carpets to test the quality of the carpets. The carpets are manufactured or bought by the Ildız Company, one of Turkey's leading carpet exporters and producers. Ildız specializes in the production of pastel-coloured Milâs carpets. Visitors to the carpet farm should ask the young attendants inside to unroll some of the Milâs carpets for them to see.

Near the carpet farm a road forks right to **Güllük**, a fishermen's town with a pretty port and numerous pensions and small hotels. An airport near Güllük which provides international connections opened in 1997, making it more accessible to tourism.

Boats can be chartered from Güllük for a one-hour trip to the ruins of **Iasus**, a Greco-Roman city. Iasus can also be reached by a rough dirt road that turns west on the Izmir-Milas highway near the ruins of Euromos.

Peloponnesians from Argos, having fought a long and bitter war with the local Carians, colonized Iasus and surroundings. But the city, which prospered from its fishing industry and trade, was ruled successively by the Persians, the Athenians, the Spartans, Alexander the Great, the Seleucids, the Rhodians, the Romans, the Byzantines, the Knights of St John and now the Turks. The town was often sacked by rival powers.

BODRUM

The most international of Turkey's summer towns, **Bodrum** is renowned for its foreign restaurants, party town atmosphere and bohemian lifestyle. This combination is appealing, especially to young foreigners and western-oriented Turks, who flock there in summer. Bodrum has a permanent population of only 21,000 (1990), yet it boasts sundry Indian, Italian, and Chinese restaurants. It is fast competing with the cosmopolitan dining scene of Istanbul, Turkey's largest city with 10 million inhabitants.

Sex city: In recent years, the town has attracted crowds of young British men and women, who come on cheap charter flights and package tours, looking for fun and romance. Visitors to Bodrum go swimming and sunning by day on the many nearby beaches. Come night, they gather at the town's many outdoor pubs, discotheques and bars to drink, dance and party till the wee hours of the morning. At these pubs love stories often begin. "Bodrum," local denizens are fond of saying, "is 30 percent sex, 25 percent love and 45 percent relaxation."

Located on the southeastern shore of the Bodrum Peninsula, the town is built on twin bays separated by the massive Castle of St. Peter. Tiny, white soapbox houses, characteristic of Bodrum, rise from the town and carpet the surrounding hills and mountains. The dark silhouette of Karaada, a virtually uninhabited Turkish island, can be seen at the mouth of the bay with the shadows of the Greek island of Cos visible on the distant horizon.

Sailing centre: Bodrum's harbour is protected by a long jetty, and scores of yachts and sailboats are moored along the quayside. Dozens of restaurants serving seafood and small outdoor coffeehouses line the harbour. Bodrum has a 125-berth marina. The town is the most important starting point for the Blue Voyage, a yachting cruise into the neighbouring Gökova Bay.

Downtown Bodrum, starting from the foot of the castle and winding along the narrow **Dr. Alim Bey Caddesi** and **Cumhuriyet Caddesi**, bustles with activity in summer. These two connected streets are lined with lively bars, restaurants, tavernas, small stores and giftshops selling carpets, leatherware, local jewellery, handmade sandals (for which the town is especially famous), and more. Young artists display their paintings on street corners, old men peddle colourful sponges, and vendors in traditional costumes sell *Kahramanmaraş dondurması* (ice cream).

The town has been a centre for boat building since the days of Mark Antony and Cleopatra. Sturdy, luxury yachts, known as gulets, are built all along the Bodrum Peninsula, but the biggest shipyards are located at **Içmeler**, a ten-minute drive from Bodrum.

Knights and conquests: Bodrum has a rich 3,000-year history, replete with military campaigns, naval victories, knights and conquests. In ancient times the city was known as **Halicarnassus**. In 546 BC, like most Anatolian cities, it came under Persian domination. Sixty years later, at the time of the Persian-Greek wars, the city was ruled by a Carian dynasty whose most famous member was Queen Artemesia. When Xerxes, the Persian King of Kings, was preparing his invasion of Greece, Artemesia joined his forces contributing several fighting ships. During a naval engagement in 480 BC in which the Persian fleet was routed, Artemesia displayed unusual bravery, causing Xerxes to exclaim: "My men have shown themselves women and my women men."

The golden age: Halicarnassus saw its golden age under King Mausolus, a Persian-appointed satrap belonging to the Carian dynasty. Mausolus moved his capital (from Mylasa) to Halicarnassus, turning it into a splendid city. He died in 353 BC and was succeeded by Artemesia the younger, his wife and sister. Artemesia, who ruled for only three years, built a majestic tomb in her husband's memory, from which we get the word "mausoleum."

Alexander the Great arrived in

Halicarnassus in 334 BC and conquered the city. After his death the city continued as a Greco-Roman city until AD 654 when it was completely destroyed by the Arab invasions of Anatolia, and wiped from the pages of history until the 15th century.

The Knights of St John revived the city in 1402, when they were given possession of Halicarnassus by Tamerlane, the oriental ruler whose armies swept through Anatolia. The Knights built the Castle of St Peter, after their patron saint, and named their city Petronium, from which the modern Turkish name Bodrum is derived. The Knights finally abandoned the city in 1522 when the Ottoman Sultan Süleyman the Magnificent conquered Rhodes, their stronghold.

Many Turkish writers and intellectuals have made Bodrum their home, the most famous in recent years being Cevat Şakir Kabaağaçlı (1890-1973), a British-educated Turkish writer nicknamed "Fisherman of Halicarnassus." Exiled to Bodrum in 1925 because of his unorthodox political views, Kabaağaçlı popularized the town through his essays, short stories and novels, attracting like-minded romantics, writers and artists.

Forsaken and isolated: Bodrum, in 1925, was a small, isolated fishermen's village with a population of less than 2,000, which had no road connections with the provincial capital Muğla. Thus it took Kabaağaçlı, accompanied by *gendarmes*, nearly four months to arrive in Bodrum from Ankara, the capital of the new Turkish Republic, trekking part of the way over mountain passes and trails that had not been used since the days of Alexander the Great.

Much has changed in Bodrum since the days of Kabaağaçlı. It was discovered by Istanbul's intellectual crowd in the early 1970s, who made it an "in place." Soon the country's nouveaux riches arrived, turning it into their summer hangout. Its fame spread and then came the international jet set. Celebrities like Barbra Streisand, Dustin Hoffman, Clint Eastwood and

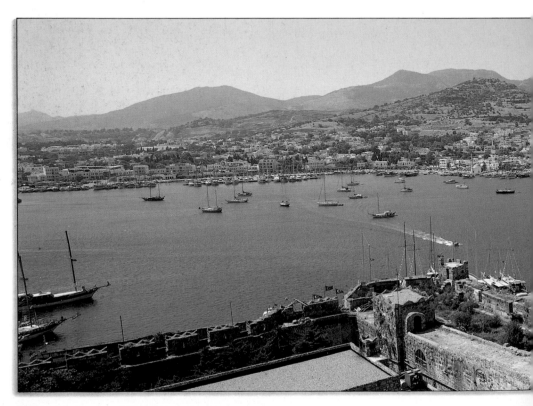

Jacqueline Onassis spent vacations in Bodrum. Ahmet Ertegün, a Turco-American who owns Atlantic Records, one of the world's leading music recording companies, bought a house there, and his guests included rock star Mick Jagger, former World Bank President Robert McNamara and ballet star Rudolph Nureyev. Today the city is a veritable Turkish Saint Tropez.

The Knights of St John: The most fascinating site to visit in Bodrum is the **Castle**, a well-preserved architectural complex. It was built between 1402-1503 by the Knights of St John, an international Catholic military monastic order, also known as the Knights Hospitaliers of St John of Jerusalem, the Knights of Rhodes and later as the Knights of Malta. The castle was used by the Knights to carry out raids on the Aegean Coast and served as a refuge for Christians fleeing Turkish captivity. To build the castle, the Knights used green stones, statuary, masonry and marble slabs from the nearby Mausoleum of Halicarnassus, which they found in ru-

ins, destroyed apparently by an earthquake sometime after the 12th century. The castle today houses the **Museum of Underwater Archaeology**.

More than 125 shipwrecks: The museum, located in several buildings in the courtyard, is one of the most impressive of its kind in the world. Opened in 1960, it contains the remains of the world's oldest known shipwrecks, discovered by scientists of the **Institute of Nautical Archaeology** (INA) along the Turquoise Coast. Founded in 1973 by George Bass, a renowned American underwater archaeologist, INA is an autonomous research organization affiliated with Texas A&M University. Using the Bodrum Castle as its headquarters, the INA has discovered and mapped more than 125 ancient shipwrecks off the Turkish Coast.

Right of the courtyard entrance is the **Bronze Age Hall.** It contains rich Mycenaean findings from a land excavation at **Musgebi** on the Bodrum Peninsula, dating from 2500 BC. It also has bronze bars and amphoras recovered by

Yachts line Bodrum's harbour, as seen from the Castle of St Peter.

George Bass and his team from a 12th-century BC shipwreck. Since 1982, Bass and his divers have been excavating the oldest known shipwreck, dating to the 14th century BC, discovered by a sponge diver off Uluburun, near the town of Kaş.

Across from the outdoor teahouse is "**Shipwreck Hall**", a large and excellently arranged room which exhibits the hull and cargo of an 11th-century shipwreck that was found at **Serçe Limanı**, a shallow cove near Marmaris.

A series of steps behind the Bronze Age Hall lead to the building displaying artifacts from the so-called "**Glass Wreck.**" This exhibition contains hundreds of colourful, almost phosphorescent glass jars, bottles and vases, retrieved in 1977 from the Serçe Limanı shipwreck.

The **Italian Tower**, which was the residence of the Italian Knights, houses the **Coin and Jewellery Hall**, a wide collection spanning several centuries. To the left of the Italian Tower is the **French Tower**, where there are two Byzantine shipwrecks, dating to the fourth and seventh centuries.

In the farthest corner of the castle is the **English Tower**. On its walls are the coats of arms of Edward the Fourth, one of the members of the House of Plantagenet, the dynasty which ruled England from 1154 to 1485, and of the captains of the Knights, Sir Thomas Shefield and John Kendall.

The **German Tower**, where the German Knights lived, is now open to the public. To its left is the structure known as the **Snake Tower**. It gets its name from a snake's frieze on its walls, taken from the mausoleum, which symbolized the serpent shape that Zeus, the supreme deity of the ancient Greeks, took before adopting human form.

The Mausoleum of Halicarnassus can be reached by walking along Neyzen Tevfik Caddesi from the castle along the harbour. Turn right at Hamam Sokak after passing the mosque and left at Turgutreis Caddesi to the Mausoleum of Halicarnassus on the left hand side of the street hidden by a wall. What re-

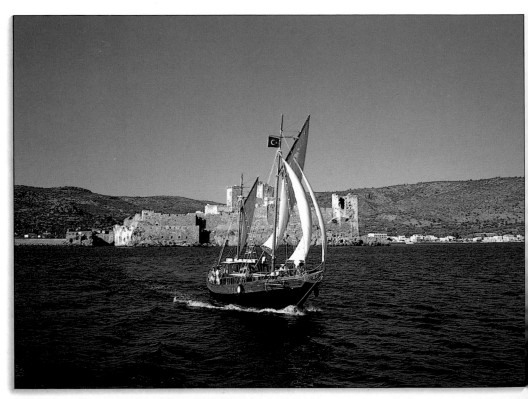

Sailing off Bodrum Castle.

mains today of the mausoleum – a foundation, a jumble of masonry and tumbled columns – belies its original greatness as one of the Seven Wonders of the Ancient World. The structure, built in the fourth century BC, consisted of a high base, a peristasis of 36 columns, a pyramid of 24 steps, crowned by a quadriga, and a four-horsed chariot, according to ancient accounts. A small model of the mausoleum can be seen inside the enclosed area. The reliefs and colossal statues of Mausolus and Artemesia uncovered by British archaeologists in the 19th century are now displayed in the British Museum.

A short walk uphill along one of the narrow streets from the mausoleum brings you to the well-preserved Roman **Amphitheatre**, located on the other side of the Bodrum-Izmir Road, with a splendid view of the town and castle.

Gümbet, a village with a long sandy beach, about three miles (five km) from Bodrum, is world renowned as a windsurfing centre. In addition to windsurfing, water skiing, banana boat riding, canoeing, parasailing and sea biking are also possible.

The modest **Cemetery of Cevat Şakir Kabaağaçlı**, the author who made Bodrum famous through his writings, overlooks Bodrum from a hill between the town and Gümbet.

Chicken princess: Arguably the best restaurant in Bodrum is **Balık Restaurant**. Located on a side street off Dr. Alim Bey Caddesi, Balık Restaurant specializes in authentic Turkish food, including *tandır kebab*, lamb on a skewer cooked on a coal fire, *tavuk prenses* (chicken princess), a tasty chicken dumpling served with black peppers. It also serves delicious seafood such as octopus salad and *kalamar*, a fried squid.

A pub crawl, involving visits to several of the town's nightclubs, bars and discotheques on the same night, is the best way to enjoy Bodrum's nightlife, starting with the upmarket and immensely popular **Halikarnas Disco and Nightclub**, and working toward Bodrum Castle. Halikarnas

Left, selling potatoes on market day, and **right**, inside a private garden.

Nightclub, with a grand view of the floodlit Bodrum Castle, caters to glamorous young foreigners and fabulously rich Turks, who dance to loud music from midnight to 5 am. The outdoor seaside disco resembles a Greek acropolis with an odeon and an amphitheatre surrounded by columns. A jet of water bursts out of a fountain by the beach near the dance floor while psychedelic lighting is flashed from behind the stage.

The main Cumhuriyet Caddesi, which runs parallel to the shoreline in the south-eastern part of town offers the greatest number of trendy bars in Bodrum. For something more typically Turkish though, one should visit the so-called **Street of Taverns**, a narrow lane off Dr Alim Bey Caddesi near the castle square. This convivial alley contains a dozen outdoor restaurants/bars which all offer lots of down-to-earth fun, music, fresh fish and tasty mezes.

The B-52: The crowded **Mola Bar** on Neyzen Teufik Caddesi and the **Hadigari Cafe Bar** on Dr. Alim Caddesi should top off the night. The Hadigari, reputed to be the best bar in Turkey, is famous for the *B-52*, a powerful cocktail concoction that is supposed to be downed in one swig.

Daily boat trips are available from Bodrum to Cos and Datça. Boats working under the principle of a shared taxi also operate daily to Karaada and nearby beaches and coves for a small fee. Leaving the harbour at 11 am, these motor driven-boats, usually Bodrum-built *caiques,* are capable of taking on 30 people at one time.

Karaada, the dark island that guards the town's bay from a distance like a sentinel, is famous for its mud baths. "These baths," the Fisherman of Halicarnassus once wrote, "are capable of nearly resurrecting the dead." After allowing passengers a short mud bath and dip in the clear waters, the boat leaves for Ortakent. Left is the Greek island Cos. Bodrum is to the right.

The boat enters **Ada Boğazı**, a shallow body of water separating a minuscule island, Iç Ada, and Bodrum Penin-

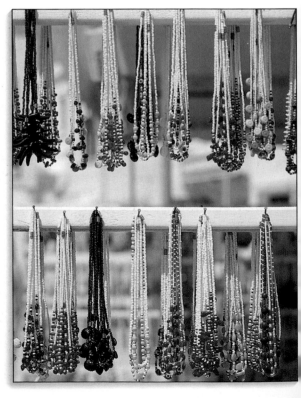

sula. The boat only stops there on the return trip to allow for swimming and snorkelling. Ada Boğazı is often referred to as the "**Aquarium**," because its sandy bottom is rich in marine life. It then passes Çelebi Island and comes to **Ortakent Beach**. Dozens of restaurants and pensions are clustered on this half-moon beach.

On the return voyage to Bodrum, the captain follows the coastline, first passing two promontories on which stands the Aktur Holiday Villas, a luxurious complex. The next wide bay is **Bitez**, one of Bodrum's most popular seaside resorts, with windsurfing, swimming, sunbathing and banana boat riding.

The Hermaphrodite: The last cove before Bodrum is **Bardakçı** (glass maker in Turkish), which has a fine beach. Bardakçı is associated with the legend of the Hermaphrodite, the son of the Olympic deities Hermes and Aphrodite, who fell in love with the nymph Salmacis. It was in Bardakçı that Hermaphrodite and Salmacis were united in a single body, having both male and female sexual characteristics. The cove lives up to its reputation for sexual diversity even today. It was the favourite beach of Zeki Müren, a popular Turkish singer who made his home in Bodrum. In the summer, you could see the Liberace-like Müren wearing high heeled sandals at his favourite coffeehouse at Bardakçı, surrounded by a flock of his gay admirers. Müren died of a heart attack in 1996.

A number of uncrowded and less noisy towns and villages are located in the vicinity of Bodrum.

Gümüşlük, at the western tip of the Bodrum Peninsula, is a gem of a village with fine fish restaurants and pensions gracing its shore. The ruins of the ancient city of **Myndus** are close by.

The town of **Turgutreis** has a number of fine hotels and pensions. It's name is derived from a 16th-century Turkish naval admiral killed during the siege of Malta, and **Yalıkavak**, a pleasant village, is renowned for its sponge fishers. **Torba**, a quiet little settlement north of Bodrum, has two holiday villages.

Strolling in Bodrum in the afternoon.

SPONGE DIVING

When May comes to coastal villages on the Bodrum Peninsula, most of the men set sail in small wooden-framed boats in search of sponges that will eventually find their way into bathrooms of homes in western Europe, Japan, Canada and the United States. For five months every year, the fishermen comb the entire Turkish Aegean and Mediterranean coast for sponges.

In the past decades, Turkey, with its relatively unpolluted waters, has been the world's biggest producer of commercial bath sponges. Other producers include Cuba, Mexico, countries in the Antilles, the United States and Greece. Turkey's annual sponge exports have totalled an average 15 tons.

Until the present tourism boom and a fungus epidemic in 1986 killed many sponges off the Turkish Coast, sponge fishing was the main livelihood of most fishermen and their families around Bodrum. Many former sponge fishermen now prefer chartering their boats to tourists to sending young divers deep down into the sea in search of sponges. Nevertheless, many young Bodrum lads still follow their fathers' footsteps and begin sponge diving at the tender age of 14.

Way of life: Sponge fishing has been a way of life for people of the peninsula for nearly 3,000 years. The ancient Greeks used sponges for bathing, or scrubbing tables and floors, for padding armour. The Romans fashioned them as paint brushes, tied them to wooden poles and used them as mops and even substituted them for drinking cups.

Dubbed the "gold of the sea depths" because of their high value, sponges are porous, multi-cellular marine animals that grow geometrically. Sponges are generally found attached to rocks at depths of between 33 feet (10 metres) to 234 feet (70 metres). Others occur at great depths. More than 5,000 varieties of sponges, mostly marine, are known in the world. A few varieties live in fresh water environments.

Known in Turkey as *sünger*, sponges vary in shapes and sizes and may reach a diameter of three feet (one metre).

"The best sponges for commercial use are those with large holes that return to their original shape when pressed," says Selim Dinçer, a Bodrum marine biologist who has studied sponges.

Lifeline: A sponge fishing team usually consists of five divers, a captain and a cook aboard a 33-foot (10-metre) *tirandil*, a wooden-framed boat that is built in the Bodrum area. Each diver takes a turn under water. The average dive is two to three hours. Equipment consists of a wet suit, mask and regulator. Air is pumped by a regulator to the diver along a lifeline, described as a *nargile*, a hubble bubble or a *hookah*. This allows the fishermen to dive to depths of 500 feet (150 metres). But the further down the sponge divers go, the greater the dangers of getting the dreaded divers' disease, the "bends" – an ailment that can permanently impair, cripple and even kill healthy people. A diver suffering from the "bends" must be treated in a decompression chamber within 24 hours.

Often sponge divers find ancient shipwrecks and amphoras. In 1988, sponge divers discovered in the Gulf of Gökova the remains of two British World War II fighter planes with the skeletons of the crew inside. The two planes had been shot down in 1942 by the Germans.

"A living sponge looks more like a slimy piece of raw liver than like the familiar sponge of the bathroom," Ralph Buchsbaum, a prominent American biologist, wrote in his two volume book, *Animals without Backbones*.

When they are taken out of the sea, sponges are covered by a membrane and a gastric bag full of visceral fluids. They are left in the boat for some time to die, put in plastic bags and lowered into the sea again. After a while, the sponges are brought back up and trampled on to remove the membranes and other fluids. The remaining skeletons are washed, rinsed, dried and chemically treated to give the sponges a pleasant white or yellow colouring.

Right, drying sponges in the sun.

BLUE VOYAGE

The area between Bodrum and Fethiye which accounts for over 90 percent of the yachting activity of the Blue Voyage can be divided into three main sailing grounds, the Gulf of Gökova, the Gulf of Hisarönü and Sömbeki, and the Gulf of Fethiye. From Bodrum to Marmaris encompasses the ancient Carian Coast. From Marmaris to Fethiye lies the Lycian Coast, which extends as far as Antalya.

Planning a cruise: Unless you are prepared to spare at least three weeks, don't try to squeeze a Blue Voyage into the three gulfs in one cruise, for you will miss a great deal while making quick leaps from one stop to the next. A wise plan would be to divide the area into three separate travel zones and allocate a week to 10 days for each but not less than five days. A fortnight is needed to make the best of two zones. If pressed for time, it is better to spend it properly

in one gulf and return for the others.

The essential spirit of the Blue Voyage is a leisurely communion with nature in the very seas where Western civilization bloomed. The Blue Voyage is not a glimpse-and-go package trip of lookalike bays. To the sophisticated traveller it is a bridge that leads to the souls and minds of the Pelasgians – the tribes of the sea – as Homer described them, who, though long gone, still haunt these shores. Unlike yachting holidays in other parts of the world, a Blue Voyage in the Aegean is a pilgrimage through 3,500 years of Western history, a homage to the past, and an understanding of ancient civilizations.

Fisherman of Halicarnassus: The **Gulf of Gökova** (also known as the Ceramic Gulf, Kerme Körfezi and Giova), is where it all began. Between the two World Wars, Cevat Şakir Kabaağaçlı, linguist, historian and a student of the classics, was sent on political exile to Bodrum. He fell in love with the tiny fishermen's village, adopted the title "Fisherman of Halicarnassus" as well

Map of the Blue Voyage Regions.

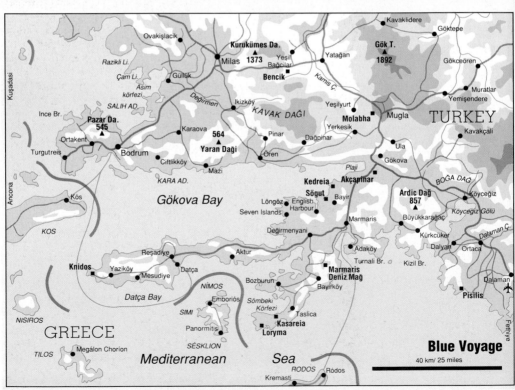

as the local fishermen's way of life. He wrote continuously of his experiences, especially of sailing in the Gulf of Gökova. After about 30 years, Turkish intellectuals finally understood what this man was telling them and the Blue Voyage became "in" among the better educated. The voyage has evolved from a trip in a small sponge diver *caique* to a journey in a luxurious Bodrum-built gulet, a 48 to 67 feet long (14 metre to 20 metre) wooden-framed yacht. Today, Turkey's intellectuals can hardly afford the Blue Voyage, and their exclusion has had an adverse effect on the journey: over commercialization.

The Gulf of Gökova extends about 35 miles (56 km) from east to west. The main places to visit, however, cover a 20-mile (32-km) strip of territory on the northeastern corner of the Datça Peninsula. The northern shores of the Gulf of Gökova offer quite a few pleasant, picturesque anchorages dominated by the 3,000-foot (900-metre) Kıran Dağı, a mountain which drops down to sea level in a sheer precipice.

Cruising off the Turkish Coast.

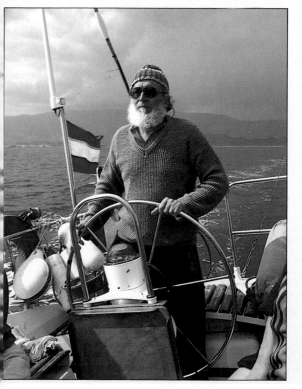

A voyage to the Gulf of Gökova logically starts from Bodrum. Not only can provisions be obtained there and the necessary boats chartered, but maintenance facilities and communications networks also abound. The prevailing winds also make it easier to sail southward to Marmaris or eastward into the Gulf of Gökova from Bodrum.

Once the loading of provisions, fuelling, watering, selection of cabins, settlement of bureaucratic procedures for leaving the port are finished, the yacht is ready to sail forth.

Mud baths: The Blue Voyage begins at Karaada, the island famous for its mud baths. Karaada is three miles (five km) from Bodrum. The mud baths, located in a grotto, are rejuvenating. Bathers emerge from the grotto resembling Indians on the war path, red mud covering their bodies.

Just across the northern tip of Karaada is the small **Pabuç Burnu** (Cape Shoe), a good safe haven for late starters from Bodrum to spend the night. Another anchorage is **Kargacık Bükü**, where an extensive and crowded holiday complex mars its beauty. Another inlet south of it, **Alman Bükü** (German Cove), is quieter, though gusts of *meltem,* a brisk summer wind, may be disturbing at times. In all of these places, it is best to anchor out and tie a mooring line ashore from the stern, leaving lots of cable.

Orak Adası (Sickle Island), 10 miles (16 km) east of Bodrum, is famous for its clear waters and abundant marine life. A derelict house stands in the middle of the bay. Strangely, the island is also notorious for its gigantic rats.

Three miles (five km) east of Orak Adası is Alakıfla Bay, also called **Kise Bükü**, a degenerated version of the word "church" (*kilise*) probably because of the ruins of a monastery in the northwest corner. Monasteries in this part of Turkey were mostly built on ruined temples or necropolises of previous civilizations.

The pleasant hamlet of **Çökertme** decorates a picturesque bay near the beginning of the mountain range that culminates in Kıran Dağı. Çökertme, or

Fesleğen (Basil), is a stopover either before or after the crossing of the gulf. In the hamlet are several restaurants, whose motorboats accost visiting yachts soon after anchoring and ask whether the yachtsmen wish to make reservations. The food served at these restaurants is good and reasonably priced. Belly dancing, accompanied by lively music, is the night's entertainment. Handwoven carpets can also be obtained in the village.

Threatened environment: Between Çökertme and Akbük, there is little else to stop for. The ugly coal-fired **Gökova Thermal Energy Plant** with a gigantic smokestack, built in the mid-1980s despite strong protests from the international environmentalists' movement, stands at what was once the village of Türkevleri, spoiling an otherwise scenic coastline. Once operational, environmentalists say, this plant will belch low grade coal fumes into the air and will pollute the entire region. It is incomprehensible why the Turkish government, which declared the Gulfs of Gökova and Fethiye environmental preservation zones, is preparing to destroy what it tries to protect for the virtues of obtaining energy. Concerned citizens hope that the decision to operate the power station will be revoked. Nevertheless, the smokestack will probably remain and, just as the ruined buildings of Hiroshima, will show the coming generations that contemporary civilization has its evil aspects too. One plan, which was proposed by the late President Turgut Özal, is to turn the plant into a five-star hotel, possibly as a face-saving measure. In 1997 the plant was still unoperational.

Ancient Ceramus, now named **Ören** (which means "ruins") is a bad anchorage, but a cheaper centre than Karacasöğüt. Various Carian, Roman and Byzantine ruins can be seen at Ceramus.

One of the magnificent, if not the most beautiful, bays in the gulf is **Akbük**. Once past Ören, yachts sail in the shadow of the majestic Kıran Dağı that tints the sea with a barely discern-

Boats tie up for the evening.

ible deep purple in daytime and gives off lapis lazuli glows as the sun sets. Young pine forests thrive on the vertical slopes of the foot hills and Kıran Dağı looms above. After a seven-mile (11-km) cruise along this breathtaking coast, yachts arrive in Akbük, a fiord-like inlet. Smaller boats may find cosy temporary anchorages in a number of coves in Akbük. These coves, unsuitable for bigger yachts, are the least spoiled in the entire Aegean. Pine forests surround Akbük and Kıran Dağı stands majestically behind. A beach stands at the end of the bay with a restaurant that is much better than expected in such wilderness. However safe it may look, Akbük is plagued by troublesome gusts and squalls, which deflect from the mountain and can disturb a yacht at anchor. As in all Aegean anchorages, it is advisable to get tern lines ashore after laying a long cable.

Cleopatra's love nest: Did Cleopatra really frolic with Antony at the islands of **Cedreae** (Cedar), south of Akbük? It is not difficult to fathom how such a cosy place could be chosen as the venue of an imperial love tryst. The main island has one of the finest and, sometimes, the most crowded beach of Turkey, known as **Cleopatra's Beach.** According to one legend, Mark Antony had the beach's fine silt sand transported from the Nile River to satisfy Cleopatra's whims.

It is best to visit Cleopatra's Beach early in the morning or in the late afternoon as it is a regular haunt for tourist hordes coming daily from Marmaris.

This group of three islands was perhaps also a holiday resort of antiquity. Little archaeological study has been conducted in the city of Cedreae, on the main island, which has remains of a castle, and an amphitheater. **Yılan Adası** (Snake Island) in the north has a necropolis of tombs.

Architectural award: Very few skippers venture east of Cedreae and Akbük to **Gökova Iskelesi**, at the extreme end of the gulf because of the presence of shoals and insufficient protection from gusts off Kıran Dağı. Those that do, however, should visit the **Residence of**

Nail Çakırhan, a Turkish poet, journalist and architect, in the nearby village of **Akyaka**. The traditional-style garden house he built there won him the 1983 Aga Khan Award for Architecture. For lunch or dinner, yachtsmen should try **Cennet Restaurant**, a pleasant eatery with old-style architecture by a natural spring.

The most logical place to anchor safely after Cedreae is **Söğüt** (often known as Karacasöğüt or Karaca Limanı), 25 miles (40 km) from Marmaris by road. One of the most magnificent bays in the Mediterranean, Söğüt has already attracted land developers and many private houses owned by rich Turks have been built near the pier. A noisy restaurant by the small pier keeps most yachtsmen up all night with music *alaturka* (Turkish-style) and belly dancing. Another calm wooded anchorage nearby is **Çanak (Bowl) Bay**.

English harbour: According to local lore, British naval vessels hid in **Ingiliz Limanı** (English Harbor), one of the bays interweaving the perfectly sheltered fiord-like **Değirmen Bükü**, during raids against the German-occupied Greek islands in World War II. One fact giving credence to the story is that entrance to the English Harbour is difficult to find. Another was the recent discovery in the bay by Turkish divers of the remains of two World War II British military aircraft with skeletons inside. Villagers say the two planes were shot down by German anti-aircraft guns in 1942 from the Greek islands.

Six good anchorages exist in Değirmen Bükü. One is occupied by a restaurant which sells water and provisions. A delicious dish served there is *oğlak çevirme*, a baby goat skewered on charcoal. But if you are unaccustomed to goat's meat, this meal may give you an upset stomach and diarrhoea.

Three miles (five km) west of Değirmen Bükü is the well-sheltered bay known as **Ballısu** (Honey Water, a name derived from the nearby watering hole), which is a perfect anchorage.

Secret bays: The entrance to **Löngöz Fiord** is half a mile (one km) west of Ballısu. Known also as Kargılı and

Gözleme, Löngöz is a narrow tree-lined inlet surrounded by steep rocks ending in a marsh. Throughout the Blue Voyage, you will often hear groans and grunts at night. These are wild bears that once lived by the shore and used to threw stones at yachtsmen in protest at the noise they were making. They seldom missed. The bears have now taken to the deep forests.

Tuzla, a sheltered bay west of Löngöz, is a good anchorage, protected by a cookie-shaped island from the strong summer winds.

A classic stop of the Blue Voyage is at **Yedi Adalar** (Seven Islands), a secluded bay south of Tuzla. The bay is ideal for swimming, snorkelling, windsurfing and spear fishing. Visitors can pull out sponges, catch crabs and watch star fish pulsate.

Three miles (five km) south of Yedi Adalar is **Bördübet**, which is said to have derived from "birdy bed", a name given by hiding English soldiers because of its abundance of bird life. It is one of the safest and most pleasant anchorages in the gulf. In the north is the area known as **Amazon**, which is now occupied by a camping site. Amazon gets its romantic name from the race of female warriors that once inhabited these shores.

The **Bay of Büyük Çatı** (Big Roof), not to be confused with Küçük Çatı (Small Roof), a cove to the east, is popular among yachtsmen because it is safe from all winds. This was once a fisherman's watering hole. The remains of a basilica and other ruins that might have once been a monastery are to be found in the hills.

Körmen on the northern shore of the Datça Peninsula is a drab windswept harbour. But it is the main point of contact between Bodrum and Datça. Ferries carrying cars and passengers stop here at least twice a day during the high season. In late September and early October, when shoals of albacorea, a distant relative of tuna, flock into the gulf, fishermen and yachtsmen in the Bodrum area cast their nets for a catch. Körmen then serves as a logical anchorage for the fishermen and yachts.

Another stop toward the end of the Datça Peninsula is **Mersincik**, a quiet, pretty cove.

Knidos, an ancient city situated at the tip of the Datça Peninsula, is usually the last stop before returning to Bodrum from a one-week to 10-day Blue Voyage in Gökova Bay. Knidos, strategically located along the major commercial sea route, was one of the most prosperous cities in the Dorian Hexapolis. It benefited from its safe harbor which sheltered ocean-going merchant ships. Knidos is famous among other things for the **Statue of Aphrodite**, the first ever of a woman in nude. Until the sculptor Praxiteles (390–330 BC) made Aphrodite's statue, the subject matter of all nudes were male gods. Even in ancient times, tourists flocked to Knidos to see the statue.

The fate of the Knidian Aphrodite is an enigma. Archaeologists can find no trace of her. One view is that the statue was destroyed in an earthquake. Otherwise it would not have escaped the plundering greed of 19th-century British archaeologists who, supported by the British Navy, removed tons of statuary from Knidos . The city was the home of Eudoxos, a fourth century B.C astronomer and mathematician who founded an observatory here which operated on the principles of modern geometry. Other wonders include two amphitheatres, the **Temple of Aphrodite** and many other buildings that are still being excavated by American archaeologists.

The ruins have a grand view of both the Gulf of Gökova in the north and the Gulf of Hisarönü in the south and the boundless open sea in the west. A series of Greek islands, including Cos, Yiali, Nisiros, Khalki and Rhodes can be seen from the headland.

Several modest restaurants serve fresh fish and lobster. As always, bargaining before ordering is recommended. The locals, whose fondness for wine drinking is notorious, throw a dancing party every night in one restaurant for the benefit of tourists and themselves. **Baba's Restaurant** in front of the harbor serves delicious fried *barbunya*, a kind of striped mullet.

Right, a Blue Voyage in the Aegean.

MARMARIS

Marmaris has come a long way since it was levelled by a devastating earthquake in 1957. The town, once a tiny fishermen's outpost isolated from the rest of Turkey, was completely reconstructed. Today Marmaris is one of Turkey's most popular resorts with hundreds of pensions and hotels and noisy night-clubs. Often described as the "Pearl of the Mediterranean," because of its magnificent natural surroundings, Marmaris has become an important yachting centre. Located in a long, wide bay, fringed by pine forests and fragrant oleander shrubs that cascade down to the shore from the surrounding mountains, the city lies at the confluence of the Aegean and the Mediterranean. The town is built around a 16th-century Ottoman citadel.

Marmaris can be reached in two hours by car from Dalaman International Airport, which is about 75 miles (120 km) from the town. A Turkish Airlines shuttle bus operates everyday back and forth from the airport to the town. Daily passenger buses carry tourists between Marmaris and most major Turkish cities, including Istanbul, Ankara, Izmir and Antalya. Regular boat services also operate between Marmaris and the Greek island of Rhodes, four hours to the west.

Marmaris has a population of 15,000 (1990) which swells to several hundred thousand (including its environs) during the long summer season when its hotels are completely booked and its streets crowded with Turks and foreigners alike.

Like Bodrum, Marmaris is very noisy in the evenings with a steady beat of amplified music coming from dozens of discotheques, bars and pubs. Visitors to Marmaris are advised to stay away from the noisy hub of the town for a good night's rest. They can always go into Marmaris by hiring a taxi or a motor launch or by taking the regular municipal trailer train, which is drawn by a big tractor and stops at every main hotel along the bay region. There are hundreds of reasonably-priced hotels and pensions around the town and in Içmeler Village. But the best hotel in Marmaris is the **Altın Yunus** (The Gold Dolphin), a five-star resort stretched out in a pine forest by the shore, 3 miles (5 km) from Marmaris. The resort is owned by the Koç group, Turkey's largest industrial company.

Turkish character: Marmaris has a distinct Turkish character, unlike Bodrum, nevertheless it is favoured particularly by German and British tourists and wealthy Turks. The five-mile (eight-km) long, two-mile (three-km) wide **Marmaris Bay** is protected by two islands at its mouth, making it ideal for windsurfing, waterskiing and jet skiing.

Palm trees, banks, restaurants and souvenir shops line Marmaris' **Kordon Caddesi** and **Barbaros Caddesi** at the northwestern end of the bay. The main shopping centre of Marmaris is on several side streets that run off **Cumhuriyet Meydanı** (Republic Square) and the **Atatürk Statue** in front of the

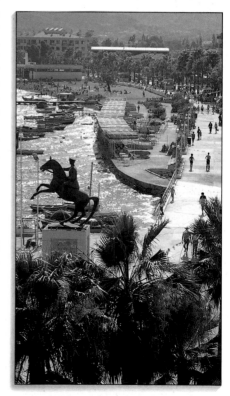

Left, Marmaris Bay, and right, Atatürk's Statue in Marmaris.

citadel. These shops sell a range of goods, from carpets and leatherware to provisions for yachts. Most shops in Marmaris stay open until 9 pm.

Silk carpets: The best place to buy carpets in Marmaris is at **Bazaar 54** near the marina. Bazaar 54 sells all brands of carpets. The Istanbul-based company, which specializes in the manufacture of fine, handmade silk carpets, can deliver carpets to customers anywhere in the world. Another carpet shop that may be worthwhile to check out is **Silk Road** on Barbaros Caddesi. Leatherware and sheepskin coats can be purchased at shops on **Barbaros Caddesi** and in **Bariş Çarşısı**.

The most famous product of Marmaris is honey, turned out by the thousands of bee keepers in the nearby villages, and sold in big jars by street vendors in the town. *Çam balı* produced by bees from the nectar of pine trees, is the tastiest honey of Turkey, far sweeter than *çiçek balı*, or flower honey.

A number of fine seafood restaurants surround the harbour, where fish and *meze* dishes are served. Many restaurants and bars line Barbaros Caddesi, including **Birtat** and **Yakamoz restaurants**, which are excellent places to socialize with western-oriented Turks and foreign women, and to eat tasty fish and meat dishes. There are several discotheques in Marmaris, the best of which are at **Martı Holiday Village** in Içmeler and at **Altın Yanus Hotel** in Pamucak.

Concrete jungle: Several charming luxury hotels and holiday villages are located in the more secluded spots of Marmaris Bay. But Marmaris has suffered from the construction of hundreds of tasteless apartment buildings and ugly concrete hotel apartment buildings that hug the shoreline, particularly around the town of Içmeler, on the other side of the bay, five miles (eight km) to the west, and Turunç, a village just outside the bay.

The **Old Quarter**, with its white houses on twisting lanes, is built on different levels on a rocky peninsula around the citadel, and is well worth a stroll. The citadel was originally constructed by Ionians who settled there in 3000 BC. It was repaired by Alexander the Great in the fourth century BC and expanded by the Ottoman Sultan Süleyman the Magnificent in AD 1522 during a military campaign to conquer Rhodes. The marina, located on the other side of the peninsula, has 800 berths, and is operated by the Net group, Turkey's fastest growing private tourism outfit.

Flourishing centre: The ancient city of **Physcus**, a deme of the Rhodian Peraea, was located at Marmaris and was a flourishing trading centre. But nothing remains to be seen of this old settlement save for some walls located at **Aşar Tepe**, on a hill overlooking the town. The hill is a recommended climb only for photographers who want to get some spectacular shots of Marmaris.

Daily excursions: Day excursions by boat can be arranged from the town to the many deserted coves around Marmaris Bay. Yachts can also be chartered in Marmaris (there are dozens of travel agencies and charter companies here) for longer Blue Voyages to the neighbouring gulfs of Bozburun, Sömbeki and Hisarönü.

The best way to get acquainted with Marmaris Bay and the outlying areas is to take a boating trip to Çiftlik (the Farm). Motorboat launches, capable of carrying up to 30 persons, leave Marmaris quay, along Kordon Caddesi, at 9 am. The round trip costs less than $10 per person.

It takes two hours to get to Çiftlik, a tiny community outside the bay which has the best and cleanest beach around Marmaris. The easiest way to reach Çiftlik and the other villages on the rugged Loryma Peninsula is by boat as road connections are still woefully inadequate, although construction is underway. The launches cruise along the northeastern part of the bay, hugging the shoreline, leaving behind Marmaris and its marina.

Paradise beach: To the left is **Günnücek Park** with its fragrant conifers. After rounding **Bedir Island**, the

Yachts in the marina.

boat comes to a stop at a little hidden cove aptly named **Cennet** or Paradise, which is surrounded by a lush forest of pine trees. Resembling a veritable Garden of Eden, Cennet is part of **Nimara Peninsula**, a bulging landmass that shelters the wide bay. The boat stays just long enough for passengers to have a quick dive into the water and swim to the sandy beach.

Once all the passengers have returned to the boat, the skipper will continue the voyage, rounding Nimara Peninsula and heading out to the open sea. Often the captain will take passengers behind the peninsula to the **Phosphorescent Grotto**, sometimes referred to as the Pirate's Cave. The boat can only partially enter the tiny cavern where the shiny bottom can be seen.

Leaving the grotto, the boat cuts across the sea to **Turunç Bükü**, a once lovely bay that has been ruined by the construction of many ugly hotels, noisy discos and bars, and sails to the next bay, **Kumlu Bükü**, which has fewer hotels and pensions. Sometimes the boat will stop at both bays to disembark or take on passengers. Next the boat glides by a long, rocky coastline that is completely uninhabited, finally stopping off at **Gerbekse**, a charming cove with interesting ruins of several Byzantine churches, allowing the passengers to take a quick dip in its clear waters.

Spear fishing: The boat turns back and goes to **Çiftlik**, a bay which is protected by a craggy island on which an Istanbul businessman has built a castle-like summer mansion. The waters of Çiftlik's mile-long beach are crystal clear and clean, a place where snorkelling, swimming with a mask and spear fishing along the rocky shoreline are possible. Except for a big hotel, several summer cottages and a few farmhouse restaurants, the bay is deserted. The restaurants serve *shish kebab*, fish, salad and melons. The most pleasant of these is the one operated by the always smiling Mehmet Yılmaz and his big family, who are known for their hospitality and generosity. Yılmaz also operates on the beach an unusual outdoor drinking bar made from the remains of a *caique*. The

passengers are allowed two more hours of swimming before the boat begins its return journey.

Leaving Çiftlik, the boat passes Kumlu Bükü and Turunç Bükü and enters Marmaris Bay, stopping off at Içmeler, which has several big hotels, including the five-star Munamar Hotel and the nearby Martı Holiday Village, owned by Halit Narin, a flamboyant textiles magnate.

Continuing along the coast, the boat next passes the luxurious Altın Yunus Hotel, the Turban Holiday Village and the renovated Hotel Lidya. To the right is the **Floating Hotel**, usually docked by Keçi Adası, the Goat's Island, at the mouth of the bay. Authorities shut down the 300-bed hotel, built on a large steel-framed barge capable of manoeuvring in the bay, in 1985 because it was discharging pollutants into the waters. The boat finally returns to Marmaris about six in the evening.

Environs: One of the most interesting side trips to take from Marmaris is to travel along Datça Peninsula to the ru-

The old lady whiles away time by knitting.

ins of **Knidos**, an ancient Carian city, situated 59 miles (95 km) west of Marmaris. Since some of the roads to Knidos are still in bad condition visitors should prefer a four-wheel drive for the three-hour trip. Especially at night, they should avoid driving on the treacherous highway, which weaves among dangerous cliffs. It's best to spend the night at Datça, an up-and-coming resort town facing the Gulf of Hisarönü. Motorists should bring spare tires before leaving as the bumpy roads to Knidos have flattened many tires.

Although difficult, the drive to Knidos is rewarding, just for its splendid scenery. After Içmeler, the asphalt road winds into the mountains for about 13 miles (20 km) only to drop gently to the fertile plains and the **Gulf of Hisarönü** below. The Datça Peninsula, a spiny, 45-mile (72-km) long, finger-like projection, separates the Hisarönü Bay in the south from the Gökova Bay in the north. The eastern part of the peninsula is verdant, covered by pine forest, valonia oak and olive trees.

Night-time in Datça.

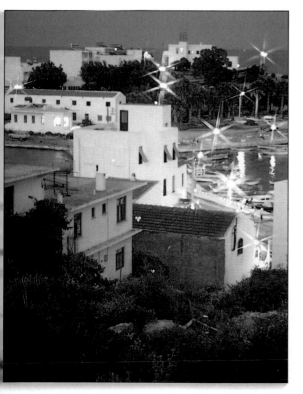

The easternmost part of the bay is silted and shallow and is known as **Kcyif**, meaning "enjoyment and bliss." Soon the narrowest point of the Datça Peninsula is reached. It is appropriately named **Balıkaşıran** (the place where fish leaps across), for here the isthmus is less than a mile wide. When the Persian army invaded Asia Minor in 546 BC and subdued the Greek cities on the coast, the Knidians began building a deep defensive canal there to separate the Datça (Dorian) Peninsula from the mainland. To get an outsider's view about the project they consulted an oracle, who replied: "Dig not nor fence your isthmus: Zeus himself had made your land an island, had he so wished." With oracle's verdict, the Knidians abandoned construction, and the Persian army swept through the peninsula and conquered Knidos.

In the 19th century, English naval Commander Graves, who was surveying the area for charting, reported to have found signs of the canal, but archaeologists George Bean and J.M. Cook, who visited the site in 1950s could find no traces of the waterway.

Solar energy: The hidden fiord facing the Gulf of Hisarönü is known as **Bencik**, a favoured anchorage among yachtsmen on the Blue Voyage. **Dişlice Island**, which means "Toothy" in Turkish, stands at the entrance of the inlet, resembling bared teeth from a distance. On the eastern end is a meteorological station and an unusual solar energy research institute, which blemish the solitude of the otherwise perfect fiord.

For the next 20 miles (32 km) the road is a series of hairpin turns into the mountains from which both bays can be viewed simultaneously from dizzying heights. A huge holiday village occupies the magnificent bays of Çiftlik and Kurucu Bükü.

Halfway up the peninsula, one reaches **Datça**, which has become a popular stopover for yachtsmen. The town has several colourful seafood restaurants, pubs and discotheques. Of the many pensions and hotels in Datça, the **Hotel Club Dorya**, on the tiny peninsula, is the best. Across the bay the

Greek island of Symi, or Sömbeki in Turkish, is visible only seven miles (11 km) away. Daily ferryboats carry passengers and cars between Bodrum to Körmen, Datça's harbour village on the Gulf of Gökova. It is possible to take daily excursions from Datça to Knidos by boat on a shared-taxi basis. The boats stop off at a number of completely deserted bays, including **Domuz Bükü** (the Bay of Pigs), where tourists can plunge into the clear waters for swimming. A British-operated holiday village is there.

Almonds and olives: A few miles out of Datça, the road becomes unpaved and very rough as it climbs the rugged vertebrae of a new mountain chain, past small villages, almond orchards and olive groves. It takes about one hour to reach the windswept town of Knidos from Datça.

The sleepy village of **Palamut**, eight miles (13 km) away, is the next settlement. Palamut, which means "bonito" in Turkish, gets its name from the abundance of fish caught in the bay. The village is the site for the ancient Knidian city of Triopium. It was in that ancient city that Dorian states held competitive sporting events in honour of Apollo, the Greek God of manly youth and beauty, that were precursors to the Olympic Games. An acropolis and some ruins are above the village, but it isn't really worth walking up the hill to see them. Palamut is famous for its fish restaurants which serve lobster. Its small harbour is good shelter for yachts seeking protection from the wind. A long strand of beach is good for swimming. The popular Emel Sayın, an attractive blonde Turkish female vocalist who has a summer house in Palamut, dines often at the **Gangün Cafeteria**, a restaurant coffeehouse by the beach.

Knidos lies next to **Cape Crio**, the tip of the Datça Peninsula.

Another possible excursion from Marmaris is up the Loryma Peninsula to Bozburun, a picturesque village. The road is rough most of the way and motorists are advised to rent jeeps. The road to Bozburun, southwest of Mar-

Temple of Aphrodite in Knidos.

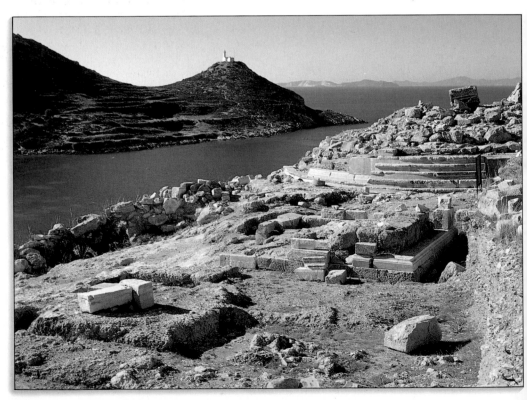

maris, forks left at the end of the Gulf of Hisarönü. The first village one comes to is **Hisarönü**. The village, by the shore, has several pleasant pensions and hotels, including the Kaplan Pansiyon and the beautiful villa-hotel called **Golden Key** with a paradisiacal garden, an outdoor restaurant-coffee house and a campsite. The village is crowded during the summer months with British and German tourists.

The ruins of **Bybassus**, an important Rhodian deme, is located on the other side of the main road. The ruins include an acropolis on a steep rocky hill surrounded by a Hellenistic fortification.

The **Sanctuary of Hemitea**, built in honour of the goddess of healing, is located on a ridge of the mountain known as Eren Dağı (900 feet/274 metres) above the plain of Hisarönü. At this sanctuary pregnant women were treated by a method resembling hypnosis, described as "incubation," believed to relieve abdominal pains. All that remains of the sanctuary is the temple's platform and crumbling theatre.

The **Bay of Orhaniye**, a deep wide inlet of the Gulf of Hisarönü protected by Eren Dağı and clad with olive trees and pine forests, is a popular stopover for yachtsmen. There is a small boat landing and a motel **Keçibükü** (goat's bay), which is at the end of the Bay of Orhaniye, has a boat landing as well. A Byzantine fortress crowns the top of the small island in the bay and a long sand bar runs along the end of the bay. A pleasant club house and several restaurants are located at Keçibükü.

After Keçibükü, the road gets rough. Another dirt road forks left uphill about half a mile (one km) to a bucolic shaded grove known as **Şelale** (Waterfalls), where peasants serve special village *böreks* and grapes by a stream. Several waterfalls plunge down the terraces, forming the stream and a deep pool in which bathing is possible.

Oregano and laurels: The village of **Bayır**, located in the mountains on the main road to Bozburun, has a pleasant square shaded by a 600-year-old oak tree under which several teahouses provide refreshments for visiting tourists. The villagers are renowned for making *kekik yağı,* the oil of oregano, which grows wild in the mountains of the peninsula. *Kekik yağı*, locals say, has medicinal properties which help cure stomach ulcers, asthma, intestinal worms and eczema. The villagers also collect aromatic *defne yaprağı*, laurel leaves, used as a flavouring in preparing *shish kebab*.

The most charming village in the area is **Selimiye**, which has a Byzantine fortress at its entrance. The bay forms a natural harbour.

Bozburun is a little town of 2,500 inhabitants. The famous boat building centre has in recent years become an important stopover for yachts on the Blue Voyage.

The biggest hotel in town is the Akvariyum Tourism Facilities, owned and operated by Korel Göymen, a well known social democrat politician. Boats can be chartered from Bozburun to the ancient site of Loryma at the tip of the peninsula and to Serçe Limanı, a bay facing the Mediterranean.

The day's catch.

MEDITERRANEAN COAST

The Turkish Mediterranean Coast begins east of Marmaris and ends at the Syrian border south of Antakya. The Turks call the Mediterranean "Akdeniz," the White Sea. The Turkish Mediterranean encompasses the eastern part of the province of Muğla and the entire coastal areas of the provinces of Antalya, Mersin, Adana and Hatay. The western part of Turkey's Mediterranean Coast is well known, but the section east of Alanya is little known among tourists and rarely visited, despite its rich past, due to the lack of sufficient hotels and information.

The western Mediterranean Coast is a mountainous region with a narrow coastal strip having many charming resorts, sunken cities and ruins of scores of fascinating ancient cities. This area was known in antiquity as Lycia, and the earliest people who inhabited it, the Lycians, were an independent-minded people noted for their bravery and their reverence for their dead. Their massive tombs, built right into the faces of the mountains, are architectural masterpieces that can't easily be copied by modern men. Towns like Fethiye, Kaş and Kemer have already become booming tourism centres, attracting travellers from all over the world. Travellers to this region go yachting, windsurfing, boating and exploring the hundreds of ancient sites which hug the coast. Saint Nicholas, better known as Santa Claus, lived in Myra in the fourth century.

Five-star hotels: Further east, the Pamphylian Coast, with Antalya as the tourist hub of southwest Turkey, is a breadbasket region, a vast plain surrounded by the towering Taurus and Bey mountains. The region produces cotton, citrus fruits and vegetables. Antalya harbour and free trade zone is one of Turkey's leading export centres.

It was from Antalya (known as Attalia in antiquity) that St Paul, with Barnabas, sailed on his last journey to Antioch (Antakya) to preach.

Many cities, including Perge and Aspendos, have flourished in Pamphylia in the past. Side and Alanya, built on ancient sites east of Antalya, are booming resorts with each having dozens of five-star hotels and holiday villages crammed with wealthy European, Japanese, Israeli, American and now Russian vacationers. These two towns also have hundreds of pensions for the middle-class traveller and the budget-conscious visitor. The beaches of the Pamphylian Coast are among the best in Turkey with soft, golden sand, favoured mainly by German tourists.

East of Alanya is the region that was known as Rough Cilicia, a place where the jagged Taurus Mountains tumble down to the sea abruptly. In the rugged Taurus Mountains, goats grow luxuriant coats. Their hair is woven into a rough fabric used in tent making. The main highway follows the ridges of the mountains and has stunning views of the Mediterranean. Anamur, the banana-growing capital of Turkey, is the most important resort in the area with its long sandy beaches and a magnificent Armenian-built castle. The mountains eventually give way to the vast Çukurova, a cotton-producing region, once known as Smooth Cilicia.

The first important town of note is Silifke – a Turkish version of Cilicia. Silifke is a touristic region with beaches and castles, including the fabled Kızkalesi, which stands on an island near the town. Silifke is located on the Göksu River delta, which is a rich breeding and wintering grounds for hundreds of species of birds, including pelicans.

Adana, Turkey's fourth largest city and a major industrial and agricultural centre, dominates the Çukurova. This region has produced two outstanding figures – literary giant Yaşar Kemal and one of Turkey's greatest industrialists, Hacı Ömer Sabancı.

Other cities in the region include the ports of Mersin and İskenderun, Tarsus and Antakya. This region is rich in history. A succession of empires ruled the area, from the Hittites, Greeks and Seleucids to the Romans, Byzantines and the Turks.

Preceding pages, Alanya Castle. Left, carrying home the goat.

THE WESTERN MEDITERRANEAN

The western Mediterranean Coast extends from a line east of Marmaris to the resort town of Alanya and covers the ancient Roman provinces of Lycia and Pamphylia. The region has about 60 percent of Turkey's tourist accommodations, with huge hotels, holiday village complexes and thousands of pensions and campsites lining the coastline. Nearly half of the tourists who visit Turkey explore this 250-mile (400-km) stretch of territory.

Fire-breathing monster: The area has many well-known destinations such as Antalya, Side and Alanya, and also rarely-visited sites such as Yanartaş, with flames from the mountains thought by the ancients to be the remains of the fire-breathing monster Chimera; the sunken cities around Kekova Island; Caunos, where archaeologists have unearthed an important city; Dalyan, one of the last breeding grounds in the Mediterranean for gigantic marine turtles. The town is also famous for its boat rides among the reeds and its rejuvenating mud baths; and the high plateaus of Lycia where townsmen pitch their tents in the summer to escape from the heat waves of the coast.

It was along the Lycian Coast that St Paul led some of his early missionary activities to spread Christianity. In Patara, St Paul embarked on his last voyage to Palestine. The rock tombs of Caunos, Fethiye and Myra are indeed incredible sites, built right into the faces of overhanging cliffs – symbols of reverence for the dead.

One of the most important events that takes place in this region is the colourful Saint Nicholas Festival held every December 4 - 6 in the town of Demre to honour the original gift-bearing saint associated with the snowy winters of northern Europe. Saint Nicholas, a controversial Christian figure, was born in Patara, a city now covered by sand dunes, and became the first official

Preceding pages, rock tombs in Fethiye.

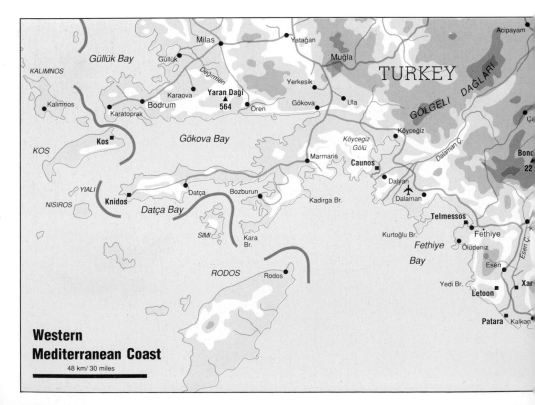

Western Mediterranean Coast

48 km/ 30 miles

Bishop of Myra. His spirit continues to this day with the exchange of gifts during the Christmas season and on New Year's day.

A Blue Voyage into the wonderful 12 Islands of the Gulf of Fethiye from the town of Göcek, which is fast becoming an important yachting centre because of its proximity to Dalaman International Airport, is strongly recommended for travellers who want to get away from the stress of modern urban living. Boat trips to the sunken cities of Kekova Sound, destroyed by earthquakes are also soothing. Travellers in these azure waters can go snorkelling among the baths which Cleopatra built, but are now partly submerged.

Pirate's hideout: The region includes Olympus, a pirates' den that is now in complete ruins in a well-hidden gorge along the rocky Lycian coast. Visitors can also go to Uluburun, a barren cave near the small town of Kaş where underwater archaeologists are excavating the world's oldest known shipwreck, discovered by chance by a sponge diver in 1982. The shipwreck has shed light on the complex trade relations that existed some 3,600 years ago in the eastern Mediterranean.

Some of the most important events of early western history have taken place along the shores of the Turkish western Mediterranean. Alexander the Great's army thundered across Pamphylian Plain in a campaign to conquer the world and build an empire. Persian and Roman armies clashed with the recalcitrant Lycians. Cleopatra and Mark Antony frolicked in the many coves. Venetian Admiral Andrea Doria raided these shores in the 16th century in a vain effort to prevent the Turks from dominating the entire Mediterranean. From 1919-1921, the region was occupied by an Italian army as part of World War I spoils. But the Italians were forced to abandon the area when Turkish nationalists put up stiff resistance.

Today, this region is the pride of modern Turkey and the centre for the nation's tourist development, waiting to be discovered and explored.

LYCIA

The Lycians, the earliest inhabitants of the rugged coast east of Marmaris known as Lycia, were a fierce sea-going people known for their exceptional bravery, pride, self-respect, and their determination to defend their independence at all costs. The Phoenicians and the Saracens of the old world dreaded encountering these warrior people. The Lycians, who inhabited this region 2,000 years ago, had their own 12-god Pantheon and dialect. More than anything else, the Lycians revered their dead. They carved their tombs, replicas of their homes, on the faces of mountains all over southwest Turkey. How they managed such engineering feats is a subject of much speculation.

Lycia can be reached from Marmaris by driving along route 400 past Köyceğiz, a town on the Köyceğiz Lake famous for its green houses, and taking the country road that forks to the right. This road leads to the charming village of Dalyan and to the ruins of Caunos, the first city of Lycia. Dalyan can also be reached by daily boating excursions from Marmaris, bypassing **Aksaz Limanı**, a bay where a big North Atlantic Treaty Organization (NATO) naval base now sits, littering the scenery. It takes about four hours to reach Dalyan by boat. The boats usually stop off at **Ekincik**, where passengers transfer to smaller boats that can navigate the shallow twisting Dalyan River, surrounded by reeds and marshes.

Dalyan, an unspoiled, cosy little resort on the Dalyan River, is one of the most relaxing sites of Turkey, facing the spooky rock tombs of Caunos. Its nights are lazy and calm and its riverside fish restaurants are superb. The best fish restaurant is the **Deniz Yıldızı** (Star Fish) just off the main square. Dalyan means fishery and it gets its name for the many fisheries along the river, which trap *kefal* (mullet) and *levrek* (seabass). These unusual breeds can live in both salt waters and fresh waters. They are caught returning to the sea after spawn-

ing at Köyceğiz Lake. Visitors who decide to spend some time in Dalyan should try *kefal*, a long gray fish, best served grilled. They should also try some tasty *pavurya* or *yengeç* (crabs) as an appetizer. The waiter usually brings a small hammer which is used to crack the shell of the animal to get at its delicious meat.

The most pleasant hotels and pensions in Dalyan are those along the river, but the Caretta Caretta Hotel, built by Nail Çakırhan, recipient of 1982 Aga Khan Architecture Award, near the village square, is regarded as one of the best.

A boat can be rented for a few hours to take tourists across the river to the ruins of **Caunos**, located on two separate levels. An ancient Carian and Lycian city, Caunos was once a thriving port. But like many ancient riverside cities along the Turkish Coast, its downfall came with the silting up of its harbour by the Dalyan River. In the fourth century BC, the town was known as a sickly malaria-ridden place with green-

Left, the "Turtle Beach" at Dalyan. **Right**, enjoying a mud bath.

complexioned inhabitants. Among the ruins to be seen are an amphitheatre, ancient walls, an acropolis hill, and of course the rock tombs, hewn right into the face of the cliff. Motorboats also travel upstream to special mud baths.

Marine turtles: Motorboats can be hired from Dalyan to Iztuzu Beach, popularly known as **Turtle Beach** at the mouth of the river. It takes about an hour to reach the six-mile (10-km) long beach, which resembles a long sand bar. Travellers can also reach the beach by car. A newly-built road from Dalyan to Iztuzu Beach winds along the marshes for nine miles (15 km). The water is shallow and safe, especially for children, and the beach is ideal for tossing frisbees, playing volleyball and building sand castles. Iztuzu Beach is one of the last remaining breeding grounds in the Mediterranean for the Loggerhead Marine Turtle *Caretta caretta.*

During the June-September turtle breeding season, the beach is closed to the public from 6 pm to 9 am to prevent tourists from trampling on the turtles' nests. Resembling amphibious landing craft and each weighing 300 pounds (136 kilos), hundreds of female turtles, travelling there from as far as the West African Coast, invade the shore in June and July, almost always at night, and lay about 100 leathery eggs that resemble golf balls in the sand. The female turtle may lay eggs four times during the breeding season. Before lumbering back to the water, the females cover their eggs with sand to protect them from predators. Nevertheless, predators such as foxes living in the hills come down to the beach at night and often find the nests by scent and feast on the newly-laid eggs.

Crawling seaward: It takes about six to eight weeks for the baby turtles to hatch. Breaking out of their shells, the baby turtles cling to one another like a double helix and claw their way up the sand for air and march to the sea. Hundreds of turtles are eaten alive by huge Ghost Crabs that lay traps for them in the sand. Hawks and other predatory birds catch the turtles which fail to reach the sea by

Rock cemeteries at Caunos.

daylight. In August and September, it is possible to see a giant army of little newly-hatched turtles crawl seaward on the beach.

Turkey's tiny environmental movement, assisted by West Ger-many's Greens Party, won its first major victory at Turtle Beach in 1987 when it successfully pressured the Turkish government to halt the building of a big Turkish-German hotel near the beach, asserting that the construction would endanger the newly-hatched turtles. The environmentalists argued that lights from the hotel would confuse the baby turtles, which would get lost and head inland instead of seeking the safety of the sea. The beach today is an environmentally protected zone. Guards keep watch over the beach area at night to prevent tourists and local farmers from trespassing – a measure to protect the turtles' nest.

From Dalyan another road leads through fertile farm lands of orange and tangerine groves to **Ortaca**, a cotton-producing town, and links up to the route 400. The town of **Dalaman**, just off the Muğla-Fethiye highway, has an international airport where hundreds of charter flights arrive daily, bringing tens of thousands of tourists daily from Europe, the United States and Japan. The only other thing Dalaman is famous, or notorious, for is a state paper mill, which is polluting the nearby Dalaman River, that empties into the Mediterranean south of the airport.

Göcek: From Dalaman the east-bound road soon climbs pine-covered mountains only to plunge to the town of **Göcek**, on the northwestern end of the Gulf of Fethiye. Göcek, only 19 miles (30 km) from Dalaman International Airport, is rapidly developing into an important yachting centre. Many local as well as foreign chartering companies have already set up shop in the town, which has a population of only 2, 500. Several resort hotels have been built around Göcek since the early 1990s.

Despite its smallness, Göcek is a town of true international character. It is one of the few places in Turkey where newspapers and magazines from all

Bays of the Turquoise Coast.

over the world are sold. The town has a small pier with scores of yachts lining it. A number of seaside restaurants and coffeehouses face the bay. At the far end of the bay facing Göcek is an old Istanbul steam boat, *Halas*, docked by the shore. Owned by Haldun Simavi, a Turkish business tycoon and former newspaper publisher, the *Halas* is now being used as a luxurious floating hotel-restaurant. Nearby is a pier operated by SEKA, the state plp and paper mills.

From Göcek it is possible to charter yachts to the 12 Islands of the **Gulf of Fethiye**, one of the most secluded and beautiful areas on the Turquoise Coast. Daily motorboat excursions to the **12 Islands** leave Göcek quay in the mornings. The day trip can also be made from Fethiye. Each passenger pays about $10 for the round trip. You can also charter a *caique*, inclusive of its captain, for about $100, if you want to be alone and have complete privacy.

As the boat heads away from Göcek, the first two islands you encounter are **Göcek Adası**, famous for its verdant pine forests, and **Zeytinli Adası**, a privately-owned estate with thousands of olive trees, both on the left.

Soon you reach **Yassıca Adaları**, an archipelago of small islands good for mooring and swimming, and the larger **Hacıhalil Adası**. The boat doesn't usually stop at any of these islands, but continues to the big island on the left, **Tersane Adası**, which has a protected cove suitable for anchorage. The boat will stop there for about half an hour, permitting passengers to swim ashore and explore the verdant island. The ruins of several buildings, which were most likely inhabited by Greek families before the 1923 population exchanges, face the cove. Tersane means "shipyards" in Turkish, and the Greek families who once lived there built wooden-framed boats.

The Pig's Island: From Tersane, the boat crosses the narrow strait to **Domuz Adası** (the Pig's Island), a rocky island that is owned by Erol Simavi, the publisher of Turkey's biggest-selling newspaper, *Hürriyet*, and one of the most

Selling watermelon from a horse-drawn carriage.

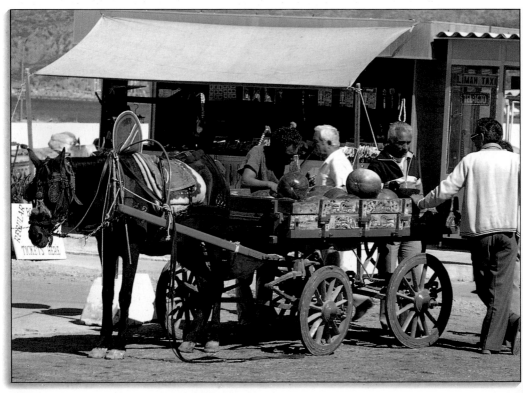

powerful men in the country. Simavi's villa stands amid what appears to be ancient ruins. Stopping at the island is forbidden. At the northwest corner of the island the remains of a nun's convent can be seen. Simavi has hosted many guests at his secret island retreat, including Prince Charles and Princess Margaret and other members of the British royal family, who have cruised along the 12 Islands on board his private yacht.

The boat continues to **Hamam Cove**, which has several partially submerged ruins of buildings that some locals claim were the **Baths of Cleopatra**. The structures sank as a result of earth tremors. The skipper of the boat will stop for 90 minutes in the bay, allowing passengers to have lunch at one of the alfresco restaurants, open only in the summer. The break will also give visitors time to swim and explore the ruins using a mask and snorkel.

From Hamam Cove, the captain will take visitors to the westernmost point of the Gulf, **Bedri Rahmi Bay**. The bay gets its name from the cubist painting of a fish on a rock by the shore. It was painted in 1974 by the late Bedri Rahmi Eyuboğlu, a well-known painter and writer who popularized the Blue Voyage with his great paintings and poetry. The region is also known as Taşyaka, or **Tombs Bay**, because of the many Lycian cemeteries and pigeonhole rock tombs along the jagged shoreline. The site was identified by the late George Bean as the ancient Lycian city of Crya. The boat will stop for about 30 minutes, enabling passengers to swim ashore and visit the rock tombs and admire Eyuboğlu's painting.

The next bay on the way back to Göcek is **Boynuzbükü**, a deep sheltered bay surrounded by pine trees where sail boats can anchor safely. A river, lined with reeds and oleander shrubs, empties into the bay. The government recently banned construction of several new hotels in this bay, including one by the former mayor of Istanbul, Bedrettin Dalan, to protect its beauty. On day trips the motorboats return to Göcek on the same day.

Fethiye: A one-hour drive east from Göcek brings the traveller to the flourishing city of **Fethiye**. Once a minor market village, Fethiye has become a thriving tourism centre in recent times. The town is immensely popular among French, German and British tourists and foreign yachtsmen. Fethiye is a yachting centre for Blue Voyages into the Gulf of Fethiye, the 12 Islands, and the unforgettable region around Kekova Island, which has some of the most mysterious sunken cities and ruins in the world.

Fethiye has always been an important centre for the export of chromium. Turkey is the world's biggest producer of this metal, which is mined all along the bulge of Lycia from the Gulf of Fethiye to Antalya.

In many ways, Fethiye resembles Bodrum. It has a rich nightlife with many pubs, discotheques and bars. Its downtown is lined with hundreds of gift shops, selling everything from carpets and leatherware to colourful T-shirts and blue glass beads to fend off the evil eye. The restaurants by the quay, the marina and the shopping district are lively during the evenings, visited by large crowds of tourists.

All this is strange for a town that had no road connections with any provincial centres as recently as 1950. At the time, all transportation was done by boat. The first organized tourist group to ever visit Fethiye came on a boat trip from Rhodes in 1963.

Telmessus: Fethiye dates back to the sixth century BC. It was once a grand Lycian city called **Telmessus**. Traces of the ancient settlement can be seen about the town, including the awesome rock tombs on the face of a cliff east of the city and several scattered heavy sarcophagi, including one next to the Town Hall (**Belediye Binası**). The town, however, is modern, having been reconstructed after the earthquakes of 1950 and 1957 levelled it.

Situated at the eastern end of the big Gulf of Fethiye, the town is surrounded by tall mountains that are snowcapped in winter. A bulging headland and an island, popularly known as **Şövalyeler**

Adası (The Knights' Island), protect the town, forming almost a big lake that is an ideal shelter for yachts.

Fethiye has many first-class hotels and holiday villages, the best of which is the spectacular Fethiye Holiday Village operated by the French Club Méditerranée, and the **Club Hotel Aries** at Çalı Beach.

Temple tomb: The rock tombs are just behind the city. Cars can be left on the base of the cliffs and the tombs can be reached by walking up a steep path. The most magnificent of these monuments to the dead is the **Temple Tomb of Amyntas**, who was a Lycian notable. A sarcophagus, weighing several tons, stands smack in the middle of the road, near the rock tombs. Neither the rock tombs nor the sarcophagus were damaged or even budged during the earthquakes that flattened Fethiye in 1950 and 1957. The local denizens have never considered pushing the sarcophagus off the middle of the road, claiming that if they were to move it even slightly "the whole world would shake." An acropolis hill at the back of the town is occupied by a castle, believed to have been constructed by the Crusader Knights of St John.

Rafet Restaurant, indisputably the best restaurant in town, is located along Kordonboyu (the quay), just off Atatürk Caddesi, the main street that runs north-south through Fethiye. The restaurant is operated by Rafet Tuna, a Turkish refugee from Bulgaria who settled in Fethiye in 1950. Tuna has run the restaurant for over 40 years. Food at the restaurant, which specializes in grilled fish and delightful appetizers, is modestly priced. Guests buy the fish at daily prices written on a board next to the display refrigerator. All the guest needs to do is point to which fish he wants and the waiter weighs it and has it cooked for you. Other good restaurants in Fethiye worth visiting are Anfora, Meğri and Yacht.

A night in town includes a visit to souvenir and carpet shops along Çarşı Caddesi, which is parallel to Atatürk Caddesi, followed by a visit to **Fethiye Holiday Village**, a sprawling resort town across the bay on **Paçaraz Peninsula**, and a pub crawl in the town. The resort village is only a six-mile (10-km) drive from Fethiye, following the coast past the marina. Automobiles are left at the entrance to the town's gate and visitors must walk through the sprawling complex along the middle promenade, to its discotheques and bars passing hundreds of fancy houses, which are part of the holiday complex but owned by Turkey's nouveaux rich, and luxury bungalows on different levels, where guests stay. From the holiday town, the flickering lights of Fethiye can been seen at night. The floodlit open air bar is at the farthest end of the peninsula, where young foreign men and women mingle with Turks.

The cosy **Entel Bar 1** on Türkocağı Sokak No. 6 in the centre of town is a good place to stop off for a nightcap. The bar is operated by Gençağa Karafazlı, a friendly Turkish journalist, and his wife. The Karafazlıs also run **Entel Bar 2** behind the state hospital (Devlet Hastanesi) near Vizon Hotel. Two other interesting nightclub/bars are **Disco Marina**, which occasionally features belly-dancing and is open until the wee small hours, and the loud **Otantik Bar**, housed inside a restored Ottoman house, with black lights and mirror balls.

Environs: Numerous excursions can be made to different resorts, towns and ancient Lycian cities from Fethiye. One of these excursions is to the ghost town of Kaya and the resort of Ölüdeniz. A dirt road, on which the massive sarcophagus stands, curves into the mountains behind the town for about six miles (10 km), passing dense pine and cedar forests, and winds down to a fertile plain. **Kaya**, formerly known as Kormylassos, stands on the side of a hill overlooking the plain. Kaya was once a wealthy Greek town of 5,000 people, the most populous in the region. The Greeks abandoned Kaya as part of the general population exchanges between Greece and Turkey at the end of the Greco-Turkish War of 1919-1922. (Nearly 1.5 million Greeks living in Turkey switched places with 500,000

Turks living in Greece in 1923.) Kaya today is an eerie ghost town that is worth an early morning or late afternoon stroll. Hundreds of houses, with their roofs crumbled from the quakes that rocked the region, remain standing along rock paths. Two well-preserved churches, one built in 1888 and still having frescoes depicting biblical scenes, remain intact. Several chapels exist below the church on the hill.

The same road continues on to **Ölüdeniz**, the "Dead Sea," another six miles (10 km) from Kaya. (Ölüdeniz can also be reached directly from Fethiye. The turnoff to Ölüdeniz is on the Muğla-Antalya Highway.) Ölüdeniz is a misnomer. Although it resembles a perfectly calm lagoon, it has a small mouth opening to the sea through which boats could once enter. Ringed by mountains, pine trees and a long sandy beach, Ölüdeniz was an ideal shelter for yachts seeking protection from the stormy sea. But Ölüdeniz was closed to yachts in 1984 to prevent pollution of its crystal waters. The **Mo-tel Meri**, a complex of private bunga-lows and comfortable hotel rooms, has the best accommodations in the area.

The **Belcekız Beach**, along the la-goon, is one of the best sand beaches of Turkey. It becomes deep very fast, how-ever, and is not suitable for toddlers or children learning to swim. The beach area is crowded and noisy in the sum-mer. Scores of camp sites and motels have opened in the past decade along the beach, and more are being built in the mountains.

Paragliding: In addition to swimming at Belcekız Beach, visitors can parasail. There are several parasailing clubs available along the beach. They can also try paragliding from the top of Baba Dağı, a rocky peak of 6,520 feet (1,976 metres) dominating the coast. Para-gliding resembles hang-gliding, except for the use of a parachute instead of a hang-glider, and is as exciting. A number of western and Turkish sports professionals lead paragliding expedi-tions daily during the summer months from Babadağ to Belcekız Beach, a 25-

The ghost town of Kaya, near Fethiye.

minute parachute glide. They work out of Deniz Camping, a privately-owned camping site with bungalows, and drive up five times a day to Babadağ to leap off the mountain with daring sportspeople.

Deniz Camping, which offers lunch and dinner and is open year round, is owned and operated by Hülya Gürkan, a British woman whose real name is Anthea, her son Osman and her husband, a former Turkish Air Force pilot. The Gürkans have been operating the campsite for over 20 years and were the first people to open a campgrounds at the beach. The precedent-setting Gürkans have also recently restored 25 houses in an abandoned former Greek village in the mountains, operating them as a motel village complex, **Ocakköy**. The pleasant village, with its library, outdoor pool, bar and do-it-yourself craft shop, is located halfway between Ölüdeniz and Fethiye. Among the activities offered by the Gürkan family at Ocakköy is donkey riding along mountain trails.

Excursions can also be made from Fethiye to the ruins of five Lycian cities in the Xanthus valley, the main area of settlement in Lycia: Tlos, Pinara, Letoon, Xanthus and Patara.

Pinara, southeast of Fethiye, located near the village of Minare, can be reached by a short dirt road that branches off the Fethiye-Kaş Highway south of Kemer. Once a great city, Pinara is believed to have existed since the Trojan War (1200 BC) and perhaps even earlier. The town is built on two acropolis hills. Only traces of the earliest city are visible, including several cisterns and rock-foundations of wood and mud-brick houses, built on a hill honeycombed with pigeonhole tombs. Many sarcophagi are scattered about the main acropolis hill, including one that is the largest in southwest Turkey.

To the south are rock cut house tombs and the remains of a Christian church, an odeon theatre, a large house-type tomb dubbed the **Royal Tomb**, believed to be the funerary monument of a prince. Inside the Royal Tomb are the reliefs of different Lycian cities. Near-

by are the agora and the main theatre.

A 20-minute drive south from Pinara brings the motorist to **Letoon**, the ancient sanctuary of the Goddess Leto, mother of both Artemis and Apollo. The turnoff to Letoon is past the town of Esen and the village of Hazırlar. The shrine is about three miles (five km) off Fethiye-Kaş highway. Leto was the principal Goddess of the Lycians.

The ruins contain the foundations of three temples, the main one dedicated to Leto, and the others to Artemis and Apollo. They also contain a nymphaion, a kind of public bath, that is partially submerged in water. The site offers a well-preserved amphitheatre too. In the middle of the **Temple of Apollo**, you can see a mosaic of a lye, the sun, a bow and arrow, the only known mosaic of the Lycian civilization.

Hera's wrath: According to popular Lycian myths, Leto was the mistress of Zeus. She incurred the wrath of Zeus' jealous wife, Hera, who hounded her and sent her into exile. In her peripatetic wanderings, Leto came upon a water

The ruins of Pinara.

fountain where she wanted to quench her thirst, but three nasty shepherds drove her away. After giving birth to Artemis and Apollo, according to the same myths, she returned to the site and turned the shepherds into frogs as a punishment.

The ancient city of **Xanthus** is just three miles (five km) away. Xanthus, the most impressive and important Lycian city, is off the Fethiye-Antalya highway, near the village of Kınık, along the Xanthus River (known today as Esen Çayı). A dirt road leads right into the ruins of the city, where cars can be parked.

On the left hand side is an outstanding amphitheatre, and next to it two tombs. The so-called **Harpies Tomb**, an elevated funerary monument, gets its name from its reliefs showing the mythological harpies, half-birds, half-women monsters, carrying away dead children to the underworld. Next to it is the **Pillar Tomb**, a squat Lycian sarcophagus on top of a long, rectangular pillar. Facing the amphitheatre is the agora on which

Parasailing over the beach.

stands the famous **Xanthian Steele**, a pillar tomb whose frame is covered with 250 lines of Lycian script, the longest ever discovered, and a Greek poem. On the other side of the road are ruins of two Byzantine basilicas and a monastery.

Mass suicides: The early history of Xanthus is obscure. It made its mark in history during Persian General Harpagus' invasion of the southwestern coast of Asia Minor around 540 BC. The Persian army, conquering the coastal cities, swept into Lycia from Caria and was opposed by the Lycians. Defeated by Harpagus in battle, the Lycians retreated into their besieged city. Rather than surrender Xanthus, the Lycians gathered their wives and children into the acropolis which they set ablaze in a defiant act of mass suicide. They then marched out to fight the Persians and were killed to the last man.

The Lycians reenacted the tragedy 500 years later during the Roman Civil Wars. In 42 BC, when Brutus arrived in Xanthus to raise money for his army for the coming showdown with Antony and

Octavian, the Lycians withdrew into the city and slaughtered their families, built a huge funeral pyre in the centre of the city and threw themselves into the flames to die. The city was repopulated by descendants of the Lycians during the Byzantine period. But its end most likely came during the Arab invasions of Anatolia in the 7th century.

The great plunder: Xanthus was discovered by Sir Charles Fellows in 1838. Four years later, sailors from the British Navy, under Lieutenant Thomas Spratt's command, removed hundreds of statues and friezes from the site in what Turks today describe as a rape of the nation's archaeological wealth. All the statuary removed from Xanthus are now exhibited at the British Museum in London in the Xanthian Hall, including the sculptures of the magnificent **Neried Monument**, a beautiful tomb.

Six miles (10 km) south of Xanthus are the ruins of **Patara**, near one of Turkey's best beaches. A sign points toward the ancient site of the Antalya-Kaş highway. Patara is the traditional birthplace of Saint Nicholas, the gift-bearing Santa Claus associated with the snowy winters of northern Europe. Patara was once a great commercial port, but today is partly covered by sand dunes and hidden by an almost impenetrable forest of thick bushes and trees, about 800 yards (728 metres) from the sea. The town has been systematically excavated by a team of devoted Turkish archaeologists since the early 1990s, against the hostility of land developers, who have been reported to have started fires to threaten the scientists.

Motorists pass an arch as they enter Patara. Vehicles can be parked in front of the restaurant behind the beach. The nearby amphitheatre is half filled with sand. On the knoll between the beach and the theatre stands an unusual structure believed to be some kind of water cistern. Next to it are ruins of what may be a lighthouse for guiding boats into the harbour, which is now silted up. Next to the harbour is the **Granary of Hadrian**, which is well preserved. An agora and a tomb are nearby.

The sand-filled theatre at Patara.

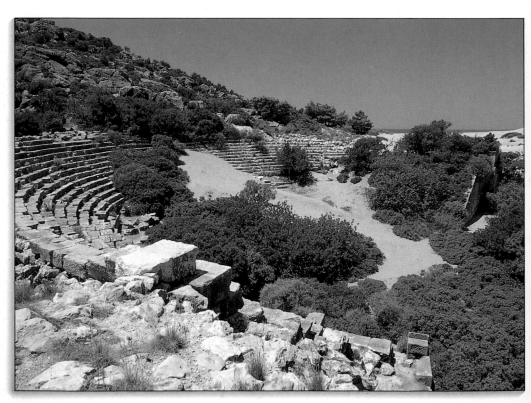

Patara's beach: Patara's 11-mile (18-km) long sandy beach is wonderful and worth bathing in. As it faces the open sea, however, Patara's waters are always turbulent. The strong undertow makes Patara's sea dangerous, especially for youngsters. There have been several reported drownings. The beach gets very hot in summer, requiring bathers to rent beach umbrellas.

The resort of **Kaş** (pronounced somewhat like "cash") is about 38 miles (60 km) east of Patara on the Fethiye-Antalya highway. The road to Kaş winds along the coast, passing **Kalkan**, a town popular with sunseekers, and many small beaches.

Like most towns on the Lycian coast, Kaş is wedged between mountains and the sea. In recent years, it has become a popular stopover for yachts on the Blue Voyage. Kaş faces the tiny island of Kastellorizon (Meis in Turkish), the farthest Greek island from mainland Greece. Meis, a resort island, gets all its supplies from Kaş, and all its hotel owners speak fluent Turkish. Each morning, several motorboats come to Kaş to carry food and other supplies to Meis.

There are several hotels and pensions in the town, but **Club Hotel Phellos** and **Kekova**, both commanding wonderful sea views, and the Mimosa Hotel near the highway, are considered among the better and more comfortable ones. Several new hotels are now built on the far peninsula away from the crowded little town, such as the **Aqua Park**.

Kaş was the location for the ancient city **Antiphellus**, but little remains of the old settlement have survived to this day. There are several sarcophagi about the town, including one by the port and an elevated one on the square above Uzunçarşı Caddesi which features the heads of lions coming out of its sides. An ancient amphitheatre is situated on Kaş' long peninsula, a walking distance from the town.

Hero carpet shop: Kaş has an extensive bazaar area, where there are numerous gift shops. The best carpet dealers in town are **Kaş and Carry** and **Magic Orient**, both of which supply a large

Sailboats in Kalkan.

and tasteful collection of old and new carpets and kilims, handmade saddlebags and other beautiful textiles.

Kaş has many fish restaurants by the port, lined with visiting yachts, and surprisingly, for such a small town, there are a few gourmet international restaurants like the **Chez Evy** French restaurant, **J P Spaghetti House** and **Smiley's**, popular for its garlic bread. Guests will find plenty of chicken and meat dishes, and fish, which is caught fresh every day in this coastal area. The restaurants of this region are known to serve goat's meat, a local delicacy, instead of mutton or beef. Those unaccustomed to goat meat may experience painful diarrhoea. Visitors should make certain that food prices are clearly listed at the front entrance of each restaurant. Compare prices with other restaurants. Several restaurants in Kaş have a reputation for overpricing food. The town also has several fine discotheques and late night bars. Check out **Mavi** and **Red Point**.

Oldest known shipwreck: A short boat trip from Kas brings one to Ulu Burun, where a team of Turkish and American underwater archaeologists have been excavating the oldest known shipwreck since 1984. The underwater archaeologists are members of the Institute of Nautical Archaeology (INA), affiliated with Texas A&M University. The team is led by Professor George Bass, founder of INA, and Cemal Pulak, a Turkish marine archaeologist of international repute. The 14th-century BC vessel was discovered in 1982 at a depth of 150 feet (45 metres) by a sponge diver, who spotted what appeared to be "metal biscuits with ears," bringing the INA divers to the scene. The metal biscuits turned out to be huge copper ingots shaped like ox hides.

The discovery has shed considerable light on rather sophisticated Bronze Age Trade in the Eastern Mediterranean. The 50-foot (10-metre) vessel was carrying a hoard of goods from one port to another when it sank, possibly in a storm. Many of the relics that have been discovered are now in Bodrum's Underwater Archaeology Museum. Besides copper ingots, the scientists recovered Baltic amber beads, the first to be discovered outside Greece, a Mycenaean vase, Canaanite amphora, ebony from Nubia, unworked ivory, stone anchors, tins and glass.

Because the shipwreck is at such great depth, the recovery work has taken many years. Divers that go down are in constant danger of getting nitrogen narcosis or worse, the "bends."

Bass has had a few mishaps. Once he ran out of air at 150 feet (45 metres) deep. "I was sure I was going to drown. But as I clawed my way to the surface, a Turkish friend grabbed me and gave me air," Bass once told a *National Geographic Magazine* interviewer.

Sunken cities: Kas is also the centre for boating trips to the nearby sunken cities around Kekova Island and the fishing village of Kale, famous for its necropolis of Lycian tombs. This is a full-day trip – boats leave for Kale from Kas each morning at 8 am and return around 6 pm With stopovers in numerous bays, it takes five hours to reach Kaleköy, the last destination. (Kekova Sound can also be reached by boat from Demre's port.

The first site one comes to is **Aperlae**, east of Kas, on the Sıçak Peninsula. Yachts can anchor in the bay and motorboats can tie up by the boat landing, known as **Sıçak Limanı**. The village of **Sıçak** is located in the hills about an hour's walk away. The boat landing is built along the ruins of Aperlae, an ancient Lycian city. The ruins include an acropolis, city walls, a necropolis of tombs and ruined houses.

The most remarkable sights in Aperlae are the harbour, quay and many streets which are now under water by the boat landing. This was caused either by a rise in the sea level or by a major earthquake. Visitors are advised to snorkel with a mask to see the astounding sunken city.

East of Aperlae is **Kekova Sound** with several deep bays, protected by the elongated Kekova Island and several smaller islands. Francis Beaufort, a British naval commander who surveyed the region in the early 19th century, recommended Kekova Sound as an anchorage for a naval fleet. "Its great extent, its bold shores and the facility for defence may hereafter point it out as an eligible place for a rendezvous of a fleet," he wrote in his book of surveys, *Karamania*.

Submerged houses: Numerous submerged houses and their foundations can be seen all along the northern shore of **Kekova Island**. At the western tip of the island, visitors can see the apse of a lone Byzantine church and remains of some houses. This was the Greek settlement of Tersane (shipyard), whose inhabitants are believed to have been boat builders.

A narrow channel across from Tersane leads to a wide hidden bay. On the shore stands the farming community **Uçağız**, with small, pleasant boat landings. Australian writer Rod Heikell who visited the hamlet in the late 1980s, reported seeing cattle wandering about the streets. East of Uçağız are the ruins of **Teimiussa**, a Lycian city, with numerous sarcophagi and rock tombs, and remains of a fortification.

The most charming village in Kekova Sound is **Kaleköy**, across the Kekova Island. A medieval crenellated castle stands dominating a craggy peninsula, surrounded by a necropolis of sarcophagi, overlooking the village.

An ancient 300-seat theatre is inside the castle. This was the site of ancient **Simena**. The villagers make their living from the sea catching fish and lobsters. The community has three jetties which double as restaurants during the tourism season. A lone Lycian sarcophagus standing in the water lures visitors to pose beside it for photographs. Nearby, in the middle of the bay is a rock with steps cut into it. This may have been a house or perhaps some kind of ancient light house.

St Nicholas Church: About 23 miles (50 km) east of Kaş is the farming community of **Demre**, famous for its many green houses. It was at Demre, known to the ancients as Myra, that Saint Nicholas, the original Santa Claus, worked in the fourth century. Visitors can see his church which stands on a

A Gypsy with his dancing bear.

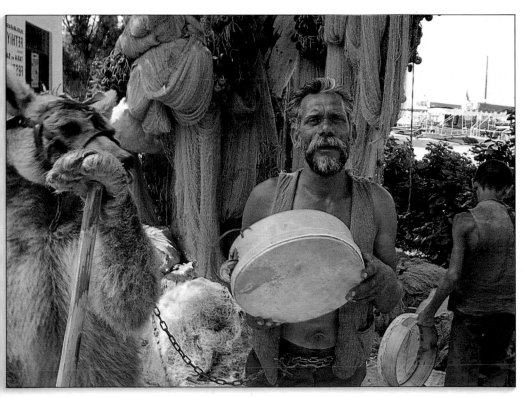

side street in the middle of the town next to a public park.

The ruins of **Myra** are north of the town. Myra's big amphitheatre, the first structure one comes to, is of Roman style. In the west gallery are the inscriptions "Place of vendor Gelasius," and this was probably the stand where theatre-goers could buy popcorn, nuts and other edibles to nibble on while watching a performance. Myra has the most impressive rock tombs on the entire Lycian Coast. The cliff facing Myra is honeycombed with rock graves, giving it a gloomy sepulchral atmosphere. Many of these tombs, to which one can climb following the trail up to the cliffs, have friezes of human figures or graffiti. The most striking cemetery is known as the **Painted Tomb** by which there are friezes of a man and members of his family, presumed to have been buried there.

Finike, Turkey's leading orange-producing community, is 25 miles (40 km) east of Demre. Finike is an unexciting market town by a river. In recent times, it has become a popular stopover for yachtsmen. Just before entering the town you come to a wide cove, known as **Andrea Doria Bay**, named after the 16th-century Venetian admiral who is said to have concealed his flagship there while fighting the Ottoman navy. There isn't much to see in the town, and its long sandy beach is unpleasant, cluttered with tons of soggy, rotting oranges thrown in the sea by nearby orange packaging plants.

The weather gets so sultry and humid in summer in this corner of Turkey that townsmen and villagers move to the cool mountain plateaus, where many have summer cottages, returning to the coast in September.

The best hotel in Finike is the clean **Baykal Motel Pension**, probably the only motel in Turkey where the owner personally provides a free taxi service for guests from the town to the pension.

Off beat site: For the next 32 miles (50 km), the road twists along the coast past the town of **Kumluca** and then winds up into the mountains blanketed by tall

Afternoon in Kaş.

pine and cedar trees. To reach the ancient pirates' hideout of Olympus, motorists must turn right off the old Finike-Antalya highway followed by another right at a sign showing Çavuş and Olympus. After driving for about another mile turn left at the Olympus sign. A rough dirt road, full of potholes, leads to the ancient town. You must drive carefully if you don't have a four-wheel drive. The humps on the road damage the transmissions of low cars. It's best to visit the site in a jeep with a full tank of gas. No service station exists in this wilderness.

Olympus, a city in ruins, is located in a gorge between two steep mountains. A stream runs through the town, once a pirates' hideout, and the ruins are on both banks, covered by a jungle of bushes and trees. A Turkish guard sits near the entrance of the ancient site. Olympus, which probably means mountain in a pre-Greek language, is one of 20 sites and mountains in the eastern Mediterranean with that name. The town has never been excavated.

Nearly 2,000 years ago, pirates controlled this settlement, raiding and plundering commercial ships plying the coast, but the Roman general Pompey finally stamped out piracy in the region after a military campaign.

Parts of a quay on the southern bank of the stream, and remains of a theatre across the knee-deep water can be seen. On the northern bank was the main section of the city, and an acropolis on the hill by the beach is still visible. Several tiny sarcophagi, probably of children, stand with their lids partly open on the side of the hill. The walls of what were probably residential houses also stand on the northern bank along the river. The main necropolis is on the southern side of the river bank and has many ornate tombs.

The sea, with a pounding surf, is just about 650 feet (200 metres) from the entrance of the settlement and the beach is a fabulous place to take a break from sightseeing, swim and have a picnic.

The eternal flames of Yanartaş (the Burning Stone) are near the village of

Sailing off on a "Blue Voyage" from Kaleköy.

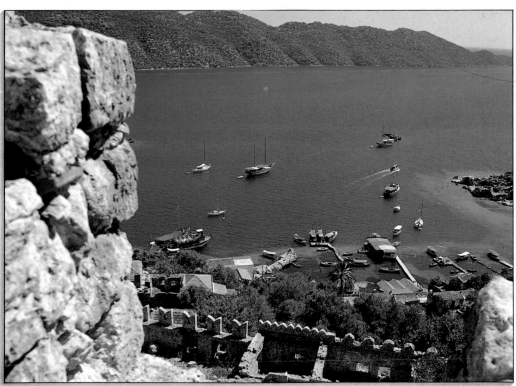

Çıralı on the face of a mountain. To get to Çıralı, motorists must backtrack to the Finike-Antalya highway and turn toward Antalya, soon reaching the new highway. They must turn right at the Çıralı sign. The poorly-paved asphalt road goes downhill for about three miles (five km).

A left turn at the small coffeehouse and a drive for another 1.3 miles (two km) will bring the visitor to a dirt road on the left that goes into the canyon. Motorists must leave the car at the end of the road and walk the rest of the way, following a trail into the mountain. The climb to Yanartaş takes about 45 minutes. **Yanartaş** is an outcrop of rocks surrounded by pine trees. Tiny flames shoot out of a dozen or more holes in these rocks.

The Chimera: The fires have been burning for thousands, perhaps millions, of years. The flames, according to myths, are the remains of the Chimera, the fire-snorting monster that once terrorized the coastal area. The Chimera, which had a lion's head, a goat's body and a serpent's tail, was slain by mythical Lycian hero Bellerophon who flew over the mountains with his winged horse Pegasus. (Mobil Oil Corp., the giant oil producing concern, uses Pegasus as its emblem.) But Turkish scientists say the fires are caused by a buildup of underground methane gas that can't be extinguished. If the flames are doused with water, they will come back burning bright in seconds. The area is volcanic by nature and may have considerable oil reserves. The state Turkish Petroleum Corp. has been searching for oil with some success over the past few years in the surrounding mountains. The fires of the Chimera can be seen burning at night from sea-going vessels sailing the coast.

Just below the Yanartaş are some unusual ruins believed to be a sanctuary for the fire God Hephaestus. One of the ruins, strangely, resembles a weird Byzantine chapel.

The Finike-Antalya road from the turnoff to Yanartaş swings through **Olympus National Park** over 44 miles

Sitting at the Chimera.

(70 km), passing through verdant pine forests. To the left are the **Bey Dağları**, a mountain range with jagged peaks resembling the Rocky Mountains. The range is good for climbing, trekking and hunting.

Phaselis: Shortly after passing the village of Beycik a dirt road forks right leading to **Phaselis**, an ancient Greek city, situated on the tip of a peninsula. There is some confusion about the early history of the town. Some say the city was founded by Rhodian colonists in 690 BC. Others claim it was founded much earlier by the seer Mopsus, who led Greek colonists to the southern coast in the wake of the Trojan War. Whatever its origins, the city today offers the visitor the chance to wander among Roman and Byzantine ruins of two harbours, a main avenue, aqueducts, baths, a theatre, an agora and a temple. Pine tree-lined bays are the favourite haunt of those who seek to swim in the Mediterranean waters or to sunbathe and windsurf.

The resort of **Kemer** is the next stop on the road to Antalya. The town has many holiday villages, including **Robinson Club Çamyuva**, and Club Méditerranée, which operates the relaxing **Kemer Holiday Village** and the **Palmiye Holiday Village**. Many luxury hotels line the secluded beaches toward Antalya, including the **Ramada Hotel** and the **Phaselis Princess Hotel**. Benefiting from its spectacular natural surroundings and hefty World Bank loans, Kemer has developed into a booming tourism centre.

The **Beldibi Caves**, where people of the Stone Age once lived, are located between Kemer and Antalya. In 1960, Turkish archaeologist Enver Bostancı discovered flint stones, bits of pottery, and a wall painting of a wild goat and other animal figures, indicating the inhabitants were hunters. The ancient findings are housed in the magnificent Antalya Museum.

The highway continues on its path north and soon the black cliffs of Antalya come into view, beginning the wide plain of Pamphylia.

A sarcophagus stands in the water at Kaleköy.

SAINT NICHOLAS

Each December 4-6, church scholars and amateur historians worldwide invade the farming community of Demre (ancient Myra), famed for its delicious red tomatoes and juicy oranges, to attend the only Santa Claus Symposium in the world.

Saint Nicholas, the original Santa Claus, a legendary man of good deeds, worked and preached in Demre 1,700 years ago, and his reputation as a gift-bearer spread throughout the Christian world, many church scholars say.

Rattling bones: Although much controversy rages in church circles over the very existence of the Christian saint, the Church officially recognizes Saint Nicholas as an authentic historical figure, the first Bishop of Myra.

While skeptics still assert that Saint Nicholas never lived, others argue he was present at the Council of Nicaea of AD 325 where he slapped the heretic Arius with such force that the victim's bones rattled.

Born in the nearby city of Patara about AD 300, Saint Nicholas came to Myra as a young man. Not long after, he was elected the town's bishop.

Since Myra was a port as well as a farming town, Saint Nicholas first became the patron saint of sailors. The abandoned Saint Nicholas Church, where he purportedly delivered sermons, is located on one of the two main streets of Demre. The church is a Christian as well as a Moslem shrine. Saint Nicholas is known among Turks as Noel Baba, or Father Christmas. A statue of the saint, surrounded by children, stands in the courtyard.

Pirates remove remains: His marble sarcophagus lies inside the church, but his remains were stolen by pirates in the 11th century to Bari, a town on Italy's Adriatic Coast, and deposited in a church named after him. Thus he became associated with pirates, robbers and thieves. Turks, however, say that some of the saint's bones were preserved and are those found in the Antalya Museum, a view that most church scholars say is farfetched.

When his fame reached northern Europe, his name was abbreviated to Claus, and Saint Nicholas became Santa Claus. The traditions of reindeer, elves, toys, sleigh and red, fur-lined attire were derived from the snowy winters of northern Europe. The gift-bearing associated with the Christmas season may have come from many tales of the original Santa. One story had him give a bag of gold each to the three daughters of a poor man as dowries to prevent them from becoming prostitutes. Another story deals with the so-called Pickled Boys: Three young famished lads came into Myra looking for work and a bite to eat. An evil, deranged butcher lured them into his shop and chopped them to pieces, intending to sell them as mincemeat. An angel, learning of the brutal killings, informed Saint Nicholas who immediately went to the butcher and restored the three young lads back to life.

Divine nature: Tales have Nicholas saving shipwrecked sailors, resurrecting the dead, parting the waters of a wide river Moses-style, and recouping lost property. He is said to have saved Myra from famine, securing the arrival of corn-bearing ships to the port in time to prevent mass starvation. While inspecting a church under construction, the building collapsed on him, but the saint emerged unhurt.

During the three-day Saint Nicholas symposium and seminar, organized by the Orthodox Churches of the United States and Orion-Tur Turizm ve Seyahat Acentesı, an Istanbul-based Turkish Travel Agency, scholars and clergymen discuss the character and the life of the saint and trace his development as a Christian figure.

On December 6, the traditional date of Saint Nicholas' death, priests from the Orthodox Church Patriarchate hold two-hour liturgical services at the small Church of Saint Nicholas. The services and symposium coincide with the Saint Nicholas festival held in Demre.

Left, the statue of St Nicholas; and **right**, Myra's theater.

ANTALYA AND ITS ENVIRONS

Antalya is the tourism centre of southwest Turkey, often described as the "Honolulu of Turkey." Surrounded on three sides by snowcapped mountains, the Bey Dağları in the west and the Toros Dağları (Taurus Mountains) in the north and east, Antalya is situated on a vast fertile plain that was known in antiquity as Pamphylia. Antalya is also the region's agricultural and commercial hub. Antalya's farmers grow everything from cotton and citrus fruits to watermelons, fresh vegetables and flowers, which they supply to all corners of Turkey. (Antalya is the name of the city as well as the province.)

With its big port and its Free Trade Zone, the city is also a key Turkish exporting base. Cotton, chromium products and citrus fruits are shipped to the United States, Europe, Japan and the Middle East.

Its long, clean sandy beaches, unpolluted waters, ancient ruins, long summers and mild winters have made Antalya province appeal particularly to travellers from northern Europe. During March through April, it is possible to ski at **Saklıkent** (The Hidden City) and swim in the Mediterranean on the same day. The ski resort, which operates in the winter season, is in the Bey Dağları, only 30 miles (50 km) from the city and takes an hour to reach.

Cave men: In addition to all forms of water sports, Antalya also offers travellers special tours for hunting, mountain climbing, trekking and cave exploration. The Beldibi and Karain caves, once inhabited by people from the Stone Age, are among the biggest in Turkey. The two caverns are within a few miles of the city.

Mountain climbing expeditions and trekking tours in the Taurus Mountains can be arranged through **Trek Travel**, an Istanbul-based travel agency.

Antalya International Airport, where hundreds of charter flights arrive daily in the summer, is only six miles (10 km) from the city centre and within two hours' driving distance to most of the resorts and historical sites of the region. A 100-mile (160-km) stretch of territory around Antalya has the greatest concentration of hotels in Turkey – these comprise nearly half of the country's bed capacity. Some 50 five-star hotels and holiday villages and thousands of smaller hotels and pensions have opened in the past ten years to accommodate the tourism expansion, and many more big hotels are being built to meet demand.

The city, which has a population of 379,000 (1990), is located on cliffs that suddenly drop into the Mediterranean. Antalya is a garden city with two parks, lined with palm trees. These are **Atatürk Park** and **İnönü Park** (known as the Karaalioğlu Park). Both offer stunning views of the Bey Dağları and the Mediterranean. Antalya's two beaches are in the suburbs: **Konyaaltı Plajı** and **Lara Plajı**.

The city's main streets, Orgeneral Kenan Evren Bulvarı, Cumhuriyet

Left, Antalya's Fluted Minaret. Right, the Konyaaltı Beach.

Bulvarı and Atatürk Caddesi run parallel to the sea and are lined with apartment buildings and clothing shops, selling the latest in European fashions.

The ancient city: The Old Quarter, known as Kaleiçi, is separated from the new city by a series of Roman walls, and faces the marina. Most of the buildings in this part of the town are splendid 18th- and 19th-century traditional wooden Turkish houses that have been restored to small hotels and pensions or gift shops.

Antalya was founded by Attalus II, king of Pergamum (159-136 BC), during the early days of his rule and was named Attaleia after him. The town was ruled successively by the Romans and the Byzantines. During the Crusades, the Crusaders used the port to carry out raids against Moslems in the eastern Mediterranean. The city was conquered by the Seljuk Turks in 1207 and ruled by their vassals, the Hamitoğlu tribe. But in 1361, Peter de Lusignan, King of Cyprus, captured the city. It finally fell to the Ottoman Turks in 1391. In 1919, the Italian army occupied the city after the Ottoman Empire's defeat in World War I but withdrew in 1921 when the Turkish nationalists, under Kemal Atatürk, put up armed resistance to the Allied occupation.

The most charming place to stay in town is the Kaleiçi Old Quarter where travellers have a choice of many delightful, modestly-priced hotels and pensions. This district can be reached by car taking the modern road downhill from Cumhuriyet Bulvarı. There is a public park just above the marina where cars must be left. Bed and breakfast at a Kaleiçi pension costs around $10. **Doğan Pansiyon**, a smartly-renovated house on the Mermerli Banyo Sokak, is highly recommended. The upmarket **Marina Hotel** and **Tütav**, both on Mermerli Sokak, and **Turban Adalya Hotel** near the marina are the best hotels in the Old Quarter. They start from $50 for two.

More luxurious hotels in town are the **Talya Hotel** (on Fevzi Çakmak Caddesi), which is favoured by business-

DİDYMA APOLLON TAPINAĞI AYDIN-TÜRKİYE

men, the **Club Hotel Sera** (near Lara Plajı) which attracts wealthy German tourists, the **Dedeman Hotel Antalya** (on the road to Lara Plajı), which has a stupendous view of the Mediterranean and the Bey Dağları and Falez, overlooking the Konyaaltı Beach.

Antalya has a number of first-class restaurants. The **Hisar Restaurant, Kral Sofrası** and **Kirk Merdiven Restaurant** in the Old Quarter combine traditional Turkish dishes and seafood with an array of *meze* appetizers.

A compact city: Most of the city's historical sites can be seen in a two- or three-hour walk. A stroll of the town can start at Kaleiçi with a walk down to the marina, a former fisherman's wharf, now a bustling port with many yachts, schooners and motorboats. Street vendors sell juicy *ajur*, locally-produced long cucumbers, and *frenk yemişi*, a cactus fruit that tastes like a cross between watermelon and cantaloupe (said to help drop kidney stones).

A short walk uphill from Iskele Caddesi, a narrow winding street, brings you to the new town. Along this street are many souvenir shops. One shop with a courtyard sells colourful handmade *Döşemealtı* carpets, and young girls show how they produce the carpets on looms. *Döşemealtı* carpets get their name from the village near Antalya where they are produced.

On one street corner a man sells local teas, spices and edibles, including aromatic *ada çayı* (island tea), *dağ çayı* (mountain tea) and *papatya çayı* (dandelion tea) and *tirmis*, which looks like corn but tastes like hazelnuts.

Fluted minaret: Soon the twisting street reaches one of the main squares of Antalya, the **Kaleiçi Square**, which is now used as the **Clock Tower**, once a part of the ancient city walls. To the left is the **Yivli Minare** (Fluted Minaret), a brick tower that today is the symbol of Antalya. The 122-foot (37-metre) high tower was constructed in 1230 by Alaeddin Keykubat, a Seljuk Sultan. The original mosque to which it was attached was destroyed and replaced in 1373 by the **Alaeddin Mosque**.

Antalya's Marina and Old Quarter.

Just south of the Fluted Minaret toward the marina at a lower level is the **Karatay Medresesi**, an Islamic religious school built in 1250 by a Seljuk notable. Near it, but on higher ground, are two tombs: **Zincirkıran Mehmed Paşa Türbe** built in 1378, and the **Nigar Hatun Türbe**, constructed in 1502. The two Islamic theological seminaries, **Atabey Armağan Medresesi** and the **Ulu Cami Medresesi** nearby are in ruins.

Immediately behind the Clock Tower is the 17th-century **Tekeli Mehmet Paşa Mosque**. The mosque is unique because the Son Cemahat Yeri (the last place of assembly) is inside the mosque, covered by domes, instead of being on the outside. Foreigners can enter mosques, but must take off their shoes at the entrance, like all Turks. Women have to cover their hair and arms with scarves. You cannot enter wearing shorts and shoes as it would be disrespectful toward worshippers and would sully the old prayer carpets inside.

Chic clothing shops: Cumhuriyet Bulvarı, which eventually becomes Orgeneral Kenan Evren Bulvarı, is the long street that runs on an east-west axis through the city. A left turn at the clock tower takes you to the main shopping district of the town with chic clothing stores and fancy seafood restaurants. To the left is the Mediterranean with the Bey Dağları in the horizon. As one walks up, one comes to **Cumhuriyet Meydanı** (The Republic Square) with the big equestrian **Statue of Kemal Atatürk**, founder and first President of the Turkish Republic.

About three miles (five km) down this street (on Orgeneral Kenan Evren Bulvarı) near the Konyaaltı Plajı is the **Antalya Museum**, which has a rich collection of prehistoric artifacts from the Beldibi and Karain caves, statuary from the Greek, Hellenistic and Roman periods and ethnographic displays of clothing and tents used by the nomadic Yörük Turks, who inhabit the surrounding mountains during the summer and the plain in the winter.

Two futuristic five-star hotels are nearby: the **Sheraton Voyager Hotel** and the **Falez Hotel**, both overlooking the pebbly Konyaaltı Plajı.

Pickle juice: Right of the Clock Tower is Atatürk Caddesi, an avenue that cuts Cumhuriyet Bulvarı on a north-south axis. Several *lokantas* (traditional Turkish restaurants) in the alleys near the intersection serve good *kebab* dishes. Shops nearby sell a variety of unusual jams, jellies and pickles. One of the most interesting jams available is eggplant marmalade. Ice cold pickle juice (*turşu suyu*) is an excellent thirst quencher.

A right turn along Atatürk Caddesi brings the traveller to **Hadrian's Gate** (Hadrianus Kapısı), a magnificent three-arch marble gate erected in AD 130 in honour of Roman Emperor Hadrian's visit to the city.

Further down the street is the **Belediye Binası** (The Municipality) and the entrance to İnönü (or Karaalioğlu) Park, which is lined with palm trees. The park, named after Ismet İnönü, the second President of Turkey, has playgrounds for children, pleasant outdoor

Hadrian's Gate.

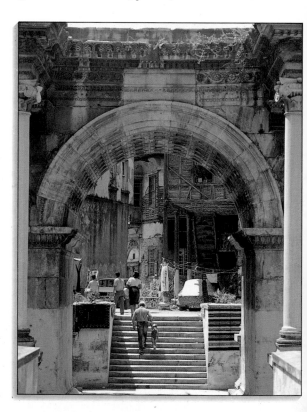

270

coffeehouses and benches to sit down and admire the stunning beauty of the sea and the distant mountains.

Roman tomb: A stroll to the eastern end of the park brings you to the pleasant **Mermerli Coffee House** and the **Hıdırlık Kulesi**, a rotund tower that is believed to be a tomb of a Roman Senator from Antalya. The tower is a miniature version of Hadrian's Tomb in Rome. Walk up the street that intersects the tower and you approach the **Kesik Minare** (the Truncated Minaret). This odd structure stands next to the **Korkut** or **Cumanın Mosque**, now in complete ruins. Built originally in the fifth century as the **Panaghia Church**, it was converted into a mosque by Korkut, the son of Sultan Beyazıt II, who added the minaret. The mosque and the minaret were destroyed in a huge fire during the 19th century.

The marina, just 10 minutes away from the Kesik Minare, has many pubs and discotheques. **Club 29, Birdland, Lece** and **Mr White's** are the most popular among the young for dancing

and socializing. Perched on the rocks above the marina, Club 29 has a swimming pool on the terrace with a magnificent view.

Antalya festival: A good time to visit Antalya is during the annual Antalya Golden Orange Film Festival and Art Festival held in autumn, usually in late October or early November, when the leading Turkish motion pictures of the year are screened and the top films, directors, actors and actresses get the Gold Oranges awards. The Festival coincides with the *Akdeniz (*Mediterranean*) Song Contest*, when soloists from nearly 20 Mediterranean countries perform in an international song contest. The song contest is usually held at the ancient Roman theatre in Aspendos, 25 miles (40 km) east of Antalya. The festivals are usually held in the first week of October.

Antalya is a paradise for hunters. The surrounding Bey Dağları and Taurus Mountains are rich in game birds and wildlife. Travellers come from all over the world to Antalya to hunt for the

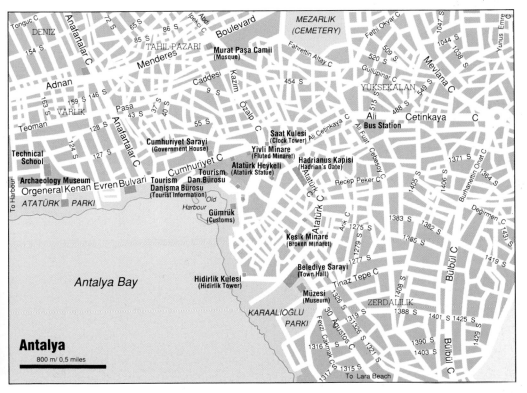

European Ibex (*yaban dağ keçisi*), an agile mountain goat with upturned horns abundant in the mountains. Game birds such as quail, turtledoves, wild ducks, and woodcocks can be found. Wildlife open to hunting include foxes, rabbits and martens. Trout fishing is possible on the Manavgat, Akçayı, Karaçayı and Köprüçayı rivers in the province of Antalya. For information on hunting and trout fishing, contact the Antalya Hunters Association (Avcılar Derneği) in Kilit Han.

Excursions from Antalya: Numerous ancient sites, caves and resorts are reachable from Antalya. One enchanting site to visit near Antalya is the **Düden Şelalesi**, a stunning series of waterfalls set in a woodland park about six miles (10 km) outside the city near the village of Varsak. The waterfalls are situated on the **Düden River**, one of several rivers that nurture the Antalya Plain, making it one of Turkey's most fertile regions. The best time to visit the site is in the morning or late afternoon when it is usually uncrowded. Several charming tea houses and outdoor restaurants, shaded by plane trees, are in the park. A Turkish version of *Snow White and the Seven Dwarfs* was once filmed in this setting.

The Düden River empties into the Mediterranean, plunging off Antalya's cliffs east of the city. A half-hour boat trip can be arranged from the marina to this site for a small fee. A smaller inland waterfalls east of the city is the **Kurşunlu Şelalesi**, which has a 17th-century water mill that was recently restored. The site is nine miles (15 km) from Antalya and can be reached by taking a road off highway E24/400 on the way to Alanya.

Nomadic carpets: The village of **Döşemealtı**, famous as a carpet-weaving centre, is located north of Antalya on highway E24/650 to Burdur. The colourful pure wool Döşemealtı carpets are made by nomadic Yörük tribesmen who inhabit the Taurus Mountains. These carpets have geometric patterns and a colour harmony of blues, dark greens and reds.

Nearby is a road that forks left to the **Karain Caves**, where men of the Stone Age lived from as early as 600,000 BC to the seventh century BC. Turkish archaeologists who excavated at Karain discovered the skull of a Neanderthal man and the fossil remains of an ancient elephant, hippopotamus and bear and tools dating back to the Paleolithic Period. Many of the findings are in the small **Karain Museum**, but some are also exhibited in the Antalya Museum. The cave is situated on the slope of the mountain above the museum. It covers a vast area consisting of several interconnected sections.

The **Kırkgöz Han**, a Seljuk inn with 40 rooms, is located on the Burdur Road, 15 miles (24 km) north of Antalya. Before reaching Döşemealtı highway 350, turn left toward **Korkuteli** off route E24 to Burdur. This road leads to **Evdir Han**, another Seljuk inn or caravansary. Evdir Han was built in 1219 and consists of a courtyard surrounded on four sides by porticoes. The southern entrance is magnificent with stalactites and geo-

Selling fancy patience beads and spoons.

272

metric designs. Nearby are the ruins of the Byzantine settlement **Eudoxia**, with several water channels and scattered sarcophagi.

Güver Uçurumu, a vast gorge forming a 705-foot (160-metre) drop down the cliffs, is located two miles (three km) north of Evdir Han. Formed millions of years ago, the gorge is indeed a stunning site.

The ruins of **Termessus**, one of the few cities in Asia that Alexander the Great could not conquer, are located in the mountains west of Güver Uçurumu. To get there take the road that forks left and has the sign reading Güllük Dağı Termessus Milli Parkı. The narrow, twisting road climbs into the mountains to the site. All cars must be left in a car park and the rest of the way (about one mile/2.2 km) must be ascended by foot. The region is considered a national park. Termessus, built on the slopes of several mountains, resembles an eagle's nest. During the Hellenistic and Roman periods it was a flourishing city with a population of 150,000 people.

Now it is in complete ruins, abandoned in the fourth or fifth century.

Termessus was a Pisidian city. The Pisidians, who inhabited the mountainous region north of Antalya fought many wars against the invading Greeks. The site includes numerous city walls, the King Street, an observation tower, water cisterns, a necropolis, a gymnasium, bathhouses, a colonnaded street, an agora and an astounding theatre overlooking the surrounding mountains. The **theatre**, built during the Hellenistic Period, has a seating capacity of 4,200 people. The orchestra is covered with rubble, which tumbled most probably because of earthquakes. A smaller odeon or assembly hall on the upper reaches of the city could seat 600 people. The most important site in Termessus is the **Tomb of Alcetas**, a general of Alexander the Great who was defeated by Antigonas in 319 BC and sought refuge in the city. He committed suicide, preferring death to being returned to his enemies. The ruins of three temples are visible, including the

Theatre at Termessus in ruins.

Temple of Zeus Solymeus, the **Minor Temple to Artemis** and the **Major Temple of Artemis**. The **Soldier's Tomb**, which gets its name from the shields, spears and helmet carved to the frieze on it, is in the necropolis. The **Founder's House**, west of the agora, is a Roman-type house in good condition.

Ancient cities: Scores of ancient ruins are east of Antalya, including Perge, Sillyum, Aspendos, Selge, Side and Seleucia in Pamphylia. Alarahan, on the road to the resort of Alanya, is famous for its castle and golden beaches.

The E24/400 highway can be eventually reached by driving east-bound from Antalya on Cumhuriyet Bulvarı and Sudi Turel Caddesi, named after a former Energy Minister from Antalya.

The first major destination east of Antalya is **Perge**, which is in the hills on a dirt road off the Antalya-Alanya highway, 12 miles (20 km) from Antalya. Signposted in yellow, the ancient Roman site lies just after a turn on the left.

Vaulted stadium: As you enter Perge, the first building you drive past is a second-century Roman amphitheatre with a seating capacity of 17,000 people. The main ruins are less than 900 yards (one km) off the amphitheatre. Visitors can park their cars and walk past the stadium, one of the best preserved in all of the eastern Mediterranean. The 772 by 112 feet (234 by 34 metre) stadium could seat about 12,000 people. The vaulted sections at the sides were probably shops.

The main city, just off the stadium, was once encircled by walls, some of which are still standing. The walls once had 30 towers. The city was laid out in a grid pattern with two main intersecting streets. Entrance to the ruins is by the **Later Gateway**, which leads to the **City Gate Complex**, a horseshoe-shaped courtyard flanked by two towers. This area is the most fascinating part of the city. Niches built inside the complex walls contained statues of gods and local heroes, such as Mopsus and Clacas, the mythic founders of the city. This complex was turned into a kind of memorial by Plancia Magna, a

The Gate Towers of Perge.

wealthy Pergaean lady. Just behind this complex is the **Monumental Gateway**, a three-arched structure of two stories, which was also adorned with statues. To the right of the circular courtyard is the agora, the city's main shopping centre.

The main thoroughfare of Perge is a colonnaded street with a water channel, running through the Later Gateway and the City Gate Complex. The water was brought to the city from a source at higher ground. About halfway up this avenue on the left is the **Church of Perge**, which was once a bishopric. At the end of the street, past the intersection, near the acropolis hill, is a **Nymphaion**. Turn left at the intersection to come first to a gymnasium, then a bath. A necropolis of several tombs are situated at the end of this street. Perge once boasted a famed temple dedicated to the Pergaean Artemis but its whereabouts today is unknown.

Nebulous early history: Perge's early history is nebulous. It is believed to have been founded by Greek migrants after the Trojan Wars. When Alexander the Great arrived in Pamphylia in the fourth century BC, the Pergaeans submitted without a struggle. Alexander used Perge as a base for mopping up operations on the coast of southwest Asia Minor. St Paul stopped in the city during his missionary adventures. The city continued as a Greco-Roman city, and was a bishopric during the early Byzantine Period. But it was probably abandoned after the seventh-century Arab invasions.

The ruins of **Sillyum** are six miles (10 km) east of Perge. A dirt road forking left from the Antalya-Alanya highway leads to Sillyum, built on a high acropolis hill. Although it hasn't been excavated and isn't often visited, Sillyum is more impressive than many of its neighbouring Pamphylian cities, according to the late George Bean. Greek settlers, possibly led by the seer Mopsus and his mixed multitudes, the same tribes that established Perge, founded the city after the fall of Troy around 1200 BC. Alexander the Great during his sweeping campaign through southern Asia Minor

The Roman theatre at Aspendos.

in the fourth century BC besieged Sillyum, but abandoned his plan to conquer it, deciding it was not worth controlling the inland city.

Ramps: The first structure travellers encounter as they ascend the acropolis hill at Sillyum is the **Lower City Gate**, a horseshoe-shaped edifice consisting of two towers and a small courtyard. Further on are the ruins of a palace and a stadium. The most impressive ruins in Sillyum are the ramps that lead up to the acropolis. The lower one, constructed in Hellenistic times, is the best preserved.

Near the top of the acropolis hill is the **Upper City Gate**, from which one can see the necropolis below as well as the city tower. Several interesting buildings are located on the acropolis, including a well-preserved Byzantine structure, a public hall and a smaller building that has the most interesting feature in Sillyum, an inscription in the local Pamphylian-Greek dialect, dating from the third century BC. Other buildings to be seen on the acropolis hill are an odeon, two theatres, a few houses, a 33-yard-long (10-metre) underground water cistern and several temples.

The Roman Theatre: The next destination in the direction of Alanya worth visiting is **Aspendos**, located near the village of Belkız, about 30 miles (50 km) from Antalya. A dirt road with the sign Aspendos forks to the left. The road continues over the **Köprüçay** (the Eurymedon River) for about three miles (five km). The first ruins you come to are the remains of two public baths. Next is the great **Aspendos Amphitheatre**, best preserved ancient Roman theatre in the world. As many as 20,000 people can be seated. The theatre, which is used today to stage the *Akdeniz Akdeniz* Song Contest, has retained its fine acoustic qualities. Visitors should test the acoustics by walking up to the very top gallery of the theatre, a steep climb, and sitting down. If someone on the stage below whispers or even drops a pin it can be clearly heard in the top gallery.

A grisly but unsubstantiated tale surrounds construction of this grand theatre in the second century. There was once a king of Aspendos who had a lovely daughter, named Belkız. As the young woman had many suitors, the king announced he would wed his daughter to the man who would construct the greatest public structure in the city. The king could not decide between the two rival contractors who sought the marriage of Belkız. One of them built the spectacular theatre. The other constructed the important and equally impressive aqueducts to supply the city with water. In the end, the king cut his daughter in half, giving each man a part of her body.

A half hour is enough to explore the theatre. The other buildings do not warrant more than a quick walk by. Near the theatre, and on the same level, is a 710-foot (215-metre) long stadium. In the vicinity of the stadium are some sarcophagi and tombs, including one hewn out of the rocks.

An acropolis behind the amphitheatre can be entered through three gates, of which the northernmost is best preserved though half-buried. The structures there include an agora, a market hall with several shops intact, a third-century basilica, a nymphaion, a council chamber and aqueducts. The aqueducts which carried water to the city from the mountains north, are the most impressive and best preserved water canals from the Roman period surviving in the eastern Mediterranean.

Visitors to Aspendos can return to the Alanya highway by crossing over the stone **Köprüçay Bridge**, built in the 13th century by the Seljuk Turks. The bridge is narrow but sturdy, and can accommodate one car at a time.

Selge: Soon another road forks left from the Antalya-Alanya Highway into the mountains through woods toward the towns of Taşağıl and Beşkonak, leading to the ruins of **Selge**. This road continues for the next 34 miles (55 km), passing Beşkonak, crossing a narrow Roman bridge, after which a side road to Karabuk must be taken. Selge is on the Zerk-Altınkay Road. Built on three hills, Selge was a Pisidian city. Pisidia was the name of the mountainous lake district north of Pamphylia. Selge has numerous ruins, including a theatre, a stadium, a customs house, tombs and sarcophagi and temples to Zeus and Artemis. A two-mile (three-km) wall encircled the city, parts of which still stand today. In ancient times Selge was famous for its wines and olives.

To reach the resort village of **Side**, a captivating settlement, motorists must return to the Antalya-Alanya highway. Side is located next to the ruins of one of the oldest and most impressive ancient settlements in Turkey. The ruins are situated on a peninsula 50 miles (80-km) east of Antalya. A road forks right to Side near a service station before reaching the town of Manavgat.

Romantic setting: The presence of an inhabited village next to the ancient ruins makes the site romantic indeed. To get the full visual impact of the town, Side should be visited during the November-March off season. Only a few tourists will be seen in the village then. Therefore the deserted ruins amidst the empty streets of modern Side will overwhelm the visitor. Many tourists who have visited Side have stayed on months, sometimes years, captivated by the charm of the village.

In summer, Side is crowded with tens of thousands of tourists and its hotels and pensions are fully booked. The village becomes commercialized. Loud music rising from scores of outdoor nightclubs, pubs and discotheques could easily drive anyone staying near the village berserk. Several five-star hotels have opened near Side, including **Novotel Turquoise**, **Le Meridien Hotel**, **Asteria Hotel**, **Iberotel Side Palace** and **Robinson Club Pamfilya**.

Side, which means "pomegranate," is a pre-Greek word that symbolized fertility. The city is believed to have been founded by migrants in the 13th or 14th centuries BC. In the sixth century, the city was dominated by the Lydians and then the Persians. It was conquered by Alexander the Great in 334 BC, and later controlled by the Ptolemites and the Seleucids. Between 188-78 BC, the Kingdom of Pergamum gained hegemony over the city, transforming it into an

Aqueduct at Side.

important commercial port, the remains of which can still be seen today. It became a Greco-Roman city, and an important Christian centre. But it was abandoned in the 12th century. The present inhabitants of Side are the descendants of Turkish refugees who fled Crete during the uprising of 1898 and settled in this village.

Pulitzer prize winner: Side was made world famous by the late Alfred Friendly, former managing editor of the *Washington Post* and Pulitzer Prize winning American journalist who lived there many years. A foundation set up by Friendly's wife has helped finance the restoration of many sites in Side, including the temples by the harbour.

The first ruins to be seen are the aqueducts, the remains of city walls and a Nymphaion. Suddenly the **Side Amphitheater** looms up on the left, next to the agora. Across is the **Bathhouse Museum**. Visitors enter the city by driving past the Vespasian Monument and the Later City Gate, an arched structure. Cars aren't allowed in the town.

The best way to see the town is to walk down the main street to the harbour, once the commercial hub of Pamphylia, now a simple fisherman's cove. To the left are the **Temple of Apollo** and the **Temple of Athena**, both dating from the second century, and a ninth-century Byzantine basilica. The eastern shore of the town brings one to the **Temple of Men**, a moon Goddess. A crescent-shaped sandy beach extends east of the site for many miles. Soon one comes back to the amphitheater. The **State Agora** and **M-Building**, which resembles a palace, are just behind the well-preserved theatre.

Stupendous view: Much of the walls around the city are either submerged in the sand or partly sunken in the sea. For a stupendous view of Side, visitors should climb to the top row of the amphitheatre. The Museum is an ancient bath that has been restored and turned into a museum. It contains many fine Roman statues and sarcophagi, several of which are in the courtyard. The bathhouse, built during the Roman Period, is well preserved. It has an *Apodyterium*

or changing room, a *Cal-darium* or hot room, a sweating room and a cooling room. The bathhouse was a place where men socialized and discussed local and political affairs.

The next town on the Antalya-Alanya highway is Manavgat, situated on the Manavgat River. Other than the pleasant riverside teahouses, there isn't much to see in the town itself, except for the bustle of the wholesale market from where trucks deliver the produce of the region, including giant melons, to other parts of Turkey. But a road forks to left before the entrance to the town toward Manavgat Şelalesi (Falls), the ancient town of Seleucia in Pamphylia and Oymapınar Barajı (Dam). This road goes 11 miles (17 km) to the **Oymapınar Dam**, one of the biggest hydroelectric dams in Turkey. A visit to the dam and its lake is worthwhile if permission to enter is granted by the guards. Three miles (five km) from the Antalya-Alanya road is the turnoff for **Manavgat Şelalesi**. A short walk leads to the falls. One of the best places in this

It's all in the family.

area to have lunch is by the picture postcard falls, along which there are several restaurants serving *alabalık* (trout) or *piliç şiş* (chicken on a skewer) or *piliç çevirme* (barbecue chicken) and tasty appetizers. The **Manavgat River** is one of Turkey's main sources for trout fishing. It is also one of the few places in Turkey where river rafting has been tried by sports enthusiasts. Motorboat rides up the Manavgat River from Side and Manavgat are possible to a point further downstream.

Seleucia in Pamphylia is one of several cities in Anatolia named after the Seleucia kings of Syria. The most famous of these is Seleucia in Pieria, the ancient port of Antioch. Seleucia in Pamphylia is located about three miles (five km) north of Manavgat Falls and is reachable from the village Şıhlar. A turnoff points in the direction of Selevkiye (the Turkish for Seleucia). The ruins to see in Seleucia include an aqueduct, an ancient bridge, city walls, a bathhouse, an agora and an odeon.

Alanya is about 30 miles (50 km)

from Manavgat along the E24/400 highway. The road follows the sea closely, passing many fine deserted beaches along the way to Alanya, including the **Incekum Beach**. About 19 miles (30 km) east of Manavgat a village road forks to the left and continues to the **Alarahan**, an inn constructed in 1232 by the Seljuk Turks, consisting of a courtyard surrounded by vaulted rooms and corridors. The inn also has a fountain and a *mescit* or small mosque. Nearby is fortress of **Alarakale**, built to protect the inn from marauders. Nearly halfway to Alanya is a 13th-century Turkish caravansary, **Serapsu Han** on the left.

Giant gastropod: Alanya (formerly Coracesium) is built around a rocky peninsula that resembles a gigantic gastropod from a distance. Jutting out to the sea like an immense mollusc, the red peninsula is crowned by a long crenellated fortress that was built by the Seljuk Turks in the 13th century to dominate the Mediterranean Coast. In ancient times, the peninsula served as

The Manavgat Waterfalls.

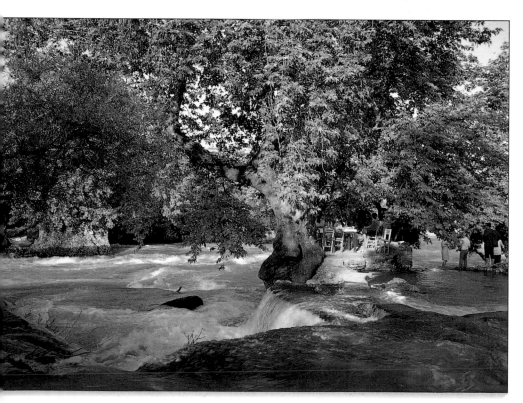

the headquarters of Pamphylian pirates who raided passing commercial ships for booty and slaves.

Alanya has some of the finest beaches in Turkey. It's worthwhile spending some time swimming and tanning on the long beach that lies before Alanya. The first site in Alanya to be seen is the **Damlataş Cave**, on the edge of the peninsula before entering the city. The damp air in this claustrophobic cave with thousands of colourful stalactites is believed to be beneficial for those suffering from asthma and other respiratory diseases. But elder people with heart ailments should avoid it.

Alanya is a pleasant touristic town, located on the foot of the peninsula, with many seaside restaurants and hotels, of which the **Club Alantur**, **Azak Hotel** and **Hotel Banana** are highly recommended. The town has a broad Board Walk-like avenue and a fine harbour where big ships can dock. Alanya is known among Turks as "Little Germany" because of the tens of thousands of Germans who visit it annually on holiday. The town's symbols are the 13th-century **Red Tower** (Kızıl Kule), a crenellated defensive building, and its ancient **shipyards**.

Alanya Castle, perched on top of the peninsula at a dizzying height of 800 feet (243 metres), dominates the coast, and overlooks the town and the majestic cliffs that plunge into the sea. The ancient walls around the old city wind four miles (seven km) uphill like the Great Wall of China, to **İçkale**, the citadel, capped by three towers. Inside is a courtyard with a Byzantine **Church of Saint George** (Aya Yorgi) and a pleasant outdoor coffeehouse.

A small outdoor shop in the courtyard sells baby dolls made from squashes, a particular art in this part of Turkey. At the northeast corner of the courtyard is the spot called the **Adam Atacağı**, (the place from where men are thrown). It was there that condemned men were hurled down the cliffs to their deaths. A condemned man would be pardoned, according to one legend, only if he could toss a pebble from that height into

A minaret spikes the sky in old Alanya.

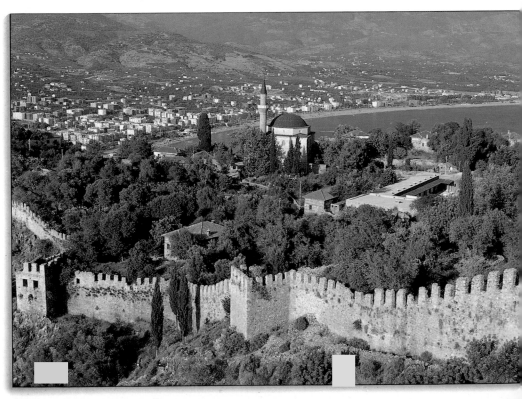

280

the sea, an impossible task. Next to it is a deep open pit covered by railings that some people suggest was a dungeon where the prisoners were kept.

From the citadel, the **Cılvarda Burnu**, a rocky promontory on which there are the ruins of three buildings, including the town's mint (**Darphane**), a tower and a monastery complex, is visible. The only way to reach these buildings is to take a boat ride along the peninsula from Alanya to the promontory and walk up.

The Old Quarter: The inhabited **Old Quarter** of the city is in the middle section of the castle. A left road as you are about to leave the castle leads to the Old Quarter, passing the fortress known as the **Ehmedek**. In the Old Quarter, you can see the **Akçebe Sultan Mescidi** (small mosque) and **Türbe** (Tomb). These structures, built in 1230 by the Seljuk Sultan Alaeddin Keykubat I, consists of three sections, two of which contain tombs. Other buildings of note in this quarter are the **Mecdüddin Cistern**, which is still in use, a caravansary

(a kind of inn) that is comprised of a rectangular courtyard surrounded by rooms, a depot and the **Bedesten** (a shopping centre). Nearby is the **Alaeddin Mosque**, a 13th-century structure that was reconstructed by Ottoman Sultan Süleyman the Magnificent in the 16th century.

Alanya is famous for its ice cream and **Bamyacı Ice Cream Parlour** in Güler Pınarı Mahalesi and in Keykubat Caddesi makes the tastiest in town.

The Kızıl Kule, a five-story, 10-foot (33-metre)-high octagonal tower which now houses the **Ethnographical Museum** is a walking distance from downtown Alanya along the harbor. The museum exhibits Yörük tents, rugs and armour. Walk further down to the **Shipyards** (Tersane) nearby. Used by Seljuks to build their fleet, the dockyard is still used today to construct small boats. During the Ottoman Period, Alanya was one of the Turks' main naval bases. In the 16th century, Turkish navies turned the Mediterranean into a Turkish lake.

Frolicking on the Turkish Riviera.

ΕΙΖ Η ΤΙϹ ΩΖ ΕΙΝΕ ΤΙϹ ΕΥ
ΕΚ ΦΗΝΑϹ ΠΗ ΓΗΝ ΤΙ
ΠΟΙΜΕΝΙΟΝ ΓΙΝ ΩϹ
ΚΕΝΗ Ϲ ΩΝ ΕΙΕΡΩΝ Λ

...ΕΤΟ ΚΑΛΛΟ ΠΕΤΡΑ
...Ν ΠΟΤΕ ΚΡΥΠΤΟΜΕΝΗ
...Ε ΦΙΛΟΝ ΒΑΣΙΛΕΥΣΙΝΕΤ...
...Σ ΑΜΕΝΟΝ ΚΑΘΑΡΩΣ

THE EASTERN MEDITERRANEAN

Turkey's eastern Mediterranean coast begins east of Alanya and ends along the Syrian frontier south of Antakya, stretching for 420 miles (672 km). The region was known to the Romans as the Cilician Coast. The area can be roughly divided into three distinct geographical zones: the rugged, mountainous terrain that stretches from Alanya to Silifke, which was known as Rough Cilicia; the vast fertile plains to the east, which was known as Smooth Cilicia, today's Çukurova; and the areas east of Adana, which extend into the Hatay, a province bordering Syria, with Antakya its capital.

Banana capital: In Rough Cilicia, the Taurus Mountains plunge into the Mediterranean over precipitous cliffs. Here and there are tiny valleys where bananas and olives are grown. The Alanya-Silifke highway winds along the ridges of the mountains. The banana capital of Turkey is Anamur, a town with a population of 35,000 halfway along Rough Cilicia. Anamur's banana growers are fond of saying their bananas taste better than the popular imported Cikita brand of South America. Anamur has miles of uncrowded golden beaches, dominated by a magnificent Armenian Castle. The ancient ruins of Anemurium are west of the town.

Rough Cilicia ends east of Taşucu and Silifke. The name Silifke is a Turkish version of Cilicia. Numerous sites of historic interest are near this coastal town, including the ghastly pits known as Heaven and Hell and the Kızkalesi (the Maiden's Castle), which stands on an island.

Neolithic settlement: Mersin, today Turkey's third biggest port after Istanbul and Izmir, started out as a neolithic settlement, rivalling in antiquity the oldest archaeological finds in Egypt and Mesopotamia.

The town of Tarsus, further east, was the birthplace of St Paul the tentmaker,

Preceding pages, the mosaic of the Three Maidens in Silifke.

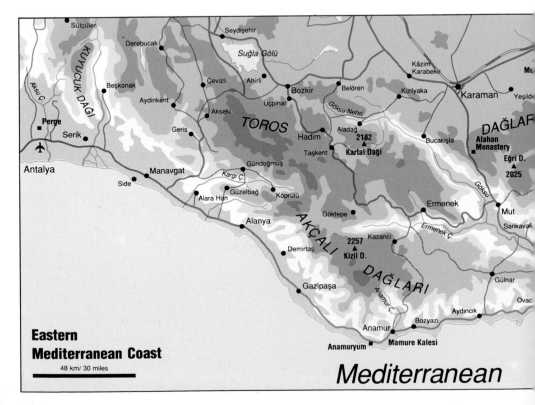

Eastern Mediterranean Coast

48 km/ 30 miles

Mediterranean

whose missionary journeys helped spread Christianity westward into Anatolia from Judea. Today it has become a booming market town. It was also in Tarsus that Antony summoned Cleopatra for their first meeting that began their big romance and ended in their tragic deaths.

North of Tarsus, high up in the Taurus Mountains, engineers nearly 3,000 years ago built an East-West short cut through Asia Minor known as the Cilician Gates. The armies of Cyrus the Younger, Alexander the Great and the Crusaders marched through this mountain pass. A modern highway today crosses the Taurus Mountains at Ulukışla east of the Cilician Gates, connecting the Anatolian steppes with the Cilician Coast.

Industrial hub: Adana, Turkey's fourth largest city and cotton boom town, stands in the centre of the vast Çukurova. It is a big industrial city, which produces cotton fabrics, tractors and harvesters and processed food, such as margarine. Numerous towns and cities can be reached from Adana, including Yumurtalık, which is the terminal of the 612-mile (980-km) Iraq-Turkey crude oil pipeline. The town has a big port which usually lined with ocean-going oil tankers.

The port of Iskenderun, where a huge Soviet-built iron and steel complex operates, is east of Adana, surrounded by the Amanos Mountains.

From Iskenderun, the road climbs the mountains to Belen Pass, the ancient Syrian Gates, to Antakya (the former Antioch). This was the site of St Paul's first ministry, the third largest city of the Roman Empire, outranked only by Rome and Alexandria. It was also in Antioch that the term Christians was first applied to the followers of Jesus. Today Iskenderun and Antakya (both of which belong to the province of Hatay) are the principal Arab-speaking cities of Turkey.

Antakya has an important museum which contains some fine mosaics from the Hellenistic, Roman and early Christian periods.

ROUGH CILICIA

Heading east beyond Alanya the highway takes to the sky on the arms of the Taurus Mountains as the first reaches of the **Cilician Coast** begin. For the next 420 miles (672 km), Cilicia's history unfolds like a colourful tapestry, its length textured with tales of conquests, corsairs and Cleopatra.

This stretch of the Mediterranean offers some of the country's most spectacular scenery and uncommon diversions. Where else can one end a day of castle-hopping with a sunset swim to a Crusader fortress, or drink from the Fountain of Knowledge after a sneak preview of Heaven and Hell?

Land of contrasts: Cilicia is a land of contrasting natural beauty that both beckons and repels. In ancient times the western region was known as "Cilicia Tracheia" (Rough Cilicia) as here, the Taurus Mountains crowd the coast, sending craggy slopes plunging into the Mediterranean. Cilicia Tracheia appeared so intimidating to the ancients that even Alexander the Great crossed it off his list after one look at its impenetrable terrain.

The eastern region, known as Cilicia Campestris (Smooth Cilicia), begins at the Lamus River, past Silifke, where the Taurus pull back from the coast, leaving a vast fertile delta that has long sustained civilization.

Cilicia was forever caught in the tug-of-war between rival kingdoms and aspiring powers and a succession of peoples ruled the land including the Phoenicians followed by the Greeks who fought in the Trojan War.

Pirates terrorize coast: The Roman Empire claimed Cilicia as one of its provinces and the Romans embarked upon a successful mission to wipe out Cilicia's most famous denizens: pirates. These buccaneers fed the Roman slave trade during the first centuries BC, terrorizing the coastal cities and plundering Syrian ships as they passed on their way to Aegean trading ports. They ruled the waves unhindered until 67 BC

when General Pompey put an end to the motley lot and piracy disappeared until Arab ships pestered the Byzantines in the seventh century.

In the 12th century, the kingdom of Lesser Armenia flourished along the coast, allying itself during the next 300 years with the invading Crusaders, who left their Frankish touch in the string of medieval coastal castles. When Armenian rule faltered, the Lusignans arrived from Cyprus, only to be overwhelmed by the fierce Seljuk and Karamanid Turcomen tribes.

Prosperity and progress eluded Cilicia and the region succumbed to Ottoman rule in the 15th century, eventually receding into anonymity. It was only during the last half century that Cilicia reemerged, fuelled by a drive to play a role in the country's economy.

Sustaining industry: The lowland of Cilicia Campestris is now called the Çukurova Plain and is the centre of Turkey's cotton crop which amply sustains a burgeoning textile industry. Two commercial ports were built, in Mersin and Taşucu, opening trade lines with the outside world and helping establish the region as an industrial base.

A government agriculture project transformed the rugged slopes of Cilicia Tracheia into patchwork valleys, crisscrossed with banana plantations and olive, lemon and fig orchards. And best of all, centuries of obscurity have left most areas of Cilicia untouched. Cilicia Tracheia appears much the same as it did in Alexander's day: beautiful, unspoiled and treacherous.

Treacherous is just one way to describe the 136-mile (217-km) drive from Alanya to Silifke as the coast road twists its way above pine forest gorges and turquoise coves of Rough Cilicia.

Hairpin turns: If one is driving, travel must be limited to the daytime when the region's beauty can be appreciated and the hairpin turns seen!

Public bus companies serve the coast frequently and have terminals (*Oto Gar*) in Antalya, Side, Alanya, Anamur, Silifke, Mersin and Adana. Reservations need to be made a day in advance as the buses are always packed with locals, tourists and *asker* (soldiers) on their way to assignment.

Travellers should reserve a seat with a seaview, but they should prepare for the sun: none of the buses have smoked-glass windows.

Seleucid fortress: The first remains of ancient civilization in Cilicia lie in **Aydap**, ancient Iotepe, one of three fortress-cities established in the second century BC by Seleucid King Antiochus IV to protect Seleucid interests from invading pirates and mountain tribes. **Gazipaşa**, the next town, is the site of the king's second city (Selinus) now marked by meagre ruins by the beach. Selinus made the social column in AD 117 when Roman Emperor Trajan died while passing through after the Parthian War. His death is considered by many to be the very point marking the beginning of the Roman Empire's decline.

The third and best preserved city is **Antiochia-ad-Cragum**, and it's exactly as its name suggests – on a crag. Ruins run helter-skelter onto a rocky promontory which once bore the brunt of continuous pirate attacks.

Leaving behind the ghost of Antiochus to fend for himself, the highway glides into a magnificent valley overgrown with terraced banana plantations which embroider the mountainside and run to the shores of a beautiful bay. This is **Kaledıran**, the ancient Calendiris, above which the skeleton of a Byzantine fortress keeps watch from a rocky ledge. The settlement is a good place to stop for a swim and sample the sweet *muz* (bananas).

Tasty carobs: Cilicia's forest is one of the most beautiful and well-tended in Turkey. Sleepy men sell *muz* under straw huts while young girls work the dangerous roads, balancing trays of nuts and fruit on top of their heads hoping to tempt tourists. The weird-looking brown pod stacked on a string is the carob (*keçiboynuzu*).

With Kaledıran in the distance, the road descends to a wide fertile delta, the Anamur Plain.

Straight ahead is **Anamur**, a town

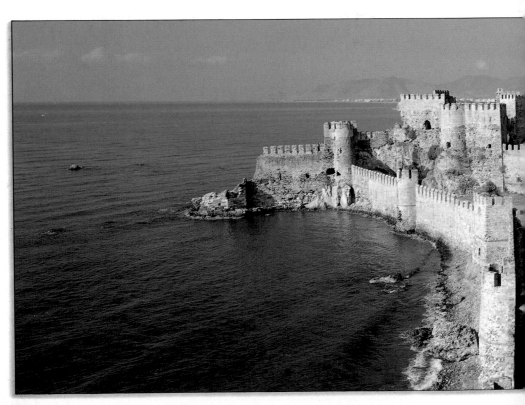

with about 35,000 residents, many of whom are unhappy that they have been ignored by travel books and tourists. Despite little historical significance, Anamur is a convenient base from which to visit surrounding sites. The town has an interesting Seljuk period mosque dating from the early 14th century, pleasant beachfront camping and a comfortable, sprawling three-star hotel, the Anahan.

Phoenician colony: Four miles (seven km) from the ancient city of Anemurium (Greek for windy place), sits **Anamur Burnu** (Cape Anamur). Originally a Phoenician colony, it later became a Hellenistic city and was incorporated into Roman Cilicia in AD 72. After continual harassment by pirates and mountain tribes, Anemurium was abandoned in the seventh century as the Arabs showed up.

A defensive wall climbs to a citadel and two aqueducts run parallel to the main road through town. It's worth hiring a guide to help you uncover the many mosaics and frescoes which are hidden throughout the site of domed tombs and churches.

Cape Anamur is Turkey's closest point to Cyprus, only 40 miles (64 km) away. On a clear day one can easily distinguish the Beşparmak Dağları (the Pentadaktylos or Five Finger Mountains) that run along the northern coast of the Mediterranean island. Gigantic radars on Cape Anamur sweep the eastern Mediterranean for enemy aircraft and naval vessels.

Crusader fortress: The massive outline of **Mamure Castle** commands the coastline two miles (three km) east of Anemurium. One of the largest and best preserved Crusader fortresses in Asia Minor, it was first mentioned in the third century as a Roman stronghold before becoming a pirates' den. During the 12th century the castle was incorporated into Armenia's defence system, and later passed to the Lusignans of Cyprus, the Seljuks and the Karamanid Turcomens. The Ottomans moved in, added the mosque and other restorations and remained there until the sun

The Castle of Anamur dominates the coast.

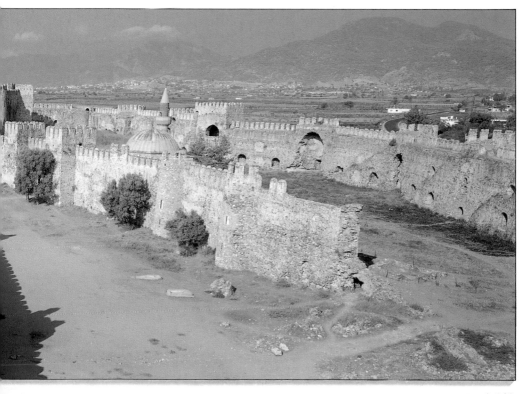

set on their empire in 1923. The circular stairway leads up the huge defence tower to a panoramic view of the castle's 36 towers and massive ramparts. Matches are needed to light its paths.

The **Köşebükü Mağarası**, one of Cilicia's famous wishing and asthma curing caves, is 11 miles (17 km) from Anamur in a lovely pine forest on the Taurus foothills. Locals believe the cave's air cures asthma while others make pilgrimages to the cavern depths to throw money into a pit and ask for Allah's blessing.

Taxis are found at the bus station but meters seem out of fashion and price haggling is a necessary evil.

Softa Kalesi (Scholar's Castle) looms high on a ridge just eight miles (12 km) east of Anamur. A hardy hike is required to reach the massive defensive walls of this 12th-century fortress. Before Softa Kalesi, the road winds through a beautiful forest and passes the government-run **Pullu Camping Grounds**, situated in a pine grove on its own private beach.

Aydıncık sits on a bay tucked between the arms of the Taurus Mountains 35 miles (57 km) from Anamur. Also known as Gilindere, it is the impressive site of ancient Kelenderis, one of the oldest colonies in Rough Cilicia, founded in the fifth century BC by Greeks from Samos.

Further on, the village of **Boğsak** rings a turquoise bay punctuated by the ghostly **Provencal Island**, a perfect Halloween haunt as the island is blanketed with tombs, sarcophagi and medieval ruins. The Gothic arches of a Crusader chapel, built by the Knights of St John, add to the general gloom.

On the western reaches of the bay sits **Liman Kalesi** (Harbour Castle), another medieval fortress built by the Armenians in the 14th century.

Taşucu, once a small village, is now a commercial port and one of two coastal departure points for the Turkish Republic of Northern Cyprus (the second is Mersin). Hotels and restaurants line the bay and on the edge of town a sprawling paper factory makes use of the abundant Cilician timber. Travellers who want to take the ferry to Northern Cyprus should stay here. Those travelling to Greece or to the Greek-controlled Southern Cyprus should not have their passports stamped for Northern Cyprus. (Officials will stamp a separate sheet of paper instead). A 14th-century Turkish fortress guards the pretty beachhead.

Before Silifke, a sign points to **Aya Thekla** (Meryemelik in Turkish), a Christian pilgrimage site devoted to St Thekla, St Paul's first convert and Christianity's first female martyr. Thekla became one of Byzantium's most popular saints and her life story was the basis for book the *Acts of Paul and Thekla*.

According to the Acts, Thekla met Paul in Iconium (Konya) and was so moved by his preaching on the virtues of chastity that she cried out, "I shall cut my hair and follow thee whitersoever thou goest." With that pious promise, she ended her engagement and incurred the wrath of a jilted fiance who his plotted revenge.

Divine intervention: Upon his orders, Thekla was stripped naked, set upon a pyre in a crowded amphitheatre, and wild lions were sent in for the kill. Divine intervention prevailed, and as the Acts report, "there was about her a cloud, so that neither the beasts did touch her nor was she seen naked."

Thekla was released, became St Paul's chief follower and founded a convent in a cave in Seleucia. One version has Thekla living to a ripe age, another claims she was murdered by thieves. Two basilicas were built in her honour. The first by Constantine after his conversion to Christianity and the second, located over the cave, was built in the fifth century by Emperor Zeno.

The underground chapel has frescoes and mosaics and has been turned into a small museum exhibiting locally-found sculpture.

One mile (1.6 km) inland is **Silifke**, the ancient Seleucia-ad Calcynum, founded in the third century BC by Seleucus I Nikator. Silifke is the largest town in Rough Cilicia and is divided by the **Göksu River**.

Silifke's **Archaeological Museum** is 190 yards (200 metres) from the bus station and opens daily. Numismatists will revel in the large collection of Hellenistic coins. Close by is the ruin of a Roman temple dedicated to Zeus.

Silifke is renowned for its folk dancers and each May hosts the international Music and Folklore festival.

The town's most visible site is a massive medieval fortress which looms atop a flat hill. This citadel was built by Byzantines in the seventh century as a bulwark against Arabs and passed to the Crusaders, Armenians and Seljuks before finally becoming Ottoman property in 1471.

Byzantine cistern: Below the hill lies **Tekir Ambarı**, a Byzantine cistern built from an ancient cave. Restaurants offering Silifke's famous creamy yogurt and a "*manzara*" (a view) have invaded the grounds. One detour from Silifke must not be missed. The road winds through the **Göksu Valley** along one of the most scenic drives in Turkey and leads to the Alahan Monastery.

Alahan Monastery is perched on a narrow mountain terrace nearly 7,000 feet (2,100 metres) above sea level and overlooks a fabulous view of winding the Göksu Valley.

Twenty-eight miles (45 km) out of Silifke the pine forests give way to olive orchards as life takes on a harsher edge and the first reaches of the Anatolian plateau begin. This is the domain of the nomad, whose straw huts line the roadside, their sides bulging with colourful *kilim* cushions (*yastıks*).

Mut, the proverbial town-in-the-middle-of-nowhere appears on the horizon. The site of ancient Claudipolis, it was founded in 50 BC by Marcus Aurelius Polemo, who undertook the crazy task of uniting the wild mountain tribes under one kingdom.

After Mut, the Taurus range reappears and 15 minutes later a sign marks a 1.3 mile (two km) road to the fifth-century Alahan Monastery. A one-hour trek through the pine forest to the mountain ledge in the early morning is an exhilarating experience. Before the final bend, north toward Aloda, one can see early Christian cave churches carved into the cliff sides.

The Evangelist Church is the first part entered from the western terrace. The church's surviving portal has detailed friezes symbolizing the triumph of Christianity over paganism. A close examination shows saints Gabriel and Michael trouncing the likes of Cybele, the Anatolian mother goddess, as well as a bull and a priest of Isis.

The portal leads to a circular baptistery, which is next to the Eastern Church, a simple yet beautiful doomed basilica crafted by expert masons in the early-sixth century. Three interior arches, held by Corinthian columns, grace the central aisle.

Tempting trails offer short-cuts down the mountain, but a layer of pine needles make the going dangerous. Unless the traveller is a mountain goat or a sure-footed villager, he should stick to the beaten path. Buses passing from Konya to Silifke will stop to pick up travellers who wait by the road at Alahan's one and only café.

Alahan
Monastery,
north of
Silifke.

SMOOTH CILICIA

The second detour from Silifke is to **Uzuncaburç**, just 19 miles (30 km) to the north. This is the site of the former Olba/Diocaesarea, founded in the third century BC by Seleucis I Nikator. It is a peaceful and impressive site, displaying a medley of Hellenistic, Roman and Byzantine ruins.

It's business as usual in Uzuncaburç as villagers tend to vineyards, goats and apple orchards. Enterprising women have set up black wool nomad tents under which they sell their much-prized handiwork – ancient crafts at thoroughly modern prices.

Corinthian Order: After paying the attendant, you enter the city through the Roman parade gate. Head down the colonnaded street to the **Temple of Zeus Olbios** which was erected at the end of the third century BC, making it the oldest known structure of the Corinthian Order in the world. Thirty of its columns still stand; four are topped with Corinthian capitals. In the grassy square to the side of the temple, sculpted friezes display the exaggerated visages of lions, bulls and monsters.

To the west stands the **Temple of Tyche**, goddess of fortune. Five Corinthian columns, each reportedly cut from a single slab of Egyptian granite, tower above a massive foundation. To the north rises an original city gate with three well-preserved arches; one proclaims the town's name, Diocaesarea. Out by the entrance, the road leads north past a small cafe where the village men play perpetual games of *okey*, a simplified version of *mahjong*, between glasses of *çay* (tea).

The Long Tower: To the right stands a five-storey, 73-feet (22-metre) Hellenistic tower which once served as a priest's tomb and later formed part of a defence and communication network with other towers throughout the region. The village took its name from the tower. Uzuncaburç means "long tower" in the Turkish language.

The road to Uzuncaburç winds through pine forests, passing through Demircili, the first-century Roman city of Imbrogin. Several unusual temple-like tombs can be seen, the most interesting is the double-decker **Çifte Anıt Mezarları** (Twin Monument Tombs), which is visible from the road.

Taxi anyone? *Dolmuş* depart for Uzuncaburç at 11 am daily across from Silifke's Tourism Office. If you miss the *dolmuş*, share a cab. A private taxi will cost you as much as five times the shared amount.

Back on the coast road, stop at **Yapraklı Eşik** (The Cove with Leaves), a perfectly sculptured cove with enticing turquoise water. Its currents are of two different temperatures: the top layer is a chilly 8°C, but the bottom layer is a soothing 23°C.

Susanoğlu, the next village, has a wide bay and long beach. Local vacationers have turned this once pretty setting into an eyesore. Military-style barb wire fencing encloses the beach and the clutter of pensions, motels and cafés and the people crowding it.

In kinder days, Susanoğlu was known as Corasium, a major Byzantine port specializing in the trading of salt. Traces of salt pans and catch basins are carved into the rocks on the east side of the bay.

Phallus of Priapus: A detour eight miles (12 km) north through Susanoğlu leads to the ancient city of **Paslı**, the best-preserved Roman site in the region and home of the famous **Mezgit Kalesi**, the **Temple Tomb of the Fearless Satrap** (Persian governor). From the monument's right side appears a remarkable relief – the outstanding **Phallus of Priapus**, the god of fertility and vitality, whose glorious presence bears testimony to the courage and fearlessness of the deceased. As the tale goes, Priape was the illegitimate son of Zeus and Aphrodite, and Hera, in a jealous fit, deformed the child, giving him a phallus equal to his height.

Priape, also known as God Bes, ranked high with the ancient Anatolians who erected temples and sacrificed donkeys in the deity's honour. Sacred wishing rocks, scattered throughout the countryside, were visited by young women who begged the God of Fertility for a good husband.

Rumour has it that village girls still make the pilgrimages to the monument in Paslı, and whisper, "Wake up oh my good fate, before my roses fade." Tiny bronze Priape statues and postcards are extremely popular with tourists who twitter at the prospect of shocking friends back home.

Narlıkuyu (Pomegranate Spring), is a sliver of bay lined with lively seafood restaurants and a small hotel, but it's the **Kızlar Hamamı** (the Bath of the Maidens) that lures visitors. This fourth-century Roman bath has a lovely floor mosaic depicting the **Three Graces**, Aglaia, Euphrosina and Thalis, the daughters Zeus had with Eurynome, daughter of the Ocean. The bath is housed in a small nondescript shed in the village and is open daily. A small fee is charged.

On the shore a spring sprouts fresh water into the sea – this is the **Fountain**

A farmer drives his tractor through a colonnaded field.

of Nus (the Fountain of Knowledge). Its powers must be taste tested!

Across Narlıkuyu await the other worldly sites of Cennet Deresi and Cehennem (Heaven's Stream and Hell), which form the **Corycian Cave Complex**. These massive sinkholes were created centuries ago when the ground collapsed from chemical erosion by an underground stream.

Cennet (Heaven) is an enormous pit, measuring 285 yards (250 metres) long and 77 yards (70 metres) at its deepest point. The stairway to heaven is lined not with "pearly gates" but with sagging trees, littered with paper talismans and petitions placed by superstitious visitors asking for cures and good luck. Obviously, anything will suffice, as snack bags and candy wrappers join hundreds of ribbons and shredded tissue paper strewn on the branches of the trees. It isn't a heavenly sight.

Descending the 452 rock steps into heaven's bowels may convince the visitor that he has accidentally landed in hell. The descent is foreboding as the air becomes stifling and the sun is blotted out by trees. A roaring sound, which grows louder with each step, does nothing to soothe the nerves.

At the grotto's end, the **Church of St Mary** guards the entrance to the gloomy cavern, which according to mythology, was the Home of Typhon – the monster with 100 dragon heads and snakes for feet. The roaring sound comes from a river deep inside the cavern, which ancients believed was the River Styx, the river encircling Hades over which boatmen known as Charon ferried dead bodies.

Symbolic assurance: When the Byzantines arrived they were uneasy with the site's evil connotations and ascribed it heavenly powers, building a fifth-century basilica to honour the Virgin Mary at the cave's entrance, as symbolic assurance that Typhon was put to rest forever. The Church of St Mary has well-preserved frescoes showing Christ with two saints.

Venture into the cave with the help of a guide and a lantern, but save your

The church in Heaven.

breath because the climb back to the real world is definitely hellish.

Cehennem (Hell) lives up to its reputation. The path to this chasm is lined with littered trees sporting paper petitions, this time asking to keep the hounds of hell at bay. The chasm resembles the open jaws of a monster; it is the perfect façade for the entrance to the underworld, as the ancients believed.

If the stairs of Heaven and sight of Hell leaves you gasping for breath, you should head to the **Wishing and Asthma Caves** (Dilek Astım Mağarası), also part of the Corycian Cave complex, and 330 yards (300 metres) west of Heaven.

The tiny resort village of **Kızkalesi** (Maiden's Castle) lies a few minutes east. Known as Corycus in ancient times, the Turks call it Kızkalesi after the Byzantine fortress of the same name which floats in a storybook setting 660 feet (200 metres) offshore. Its landlocked partner, the massive 12th-century Corycus rambles on the coast just east of the sea castle. At one time the fortresses were connected to each other by a sea wall which formed a secure port for Corycus.

Pirates' haunt: Corycus is believed to have been settled before the fourth century BC and during the second and third centuries BC it was a strategic harbour and a famous pirates' haunt. The region prospered under Roman and Byzantine rule but declined slowly over the following centuries and was eventually abandoned; only during the past 40 years have people returned.

However, Kızkalesi of today, with its wild frontier town atmosphere, is far from its former days of splendour. The beach is crowded with hotels, motels and pensions – many only half-finished, and in the peak summer months the streets are filled with vacationers, mainly locals from Adana, with a sprinkling of curious foreigners. Club Barbarossa offers a decent escape from the maddening crowd and has a pleasant beach, nice pool and straight-on view of the Maiden's Castle.

Left, the Guardian to Hell. Right, a frieze at Kanlıdivane.

Taxis are rare but *dolmuş* leave every 15 minutes from the main Mersin-Silifke road, leading in either direction. There are good places to swim all along the coast and they are best tested in late spring or early fall when the crowds are thinner. To explore the sea castle, you should either swim to it (a brave feat) or rent a canoe from the public beach, or hire a guide and row a boat across.

Maiden's legend: Although built for military reasons, the fortress carries the standard medieval castle legend involving a maiden and the premise that neither love nor care can change the course of human fate.

The tale describes the King of Corycus, who upon learning that his daughter's fate was to die by a snake bite, shipped her off to the island castle, far away from the world's dangers. Naturally, a lowly reptile made its way to the princess (in a basket of figs sent by a well-intentioned suitor) and the princess met her fate.

Area police suggest young maidens remain sequestered in hotel rooms at night (to ignore this advice is to tempt fate), as Kızkalesi retains a rambunctious personality left over from its days as a pirate's hangout.

Bushes and snakes: The land castle of Corycus can be explored but it is not as exciting as its sea-girt partner. The interior is overgrown with bushes and oftentimes occupied by modern day, two-legged snakes of the village species.

Two miles (three km) from Kızkalesi is **Ayas**, ancient Elaeusa-Sebaste, founded partly on an islet, and known to the Romans as Elaeusa (Olives) and Sebaste (Augustus) to the Greeks. Three columns, a theatre and necropolis can be seen.

The entrance to **Kanlıdivane**, the ancient settlement of Kanytelis, lies four miles (seven km) east in Kumkuyu. A two-mile (three-km) road leads to the city, which was founded around a huge sacred chasm. Houses, churches, cemeteries and cisterns remain. A Hellenistic tower, like that in Olba/Diocaesarea, stands at the hellish pit's southwest corner. Carved into the cliff underneath is a rock bas-relief showing a family of six. Of the five churches, the most impressive is the **Church of Papylos** at the northeast end of the hole.

Necropolis: Visitors must see the necropolis which lies in a small valley 330 yards (300 metres) away. Walk down the road that leads to **Çanakçı** and head left down the footpath to the south side of the gorge. There, nine reliefs glow from the red rock; one tomb shows a woman fashionably dressed in a tight gown; another is of a man reclining with a glass of wine.

The road to Mersin is dotted with aqueducts in almost every valley, which long ago tunnelled water from the **Lamas Çayı** (the ancient Lamus River) to the ancient cities, before winding through the Cilician Plain and flowing into the Mediterranean. Although many ancient geographers placed Smooth Cilicia east of the Göksu River (the Calycadnus), Strabo, the most famous of Greek geographers, considered the Lamus River the boundary between Rough Cilicia and Smooth Cilicia, as here the Taurus disappears into the

The Banana Man in Anamur.

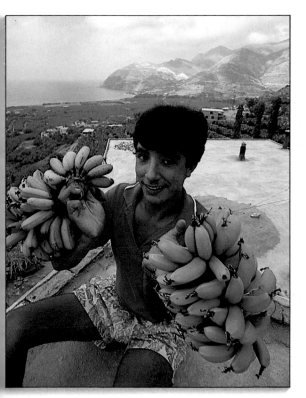

backdrop, leaving a wide fertile delta stretching to the foothills.

A right turn at Mezitli will take you to **Viranşehir**, less than one mile (1.6 kilometres) away. Viranşehir was founded in the seventh century BC by settlers from Rhodes who set up an important trading post. Shortly after, Attic colonizers took over, naming it Soli (sun in Greek). These people spoke a strange harsh dialect that both puzzled and amused their neighbours, giving birth to the word "solecism," which means an offence against grammar.

The Stoic School: Soli was also the birthplace of Chrysippus, a founder of the less-than-fun Stoic School of Philosophy, who in the third century BC wrote 750 books on stoicism, decreeing that "the wise man should be free from passion, unmoved by joy or grief and submissive to natural law." Stoicism, according to Dionysus of Halicarnassus, was a "monument of dullness."

In 91 BC the Armenian Tigranes chased the population out of Soli, and then pirates raised havoc until 67 BC when Pompey cleaned the coast of corsairs, burning 1,300 pirate ships and ending the buccaneering business in just three months. He repopulated Soli with his prisoners of war – demanding they behave – and renamed the city Pompeiopolis. The city originally was entered through a 500-foot (150-metre) long Via Sacra (Sacred Way), lined with 200 Corinthian columns which led to the harbour. Today twenty columns remain, standing firmly in a field of raspberry bushes.

Mersin is one of the oldest inhabited spots on earth and the capital of İçel Province. It has undergone positive changes in the past years – with a new harbour (third largest in Turkey) and oil refineries boosting its stature as a modern industrial city.

There isn't much history to see in Mersin unless you are a fanatic about excavation sites. Two miles (three km) away is the terraced mound of **Yümüktepe** – the original site of the city, which was excavated in the 1930s and 1940s. The oldest stratum dates back to the Stone Age.

Mersin has many quality hotels, like the five-star Merit and the good old Hilton, which dot a lovely palm-lined boulevard. English is spoken at the Tourism Office, located on the east side of the harbour, and its personnel provide information about the Turkish Republic of Northern Cyprus. There is a regular ferryboat service from Mersin to Gazimagosa (Famagusta) in Cyprus. *Dolmuş* buses run frequently through the city to Mersin Bus Station. From there, buses leave for all points east, west and north.

Soap opera: Sixteen miles (25 km) east of Mersin, **Tarsus** languishes on the banks of Tarsus Çayı, the ancient River Cydnus. The city commands a strategic position on the rich, fertile Cilician Plain and has a long history dating to the 14th century BC. Rome was impressed by Tarsus and proclaimed it the capital of its Cilician province in 64 BC. And it was here that the world's first soap opera unfolded, as Mark Antony summoned Cleopatra to Tarsus with intentions of slapping her

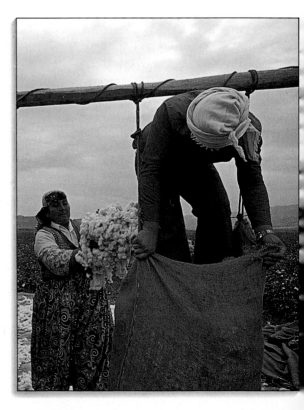

Farmers pile cotton in sacks.

hand for supporting the rival Cassius. But poor Antony buckled under his surging male hormones as Cleopatra floated up the Cydnus in her gleaming golden barge under purple sail, and she was swathed to the teeth in flowing silks and reclining under the attentions of fawning slave boys.

Tarsus is best known as the birthplace of Paul the Apostle who worked as a tentmaker in the city until his preachings took him on the road. A well marks the site of his house.

A few ho-hum sites remain in Tarsus. There's **Cleopatra's Gate**, one of the city's original six entrances. Down from the gate is the "**Özgürlük Anıtı,**" an inscription of independence carved into a stone which dates from the reign of Emperor Severus Alexander and proclaims that Roman Civil law will apply in Tarsus.

The local museum is worth a quick trip. Located in the **Kutupaşa Medresesi**, it contains numerous friezes, statuary and a Roman sarcophagus. The forbidding-looking mosque to the north was once a Gothic church. Most noticeable in Tarsus are the endless carts, stands and markets overflowing with fruit and vegetables, adding the only splash of colour against the gray town. Against this oriental backdrop sits a 19th-century American high school which is still regarded as one of the best in Turkey.

The **Cave of the Seven Sleepers** is nine miles (14 km) from Tarsus, and legend says early Christians hid here to avoid persecution by the Roman governor Dacianus. After awakening from a 100-year slumber they returned to town and attracted attention with their out-of-date fashions.

About 31 miles (50 km) north of Tarsus, after the town of Ulukişla, are the infamous **Cilician Gates** (Gülek Boğazı), actually a 4,160-foot (1,286-metre) narrow passage blasted through the Taurus range. It was one of the most important, and dreaded, mountain crossings in history and until recently was the only main connection between Tarsus and the Anatolian highlands.

Harvesting the crop in the Çukurova Region.

ADANA AND THE EAST

In the middle of the Cilician Plain, now called Çukurova, lies **Adana**, Turkey's fourth largest city with about one million inhabitants (1990). This fertile region 25 miles (40 km) east of the Taurus Mountains owes much of its wealth to the Ceyhan and Seyhan rivers, which for centuries have irrigated the vast fields. But the area's wealth has only recently trickled down to the inhabitants, whose abject poverty as virtual serfs to greedy landowners is so aptly described by Adana's favourite scribe and perennial Nobel Prize nominee, Yaşar Kemal.

In fields near the city people continue to toil as they have for 100 years, backs bent and heads covered to protect against the harsh Adana sun. Yet here and there are signs of change: brightly painted houses, cars parked alongside the fields, the increasing number of schools and bustling markets.

Economic boom: In Adana, an economic boom is unmistakable. The city's strategic location as a major transport hub to Syria and Iraq, coupled with the growth of Turkey's textile industry and the nearby presence of a major US Air Force base have all contributed to the growing economy. Construction is booming, particularly of five-star hotels and new apartment blocks – and the old village character of Adana has given way to a city feel.

Downtown Adana exudes a pleasant small/big city ambience with its spacious, tree-lined boulevards, elegant clothing shops and the latest European and Japanese cars.

Beyond the main avenues lies the real city, a settlement of shanties, substandard *gecekondu* housing and peasant farmers from the east who migrated to the city in search of work. City officials estimate that nearly nine out of 10 buildings of Adana are *gecekondu* dwellings, illegally built on private or public property by rural migrants. Vast *gecekondu* neighbourhoods built

Left, emptying red peppers. Right, downtown Adana.

around downtown Adana lack proper drinking water, electricity and sewage treatment facilities. Nearly half of Turkey's malaria cases had been reported within the boundaries of the city. The disease is now almost eradicated.

Urban renewal: As part of an urban renewal project, a new city is being built on the outskirts of Adana that will provide housing for another one million people by the year 2000. Started by the former Mayor Aytaç Burak, a progressive contractor, the construction project will give Adana a new look. The new city is bisected by two avenues – **Orgeneral Kenan Evren Bulvarı**, named after the former President of Turkey, and **Turgut Özal Bulvarı**, named after his successor who died in 1993. The two men were responsible for sponsoring the construction of the new city.

The Cilician Plain is steeped in history from the Hittites onward, but in Adana itself there are few ancient sites. The Roman Bridge **Taşköprü**, built by Hadrian in the second century, is still useful and pretty, due to old age.

The most impressive structure has to be the **Ulu Cami**, located in the historic district between an uninspiring bazaar and the auto repair and spare parts district. The exact date of the mosque's construction is debatable. Some say it was built in 1507 by Halit Bey, emir of the Ramazanoğlu Turks, and ruler of the region until the Ottomans conquered Adana in 1517. However, a plaque above the door puts the date of completion at 541, attributing it to both Halit Bey and his son, Mehmet Pasha.

Iznik tiles: The mosque has an interesting squat minaret and the tiles inside are said to come from the famed Iznik kilns. Adjacent to the mosque is a charming if a bit dilapidated park containing Halit Bey's Iznik-tiled mausoleum, a perfect place to sit and wait for an attendant to unlock the door and allow you into the mosque.

Across the street from Ulu Cami is a little teahouse, set in the midst of an old complex for religious studies. Despite its proximity to the mosque, the only thing being studied there now is back-

Adana during the Ottoman Period.

gammon and the fine art of conversation beneath shady trees.

Two other sites of interest are close by. The Ethnographic Museum, located on a small alley just off Inönü Caddesi and Ziya Paşa Bulvarı, houses a small but adequate collection of *kilims*, jewellery, weapons, musical instruments and clothing. The building may have been built by the Crusaders as one of their numerous churches, but an inscription above the entrance dates it in Greek letters to 1845.

Roman ruins: The **Adana Regional Museum** is an airy modern construction on Fuzuli Caddesi, the main road running along the Seyhan two blocks west of Inönü Caddesi. There is a generous collection of Roman ruins and a little garden filled with more ruins and old tombstones.

Apart from cotton, this region is best known for spicy *Adana kebab*. Although every restaurant menu sports this dish, the best ones are clustered on **Atatürk Bulvarı**, across the street from the Tourism Office. Those longing for an American-style snack can find comfort in the neighbourhood around the US Consulate, where restaurants offer hamburgers, french fries and lots of Coca-Cola memorabilia.

One other dish worth trying in Adana is *piliç şiş* (a *shish kebab* made from chicken instead of mutton). Visitors to the city should also try *şalgam suyu*, a salty, crimson drink made from the juices of turnips, beets and carrots, served in most Adana restaurants.

Adana is also famous for *bici*, a dessert of crushed ice, rice pudding, rose water and powdered sugar. Served in pretty glass bowls by men with pushcarts, *bici* is a nice change from the gallons of water you have to drink in the hot, hot weather.

Adana has several first class hotels, including the **Büyük Sürmeli** and **Zaimoğlu**, both on Özler Caddesi, and Seyhan Hotel on T. Cemal Beriker Bulvur.

Marco Polo's town: Some 31 miles (50 km) south of Adana on the delta formed by the Ceyhan and Seyhan rivers lies **Karataş**, a sleepy port and summer resort town with little attraction save for its bathing beach. Another 25 miles (40 km) east of Karataş is the port of **Ayas**, noted by Marco Polo in the early-13th century as a bustling market spot for spices and fabrics. The contemporary visitor, however, must exercise his imagination to picture such a scene.

Much more splendid are the sites east of Adana off the E-5 highway on the way to Ceyhan. About 19 miles (30 km) past fields of cotton and more auto repair shops lies **Yılan Kalesi**, or Snake Castle. In an area where castles and fortresses are so numerous as to almost become mundane, this eerie structure high atop a hill that looks black from the road should not be missed. Reportedly built by the Armenians in the early-13th century, it was extended by the Crusaders. The origin of its name is unknown, although this area is rife with snake legends and possibly snakes.

Continuing on E-5, one turns inland towards Kadirli at the intersection for Ceyhan on the right to reach **Anavarza**, founded by the Romans in the first cen-

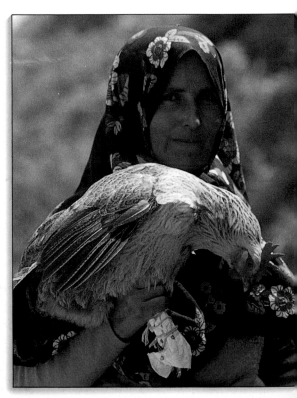

Holding up the prizefighter.

tury BC. Driving on this narrow road you are thrust back decades, passing miles and miles of cotton fields broken up by the occasional splotch of colour as women and men arduously pick the ripe cotton by hand, or a cluster of houses with sun-bleached clothing hanging out to dry.

Anavarza, which is off the road to the right (one should look for a yellow sign on the left-hand side of the road facing the opposite direction), is a picturesque village of 1,000 people living amidst Roman ruins.

Just across from the ancient walls, which are more or less intact, is a small sign saying "Museum." It looks more like a private house, which in fact it is, but the few Roman ruins and tombstones in the front garden are misleading on the quality of the exhibits inside.

A small bath that has been excavated contains a fine mosaic in honour of ancient gods, and when water is thrown on it – as surely will be done by some of the people sitting around a table outside – it takes on an almost new character. A short hike through the family's backyard leads to another bath, this one is slightly larger with a fish mosaic design on the bottom.

A little further past the museum is the ancient city gate, still standing, beyond which lie seemingly indistinguishable rocks. Some of the young boys who hang around the arched gate will show the visitors where the amphitheatre was and so on, but the area has never been properly excavated. In the distance looms a handful of castles atop a hill whose ascent is not easy, which is probably why the climb is used as an exercise course for soldiers at Adana's **Incirlik Base**.

Frustrating trip: In theory the road slicing between the two hills should lead straight to **Karatepe National Park** about 13 miles (20 km) southeast of Anavarza. In practice, driving along this road is likely to end in frustration and failure as the dirt roads, zig-zagging through the endless cotton fields, are unmarked. The various villages amidst the fields contain helpful ➡**306**

Placing bets at the cockfights.

CRUSADER CASTLES

Silhouettes of Crusader castles even in their ruined state beckon to explorers and hint of ancient glory and adventure. They bring up dreams of knights in shining armour, stirring battles, and colourful pageantry. The stone buildings which stand along the western coast of Turkey also give a real history. They witness to the skill, the energy and the artistry of their successive owners, in particular the Crusaders who invaded Anatolia from Europe in the 12th and 13th centuries.

Precision-made: The castles were precision-made instruments of military strategy. Generally they were composed of two concentric curtain walls interrupted with towers, a main gate and one of several postern gates in the outer wall. In the central area were living quarters for the lord, his accompanying knights, squires and the farming community who would retreat behind

the walls during an attack, a chapel, cisterns, storage space and stables for the animals.

During the time of the Crusades, knights, because of their versatility, were often indispensable to any army. The armoured knight on horseback wielding a sword, coupled with courage and resourcefulness, was capable of overwhelming opponents with more formidable weapons. Castles, in a way, were the knights' armour.

Battering rams: The varieties of forces employed against the men and their castles included catapults, archers' fire, battering rams, siege towers and sappers' tunnels. Under the protection of the archers' fire, men wielding a metal-pointed log could pick at the loose mortar in the wall, changing the point for a battering ram when the stones started to come apart.

Protected by towers: Entrances to castles posed special security problems. Often they were at the end of a sloping ramp to make the attackers work uphill. At Silifke (southwest of Mersin) the ramp was protected by a tower which exposed anyone approaching the gate to fire from behind. There might be several turns in the entrance to foil the rush of a battering ram, as at Bağras (south of Iskenderun). The confusion could be impounded by the entrance being dark, thus temporarily blinding those who had broken through.

Wooden siege towers higher than the ramparts of a castle that could be rolled up to its wall gave the attackers the advantage of firing down on the defenders. They, however, were subject to fire and being toppled by well-placed missiles from the castle.

More frightening in the long run to the defenders because they could not see them was the steady thud of sappers digging a tunnel below their walls. As the sappers proceeded, they shored up the tunnel with wooden struts which, when they reached their goal, they set fire to. The collapse of the burning tunnel brought down the walls above it. This method was employed successively by the Arabs against Edessa (Urfa) in 1144.

Villagers and Anavarza Castle.

Maximizing control: Always the castle was sited to maximize the owner's control of his territory. It also was placed so that friends could communicate. From Yılan Kalesi which dominates the Cilician Plain above a curve in the Ceyhan River, one could see at least eight other castles in a 31-mile (50-km) radius, including Sis (Kozan), Anavarza and Toprakkale.

Castles were often on cliffs in mountain passes. **Güllek** stood above the Cilician Gates; the watchman there could spot the dust of an approaching horde two-days' away to the south, giving the defenders time to lay their supplies. Its rock base made it invulnerable to attack by sappers.

The surrounding rugged countryside was part of the defence of seaports such as **Corycus** (Kızkalesi). Corycus was linked by a sea wall to the offshore castle for military reasons.

Blind spots: The height of the walls was improved by a moat, usually filled with water. The moat gave protection to the archers on the walls who, without it, were hampered by the blind spots at ground level.

Towers which jutted out from the curtain walls enabled the defenders to outflank the attackers. In Yılan Kalesi, the natural contours of the hill were incorporated into the angles of the walls to give the best advantage from several sides for defence.

The walls and entrance could be further protected by openings in the upper floors as at Silifke through which defenders dropped stones and boiling oil on the attackers.

Military architecture: The last-built of the Crusader castles in Turkey is that of the Knights of St. John at Bodrum. Dating from 1402 and built using stones from the Mausoleum of Halicarnassus, it survives as a magnificent example of 15th-century military architecture. Construction was stopped in the 16th century, for with the advent of gunpowder as a propellant, castles had quickly become obsolete. Today a museum of underwater archaeology enhances its attraction. ∎

Yılankale in Adana.

residents, only none of them possess vehicles, so in each village conflicting directions are given. The best plan is to return to Anavarza and from there continue on to Ceyhan.

Safely back on the E-5, the trip is straight to **Osmaniye**, where you turn left at the junction for Iskenderun south and Karatepe north. For here the road is well marked although a few miles up it turns to dirt and gravel but the scenery – lush green and rolling mountains – makes the pain worthwhile.

Karatepe, situated in a forest overlooking a breathtaking lake formed by a dam on the Ceyhan River, is a major site of Hittite remains dating approximately to the 12th century BC. Knowledge of this culture is still fairly scant as only a few records have been unearthed.

In fact, the existence of this group of people – at the height of their power (from the 19th century BC to the 13th century BC they ruled Anatolia) they had clout and imperialistic appetite matching that of the Egyptians – was discovered only a century ago.

The open-air museum houses some two dozen sculptures and reliefs, all restored and exhibited one after the other under shady trees. The pieces seem in very good condition and some are extremely beautiful; there are animals, domestic scenes including a mother suckling an infant, and figures holding menacing-looking spears. For archaeologists, one of the more fascinating aspects of the discoveries here was the unearthing of tablets containing the first known examples of Hittite writing. Sadly, it is forbidden to take pictures, but at the entrance of the site it is possible to buy postcards and slides of what is displayed.

Another memorable site in the area is **Kadirli**, north of both Anavarza and Karatepe and situated on the banks of the Ceyhan River. Development has been slow in coming to this spot, which is perhaps why a wealth of ancient ruins remains. There are neolithic mounds, almost a dozen castles nearby and some Hittite reliefs. The road is rather torturous and given the number of ruins else-

Village girls skip rope during a Sunday outing.

where and the almost surfeit of castles you can give this a pass.

The Earth Castle: Leaving the national park and heading back to the E-5, you pass **Toprakkale**, or Earth Castle, built in the 10th century by Byzantine Emperor Nicephorus II Phocas. This castle was bitterly fought over by the Armenians, the Crusaders and the Arabs as it was a vital outpost guarding the route leading from the Cilician Plain to the Hatay region, the same route travellers must still follow to reach Iskenderun and beyond.

Toprakkale also signals the beginning of the Plain of Issus, where Alexander the Great defeated the Persian armies under Darius III in 333 BC. Darius is said to have fled the field, leaving behind even his harem. The victory thus gave Alexander room to begin his sweep of Syria and finally ancient Palestine. Turning south at the intersection at Osmaniye and Toprakkale, the E-5 road enters the Hatay, Turkey's southernmost province.

The **Hatay** was given to Syria under a French mandate after the collapse of the Ottoman Empire, but was returned to Turkey in 1939. For many years Syria has wistfully claimed the Hatay as part of its territory, saying that Turkey's sovereignty over the province is illegal. Contrary to international realities, Syrian maps still show the Hatay as part of its national boundaries. Turkish authorities find Syrian claims absurd. But because of its proximity to Syria and its historic importance as a major port and trading centre, the Hatay attracted numerous minorities and nationalities, leaving to the region a rich heritage of languages, cultures and religions.

Cheap accommodations: In general, this region tends to be very inexpensive for the traveller. The price of food can run as low as half of what one would pay in Istanbul, while the best hotels (so far nothing available higher than four-stars) often cost $60 for a double. Partly because the Hatay draws few tourists, and partly because it is a region noted historically for a mix of peoples, the locals are friendly solely because they are pleasantly surprised to see a stranger. While there is little in terms of local crafts to buy (unless one counts boxes of laundry detergent and cigarettes smuggled from Syria), in Antakya particularly it is possible to find interesting pieces of carved wood.

The northern part of the Hatay is now dominated by oil refineries and steel plants, which fill the sky with evil-smelling smoke. The first town is **Dörtyol**, the end of the line for the oil pipeline travelling from the Kirkuk oil fields in Iraq.

Dörtyol is followed by the ancient port of **Payas**, now alternatively referred to as Yakacık on most maps but Payas on road signs. The harbour has long since been filled up, but is still worth visiting because Payas is the site of an extremely well-kept 16th-century Ottoman mosque complex reportedly built by Yavuz Pasha under advise from the most celebrated of all Ottoman architects, Mimar Sinan.

Truck route: It is easy to drive right past Payas town, as you will probably be boxed in between precariously **310**

Mecca or Elvis Presley rugs for all faiths.

YAŞAR KEMAL

Yaşar Kemal, Turkey's most eminent novelist and a perennial candidate for the Nobel Prize, likes to emphasize his rural roots. "I am a peasant," says the burly, six-foot (1.8-metre) tall author. "I was born in a village."

Best known for his novels of social protest that take place in the rural settings of his native Çukurova (Cilician Plain), Kemal has been compared to William Faulkner and Nikos Kazantzakis for his depth and keen observations, and penetrating factual accounts of changing village life in Turkey and of his rich use of the Turkish language. His use of colloquial language, dialect and curses, taken straight from the villages of the Çukurova Plain, is extraordinary and natural.

The transformation of the Çukurova from an underdeveloped rural farm belt to an industrial region, where feudal ownership of land still prevails, is a theme widely used in Kemal's novels. His chief characters are the common people: cotton farmers, peasant villagers, seasonal migrant workers, and brigands, fighting against an oppressive class of feudal landlords, who own entire villages.

Kemal was also the first writer in Turkey to describe in detail rural blood feuds between rival family clans, instigated by conflicting claims over women and property.

The Financial Times once described Kemal as "a man who tells, like no other, the tale of Turkey under change."

His best known novel, *Memed, my Hawk*, has been translated into many languages. The four-book epic tells the life story of Memed, a young Çukurova lad who escapes his village, controlled by a tyrannical, exploitative feudal landlord, to become a Robin Hood-like bandit. From his hideout in the Taurus Mountains, Memed leads a pack of *eşkiya* (brigands) who steal from the rich and give to the poor and plots his revenge against the evil landlord who murdered his loved one, a young village girl he tried to elope with. Memed, Kemal says about the protagonist: "I can't kill the son of a bitch. He has taken me over. When I started writing *Memed, my Hawk*, I was 24 years old and he was 21. When I completed the fourth book on him, I was 65 and the bastard was still 24."

Yaşar Kemal is a pen name he started using in the 1950s. He was born Kemal Sadık Gökçeli in the village of Gökçeli near Adana in 1922. His father came from a line of feudal landlords and his mother from bandits. He was five years old when he witnessed the stunning murder of his father in a mosque, a shocking event that was to propel him toward a career as a writer.

As a young lad, he worked as an apprentice to the *aşıks*, the travelling bards of Anatolia who roamed the countryside with their *saz*, a banjo-like instrument, singing songs about love and heroism and religion. From these traditional minstrels, Kemal learned the art of story-telling.

Kemal dropped out of high school to take an odd assortment of jobs, including working as a cotton picker, factory worker, and as a petition writer. He worked three years as a night watchman in a public library in Adana, where he read every book on the shelves during the long, lonely nights and memorized some of the great Greek classics, including Homer's *Iliad* and the *Odyssey*. In 1950, he migrated to Istanbul to start a journalism career with the newspaper *Cumhuriyet*, where he quickly became a star feature writer.

His first novel, *Memed, my Hawk*, brought him national recognition and international acclaim. In the early 1980s Peter Ustinov made a motion picture based on the book, filmed in Yugoslavia.

In his book *Iron Earth, Copper Sky*, Kemal describes the sufferings and hardships of the seasonal migrant workers arriving in Çukurova from nearby impoverished mountain villages to harvest cotton.

In *A Murder in the Iron Workers Market*, written in 1974, and *Yusufcuk*

Yusuf, published a year later, Kemal tells of an emergence of a new type of feudal landownership system, influenced by the arrival of industrial development in the region. The new landowners, cunning as ever but not as effective as in the past, fear that the workers will one day unite to undermine them. These landowners attempt to dominate the workers by fomenting squabbles and clashes among them.

More than 112 editions of his books have been published overseas, and his works have been translated into English, French, German, Russian, Spanish and other languages.

In 1982, the French Critics Association awarded him the *Del Duca Prize*, a $30,000 award whose earlier recipients included Jean Anouilh of France, Argentinean poet Jorge Luis Borges, Italian novelist Ignazio Silone and Senegal's former President, the poet Leopold Sedar Senghor.

Two years later, French President François Mitterand presented him with the *Legion of Honour*, an honour he shared with Italian film director Federico Fellini, the late Dutch documentary film maker Joris Ivens and Elie Wiesel, a Nobel Prize-winning American novelist who achieved fame through his books about the Jewish holocaust during World War II.

Many of his novels have been translated into English by his wife Thilda, a woman Kemal describes as "my most important and trustworthy friend in the whole world."

He despises many of the inevitable changes taking place in Çukurova where mechanized agriculture has replaced the horse and plough.

In a recent interview given to a journalist at the *International Herald Tribune*, he described how these changes are altering the environment for the worse: "In the 1920s there were 10 large marshes in Çukurova, filled with all kinds of birds – there were even flamingos. There were gazelles. Then in the 1950s the tractor arrived and nature changed immediately – no more marshes, no more gazelles." ■

Novelist Yaşar Kemal.

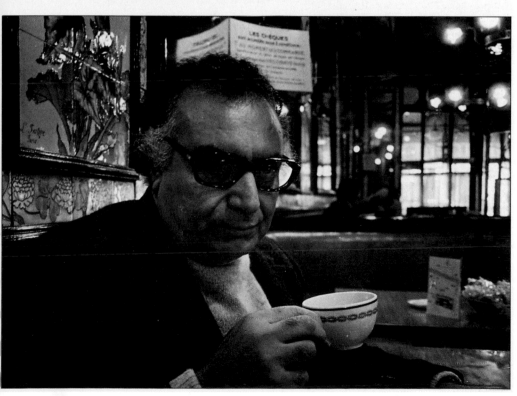

balanced trucks journeying to the Syrian border. From the road, the town looks uninteresting, filled with car repair shops, dirty teahouses and down-at-the-heels hotels.

There are no signs off the main road pointing to the complex, so it is best to turn right after the first block of shops, and then simply head towards the sea and the castle, slightly visible in the distance. For all the dirt and traffic of the main road, the back of Payas is remarkably clean and quiet. Sheep and cows graze idly by the walls of the caravansary, while olive tree groves, wandering bushes and flowers give the area a sleepy character.

As you enter the caravansary, immediately on the right are the old baths, now boarded up and guarded by wayward cows. Beyond the squat roof of the *hamam* is a 13th-century Crusader Castle, later repaired by the Ottomans and used as a sort of housing complex centuries ago. In surprisingly good condition, the huge iron door will be opened by the elderly watchman, who can usu-ally be found sitting by the crumbling stairs. It is best to ascend to the top of the castle walls, from which you have a spectacular view out to the Mediterranean and across the town. Little remains within the castle grounds save for a few ruins of old houses now partly obscured by overgrown grass.

Islamic schooling: As you leave the castle, you will see, almost straight ahead, a courtyard framed by a mosque and a students' quarters. Whether official or not, the mosque is back in use, and visitors are likely to see a group of young children busy studying the Koran. The students' quarters have been transformed into latter-day apartments, with laundry drying from trees and women squatting by the courtyard's walls chopping vegetables and playing with babies.

Coming out of the courtyard you turn right to enter the covered bazaar, a narrow hallway with a vaulted ceiling. At the time of our visit there were plans to reopen the bazaar for the shops are all newly numbered and framed by plate- **Planting crops in the Çukurova.**

glass windows. If you exit the bazaar from the entrance, you will see on the right buildings that were probably used to house the soup kitchen and more apartments.

Travellers must return to the E-5 to drive to Iskenderun. Driving at night is perhaps one of the best times to make the one-hour trip. By sunset, the road clears a bit of cars, and what during the day is a horribly crowded, polluted site is transformed after dusk: puffs of smoke from steel plants disappear gently into the night against a backdrop of blinking factory lights and bright red, yellow and white flames.

Iskenderun: At first sight **Iskenderun** is not very exciting. The streets are narrow and crowded with cars, pedestrians and fruit sellers pushing wooden carts. The city is bordered on one side by a busy port – whose position is slowly being usurped by Mersin – and on the other side by the Amanos Mountains rolling into Syria.

Iskenderun was known as Alexander-atta after its founder Alexander the Great, and Iskender is the Turkish equivalent for Alexander. The 175,000 people in the city are a mix of the multinationals who populate the Hatay.

Now Turkey's southernmost port, it was originally founded as a port town by Alexander the Great to celebrate his victory over Darius III, but its importance dwindled after the founding of a rival Seleucid port near Antioch a few years later.

Tasty prawns: There isn't much to see or do in Iskenderun, although there is a wide promenade along the Mediterranean which offers a pleasant walk and numerous beer and teahouses. Across the street from the promenade are large, outdoor restaurants serving traditional Turkish *meze* dishes with fresh fish and giant-sizes prawns. One *meze* dish that must be tried in Iskenderun is *humus*, an appetizer made from crushed chick peas, flavoured with lemon and parsley. This and other Arabic dishes found in Iskenderun have been influenced by the city's proximity to Syria.

The only hotel of note in ➧**314**

The port of Iskenderun.

HACI ÖMER SABANCI

If Yaşar Kemal is the man who introduced central Anatolian life to the world through his vivid portrayals of a young peasant boy struggling against an exploitative landowner in *Memed, my Hawk*, then Hacı Ömer Sabancı is the man who showed that it is possible to overcome these harsh conditions.

For Hacı Ömer started as a peasant boy toiling in the region called Çukurova, a fertile plain whose vast spreads of cotton turned into great wealth in the late 1800s as American and European demands for cotton could no longer be met by their own farmers. But unlike Memed and other peasants who fill Kemal's novels, Hacı Ömer's fight against poverty ended not in gunshots and mountain pursuits, but in the creation of the world-renowned Hacı Ömer Sabancı Holding Company.

In the New York-based *Fortune Magazine*'s list of 500 top overseas corporations, Sabancı Holding repeatedly ranks among the top 200, one of two Turkish groups to make the list. With assets of $4 billion, thousands of employees, more than 600 bank branches and holdings in education, health and cultural institutions in addition to over 100 factories in textiles, food, plastics, tires, automobile parts, cement, paper, electronics, pharmaceuticals and agribusiness, Sabancı Holding is a testament to one man's ability to conquer the greatest odds.

In many ways, Hacı Ömer's life mirrored that of the dissolution of the Ottoman Empire and the founding of the Turkish Republic. Born in Akçakaya village in Kayseri province in 1906 or 1903 (there is some dispute over the exact date), he left to seek his fortune in Adana in the early 1920s, just after Turkey's eventual founder, Mustafa Kemal (Atatürk), delivered the region from its three-year occupation by the French following the Ottoman Empire's defeat in World War I.

The whole country was reeling from shock of defeat and the threats to its ever-diminishing borders. Hundreds of thousands of Turkish men were wounded or died in the war, and the economy lay in tatters. Hacı Ömer's father had been killed in the war too, fighting the enemy in some distant battlefield. But in the Çukurova region, there was great hope for the world still wanted cotton and the fields were still blooming. So like many other young men who trooped off to Adana in search of a livelihood, Hacı Ömer started off in a cotton factory, washing cotton for 85 piasters a day. But this young man, who not only had the desire to make money but had the will as well, slowly became well-known in Adana for his thriftiness and, more important, his commercial drive and sense. Soon, he was acting as an employment agency, matching workers with job openings. After the founding of the Republic in 1923, Hacı Ömer was picked to restart factories abandoned in Adana by Armenian and Greeks during the intercommunal strife both before and immediately following the end of the French occupation.

Industrialist Hacı Ömer Sabanci.

When it was legislated in 1934 that all people must take a surname, Hacı Ömer, by then a wealthy factory owner, took the name Sabancı – meaning ploughmaker – so he would never forget his roots.

By the end of World War II, the country embarked on a modernization programme through the help of the Marshall Plan, and businessmen were at the forefront of the changes. Hacı Ömer, already a millionaire, was never a man to pass up a business opportunity and he quickly realized that if he wanted to expand his holdings even further, he would need a bank. With a bank, he could easily obtain money for his new enterprises and still practice his renowned thriftiness by encouraging others to save their money which in turn could finance his new operations.

At the time, banking was still a profession mainly left to foreign minorities, and the general public was usually too poor to worry about savings or kept their savings hidden under their beds or stashed somewhere else. But Hacı Ömer, with an appetite for risk and the insight that made him a successful businessman, realized that a stronger economy would support and need banks, and so he became a founding partner of Akbank in 1948. Akbank today ranks among the 200 largest banks in the world in assets and profits.

By the mid-1950s, he had moved into apartment construction and textiles, establishing in Adana the giant Bossa factory, one of the world's largest textile mills. A few years later he acquired majority shareholding in the bank and started up an insurance company.

In his personal life, he was just as demanding, teaching his six sons the value of thrift, insisting they take advantage of the formal education he could not pursue. His wife, Sadıka, whom he married in 1928, stood by him as he dreamt and built his family fortune. In 1949, Hacı Ömer acquired a mansion along the Bosphorus in Istanbul, which continues to serve as the family home.

Hacı Ömer never forgot his Anatolian roots, but he also remembered that modern Turkey grew out of the splendours of the Ottoman Empire, and this fanned his love for fine antiques and furniture. Each piece to him symbolized more than sheer economic or utilitarian value, but it represented a story much like his own: creation, use and appreciation for fine craftsmanship. If he had one spendthrift side to him – and tales of him avoiding taxes to save money even when he was a wealthy man are legendary – then it was in the pursuit of collecting pieces of the past. His love of art was best exemplified at the Sabancı Villa on the Bosphorus, where many objects of master painters and sculptors can still be seen today. His only other pastime was chatting with friends about business or smoking a *nargile*, or hookah, in Emirgân, a town on the Bosphorus near his home.

An earthy man who spoke with an atrocious rural accent, Hacı Ömer always dressed like an Anatolian peasant and never wore a tie in his life, even when meeting the President of the Republic. He hung up on the wall of his house a harness he had used while working as a young *hamal* – a beast of burden – to carry huge bales of cotton on his back, as a reminder to himself and his family of his humble origins as a cotton worker.

Hacı Ömer died in 1966, but the fortune he so carefully amassed and the friendships he maintained with people from peasants in Adana up to high government officials did not disappear. Thousands mourned his passing and Adana today has countless signs of his love for Turkey, from his factories and banks to a cultural centre and educational institutions established by Sabancı Holding.

His eldest son died in 1979, but the other five sons continue to work in the company now headed by Sakıp Sabancı, the second oldest son.

It is virtually impossible to travel anywhere in Turkey today without seeing the SA initials in front of a factory or company name, a symbol now not only of one man's ability to amass great wealth, but of Turkey's growing economic power. ∎

Iskenderun is the **Grand Hotel Ontur** on Muam-mer Aksoy Caddesi.

Iskenderun is also an important naval base. A boot camp for Turkish naval infantry, with a live-sized concrete destroyer in its midst, can be found on the road to Antakya.

After leaving Iskenderun, a right turn off the E-5 will take the motorist along the Gulf of Iskenderun to **Arsuz**, a little resort village thought to be the site of the Seleucid town of Rhosus, built in 300 BC. The hamlet, which has a pleasant beach, contains the remains of several ancient buildings and city walls. Many of the old mansions in Arsuz were built by the French when they ruled the area under a League of Nations mandate from 1919-1939. A Crusader castle stands further south near the promontory known as **Hınzır Burnu** (the Cape of Pigs), which is the western side of the peak known as **Musa Dağı** (The Mountain of Moses). The mountain was the scene of intense fighting in 1915 between insurgent Armenians and the Turkish army. The stand of the Armenian rebels was made famous by Franz Werfel in his acclaimed novel, *Forty Days in Musa Dagh*.

Returning to the E-5, the road turns away from the sea and into the **Amanos Mountains**. A road forks to the right to **Soğukoluk**, a breezy plateau town where many of Iskenderun's wealthy families have summer villas. Numerous hotels in the town serve visiting Arab businessmen. Before the 1980 military coup, Soğukoluk was an infamous, naughty brothel city, where young Turkish girls trapped into prostitution were literally sold as concubines to visiting Arab sheiks. Despite official disclaimers, rumours persist that prostitution and white women slave trade continues there.

The Syrian Gates: Back on the E-5, the road narrowly winds its way around the Amanos Mountains, from which you have a terrific view of the **Orontes Valley** – part of the **Amik Ovası** – whose flowing fields and generous greenery attest to the area's fertility and source of the region's wealth. This sec-

A young woman carries her baby on her back.

tion of the road is called the **Belen Pass**, formerly known as the Syrian Gates for its strategic location between the sea and Antioch. **Belen** itself is a small village whose fame rests upon the belief that its waters hold curative powers. For those who dare, open water fountains in the city centre offer the traveller a cool, tasty drink.

As you drive towards Antakya (Antioch), you will notice that the sides of the road are dotted with ancient Roman walls and mounds, all unexcavated sites of earlier life. After the pass there is a turnoff for **Bağras Castle**, a medieval fortress reportedly built by the Byzantines in the 10th century. This fortress passed through the hands of the numerous empires that stormed the region, finally falling to the Crusaders in 1097. After the Ottomans conquered the region in the 16th century the fortress was abandoned.

The road continues its slow dip into Antakya – set on the banks of the **Asi Nehiri** (the Orontes River) – through the fertile Amik Plain. Virtually every hill along the way contains stone outcroppings from previous civilizations, but most are unmarked and barely visible, so it is best to wait until Antakya for your exploration.

Antakya, better known by its ancient name of Antioch, was founded in 300 BC by Seleucus Nikator, a lesser general in Alexander's army. Following Alexander's death, Seleucus added Syria and Mesopotamia to his empire that started in Babylonia. Antioch became the capital city of the Seleucid Empire and made a name for itself as a busy commercial centre.

Antioch passed to the Romans in 81 BC, and in 64 BC it was made capital of the Roman province of Syria. Antioch's splendour became known throughout the Hellenistic world and the population grew to almost half a million. Numerous Roman rulers, including King Herod of Judea, gave public buildings to the city, and spacious villas and temples cropped up in the area. Many of the beautifully detailed mosaics that were so popular with the Romans – used as bath floors and as decorations in salons and gardens

Having a close shave.

– are now on display in the **Antakya Archaeological Museum**.

Antioch was the scene for St Paul's first ministry. It was here that the term "Christian" was first used to describe the followers of Jesus.

But the city suffered from devastating earthquakes and, as the Roman Empire began to disintegrate, Antioch came under attack. It was sacked numerous times by the Persians and the Arabs, the latter of whom captured the city in AD 638. The Byzantines took it back in 969, only to lose it again – this time to the Crusaders. Once again made the capital, its glorious history ended in tragedy in 1268, when the Mamelukes of Egypt sacked the city and drove out the remaining inhabitants.

Virtual decay: For centuries Antioch lay in a state of virtual decay. Old engravings made by 19th-century travellers show Antioch as a scattering of ruined buildings along the Orontes, with sheepherders the only sign of life in the once-bustling city.

Since the founding of the Republic

and the development of this region as an important farming and once again commercial centre, Antioch's population has grown to over 200,000 and the city is full of new apartment blocks and streets crowded with boutiques such as **Benetton** and **Levi's**.

Excavations conducted in the 1930s discovered numerous ancient sites within and around the city, most famous of which are the many mosaics dating from early Roman times, now on display in the Archaeological Museum. For a sight of these mosaics alone it is worth travelling to Antakya. The majority of these mosaics date to the second and third centuries. The collection is the world's most extensive gatherings of Roman mosaics. Many were found virtually complete and the colours are almost as brilliant as they once were. The museum also includes an interesting collection of Roman coins, along with pottery and jewellery.

Otherwise Antakya is filled with various sites of Christian and Roman significance. Within the city itself is a Roman bridge (circa AD 200) crossing the Asi River, a very small but charming bazaar in the centre of town, and numerous beautiful mosques. The outline of the ancient city walls, about 19 miles (30 km) in length, gives some idea of the city's former fame.

Daily tours: Primarily because of the amazing mosaics found in the museum, and because of the city's location on the road to Syria, Antakya has built itself up as a tourist centre, and almost daily tour buses disgorge their French and German passengers outside the Büyük Antakya Hotel, located across the street from the museum. The people who work at the Tourist Information Office off **Atatürk Caddesi** at the first roundabout into the city are very helpful and will often offer to personally accompany the visitor if he has trouble locating a specific site.

The food tends toward *humus*, *shish kebab* and *meze* dishes, served in the best restaurants found along **Hürriyet Caddesi**, which runs from the left bank of the Asi River south. On the streets,

The Hittite Lions in Antakya Museum.

vendors sell fresh fruit drinks and *bıcı*. The refreshing and eye-catching *bicis* are best eaten with lots of ice. The best hotel in town is the four-star **Büyük Antakya** Hotel on Atatürk Caddesi.

Like the whole of the Hatay, Antakya's population is mixed, and Arabic vies with Turkish as a first language. A majority of the Arabs of Antakya are Alevis, members of Turkey's Shiite community. There is a small Jewish population living here, numbering about 150 people, and an equally tiny Christian population.

Jewish community: The **synagogue** is located on the eastern bank of the Asi River, right behind the **Old Market District** on Kurtuluş Caddesi. It is only open on Saturday mornings and Jewish holidays. Disguised as a government building with a picture of Atatürk above the doorway, it is not easy to locate. Walk to the Habib Naccar Camii and then ask directions of one of the small tradesmen sitting outside their shops drinking tea. The **Habib Naccar Camii**, constructed in the 17th century,

is one of the finer mosques in the city and is well worth a visit.

Kurtuluş Caddesi itself is the new version of ancient Antioch's famed main street. The ancient street, constructed around 30 BC with colonnades running on either side of the street that was supposedly over 30 feet wide and two miles long, has been replaced by modern buildings and *hans* (commercial centres) and pavements with automobiles and trucks.

The first Christian community: Antakya is famous for the grotto **Church of St Peter**, just outside the city on the road to Halep (Aleppo). This is allegedly the oldest working church in existence, and it is here that St Peter together with St Paul and Barnabas reportedly preached from a cave around AD 47 and the world's first Christian community was founded. The grotto church is said to have a secret tunnel through which believers could escape when they were under threat of persecution.

During Antioch's heyday, it was renowned for its **Shrine of Daphne**, now

A mosaic of the sea god Poseidon at the Antakya Museum.

located in Harbiye, a cool verdant plateau eight miles (13 km) south of Antakya on the road to Samandağ.

According to myth, this is the spot where Apollo pursued Daphne and she was changed into a laurel. There is some contention over whether this was really the setting, but its beauty – cascading waterfalls set among small ledges of pine trees above the Asi River – makes it an appropriate setting.

The conqueror of the region, Emperor Seleucus, built a temple and oracle complex to Apollo here, and later Roman rulers added even more temples and palaces. It was allegedly here that Cleopatra and Antony were married and where the Antioch Games, precursor of the Olympics, took place. But Daphne fell along with Antioch, and although it remains a favourite holiday spot for locals and visiting Arabs, one's imagination must be put into full force to see its former beauty.

The grove itself is filled with little open air *kebab* restaurants whose patrons sit around tables balanced precariously on rocks along the bubbling, torrential streams. Garbage is everywhere and the waterfalls are obscured by the hordes of people who tramp around looking for an empty picnic table. Above Daphne is a street of hotels and fish restaurants, except that fish is rarely on the menu and the ones available look like they swam too long near the oil terminal of Dörtyol.

The area was also made famous during the Roman-Byzantine reign by the activities of St Simeon the Elder, who around AD 420, having decided that the way of faith was to avoid the world, climbed up to a mountain top east of Antioch, and perched himself on a pillar. He kept moving to higher and higher pillars before finally settling on a point falling across the Syrian border near Yayladağı.

But his style of faith proved popular, and his most faithful disciple, St Simeon the Younger, ascended **Samandağ** (the Mountain of St Simeon) reportedly at the age of seven, to preach and pray around AD 520. The two churches dedicated to him atop the mountain remain in a state of disrepair due to tremendous earthquakes, but reaching them is not easy.

Samandağ (also the name for the city), about 12 miles (19 km) from Antakya, is Turkey's southernmost city where the Asi River feeds into the Mediterranean. This city is the modern town of Antioch's ancient port, **Seleucia ad Peiria**. Seleucia was the original capital of the Seleucid Empire until 281 BC, when Seleucus was assassinated and his son Antiochus took the throne and moved the capital to Antioch. It was originally one of four cities founded by Seleucus.

Ruined harbour walls still dot the beach front, while nearby is the **Tunnel of Vespasian**, a huge series of water sluices carved out of rock near the sea and dated to AD 79. You can hike around in the water tunnels, enjoying the solitude of the spot, which makes for a refreshingly pleasant change from the noisy beach below.

As a resort area, Samandağ is less than attractive. Garbage tossed in the sea by passing ships is regularly washed ashore, the sea looks dirty and the undertow is treacherous. Many people have drowned offshore.

From the centre of the town itself there is an interesting albeit rough road that leads to **Hıdırbey**, a tiny village which boasts **Hıdır's Tree**, reportedly sprouted from the staff of a Moslem Prophet Hıdır. Legend has it that the Old Testament Prophet Moses met with Hıdır for instruction near this spot. In Turkish, Hıdır – or Hızır – refers to an extraordinary being who wanders the earth performing miracles.

Facing Musa Dağ, Hıdırbey is set in a sort of valley through which runs a pretty creek. The tree is definitely there, although it is not quite as large as some people say. After the long, hot drive, it is best just to buy a refreshing drink from the nearby shop and like all locals sit and stare at the tree and the creek. Unless you are very adventuresome and have a full tank of petrol, it is better to return on the same road you have come in on, for it is unclear where the road goes after Hıdırbey.

Right, old men with watermelons.

318

INSIGHT GUIDES
Travel Tips

Insight Guides portray destinations in depth, providing the complete picture and the top photography

Insight Pocket Guides focus on the best choices for places to see and things to do and include large fold-out maps

Insight Compact Guides' portability makes them the perfect books to carry with you for on-the-spot reference

Three types of guide for all types of travel

INSIGHT GUIDES Different people need different kinds of information. Some want *background information* to help them prepare for the trip. Others seek *personal recommendations* from someone who knows the destination well. And others look for *compactly presented data* for on-the-spot reference. With three carefully designed series, Insight Guides offer readers the perfect choice. Insight Guides will turn your visit into an experience.

The world's largest collection of visual travel guides

Getting Acquainted

The Place

Turkey has a population of more than 60 million. Six out of ten Turks live in cities while the rest inhabit villages. The nation is one of the l argest in Europe and is about the size of Britain and France combined. It is surrounded by the Mediterranean, the Aegean and the Black Sea. The country has 300,000 square miles (780,000 square km) of territory. Three percent of Turkey lies in Europe, and this region is known as Trakya, or Thrace. Ninety-seven percent of the country lies in Asia and is called Anatolia, a rugged region covered by mountainous terrain surrounding vast fertile plains and steppes, nurtured by several winding rivers, including the Euphrates and Tigris rivers. The European and Asian parts of the country are separated by the Dardanelles in the southwest, and the Sea of Marmara and the Bosphorus in the northwest. Most of the population lives in the west along the verdant coastal plains.

Time Zone

Turkish Standard Time is seven hours ahead of Eastern Standard Time and two hours ahead of Greenwich Mean Time.

Electricty

Electricity in Turkey is 220 volts. The speed for electronics is fifty cycles. Two-round prongs are the standard plugs for normal appliances.

Maps

General maps of Turkey can be obtained free of charge from the various Tourism Information Bureaux along the Turkish Coast. Detailed regional, provincial and city maps are available at most booksellers.

Climate

The Aegean and Mediterranean shores of Turkey have hot and dry summers and mild winters. Average temperatures in Celsius are:

	Jan.	April	July	Oct.
Izmir	9	20	30	21
Antalya	11	22	32	23

Economy

Turkey is a secular republic with an elected parliament. Organized into 80 provinces, Turkey is bordered by Bulgaria, Greece, Russia, Iran, Iraq and Syria. It is a member of the North Atlantic Treaty Organization (NATO), the Organization of Economic Cooperation and Development and the Council of Europe. The nation is also an associate member of the European Community, and a full member of the European Customs Union. With 800,000 men under arms, it has the second largest army in NATO after the US. Its capital is Ankara.

Turkey's main crops are wheat, cotton, tea, tobacco, hazelnuts, fruit and vegetables. Major exports include textiles, steel, chromium, bauxite, manganese and hazelnuts.

Turkey is one of the world's leading producers of textiles. Its production is so vast that Turkish textiles are often imported by countries with quota limitations under labels of other foreign manufacturers.

Culture & Customs

Emphasis is placed on the family in Turkey. Children are very important and are expected from every couple. They are the future of each family. Although the economics of supporting a family in Turkey are strained, the average family has two or three children. In rural areas, where big families are emphasized, couples may have eight to nine children, but how they manage to survive is uncertain.

Women are still expected to marry by the time they reach 25. The role of the woman is changing. In larger cities there are plenty of women in the work force, serving in all the professions. Many women are teachers, doctors, lawyers, scientists, administrators and business managers. But in many Turkish families the tradition of male

bread-winner and female housewife lives on.

Because Turks are so family-oriented, the Turkish language has provided for the specific naming of each family (gender is always evident) member. An older brother is an *agabey*. An older sister is an *abla*. An aunt from the mother's side is a *teyze*, while an aunt from the father's side is a *hala*.

An uncle from the mother's side is called *dayı* while an uncle from the father's side is known as an *amca*. The bride's sister-in-law is called *görümce* while the groom's sister-in-law is a *baldız*.

Some words clarify age. Call an older person as *siz* – the formal you or thy. A younger person or close relative is *sen*.

The family structure is still very tight. Retirement homes are rare in Turkey. Often three generations live together under one roof, partly because it is more economical but also because the displacement of an older member is seriously frowned upon by society.

Planning the Trip

What to Bring

Clothing

Dress differs from region to region. In the cities, shorts are not very common, but in coastal towns and resorts on the Aegean and Mediterranean, colourful Hugo Boss beach shorts and La Coste T-shirts are popular. Beachwear and light cotton clothing are recommended.

During the hot, sultry summer months, it is a good idea to wear a hat or cap, and use plenty of sunscreen. Rubber sandals and slippers can also be worn on the beaches of southern Turkey.

Most Turkish women adopt western dress. Women wearing *çarsafs*, black veils covering the body from head to toes, are usually peasant villagers or Saudi tourists. As a sign of respect for

Islam, women must wear head scarves and cover their arms and legs when visiting mosques. Miniskirts and shorts should not be worn in mosques. Women should dress conservatively in rural areas and small towns away from coastal resorts.

Entry Regulations
Visas & Passports

For visits up to three months, nationals of the following countries may enter Turkey with current passports without a visa: Argentina, Australia, the Bahamas, Bahrain, Barbados, Belgium, Belize, Brazil, Canada, Chile, Denmark, Morocco, Finland, France, Germany, Greece, Holland, Iceland, Israel, Jamaica, Japan, Liechtenstein, Luxembourg, Malta, Mauritius, Monaco, Norway, New Zealand, Singapore, Sweden, Switzerland, Trinidad, Tunisia, Vatican City.

Nationals of the following countries need a visa, but can easily get a sticker visa at the border gates for up to three months: Austria, Ireland, Italy, Portugal, Spain, United Kingdom and USA.

Nationals of other countries require a visa, which can be obtained from the nearest Turkish embassy or consulate.

All EU citizens, Swiss, Maltese, and the citizens of the Turkish Republic of Northern Cyprus may enter Turkey with the proper identity cards in place of a passport.

Customs

Visitors to Turkey may bring in the following duty free: 400 cigarettes, 50 cigars, 2.2 pounds (one kilogram) of tobacco, 2.2 pounds (one kilogram) of coffee, 3.3 pounds (1.5 kilograms) of instant coffee, up to seven bottles of spirits of which no more than three shall be of the same brand.

Valuable items such as fur coats, electronics, antiques, sports and camping equipment, and video cameras brought into the country will be registered into the owners' passports. Travellers leaving without these imported items would have to pay duties. Entry of firearms and diving equipment are subject to authorization.

Sharp instruments such as knives cannot be transported in hand luggage in transit to Turkey. They should be placed in check-in baggage.

Gifts not exceeding $285 in value may be brought into the country duty free. Gifts up to $285 may be sent by mail one month before and after the *Kurban Bayram, fieker Bayram* (following Ramadan), Christmas, New Year, and Easter.

Taking antiques (100 years or older) out of Turkey is illegal and considered an act of smuggling. Proof of purchase is needed for items such as handmade carpets. A certificate from a directorate of a museum is required for old objects.

Health

No vaccinations are required, but it is a good idea to have cholera shots if you are planning to travel in the countryside. The change in bacteria content in food may cause diarrhoea.

Fruits and vegetables should be washed well. Tap water can be used for washing but should not be drunk. Always use bottled water for drinking everywhere you go in Turkey.

Be cautious with local animals, such as dogs and cats, since many do not have rabies shots.

Animals

A rabies vaccination certificate for domestic animals and hunting dogs is required. It must be issued 48 hours before departure for Turkey and translated into Turkish by a Turkish Embassy or Consulate.

Possession of Drugs

It is hoped the visitor to Turkey hasn't been introduced to the country through the film *Midnight Express*. Penalties are heavy for possession of drugs (which includes hashish), but being Hollywood, there was much exaggeration in this film. Drugs are produced for medical purposes, and drug abuse and alcoholism are low.

Money

The Turkish Lira (TL) comes in coins of 5, 10, 25 and 50 thousands, and the notes in 50, 100, 250, 500 thousands, and 1 and 5 millions. Turkey has an inflation rate varying between 80%–120%. Foreign exchange rates are published daily in newspapers, including the English-language *Turkish Daily News*, and posted in banks.

There is no limit on the foreign currency that can be brought into or taken out of Turkey.

Money transfers can be withdrawn as Turkish Lira with no problems. If a transfer is withdrawn as a foreign currency, a commission of up to three percent is usually charged. ATM's of major Turkish banks, such as İş bankası, Yapı Kredi Bankası and Pamukbank, give cash advances against major international credit cards.

Foreign Exchange

Money can be changed almost any time at the airports. Banks have 24-hour operations at Istanbul Atatürk Airport; plenty of automatic teller machines are to be found in larger towns and sightseeing areas.

Public Holidays

Jan. 1	New Year's Day
April 23	National Sovereignty and Children's Day
Beginning of February	Şeker Bayramı (The Sweet Holiday). This Moslem holiday, which follows the Ramazan fasting period comes 10 days earlier each year.
Early April	Kurban Bayramı (The Sacrificial Holiday). This Moslem holiday is observed after the pilgrimage to the Islamic holy lands and comes ten days earlier each year.
May 19	Youth and Sports Day
August 30	Victory Day
October 29	Republic Day

Religious Festivals

Mid January	Camel Wrestling Festival, Selçuk
18th March	1915 Sea Victory Celebration and Memorial Ceremonies, Çanakkale
May	Efes International Festival of Culture and Tourism, Selçuk
May	International Music and Folklore Festival, Silifke

May	International Yachting Festival, Marmaris	Sept.-October	Akdeniz Song Contest, Antalya	

May	International Yachting Festival, Marmaris
Late May	International Beach Volley Tournament, Alanya
June	International Offshore Races, Istanbul-Izmir
June	Foça Music, Folklore and Watersports Festival, Foça
June	Marmaris Festival, Marmaris
June	Bergama Festival
June	International Sea and Music Festival, Çeflme
June	International Song Competition, Pamukkale
June	Finike Festival, Finike
June-July	Istanbul International Music Festival, Istanbul
June-July	Izmir International Music Festival, Izmir and Ephesus
June-July	Traditional Kırkpınar Grease Wrestling Festival, Edirne
July	Tourism and Culture Festival, Iskenderun
July	Tourism Festival, Kufladası
August	Troy Festival, Çanakkale
September	Izmir International Fair, Izmir
September	Kemer Carnival
September	International Fair, Mersin
September	Altın Portakal (Golden Orange) Film Festival, Antalya
September	Yağcı Bedir Carpet Festival, Sındırgı, Balıkesir
Late September	Assos International Theatre and Dance Festival, Assos, Behramkale (Ayvacık)
Sept.-October	International Fine Arts Biennale, Istanbul
Sept.-October	Akdeniz Song Contest, Antalya
Sept.-October	Art and Culture Festival, Mersin
October	International Regatta and Cup, Bodrum
October	International Gullet Biennale, Bozburun, Marmaris
Late October	International Triathlon Races (swimming, biking, running), Alanya
November	International Yacht Races, Marmaris
December	International St Nicholas Symposium, Demre
December	Mevlana (Whirling Dervishes) Commemoration Ceremonies, Konya

Getting There

By Air

There are many daily flights from major European, American, Middle Eastern and Far Eastern cities to Istanbul's Atatürk International Airport, from where you can get regular Turkish Airlines connecting flights to Izmir, Antalya, Dalaman Bodrum and Adana. Many charter flights operate from Europe to Antalya, Dalaman and Izmir, making it easy to get to the Turkish Coast. Turkish Airlines (THY) has a direct flight to Bodrum from London's Gatwick Airport, too.

A number of private Turkish airline companies, such as **Top Air** (Istanbul, tel: (212) 599 0227, and Bodrum, tel: (252) 313 0626 and **Istanbul Airlines** (Istanbul, tel: (212) 231 7526, Bodrum tel: (252) 316 1781), provide direct flights from Istanbul to Izmir and Bodrum daily on small passenger planes.

Istanbul, Ankara, Izmir, Dalaman and Antalya all have international airports. Adana airport can be reached by domestic transfer.

A British-Turkish joint venture constructed an international airport at Güllük, Milas, to the north of Bodrum which became operational in 1996.

Duty free shops in the arrival lounges sell cigarettes, gift, souvenirs and something quite expensive in Turkey: perfume and cosmetics.

Air Transport

TURKISH AIRLINES RESERVATION OFFICES

Adana, Stadyum Caddesi 32, tel: (322) 453 0867.
Ankara, Atatürk Bulvarı 231/A, Kavaklıdere, tel: (312) 419 2800/ 468 7340.
Antalya, Cumhuriyet Caddesi 2, tel: (242) 243 4383.
Bodrum, Güllük, Milas Airport, tel: (252) 536 6595.
Dalaman, Dalaman Airport, tel: (252) 692 5899.
Istanbul, Cumhuriyet Caddesi 199-201, Harbiye, tel: (212) 247 1338 and Hamidiye Caddesi, Doğubank 27, Sirkeci, tel: (212) 522 8888.
Izmir, Gaziosmanpafla Bulvarı, underneath Büyük Efes Hotel, tel: (232) 484 1220/425 8280.
Marmaris, Atatürk Caddesi 50/B, tel: (252) 412 3751.
Mersin, Istiklal Caddesi, 27 Sokak, Çelebi Iflhanı, tel: (324) 231 5232.

OTHER DOMESTIC AIRLINE RESERVATION OFFICES

Istanbul Airlines, Cumhuriyet Caddesi 289, Harbiye, Istanbul, tel: (212) 231 7526. Istanbul Atatürk Airport, tel: (212) 509 2100.
Flights to Bodrum, Antalya, Dalaman.
Top Air. Tel: (212) 613 8150/599 0227.
Flights to Bodrum and Antalya.

By Ship

Regular boat services operate during the summer from various Greek islands to Turkish resort towns on the Aegean, including Ayvalık, Izmir, Kusadası, Bodrum and Marmaris. Turkish Maritime Lines (Deniz Yolları) has a regular passenger boat service along the Turkish Coast from Istanbul.

It also operates a weekly service between Venice and Antalya in the summer season. Turkish Maritime Lines, Antalya, tel: (242) 241 1120; Istanbul, tel: (212) 249 9222.

TURKISH MARITIME LINES OFFICES

Antalya, Kenan Evren Bulvarı, Konyaaltı Caddesi 40/19, tel: (242) 241 2630; fax: (242) 247 5095.
Istanbul, Rıhtım Caddesi, Karaköy, tel: (212) 249 9222/293 7454; fax: (212) 251 9025.

Izmir, Yeni Liman (Harbour), Alsancak, tel: (232) 421 1484/421 0077; fax: (232) 421 1481.

By Train/Bus

There are regular train services from Istanbul and Ankara to Izmir, Aydın, Denizli, Tarsus, Mersin and Adana. Izmir can also be reached from Bandırma.

There are also regular train services operating between Istanbul and Venice, Munich, Vienna and Paris, stopping off in many major cities in between.

The train is the cheapest form of transportation in Turkey. Breakfast, lunch and dinner are served aboard the train, but are not included in the price. It is a good idea to book a private compartment if you are travelling on an overnight train. Istanbul's terminal train station on the Asian side is in Haydarpasa, tel: (216) 336 0475/348 8020.

By Road

Frequent bus services operate between major Turkish cities and any of the popular spots on the Turkish Aegean and Mediterranean. Those journeying long distances in summer often travel at night, when it is cooler. Bus travel is inexpensive and varying in comfort, depending on the company. Most of the buses are modern and well-kept, but not all have air conditioning. Deluxe Varan buses are almost always air conditioned. Bus companies having the most routes in the southern coast are Pamukkale, Kamil Koç, Varan and Ulusoy. Bus travel is not recommended for visitors who dislike cigarette smoke, but more and more major bus companies provide a deck for non-smokers, including Varan and Ulusoy. Both companies operate from Germany as well. Varan's Istanbul office in Taksim, tel: (212) 251 7481; Ulusoy's Istanbul office in Taksim, tel: (212) 249 4373. The northern Turkish Aegean can easily be reached from Bulgaria and Greece. Motorists can also drive to the eastern Turkish Mediterranean from Aleppo, Syria.

Entry by Yacht

Upon docking the yacht at a Turkish port, the captain must meet with the authorities and make necessary decla-rations. Entry into Turkish waters will be recorded in the captain's passport and cancelled upon departure. Ports acceptable for entry are: Trabzon and Samsun (on the Black Sea); Tekirdağ and Bandırma (on the Sea of Marmara); Istanbul (on the Bosphorus); Çanakkale (on the Dardanelles); Akçay, Ayvalık, Dikili, Izmir, Çeşme, Kuşadası, Güllük, Bodrum, Datça and Marmaris (on the Aegean); Fethiye, Kaş, Kemer, Antalya, Alanya, Anamur, Taşucu, Mersin and Iskenderun (on the Mediterranean).

Registration must be renewed if yachts depart from Turkey. Yachts are to be moored for winter lay-up, replacement of person registering, or completion of the specified sailing route. Registration of log is valid for three months.

Yachtsmen must adhere to their registered sailing routes. Health certificates issued for foreign yachts are valid for three months under condition that no foreign port has been entered. In the case of death or contagious disease, port authorities must be notified.

Foreigners entering Turkey may leave their vessel at a licensed marina up to two years for winter lay-up, repair and maintenance services and can leave the country by other means. Yachts over 30 NRT must pay a lighthouse fee.

Practical Tips

Business Hours

Government offices are open from 8:30am to noon and 1:30pm to 5:30pm. Commercial banks are open from 8:30am to noon and 1:30pm to 5pm. The main post offices in cities and resorts, from where you can make phone calls, are open 24 hours, even during public and religious holidays. In resorts, some banks have exchange offices which open till late in the evening, and 24-hour ATM's give Turkish Lira or hard currency cash against major credit cards.

Religion

Turkey is 99 percent Moslem, but small pockets of Christians and Jews live in the big cities and in the rural areas of eastern Turkey. Turks are predominantly Sunni, but one out of every six Turks is Alevi (Shiite). Pious Turks pray in mosques which conduct services five times a day. The call to prayer, known as the *ezan*, is sung by *muezzins*, and sometimes even played on tape, from minaret tops. Izmir, Istanbul, Adana, Iskenderun and Antakya have churches serving different Christian denominations and synagogues for the Jewish community.

Media

Newspapers & Magazines

Cumhuriyet is considered the most serious national newspaper with special emphasis on the arts, national and local politics, economy and foreign news. Other major newspapers are *Hürriyet*, *Sabah*, *Yeni Yüzyıl* and *Milliyet*. More gossip-oriented papers are *Akşam*, and *Güneş Posta*, etc.

An English-language newspaper published daily in Ankara and distributed country-wide is the Turkish *Daily News* . It provides concise coverage of Turkish and international political and economic issues and contains a variety of helpful facts and information for English-speaking foreigners in Turkey.

The bi-monthly, English-language city culture magazine, *The Guide Istanbul*, runs its updated Antalya and Bodrum editions every year in June. The colourful and well-researched geography and travel magazine, *Atlas*, publishes interesting articles on Turkey (and international places) that initiated visitors to this country will find worthy of attention.

Radio

The *BBC World Service* can be heard on shortwave 15070kHz, 12095kHz and 15400kHz. *Voice of America* can be picked up on 1260kHz or 15205kHz.

There are now dozens of local FM radio stations in larger towns throughout the country running international and Turkish music programmes with news broadcasts thrown in. Based in Istanbul, *Power FM* and *Kiss FM* also broadcast for the major holiday towns along the Turkish coast, featuring dynamic western pop and rock music. The state-run *TRT 3 Radio*, which is aired country-wide on FM 88.2, broadcasts excellent classical, jazz, latin, pop and rock music, and gives news bulletins in English, French and German at 9am, 12am, 2pm, 5pm, 7pm and 10pm.

Television

More than 15 television channels now operate in Turkey, most of them being privately owned by a few media giants. *Show TV*, *Interstar*, *ATV*, *Kanal D*, and *TRT* channels are among the most popular with Turkish viewers. The state-owned *TRT 2 Television* runs the news in English, French and German every night at 10pm. The home-tv channel, *Cine 5*, shows live programmes of first league Turkish football matches, and the latest Hollywood films, which are sometimes broadcast in the original language.

Turkish postal services are among the most reliable in the world. A post office is called a PTT. In addition to mailing letters and sending telegrams from a PTT, you can make local, long distance and foreign phone calls. All PTTs now also have fax and telex services.

Telecommunications

Public telephones operate with tokens (*jeton*) sold in three sizes. Small tokens are for one-minute calls, medium and large tokens for long distance and overseas calls. Telephone cards are more useful for busy callers. They can be purchased at PTT offices and used at telephone booths located on busy street corners, large hotels, marinas and, of course, at post offices. When making a long-distance call to a foreign country from Turkey, dial (00) first and then the code of the country (see international codes, below), then the city code and the specific number. All these numbers should follow each other without waiting.

International Codes

Australia	61
Canada	1
Great Britain	44
United States	1

Turkish Telephone Codes

The following are the international telephone code numbers of Turkey's major cities and resorts on the Aegean and Mediterranean. To use the codes within Turkey itself, the numbers must be preceded by 0.

City Name	Telephone Codes
Adana	322
Alanya	242
Anamur	324
Ankara	312
Antakya	326
Antalya	242
Aydın	256
Ayvalık	266
Balıkesir	266
Bergama	232
Bodrum	252
Bursa	224
Çanakkale	286
Çeşme	232
Çeşme-Ilıca	232
Dalaman	252
Dalyan (in Muğla province)	252
Datça	252
Denizli	258
Eceabat	286
Edirne	284
Enez	284
Fethiye	252
Finike	242
Foça	232
Gelibolu	286
Ipsala	284
Iskenderun	326
Istanbul	European side 212
	Asian side 216
Izmir	232
Kalkan	242
Kaş	242
Kemer	242
Konya	332
Köyceğiz	252
Kuşadası	232
Manisa	236
Marmaris	252
Mersin	324
Muğla	252
Pamukkale	258
Selçuk	232
Silifke	324

Other Useful Numbers

Directory Assistance	118
Intercity Operator	131
International Operator	115
Telegrams by Phone	141

Tourist Information

Overseas Tourist Information Offices

The following is a list of the overseas bureaux of the Turkish Tourist Information Department.

United Kingdom, 170–173 Piccadilly, First Floor, London W1V 9DD, tel: (44-171) 629 7771.

USA, 821 United Nations Plaza, New York N.Y. 10017, tel: 1-212-687 2194).

Local Tourist Information Offices

Adana, Atatürk Caddesi 13, tel: (322) 359 1994/352 4886.

Alanya, Çarşı Mahallesi, Kale Arkası (behind citadel), tel: (242) 513 1240; also, next door to Damlataş Mağarası, tel: (242) 513 1240/513 5436.

Ankara, Gazi Mustafa Kemal Bulvarı 121, Tandoğan, tel: (312) 229 2631/ 231 5572.

Antakya, Vali Ürgen Alanı 47, tel: (326) 216 0610.

Antalya, Selçuk Mahallesi, Mermerli Sokak, next door to Ahi Yusuf Mosque, tel: (242) 247 5042/247 0541; also Cumhuriyet Caddesi, Özel ıdare Altı, No. 2, tel: (242) 241 1747.

Ayvalık, Opposite Yacht Marina, tel: (266) 312 2122.

Bergama, Zafer Mahallesi, Izmir Caddesi 54, tel: (232) 633 1862.

Bodrum, Barış Meydanı, tel: (252) 316 1091/316 7694.

Çanakkale, Iskele Meydanı (Harbour Square) 67, tel: (286) 217 1187.

Çeşme, Iskele Meydanı (Harbour Square) 8, tel: (232) 712 6653.

Dalaman, Airport, tel: (252) 692 5220.

Datça, Hükümet Binası, Iskele Meydanı (Marina), tel: (252) 712 3546/712 3163.

Edirne, Hürriyet Meydanı 17, tel: (284) 225 1518.

Fethiye, Iskele Karflısı 1 (opposite the marina), tel: (252) 614 1527.

Foça, Atatürk Bulvarı, Foça Girifli 1, tel: (232) 812 1222.

Istanbul, Atatürk Airport, tel: (212) 663 0793; Sultanahmet Square, tel: (212) 518 1802; Sirkeci Train Station, tel: (212) 511 5888; Meşrutiyet Caddesi 57/1, Tepebaşı, Beyoğlu, tel: (212) 245 0109; Turkish Maritime Port, Karaköy, tel: (212) 249 5776.

Izmir, Gazi Osmanpaşa Bulvarı, under Büyük Efes Hotel, tel: (232) 489 9278; Atatürk Caddesi 418, Alsancak, tel: (232) 422 1022; Airport, tel: (232) 274 2214.
Kaş, Cumhuriyet Meydanı 5, tel: (242) 836 1238.
Kemer, Belediye ve Turizm Binası, tel: (242) 814 1112/814 1537.
Köyceğiz, Atatürk Kordonu, tel: (252) 262 4703.
Kufladası, Liman Caddesi 13, tel: (256) 614 1103/614 6295.
Marmaris, Iskele Meydanı 2 (Harbour Square), tel: (252) 412 1035/412 7277.
Mersin, Ismet Inönü Bulvarı 5/1, tel: (324) 238 3271.
Muğla, Marmaris Bulvarı 24, tel: (252) 214 1261; Cumhuriyet Meydanı, Belediye Atapark Sitesi, tel: (252) 214 3127.
Pamukkale, Ören Yeri (Archaeological Site), tel: (258) 272 2077.
Selçuk, Atatürk Mahallesi, Agora Çarşısı 35, tel: (232) 892 6945/892 6328.
Side, Side Yolu Üzeri, Manavgat, tel: (242) 753 1265.
Silifke, Gazi Mahallesi, Veli Gürten Bozbey Caddesi 6, tel: (324) 714 1151.

Embassies

Listed below are the foreign embassies and consulates located in Ankara, Istanbul, Adana and Izmir.
Australia, Nene Hatun Caddesi 83, Gaziosmanpafla, Ankara, tel: (312) 446 1180; Tepecik Yokuflu 58, Etiler, Istanbul, tel: (212) 257 7050.
Canada, Nene Hatun Caddesi 75, Gaziosmanpaşa, Ankara, tel: (312) 436 1275.
United Kingdom, Şehit Ersan Caddesi 46/4, Çankaya, Ankara, tel: (312) 468 6230; Meşrutiyet Caddesi 34, Tepebaflı, Beyoğlu, Istanbul, tel: (212) 252 6436/293 7540; Kızılsaray Mah. Dolaplıdere Caddcsi, Pırıl Sitesi, 1st floor, Antalya, tel: (242) 247 7000; Atatürk Caddesi, Adliye Sokak 12/C, Bodrum, tel: (252) 316 4992.
USA, Atatürk Bulvarı 110, Kavaklıdere, Ankara, tel: (312) 468 6110/426 5470; Meşrutiyet Caddesi 104-108, Tepebaşı, Beyoğlu, Istanbul, tel: (212) 251 3602.

Emergencies

Violent crime is rare in Turkey. Theft by pickpockets is on the rise in crowded urban settings. Cars with cassette players and radios are also a popular target. In larger cities, parking in well-lit places is a good safe-guard.

Useful Numbers

Police	155
Gendarme	156
Emergency ambulance	112
Fire	110

Medical Services

Unless it is an emergency, wait until you've returned home for medical treatment. English, German or French speaking doctors who have been trained abroad, can be found in the cosmopolitan areas. Local pharmacies (Eczane) can provide antidotes for minor ailments, bruises and cuts. Antibiotics can be purchased without a prescription. A list of hospitals follows:

ANTALYA

Akdeniz University Medical School Hospital, Kepez Mahallesi, tel: (242) 227 4343.
Antalya Private Hospital, Bayındır Mahallesi, 325 Sokak 8, tel: (242) 335 0000. (English- and German-speaking doctors).
Antalya Private Clinic, Iflıklar Caddesi 55/2, tel: (242) 243 3159.
Akdeniz Hospital, (Private), Sorgun Yolu, tel: (242) 746 0013.
Specialists' Polyclinic, (Private), 100 Yıl bulvarı, Devlet Hastanesi Kavflağı, tel: (242) 241 3187.

BODRUM

Bodrum State Hospital, Turgutreis, Caddesi, tel: (252) 313 1420.
Bodrum Clinic, Sağlık Ocağı, Turgutreis Caddesi, tel: (252) 316 1353.
Halikarnas Clinic, Kıbrıs Şehitleri, Caddesi 97, tel: (252) 316 3635.
SOS International. Tel: (532) 215 3780.

IZMIR

American Hospital, 1375 Sokak, Alsancak, tel: (232) 484 5360.
Karakaş Jewish Hospital, (Musevi Hastanesi), Inönü Caddesi 336 Sokak 30, tel: (232) 484 9832.

ALANYA

Hayat Hastanesi, (Private), Yeni Hastane Caddesi, Yayla Yolu Civarı, tel: (242) 512 1455.

Doctors

ANTALYA

Kadri Yakut, (General surgeon), Konyaaltı Caddesi, Mehmet Konuk Apt. No. 17, tel: (242) 241 9911.
Haluk Yeğin, (Heart diseases), Güllük Caddesi 73, tel: (242) 248 0854. (Speaks English).
Mürüvet Kıvran, (Paediatrician), Güllük Caddesi, Alimoğlu Apt. No. 52/1, tel: (242) 242 9849. (Speaks German).
Fuat Kivran, (Gynaecologist), Güllük Caddesi, Alimoğlu Apt. No. 52/1, tel: (242) 242 9849. (Speaks English and German).
Mehmet Ali Uçar, (Internal diseases), Konyaaltı Caddesi 131, Güneş Apt. No. 2, tel: (242) 242 0530.

BODRUM

Kazım Kocagil, (Paediatrician). Tel: (252) 316 8138/(542) 212 0360.
Hüseyin Ünsal, (Internal diseases). Tel: (252) 313 1415.
Mehmet Akif Yılmaz, (Internal diseases and ultrasound). Tel: (252) 316 6834/(532) 231 0392.
Celal Tosun, (Gynaecology and ultrasound). Tel: (252) 316 4775.

Getting Around

On Arrival

Taxis are readily available at all airports 24 hours during the summer months. Most car rental services have offices at the major airports along the coast, at major tourist destinations, and in Istanbul.

Regular shuttle buses also operate at Istanbul Atatürk Airport, Izmir Adnan Menderes Airport, Antalya and Adana airports to the main Turkish Airlines ticket offices in the cities which are usually not more than a half hour's drive away. They also carry passengers for a small fee. A regular service bus operates from Dalaman Airport to Marmaris, two hours away.

Water Transport

The Turkish Maritime Lines (Türkiye Deniz Yolları) operates a regular passenger line service to the Turkish Aegean and Mediterranean from Istanbul with stops at major ports and resorts. They provide first-class accommodation and service and excellent opportunities for sightseeing. All boats depart from Sirkeci or Eminönü, and it is advisable to make early reservations for touristic cruises.

One of the best and cheapest ways to reach Izmir from Istanbul is a combination boat and train trip: passenger boats leave from Sirkeci every day except Sunday, to Bandırma, a pleasant town on the Asian shores of the Marmara Sea in the south. Departure time is 8pm on Fridays and 9am on other days. There is a train from Bandırma to Basmane Station in Izmir. The trip takes about 10 hours.

Çanakkale Car Ferry Service

Regular passenger and car ferryboats operate on the Dardanelles every hour between Çanakkale on the Asian side separately to Eceabat, and Kilitbahir on the European side. Ferryboats on the Gelibolu-Lapseki line operate every two hours. Daily ferryboats also operate to the Turkish Aegean island of Gökçeada (Imroz) from Çanakkale and Kabatepe on the Gallipoli Peninsula. The Turkish Aegean island of Bozcaada (Tenedos) can be reached by daily ferryboats from Geyikli Iskelesi south west of Çanakkale. Bozcaada is a pretty, and usually sleepy, little island whose main livelihood is wine production. Gökçeada is both residential and a military base. Both islands welcome foreign visitors and there is no obligation for foreigners to get permission to visit the island.

Izmir Ferry

The pleasant and comfortable car and passenger ferryboats leave for Izmir from Istanbul weekly on Fridays at 5.30pm. Arrival is early next morning.

Passenger Ferries

Apart from the numerous cruises by Turkish Maritime Lines in the Mediterranean, several foreign shipping companies have regular boat services to the ports of Istanbul, Izmir, Kuşadası and Bodrum.

Car Ferries

Turkish Maritime Lines (TML) operates an Izmir-Venice line weekly during the summer. The boat leaves Izmir on Wednesday at 4pm, and arrives in Venice on Saturday. The return trip to Izmir is on Saturday at 9pm, arriving on Tuesday. From June to October, TML also sails to Venice from Antalya, leaving every other week.

Ferryboats operate between Mersin and Magosa (Famagusta in the Northern Cyprus) three times a week. A private company operates ferryboats regularly between Tasucu and Girne (Kyrenia) in Northern Cyprus.

Ferry Lines between Turkey and Greece:

Ayvalık-Lesbos: April through October daily boat service except Sundays. Price $15 adult one-way; $25 return on same day; $15 motorcycles; $120 caravans. Crossing: two hours.

Bodrum-Cos: Daily service in summer. Price $10 adult one way; $15 return same day; $25 return open date; $15 motorcycles; vehicles $40 up to 1,650 pounds (750 kg); $60 up to 2,200 pounds (1,000 kg); $80 up to 2,750 pounds (1,250 kg); and $100 for caravans. Crossing: one and a half hours.

Marmaris-Rhodes: Daily service in summer. Price: $20 adult one way; $50 motorcycles; $65 cars; $100 minibus; $150 caravan. Crossing: three and a half hours.

Kuşadasi-Samos Island: every day in the summer.

Private Transport

Driving within Turkey requires the utmost alertness of the driver at all times. Winding coastal roads, while breathtakingly scenic, can be dangerous. Above all, beware of aggressive male drivers.

Numerous car rental agencies, such as Avis, Hertz, Europcar, Budget and Airtour have offices in major cities and resort towns on the Turkish Coast. Renting a car costs about twice as much in Turkey than it does in Europe and the US. Jeeps as well as chauffeur-driven cars and limousines can also be rented.

Car Rental Services

AVIS OFFICES

Adana, Ziya Paşa Bulvarı, Hürriyet Apt. 11/B, tel: (322) 453 3045; Airport: tel: (322) 435 0476.

Alanya, Atatürk Caddesi 13, tel: (242) 513 3513/513 4990.

Ankara, Tunus Caddesi 68/2, Kavaklıdere, tel: (312) 467 2313; Airport: (312) 398 0315.

Antalya, Fevzi Çakmak Caddesi, Talya Apt. 67/B, tel: (242) 242 5642/241 6693; Airport, tel: (242) 330 3073.

Ayvalık, Talatpaşa Caddesi 67/B, tel: (266) 312 2456.

Bodrum, Neyzen Tevfik Caddesi 92/A, tel: (252) 316 1996/316 2333; Imsık Airport, Bodrum, tel: (252) 373 5707.

Çeşme/Izmir, Cumhuriyet Meydanı, underneath Rıdvan Hotel, 11/1C, Çeşme, tel: (232) 712 6706.

Dalaman, Airport, tel: (252) 692 5410/692 5588.

Fethiye, Fevzi Çakmak Caddesi 1/B, tel: (252) 614 6339/612 1385.

Göcek/Muğla, Setur Travel Company Office, Göcek Village, Muğla, tel: (252) 645 2079/645 1323.

Iskenderun, Pac Meydanı, Pınarbaşı Caddesi 1/A, tel: (326) 615 4949.

Istanbul, Hilton Hotel Arcade, Elmadağ, tel: (212) 246 5256/241 7896; Selamiçeşme (Asian side), Bağdat Caddesi 162/7, tel: (216) 355 3665/350 4878; Airport, International Lines, tel: (212) 663 0646; Chauffeur-drive service, tel: (212) 241 7896.

Izmir, Şair Eşref Bulvarı 18/D, Alsancak, tel: (232) 441 4417; Airport, tel: (232) 274 2172.

Kemer/Antalya, Atatürk Bulvarı 8/G, Kemer, tel: (242) 814 3936/814 1372.

Kuşadaı, Atatürk Bulvarı 26/A, tel: (256) 614 4600.

Marmaris, Atatürk Caddesi 30, tel: (252) 412 2771/412 6412.

Mersin, Ismet Inönü Bulvarı 100, Uysal Apt., tel: (324) 232 3228.

Selçuk/Ephesus, Atatürk Caddesi, Belediye Pasajı 7/10, Selçuk, tel: (232) 892 2226/892 2469.

Side, Fatih Caddesi 25, tel: (242) 753 1348/753 2813.

BUDGET RENT-A-CAR OFFICES

Alanya, Saray Mahallesi, Atatürk Caddesi, Oral Apt., tel: (242) 513 7382.

Ankara, Tunus Caddesi 38/A, Kavaklıdere, tel: (312) 417 5952; Airport, tel: (312) 398 0372.

Antalya, Gençlik Mahallesi, Fevzi Çakmak Caddesi 27, tel: (242) 243 3006; Airport, tel: (242) 330 3079.

Bodrum, Neyzen Tevfik Caddesi 86/A, tel: (252) 316 7382.

Bursa, Çekirge Caddesi, Kültür Park Karşısı, Kerem Apt., tel: (224) 222 8322.

Fethiye, Karagözler Yokuşu, tel: (252) 614 6166.

Istanbul, Cumhuriyet Caddesi 13/1, Taksim, tel: (212) 253 9200/237 2919; Airport, International Lines Arrival, tel: (212) 663 0858; Feneryolu (Asian side), tel: (216) 449 3646.

Izmir, Şair Eşref Bulvarı 22/1, Alsancak, tel: (232) 441 9224; Airport, tel: (232) 274 2203.

Kuşadası, Sağlık Caddesi 58, tel: (256) 614 4956.

Marmaris, Ulusal Egemenlik Caddesi 12, Girginç Apt., tel: (252) 412 4144.

Side, Side Girişi (at the entry to Side Town), tel: (242) 753 1486.

Where to Stay

1) "SL" indicates "special licence" hotels which are housed in restored historic buildings. They normally have a limited number of rooms with many of the luxuries offered by the larger hotels.

2) *It is understood that hotels with more than 3 stars, and holiday villages/clubs have private bathroom, direct-dail phone, music, TV, and hairdryer in each room.*

The Northern Aegean
Assos

Assos, Behramkale Iskele, Ayvacık, tel: (286) 721 7092; fax: (286) 721 7249. (SL). 36 rooms with shower and toilet, direct-dial phone, TV, minibar, air conditioning. Restaurant, bar.

Behram, Behramkale Iskele, Ayvacık, tel: (286) 721 7016; fax: (286) 721 7044. (SL). 17 rooms with shower and toilet, direct-dial phone, central heating. Restaurant, bar.

Nazlıhan, Behramkale Iskele, Ayvacık, tel: (286) 721 7064; fax: (286) 721 7387. (SL). 37 rooms with shower and toilet. Restaurant, bar.

Bayram Motel, Kadırga Koyu, Behramkale, Ayvacık, tel: (286) 721 7041; fax: (286) 721 7141. 30 rooms with shower and toilet, direct-dial phone, central heating. Restaurant, bar, campsite, beach, parking.

Eden Beach, Kadırga Koyu, Behramkale, Ayvacık, tel: (286) 721 7039; fax: (286) 721 7054. 68 rooms with shower and toilet, phone, central heating. Restaurant, bar, playground, beach, water sports, parking.

Troas, Büyük Hüsun Köyü altı, Ayvacık, tel: (286) 762 9330. 18 rooms with toilet and shower. Restaurant, bar, beach, parking.

Bozcaada (Tenedos) Island

Ege Bozcaada, Kale Arkası, tel: (286) 697 81 89; fax: (286) 697 8389. (SL). 36 rooms with toilet and shower. Bed and breakfast. Bar and TV room. Garden.

Thenes, Iğdelik Mevkii, tel: (286) 697 8888; fax: (286) 697 8367. 28 rooms with toilet and shower, direct-dial phone, central heating. Restaurant, bar, water sports. ☆☆

Ümit, Iğdeli Sokak 14, tel: (286) 697 8880; fax: (286) 697 8278. 6 rooms with direct-dial phone, bathroom, central heating. Bed and breakfast.

Çanakkale

Akol, Kordonboyu Caddesi, tel: (286) 217 9456; fax: (286) 217 2897. 135 rooms with bathroom, balcony, direct-dial phone, air conditioning, minibar, TV, central heating. Restaurant, bar, swimming pool. ☆☆☆☆

Anzac, Saat Kulesi Meydanı 8, tel: (286) 217 7777; fax: (286) 217 2018. 27 rooms with bathroom, phone, TV, central heating, minibar. Restaurant, bar, meeting room. ☆☆

Büyük Truva, Cevatpaşa Mahallesi, Mehmet Akif Ersoy Caddesi 2, tel: (286) 217 1024; fax: (286) 217 0903. 66 rooms with toilet and shower, direct-dial phones, TV, minibar, central heating. Restaurant, bar, meeting room. ☆☆☆

Guleç, Cevatpaşa Mahallesi, Velibey Sokak 6, tel: (286) 217 2500; fax: (286) 217 6409. Pension with 21 rooms with shower and toilet, direct-dial phone, TV, central heating. Bed and breakfast.

Kestanbol, Hasan Mevsuf Sokak 5, tel: (286) 217 0857; fax: (286) 217 9173. 26 rooms with shower and toilet, phone, TV, central heating. Bed and breakfast. ☆

Tusan, Güzelyalı, Çanakkale, tel: (286) 232 8210; fax: (286) 232 8226. 64 rooms with bathroom, direct dial phone, air conditioning, central heating, minibar, TV. Restaurant, meeting room, playground, disco, sports. ☆☆☆

Edirne

Balta, Talatpaşa Asfaltı 97, tel: (284) 225 5210; fax: (284) 225 3529. 75 rooms with bathroom, direct-dial phone, TV. Restaurant, bar, meeting room. ☆☆

Gelibolu

Abide, Morfo Bay, Alçıtepe Köyü, Eceabat, Gelibolu Peninsula, tel: (286) 844 6158. Hotel, restaurant, beach.

Boncuk, Sütlüce Kale Köyü, Gelibolu, tel: (286) 576 8292; fax: (286) 576 8158. 48 rooms with toilet and shower, direct-dial phone, central heating. Restaurant, bar, swimming pool, sports. ☆☆☆

Kum Motel & Camping, Birinci Paşa Mahallesi, Evren Sokak 2/2, 16km from Eceabat, Gelibolu, tel: (286) 814 1455; fax: (286) 814 1917. 56 rooms with toilet and shower, phone, central heating. Camping, restaurant, beach, sports, parking.

Gökçeada (Imbros) Island

Gökçe Hotel, town centre, Gökçeada Island, tel: (286) 887 3473. Rooms with toilet and shower, direct-dial phone, central heating. Bed and breakfast. ☆☆

Keflan

Yener, Yukarı Zaferiye Mahallesi, Demirciler Caddesi 18, tel: (282) 714 3660; fax: (282) 714 5755. 68 rooms with bathroom, direct-dial phone, TV, central heating. Restaurant, bar, meeting room. ☆☆☆

The Southern Aegean
Akçay-Altınoluk-Edremit

Afrodit Holiday Village, Altınoluk, tel: (266) 378 5380; fax: (266) 378 5222. 25 apartments, 12 suite rooms. Restaurants, bars, beach, Turkish bath, fitness centre, swimming pool, disco, market, sports.

Güneş, Buruncu Mevki, Altınoluk, tel: (266) 396 1313; fax: (266) 396 1370. 83 rooms with toilet and shower, direct-dial phone. Restaurant, bar, beach, pool, disco, sports. ☆☆☆

Idaköy Çiftliği, Çamlıbel Köyü, Edremit, tel: (266) 387 3402. A farm house/pension with a small number of rooms, set on the outskirts of the village of Kaz Dağları (Mt Ida). (Istanbul office tel: 216- 337 1962; fax: 216-347 2224).

Linda Hotel, Barbaros Meydanı, Akçay, tel: (266) 384 3500; fax: (266) 384 2524. Pension with 18 rooms all with toilet and shower, direct-dial phone, TV, central heating. Restaurant and bar.

Mare & Monte,Iskele Mahallesi, Fatih Caddesi 7, Altınoluk, tel: (266) 396 1730; fax: (266) 396 0675. Pension, 23 rooms with toilet and shower, central heating. Restaurant, bar, beach, sports.

Aliağa

Afacan Motel, Incirlik Mevkii, Aliağa, tel: (232) 628 7030; fax: (232) 463 0975. 36 rooms with bathroom. Restaurant, bar, swimming pool, garden, playground, campsite, disco, sports.

Ayvalık

Florium, Lale Adası, Ayvalık, tel: (266) 312 9627; fax: (266) 312 9631. 135 rooms with air-conditioning, minibar, and balcony. Restaurants, bars, swimming pool, Turkish bath and sauna, pâtisserie, sports. ☆☆☆☆☆

Club Washington, Tuzla Mevkii, Ayvalık, tel: (266) 343 7395; fax: (266) 343 7399. 230 rooms with bathroom, direct-dial phone, air conditioning, central heating. Restaurants, bars, swimming pool, playground, disco, game room, shops, sports, meeting room, parking. ☆☆☆

Billurcu, Sarımsaklı, Ayvalık, tel: (266) 324 1188; fax: (266) 324 1751. 60 rooms and 30 apartments, with bathroom, direct-dial phone, TV. Restaurants, bars, swimming pool, sports, meeting room. ☆☆

Kaptan Hotel, Balıkhane Sokak, Ayvalık, tel: (266) 312 8834. 15 rooms with bathroom, phone, hot water. Bed and breakfast.

Ilker, Halk Caddesi 10, Alibey (Cunda) Island, tel: (266) 327 1034. Pension with five rooms. Shared bathrooms and kitchen.

Taksiyahis, Mareşal Fevzi Çakmak Caddesi 71, Ayvalık, tel: (266) 312 1494. Pension with five rooms. Shared bathrooms and kitchen, washing machine, Turkish bath.

Yalı, Behind PTT building 20, Ayvalık, tel: (266) 312 2423. Pension with five rooms. Shared bathrooms and kitchen, hot water, washing machine.

Bergama

Berksoy, Izmir Asfaltı 19, Bergama, tel: (232) 633 2595; fax: (232) 633 5346. 57 rooms with bathroom, phone, TV, minibar, central heating. Restaurants, bars, meeting room, swimming pool, play ground, sports. ☆☆☆

Iskender, Izmir Asfaltı, Ilıca Önü Mevkii, Bergama, tel: (232) 633 2123; fax: (232) 633 1245. 60 rooms with bathroom, phone, central heating. Restaurant, bar. ☆☆☆

Efsane, Izmir Asfaltı 86, Bergama, tel: (232) 632 6350; fax: (232) 632 6353. 24 rooms with toilet and shower, phone, central heating. Restaurant, bar, swimming pool. ☆☆

Tusan Motel, Yolçatı Mevkii, Bergama, tel: (232) 633 1173; fax: (232) 632 6284. 44 rooms with bathroom, central heating. Restaurant.

Böblingen, Asklepion Caddesi 2, Bergama, tel: (232) 633 2153. Pension with 11 rooms with shower. Bed and breakfast.

Bodrum

Bodrum Cesars, Okaliptus Sokak 4, Gümbet, tel: (252) 316 9571; fax: (252) 316 9570. 100 rooms with air conditioning, minibar. Restaurants, bars, swimming pool, Turkish bath, health club, shop, casino, night club, sports. ☆☆☆☆☆

Kariye Princess, Canlıdere Sokak 15, Bodrum, tel: (252) 316 8971; fax: (252) 316 8979. 52 rooms all fitted with air conditioning, minibar, central heating. Restaurant, bars, meeting room, swimming pool, Turkish bath, gym, garden, casino, night club. ☆☆☆☆☆

Sea Garden, Yalıçiftlik, tel: (252) 368 9015; fax: (252) 368 9048. 285 rooms with air conditioning, minibar, central heating. Restaurants, bars, swimming pools, beach, garden, night club, Turkish bath, fitness centre, sports. ☆☆☆☆☆

Ambrosia, Bitez Yalısı, tel: (252) 343 1886; fax: (252) 343 1879. 84 rooms minibar, balcony, central heating. Restaurant, bars, conference rooms, Turkish bath, gym, jacuzzi, health room, swimming pool, beach, shop, sports. ☆☆☆☆

Bona Dea, Bardakçı Koyu, Bodrum, tel: (252) 313 0371; fax: (252) 313 0375. 138 rooms with air conditioning, minibar, balcony, central heating. Restaurants, bars, meeting room, swimming pools, medical room, health centre, baby sitter, beach. ☆☆☆☆

Club Hotel Hebilköy, Türkbükü, Hebilköy, tel: (252) 377 5477; fax: (252) 377 5546. 70 rooms with air conditioning, minibar. Restaurant, bars, Turkish bath, swimming pool, disco, animation, shop, sports. ☆☆☆☆

Medisun, Yahşi Yalısı, Ortakent, tel: (252) 348 3207; fax: (252) 348 3487. 75 rooms with air conditioning, minibar, safe, central heating. Restaurant, bars, garden, Turkish bath, sauna, gym, swimming pool, garden, hairdresser, shop, disco, sports. ☆☆☆☆

Olfiya, Yalıçiftlik Mevkii, tel: (252) 368 9111; fax: (252) 368 9112. 200 rooms with air conditioning, minibar. Restaurants, bars, conference rooms, swimming pool, beach, sauna, health cabin, hairdresser, shops, disco, children's club, sports. ☆☆☆☆

Anka, Eskiçeşme Mahallesi, Aşarlık Mevkii, Gümbet, tel: (252) 316 8217; fax: (252) 316 6194. 90 rooms with toilet and shower, phone, balcony. Restaurant, bars, swimming pool, beach, garden, disco, health cabin, sports. ☆☆☆

Bitez Han, Bitez Yalısı, tel: (252) 343 1766; fax: (252) 343 1968. 80 rooms with toilet and shower, phone, balcony. Restaurant, bars, swimming pool, beach, Turkish bath, garden, shop, sports. ☆☆☆

Club Yalıkavak Boydaş, Tilkicik Köyü, Yalıkavak, tel: (252) 316 3548; fax: (252) 316 1365. 123 rooms with toilet and shower, phone. Restaurants, bars, swimming pool, beach, health cabin, shop, sports. ☆☆☆

Myndos, Mindos Caddesi 1, Bodrum, tel: (252) 316 3080; fax: (252) 316 5252. 51 rooms with toilet and shower, phone, central heating. Restaurant, bars, swimming pool, TV room. ☆☆☆

Torbahan, Sahil Yolu 36, Torba, tel: (252) 367 1073; fax: (252) 367 1075. 50 rooms with toilet and shower, phone, fan. Restaurant, bars, swimming pool, garden, sports. ☆☆☆

Aksu, Cumhuriyet Caddesi 159, Bodrum, tel: (252) 316 8883; fax: (252) 316 9111. 21 rooms with toilet and shower, phone, fan, central heating. Restaurant, bars, swimming pool, beach, garden. In city centre. ☆☆

Bodrum Maya, Gerence Sokak 49, Bodrum, tel: (252) 316 4741; fax: (252) 316 4745. 72 rooms with toilet and shower, phone, air conditioning, central heating. Restaurant, bars, swimming pool, gym, sauna. In city centre. ☆☆

Domino, Gümbet, tel: (252) 316 0152; fax: (252) 316 0153. 39 rooms with toilet and shower, phone. Restaurant, swimming pool, TV room. ☆☆

Seçkin Konaklar, Neyzen Tevfik Caddesi 246, Bodrum, tel: (252) 316 1351; fax: (252) 316 3336. 37 rooms with toilet and shower, phone, central heating. Breakfast room, bar, swimming pool. In city centre. ☆☆

Yaprak, Kadıkalesi, Turgutreis, tel: (252) 382 2017; fax: (252) 382 4982. 43 rooms with toilet and shower, phone, balcony. Restaurant, bar, swimming pool, beach, sports.

Mylasa Pension, Cumhuriyet Caddesi 34, Azmakbaşı, Bodrum, tel: (252) 316 1846; fax: (252) 316 1254. 16 rooms with toilet and shower, phone. Breakfast room, bar, TV room. Bed and breakfast. In city centre.

Club Hotel M Holiday Village, Değirmen Mevkii, Haremtan, Bodrum, tel: (252) 316 6100; fax: (252) 316 2581. 209 rooms with bathroom, TV, minibar, air conditioning, phone. Restaurants, bars, conference room, swimming pools, beach, Turkish bath, gym, health cabin, sports.

Club Med Palmiye Holiday Village, Çiftlik Köyü Yalısı, tel: (252) 368 9152; fax: (252) 368 9138. 176 rooms with toilet and shower, phone, air conditioning. Restaurants, bars, conference hall, swimming pool, beach, Turkish bath, gym, health cabin, shop, sports.

Club Müskebi Holiday Village, Ortakent, tel: (252) 358 5086; fax: 358 5067. 138 rooms with toilet and shower, phone, balcony. Restaurant, bars, swimming pool, beach, disco, health cabin, garden, sports.

Burhaniye-Ören

Artemis Holiday Village, Ören, tel: (266) 412 5420; fax: (266) 422 1317. 112 rooms. Restaurants, bar, disco, beach, swimming pool, shops, sports, playground.

Konak Lale Hotel & Fer-Tur Villas, Ören, tel: (266) 422 1343; fax: (266) 422 2366. 25 suite rooms and 15 apart villas. Restaurant, bar, garden, sports, disco. ☆☆

Club Orient Holiday Village, İğdeburnu Mevkii, Ören, tel: (266) 412 6943; fax: (266) 412 7292. 62 rooms with bathroom, phone, refrigerator. Restaurants, bar, beach, swimming pool, disco, shops, sports, playground.

Urut 1, Hürriyet Meydanı 14, Burhaniye, tel: (266) 422 1105; fax: (266) 412 5250. 72 rooms with bathroom, phone, central heating. Restaurant, bar, meeting room. ☆☆☆

Urut 2, Meco Caddesi, Ören, tel: (266) 422 1205; fax: (266) 412 5250. 34 rooms with toilet and shower. Restaurant, bar, garden.

Çesme-Ilıca

Framissima Boyalık Beach, Boyalık Mevkii, Çeşme, tel: (232) 712 7081; fax: (232) 712 7331. 210 rooms. Restaurants, bars, meeting rooms, swimming pool, beach, play ground, disco, shops, sports. ☆☆☆☆

Çeşme Ladin, Dalyan Köy, Çeşme, tel: (232) 724 8327; fax: (232) 724 7039. 71 rooms with toilet and shower, phone, central heating, balcony. Restaurant, bars, swimming pool, garden, fitness centre, sauna, shop, playground, sports. ☆☆☆

Farm, Çiftlikköy, Çeşme, tel: (232) 722 1236; fax: (232) 722 1235. 52 rooms with toilet and shower, phone, balcony. Restaurant, bar, swimming pool, garden, beach. ☆☆☆

Inkim, Izmir Caddesi, PTT Karşısı, Ilıca, tel: (232) 723 3900; fax: (232) 723 3904. 71 rooms with toilet and shower, phone, central heating, balcony. Restaurant, bar, swimming pool, beach, sports. ☆☆☆

Rıdvan, Cumhuriyet Meydanı 11, Çeşme, tel: (232) 712 6336; fax: (232) 712 7627. 36 rooms with toilet and shower, phone, TV, minibar, central heating. Restaurant, bar. ☆☆

Altın Yunus Holiday Village, Boyalık Mevkii, Çeşme, tel: (232) 723 1250; fax: (232) 723 2252. 514 rooms. Restaurants, bars, conference rooms, casino, indoor and outdoor pools, beach, multi-functional health club, hydrotherapy, sports, shops.

Club Kardia Holiday Village, Çiftlik Mahallesi, Çeşme, tel: (232) 722 1111; fax: (232) 722 1227. 257 rooms with toilet and shower, phone, fan, balcony. Restaurants, bars, meeting rooms, Turkish bath, fitness centre, indoor and outdoor swimming pools, beach, children's club, sports.

Golf Holiday Club, Çiftlik Mahallesi, Çeşme, tel: (232) 722 1003; fax: (232) 722 1225. 62 suite rooms with toilet and shower, balcony. Restaurant, bars, swimming pool, beach, garden, disco, sports.

Omarland Holiday Village, Narlıca, Ildırı, Çeşme, tel: (232) 715 2153; fax: (232) 715 1421. 75 apartment villas with bathroom, phone, TV, refrigerator, fireplace, air conditioning, balcony. Restaurant, bars, swimming pool, beach, night club, disco, sports.

Kaptan, Yeni Çevre Yolu, Çeşme, tel: (232) 712 6186. Pension with 40 rooms with toilet and shower, phone. Swimming pool. Bed and breakfast.

Datça

Mare, Şükrü Efendi Caddesi, Datça, tel: (252) 712 3211; fax: (252) 712 3396. 50 rooms with toilet and shower, phone, balcony. Restaurant, bar, swimming pool, garden, beach, shop, sports. ☆☆☆

Soytok, Yalı Caddesi 5, Datça, tel: (252) 712 2160, fax: (252) 712 3065. 39 rooms with toilet and shower, central heating. Restaurant, bar, garden. Bed and breakfast. ☆☆

Fuda Yalı, Dr. Turgut Dündar Caddesi, Datça, tel: (252) 712 2237; fax: (252) 712 4066. 20 rooms with toilet and shower, phone. Restaurant, bar, garden, beach, sports. ☆

Olimpos, Koru Mevkii, Datça, tel: (252) 712 2001; fax: (252) 712 2653. 30 rooms with toilet and shower, phone, balcony. Restaurant, bar, TV room. (SL)

Didim

Holipark Swan, Akbük Mevkii, Didim, tel: (256) 846 1830; fax: (256) 846 1797. 197 rooms with air conditioning, balcony. Restaurant, bars, Turkish bath, fitness centre, swimming pool, beach, garden, hairdresser, shop, disco, sports. ☆☆☆☆☆

Tuntaş, Altınkum, Didim, tel: (256) 813 2905; fax: (256) 813 1391. 134 rooms with toilet and shower, phone, balcony. Restaurant, bars, swimming pool, garden, beach, sports. ☆☆☆

Grand Didyma, Üç Mevsim Sitesi, Altınkum, Didim, tel: (256) 813 2038; fax: (256) 813 3468. 63 rooms with toilet and shower, air conditioning. Restaurant, bars, swimming pool, playground. ☆☆

Club Patio Ligamar Holiday Village, Çamburun Mevkii, Akbük, Didim, tel: (256) 856 4273; fax: (256) 856 4281. 134 rooms with air conditioning, balcony. Restaurants, bars, health cabin, swimming pool, garden, shops, disco, children's club, sports.

Dikili

Mysia, Geren Mevkii, Dikili, tel: (232) 671 7010; fax: (232) 671 4987. 136 rooms with bathroom, phone, TV, air conditioning, minibar. Restaurants, bars, meeting room, pâtisserie, swimming pool, garden, health cabin, shop, sports. ☆☆☆

Sinka, Iskele Caddesi, Park Karşısı 2, Dikili, tel: (232) 671 4433; fax: (232) 671 4717. 24 rooms with bathroom, phone, central heating. Restaurant, bar.

Foça

Hanedan Beach Hotel, Dördüncü Mersinaki, Foça, tel: (232) 812 3650; fax: (232) 812 2451. 70 rooms with bathroom, phone, TV, minibar, central heating. Restaurants, bars, meeting room, swimming pool, Turkish bath, shop, disco, sports. ☆☆☆

Club Mavi Holiday Village, Çanak Mevki, Foça, tel: (232) 825 1002; fax: (232) 825 1030. 250 rooms with bathroom, phone, refrigerator. Restaurant, bars, health cabin, playground, sports.

Club Mediterranee, Eski Foça, tel: (232) 812 3691; fax: (232) 812 2175. 350 rooms with bathroom, safe. Restaurants, bars, Turkish bath, swimming pool, disco, children's club.

Amphora, Ismetpaşa Mahallesi, 208 Sokak 7, Eski Foça, tel: (232) 812 2806; fax: (232) 812 2483. 27 rooms with bathroom, phone, minibar, central heating. Restaurant, bar, garden, swimming pool. (SL).

Karaçam, Sahil Caddesi 70, Eski Foça, tel: (232) 812 1416; fax: (232) 812 2042. (SL).

Evim, 216 Sokak 40, Eski Foça, tel: (232) 812 1360. Pension with seven rooms. Shared bathrooms, garden. Bed and breakfast.

Güllük (Bodrum)

Labranda Corinthia, Sıralık Mevkii, Güllük, Milas, tel: (252) 522 2911; fax: (252) 522 2009. 138 rooms with air conditioning, minibar, balcony, central heating. Restaurants, bars, swimming pool, beach, meeting rooms, shops, gym, health cabin, disco, animation, sports. ☆☆☆☆

Gümüldür

Euro Sun Club, Atatürk Mahallesi, Gümüşsu Caddesi 17, Gümüldür, tel: (232) 793 1407; fax: (232) 793 1850. 173 rooms with bathroom, phone, air conditioning, refrigerator, central heating. Restaurants, bars, health cabin, beach, swimming pool, garden, disco, sports. ☆☆☆

Denizatı Holiday Village, Büyükalan Mevkii, Gümüldür, tel: (232) 793 1333; fax: (232) 793 1692. 70 rooms with toilet and shower, balcony. Restaurant, bars, beach, swimming pool, garden, health cabin, disco, shop, sports.

Izmir

Büyük Efes Hotel, Gaziosmanpaşa Bulvarı 1, tel: (232) 484 4300; fax: (232) 441 5695. 446 rooms air conditioning, minibar, central heating, balcony. Restaurants, bars, meeting rooms, Turkish bath, fitness centre, shops, garden, indoor and outdoor swimming pools, casino, sports. ☆☆☆☆☆

Hilton, Gaziosmanpaşa Bulvarı 7, tel: (232) 441 6060; fax: (232) 441 2277. 381 rooms with electronic lock, sprinklers, air conditioning, minibar, hairdryer, electronic safety box. Rooms for handicapped, no-smoking floor, CD and video players in some rooms. Restaurants, bars, meeting rooms, fitness centre, hairdresser, indoor swimming pool, solarium, casino, shops, sports. ☆☆☆☆☆

Mercure, Cumhuriyet Bulvarı 138, tel: (232) 489 4090; fax: (232) 489 4089. 168 rooms with air conditioning, minibar, hairdryer. Restaurants, bars, meeting rooms, night club, casino, shops, indoor and outdoor swimming pools, gym, sauna, solarium, hairdresser. ☆☆☆☆☆

Thermal Princess, Balçova, Izmir, tel: (232) 238 5151; fax: (232) 239 0939. 300 rooms with thermal bath, air conditioning, minibar, hairdryer, safe. Restaurants, bars, pâtisserie, meeting rooms, Turkish bath, sauna, gym, hairdresser, shops, indoor and outdoor swimming pools, casino, night club, disco, sports. ☆☆☆☆☆

Ege Palas, Cumhuriyet Bulvarı, Alsancak, tel: (232) 463 9090; fax: (232) 463 8100. 112 rooms with air conditioning, hairdryer, minibar, balcony. Restaurants, bars, meeting rooms, outdoor swimming pool, fitness centre with sauna, hairdresser, shops. ☆☆☆☆

Balçova Termal, Vali Hüseyin Öğütgen Caddesi 2, Balçova, tel: (232) 259 0102; fax: (232) 259 0829. 198 rooms with bathroom, phone, air conditioning. Restaurants, bars, meeting rooms, garden, physical rehabilitation centre, indoor and outdoor swimming pools, health cabin, sauna, jacuzzi, sports. ☆☆☆

Ismira, Gaziosmanpaşa Bulvarı 28, Çankaya, tel: (232) 445 6060; fax: (232) 445 6071. 78 rooms with bathroom, phone, TV, minibar, air conditioning, central heating. Restaurant, bar, pâtisserie, meeting room. ☆☆☆

Izmir Palace, Vasıf Çınar Bulvarı 2, Alsancak, tel: (232) 421 5583; fax: (232) 422 6870. Seafront hotel. 152 rooms with bathroom, phone, minibar, TV, air conditioning, central heating. Restaurant, bar, meeting room, 24-hour room service. ☆☆☆

Karaca, 1379 Sokak 55, Sevgi Yolu, Alsancak, tel: (232) 489 1940; fax: (232) 483 1498. 73 rooms with bathroom, phone, TV, minibar, air conditioning, central heating. Restaurant, bar, laundry, hairdresser, 24-hour room service. ☆☆☆

Devak, Mustafa Kemal Sahil Bulvarı 273, tel: (232) 445 9480; fax: (232) 483 1516. 40 rooms with bathroom, phone, TV, air conditioning, minibar, central heating. Restaurant, bar, meeting room, garden. ☆☆

Ege Çınar, 9 Eylül Meydanı 2, Basmane, tel: (232) 441 3113; fax: (232) 489 5068. 35 rooms with bathroom, phone, TV, air conditioning, minibar, central heating. Bed and breakfast, bar. ☆☆

Küçükkuyu

Çetmi Han, Yeşilyurt Köyü, Küçükkuyu, Kazdağları (Mt Ida), Çanakkale, tel: (286) 752 6169; fax: (286) 752 6170. 10 rooms with toilet and shower, central heating. Restaurant, bar with fireplace, garden. (SL).

Kuaşdası

Fantasia De Luxe, Söke Yolu, Yavansu Mevkii, Kuşadası, tel: (256) 614 8550; fax: (256) 614 2765. 324 rooms all with air conditioning, minibar, balcony. Restaurants, bars, conference rooms, indoor and outdoor pools, beach, disco, casino, Turkish bath, health club, shops, sports. ☆☆☆☆☆

Korumar, Gazi Beğendi Mevkii, Kuşadası, tel: (256) 614 8243; fax: (256) 614 5596. 248 rooms with air conditioning, minibar, balcony, central heating. Restaurants, bars, conference rooms,Turkish bath, fitness centre, shops, indoor and outdoor pools, beach, disco, casino, sports. ☆☆☆☆☆

Tusan, 31'ler Mevkii, Kuşadası, tel: (256) 614 4495; fax: (256) 614 4498. 202 deluxe rooms with air conditioning, minibar, 148 standard rooms. Restaurants, bars, Turkish bath, fitness centre, swimming pools, night club, shops, hairdresser, game room, sports. ☆☆☆☆☆

Ayma International, Kadınlar Plajı, Kuşadası, tel: (256) 614 9041; fax: (256) 614 7004. 128 rooms with air conditioning, minibar, balcony, central heating. Restaurants, bars, meeting room, swimming pool, Turkish bath, health cabin, sauna, shop.☆☆☆☆

Kısmet, Akyar Mevkii, Türkmen Mahallesi, Kuşadası, tel: (256) 614 2005; fax: (256) 614 4914. 102 rooms with bathroom, phone, TV, air conditioning, balcony. Restaurants, bars, beach, garden, sports. ☆☆☆

Macellan, Near Dilek Peninsula National Park, Güzelçamlı, tel: (256) 646 1980; fax: (256) 646 1980. 86 rooms with toilet and shower, phone, minibar, balcony. Restaurant, bars, health cabin, swimming pool, beach, garden, disco, sports. ☆☆☆

Martı, Kadınlar Plajı, Kuşadası, tel: (256) 614 3650; fax: (256) 614 4700. 112 rooms with bathroom, phone, balcony. Restaurants, bars, night club, sports. ☆☆☆

Club Solara, Güzelçamlı Mevkii, Kuşadası, tel: (256) 646 1988; fax: (256) 646 1483. 90 rooms with toilet and shower, phone, balcony. Restaurant, bar, meeting room, swimming pool, garden, night club, playground, sports. ☆☆

Club Kervansaray, Atatürk Bulvarı 2, Kuşadası, tel: (256) 614 4115; fax: (256) 614 2423. 40 rooms with toilet and shower, phone. Restaurant, bar, night club, laundry, garden. (SL).

Club Mediterranee Kuşadası, Arslanburnu Mevkii, Kuşadası, tel: (256) 614 9391; fax: (256) 614 1200. 478 rooms with bathroom and safe. Restaurants, bars, night club, swimming pool, beach, disco, children's club, sports.

Kuştur Holiday Village, Bayraklıdede Mahallesi, 31'ler Plajı, Kuşadası, tel: (256) 614 4110; fax: 614 8832. 499 rooms with toilet and shower. Restaurants, bars, conference room, Turkish bath, swimming pool, beach, children's club, disco, hairdresser, sports.

Colibri, Cumhuriyet Mahallesi, Menderes Bulvarı 7, Kuşadası, tel: (256) 614 4479; fax: (256) 612 4102. 30 rooms with toilet and shower, phone, central heating, balcony. Restaurant, bars, TV room. ☆☆

Efe, Güvercin Adası Caddesi 37, Kuşadası, tel: (256) 614 3660; fax: (256) 614 3662. 44 rooms with toilet and shower, phone. Restaurant, bar, garden, TV room, shop. ☆☆

Turistik Hotel Kelebek, Soğucak Köyü, Kuşadası, tel/fax: (256) 681 0653. 20 rooms with toilet and shower, phone, TV, refrigerator, balcony, central heating. Restaurant, bar, garden, swimming pool.

Marmaris-Hisarönü-Bozburun

Mares (formerly Altın Yunus), Pamucak, Marmaris, tel: (252) 455 2200; fax: (252) 412 1214. 420 rooms with air conditioning, minibar, balcony. Restaurants, bars, conference rooms, swimming pool, garden, beach, marina, Turkish bath, gym, casino, disco, shops, sports. ☆☆☆☆☆

Merit Grand Azur, Kenan Evren Bulvarı 11, Marmaris, tel: (252) 412 8201; fax: (252) 412 3530. 285 rooms with air conditioning, minibar, balcony. Restaurants, bars, conference rooms, outdoor and indoor swimming pools, garden, beach, gym, sauna, casino, disco, sports. ☆☆☆☆☆

Robinson Select Club Maris, 30km from Marmaris on Datça Road, Hisarönü village, tel: (252) 436 9200; fax: (252) 436 9228. 293 rooms with air conditioning, minibar. Restaurants, bars, outdoor swimming pool, beach, regeneration centre with indoor pool, Turkish bath, sauna, jacuzzi, massage, sports. ☆☆☆☆☆

Merit Laguna, Altın Sahil Mevkii, İçmeler, Marmaris, tel: (252) 455 3710; fax: (252) 455 3622. 64 rooms with air conditioning, minibar, balcony. Restaurant, bar, swimming pool, beach, garden, Turkish bath, gym, shop, sports. ☆☆☆☆

Turunç, Turunç Köyü, Marmaris, tel: (252) 476 7024; fax: (252) 476 7032. 256 rooms with air conditioning, balcony. Restaurants, bars, swimming pool, beach, garden, Turkish bath, fitness centre, shops, sports. ☆☆☆☆

Lidya, Siteler Mahallesi 130, Marmaris, tel: (252) 412 2940; fax: (252) 412 1478. 336 rooms with toilet and shower, phone, air conditioning, central heating, balcony. Restaurants, bars, indoor swimming pool, beach, garden, health cabin, casino, disco, sports. ☆☆☆

Portofino, Kayabalı Caddesi 84, İçmeler, Marmaris, tel: (252) 455 3601; fax: (252) 455 3601. 48 rooms with toilet and shower, phone, air conditioning, balcony. Restaurant, bar, swimming pool, garden. ☆☆☆

Efendi, Kenan Evren Bulvarı, İçmeler, Marmaris, tel: (252) 455 2053; fax: (252) 455 3313. 30 rooms with toilet and shower, phone, air conditioning, balcony. Restaurant, bar, swimming pool. ☆☆

Kavala, Turunç Köyü, Marmaris, tel: (252) 476 7211; fax: (252) 476 7213. 38 rooms, 6 flats, with toilet and shower, phone, air conditioning, balcony. Restaurant, bars, swimming pool, beach, garden, TV room. ☆☆

Iberotel Marmaris Park Holiday Village, Pamucak, Marmaris, tel: (252) 455 2121; fax: (252) 455 2146. 200 rooms with balcony. Restaurants, bars, swimming pool, beach, garden, shops, sports.

Magic Life Der Club Marmaris Holiday Village, Yalancı Boğazı, Marmaris, tel: (252) 412 0700; fax: (252) 412 0708. 247 rooms with air conditioning, balcony. Restaurants, bars, swimming pool, beach, garden, Turkish bath, fitness centre, shop, sports.

Martı Holiday Village, İçmeler, Marmaris, tel: (252) 455 3440; fax: (252) 455 3448. 289 rooms with air conditioning, balcony. Restaurants, bars, indoor and outdoor swimming pools, beach, garden, Turkish bath, gym, casino, disco, mini club, sports.

Golden Key Villas, off Datça Road, Hisarönü, tel: (252) 466 6211; fax: (252) 466 6042. Small villas with 30 rooms, with bathroom, air conditioning, phone, TV. Restaurant, bar, swimming pool, beach, garden, sports.

Moonlight Apart Hotel, Turgut Reis Caddesi 10/1, İçmeler, Marmaris, tel: (252) 455 2529. 14 flats with bathroom, refrigerator, kitchen, balcony. Bar, garden, swimming pool.

Sabrina's House Hotel, Bozburun, tel: (252) 456 2045; fax: (252) 456 2470. 18 rooms with toilet and shower, fan, heating, balcony. Restaurant, bar, garden, sports.

Pamukkale (Denizli)

Colossae Thermal, Karahayık, Pamukkale, tel: (258) 271 4156; fax: (258) 271 4250. 230 rooms with air conditioning, balcony. Restaurants, bars, Turkish bath, health and fitness centre, beauty treatment, indoor and outdoor swimming pools, disco, sports. ☆☆☆☆☆

Polat, Karahayıt, Pamukkale, tel: (258) 271 4110; fax: (258) 271 4092. 256 rooms with air conditioning, minibar, central heating, balcony. Restaurants, bars, meeting rooms, Turkish bath, gym, indoor and outdoor pools, health cabin, night club, sports. ☆☆☆☆

Richmond Thermal, Karahayıt, Pamukkale, tel: (258) 271 4294; fax: 271 4078. 307 rooms with air conditioning. Restaurants, bars, meeting rooms, fitness centre, indoor and outdoor pools, thermal pool, night club. ☆☆☆☆

Kur-Tur, Karahayıt, Pamukkale, tel: (258) 271 4117; fax: (258) 263 0818. 69 rooms with toilet and shower, phone, central heating, balcony. Restaurant, TV room, thermal pools, pool bar, playground.

Pamukkale Özel Idare Motel, Pamukkale, tel: (258) 272 2024; fax: (258) 272 2026. 55 rooms with toilet and shower, phone, TV, minibar, central heating. Restaurant, bars, garden, swimming pool with travertine stream, shop, tennis.

Aspava, Pamukkale, tel: (258) 272 2094. Pension with 14 rooms with toilet and shower, balcony. Thermal water swimming pool. Bed and breakfast.

Kervansaray, Pamukkale, tel: (258) 272 2209. Pension with 14 rooms with toilet and shower, balcony. Thermal water swimming pool. Bed and breakfast.

Seferihisar

Çakırağa, Sığacık Mahallesi, Akkum Caddesi, Seferihisar, tel: (232) 745 7575; fax: (232) 745 7023. 32 rooms with bathroom, phone, TV, refrigerator, central heating, balcony. Restaurant, bars, swimming pool, garden, shop. ☆☆☆

Club Teos Holiday Village, Seferihisar, tel: (232) 745 7467; fax: (232) 745 7475. 130 rooms with toilet and shower, phone, balcony. Restaurant, bars, swimming pool, garden, children's club, shops, disco, sports.

Selçuk (Ephesus)

Kalehan, Atatürk Caddesi 49, Selçuk, tel: (232) 892 6154; fax: (232) 892 2169. 54 rooms with toilet and shower, phone, central heating. Restaurant, bar, swimming pool, garden. (SL).

Şirince Evleri, Şirince Köyü, Selçuk, tel: (232) 421 3467, tel/fax: (232) 898 3099. 5 rooms with bathroom, phone, minibar, fan. Bed and breakfast, garden, laundry. Hunting and trekking area. (SL)

Ephesus Richmond Hotel, Pamucak, Selçuk, tel: (232) 892 7077; fax: (232) 892 6731. 196 rooms with air conditioning, minibar, central heating. Restaurants, bars, Turkish bath, fitness centre, indoor and outdoor swimming pools, disco, sports. ☆☆☆☆

Alanya

Ananas Altınyunus, Alanya, tel: (242) 514 0900; fax: (242) 514 0850. 176 rooms with air conditioning, minibar. Facilities include swimming pool, beach, meeting rooms, casino, fitness centre, playground. ☆☆☆☆☆

Grand Kaptan, Oba Göl Mevkii, Alanya, tel: (242) 514 0101; fax: (242) 514 0092. 268 rooms with air conditioning, minibar. Facilities include swimming pool, beach, disco, fitness centre, sports. ☆☆☆☆☆

Serapsu, Konaklı Kasabası, Alanya, tel: (0-242) 565 1476; fax: (242) 565 1072. 218 rooms with air conditioning, minibar. Facilities include swimming pool, beach, disco, fitness centre, diving school, shops, sports. ☆☆☆☆☆

Alaaddin Incekum, Incekum, Avsallar, Alanya, tel: (242) 517 1491; fax: (242) 517 1317. 232 rooms with air conditioning, minibar. Facilities include swimming pool, beach, Turkish bath, fitness centre, shops, playground. ☆☆☆☆

Banana Kleopatra, Alanya, tel: (242) 513 72 94. ☆☆☆☆

Botanik, Okurcalar Köyü, Alanya, tel: (242) 527 4850; fax: (242) 527 4072. 306 rooms with air conditioning, minibar. Facilities include swimming pool, beach, Turkish bath, fitness centre, disco, sports. ☆☆☆☆

Club Justiniano, Okurcalar Koyu, Karaburun Mevkii, Alanya, tel: (242) 527 4955; fax: (242) 527 4682. 296 rooms with air conditioning. Facilities include indoor and outdoor swimming pools, beach, Turkish bath, gym, sports. ☆☆☆☆

Özkaymak, Incekum, Avsallar, Alanya, tel: (242) 517 1245; fax: (242) 517 1724. 363 rooms with air conditioning, minibar. Facilities include swimming pool, beach, disco, gym, sports. ☆☆☆☆

Alara, Yeşilköy, Alanya, tel: (242) 527 4740; fax: (242) 527 4166. 120 rooms with bathroom, phone, balcony. Restaurant, bar, swimming pool, beach. ☆☆☆

Aspera, Fuğla Koyu, Incekum, Alanya, tel: (242) 517 1797; fax: (242) 517 1723. 180 rooms with air conditioning. Restaurant, bars, swimming pool, beach, Turkish bath, gym, disco. ☆☆☆

Azak, Atatürk Caddesi 161, Alanya, tel: (242) 513 9155; fax: (242) 513 1759. 51 rooms with air conditioning. Restaurant, bar, swimming pool, sports. ☆☆☆

Club Hotel Serda Altınyunus, Telatiye Mevkii, Konaklı, Alanya, tel: (242) 565 2535; fax: (242) 565 2537. 100 rooms with air conditioning. Facilities include swimming pool, beach, disco, health cabin, sports. ☆☆☆

Kaptan, Iskele Caddesi 70, Alanya, tel: (242) 513 4900; fax: (242) 513 2000. 48 rooms with bathroom, phone, balcony. Facilities include swimming pool. ☆☆☆

Liberty, Konaklı, Alanya, tel: (242) 565 2625; fax: (242) 565 2627. 82 rooms with air conditioning. Facilities include swimming pool, beach, Turkish bath, disco, health cabin, sports, diving school. ☆☆☆

Sunny Hill, Çarşı Mahallesi, Damlataş Mevkii, Sultan Alaaddin Caddesi 3, Alanya, tel: (242) 511 1211; fax: (242) 512 3893. 73 rooms with air conditioning. Facilities include swimming pool, health cabin, garden. ☆☆☆

Ladin, Karasaz Mevkii, Keykubat Caddesi, Alanya, tel: (242) 514 1217, fax: (242) 514 1221. 44 rooms with bathroom, balcony. Restaurant, bar, swimming pool. ☆☆

Mesut, Oba Kasabası, Göl Mevkii, Alanya, tel: (242) 514 0485; fax: (242) 514 0486. 100 rooms with bathroom, balcony; 70 with air conditioning. Restaurant, bars, swimming pool, beach. ☆☆

Crown, Güller Pınarı Mahallesi, Yenilmez Sokak 6, Alanya, tel: (242) 513 2830; fax: (242) 513 5850. 40 rooms with bathroom, phone, central heating. Restaurant, bar. ☆

Club Alantur Holiday Village, Dimçayı Mevkii, Alanyal, tel: (242) 518 1740; fax: (242) 518 1756.

Club Oasis Beach Vista Holiday Village, Konaklı, Alanya, tel: (242) 565 1451; fax: (242) 565 1449. 836 rooms with bathroom, phone, balcony. Swimming pool, beach, disco, sports.

Hamdullah Paşa Holiday Village, Bölge Trafik Karşısı, Konaklı, Alanya, tel: (242) 565 1520; fax: (242) 565 1531. 311 rooms with bathroom, phone, air conditioning. Swimming pool, beach.

Antalya

Club Hotel Sera, Lara, tel: (242) 349 3434; fax: (242) 349 3454. 223 rooms, 10 bungalows with air conditioning, minibar. Facilities include swimming pool, garden, Turkish bath, gym, casino, disco, shops, sports. ☆☆☆☆☆

Dedeman Antalya, Lara Yolu, tel: (242) 321 3930; fax: (242) 321 3873. 482 rooms with air conditioning, minibar. Facilities include indoor and outdoor swimming pools, fitness centre, Turkish bath, casino, disco, shops, many sports. ☆☆☆☆☆

Falez, Konyaaltı, Falez Mevkii, tel: (242) 248 5000; fax: (242) 248 5025. 342 rooms with air conditioning and minibar. Facilities include indoor and outdoor swimming pools, casino, disco, art gallery, Turkish bath, fitness centre, shops, sports. ☆☆☆☆☆

Sheraton Voyager, Yüzüncü Yıl Bulvarı, tel: (242) 243 2432; fax: (242) 243 2462. 409 rooms with air conditioning and minibar. Facilities include indoor and outdoor swimming pools, disco, casino, health club, Turkish bath, business centre. ☆☆☆☆☆

Talya, Fevzi Çakmak Caddesi 30, tel: (242) 248 6800; fax: (242) 241 5400. 204 rooms with air conditioning, minibar. Facilities include restaurant, swimming pool, fitness centre, Turkish bath, beach, casino, sports. ☆☆☆☆☆

Cender, 30 Ağustos Caddesi, tel: (242) 243 4304; fax: (242) 243 3987. 154 rooms with air conditioning, minibar. Facilities include swimming pool, gym, Turkish bath, disco. ☆☆☆☆

Antalya Prince, Lara Yolu, Karpuzkaldıran Mevkii, tel: (242) 349 3868; fax: (242) 349 3873. 114 rooms with bathroom, phone, TV, air conditioning, minibar. Facilities include restaurant, bars, swimming pool, beach, fitness room, Turkish bath, disco, shops, sports. ☆☆☆

Lara, Lara Yolu, tel: (242) 349 2930; fax: (242) 349 2936. 75 rooms with bathroom, phone, TV, air conditioning. Facilities include restaurant, bar, indoor and outdoor swimming pools, beach, health cabin, sauna, shop, disco, sports. ☆☆☆

Afflin, Arapsuyu Mevkii, 4105 Sokak 49, tel: (242) 229 0680; fax: (242) 229 0305. 36 rooms with bathroom, phone, TV, air conditioning, minibar. Restaurant, bar, swimming pool. ☆☆

Perge, Perge Sokak 5, tel: (242) 244 0025; fax: (242) 241 7587. 26 rooms with bathroom, phone, TV, air conditioning, minibar. Restaurant, bar, beach, garden. ☆☆

Argos, Opposite Atatürk Ortaokulu, Kaleiçi (Old Quarter), tel: (242) 247 2012; fax: (242) 241 7557. 15 rooms with bathroom, phone, TV, air conditioning, minibar. Restaurant, bar, swimming pool, garden. (SL).

Aspen, Kaledibi Sokak 16-18, Kaleiçi (Old Quarter), tel: (242) 247 0590; fax: (242) 241 3364. 36 rooms with bathroom, phone, TV, air conditioning, minibar, central heating. Restaurant, bar, swimming pool, sauna. (SL).

Marina, Mermerli Sokak 15, Kaleiçi (Old Quarter), tel: (242) 247 5490; fax: (242) 241 1765. 42 rooms with bathroom, phone, TV, air conditioning, minibar, heating. Restaurant, bar, swimming pool, garden. (SL).

Magic Mount, Tünektepe, Antalya, tel: (242) 345 7998; fax: (242) 345 0945. Hilltop hotel outside of downtown Antalya. 35 rooms with bathroom, phone, air conditioning. Restaurant, bar, disco, garden, swimming pool. (SL).

Tuvana, Tuzcular Mahallesi, Karanlık Sokak 18, Kaleiçi (Old Quarter), tel: (242) 247 6015; fax: (242) 241 1981. 15 rooms with bathroom, phone, air conditioning. Restaurant, bar, swimming pool, garden. (SL).

Tütav Türkevi, Mermerli Sokak 2, Kaleiçi (Old Quarter), tel: (242) 248 6591; fax: (242) 241 9419. 20 rooms with bathroom, phone, air conditioning, minibar, central heating. Restaurant, bar, sauna, health cabin, swimming pool. (SL).

Villa Perla, Barbaros Mahallesi, Hesapçı Sokak 26, Kaleiçi (Old Quarter), tel: (242) 248 9793; fax: (242) 241 2917. 10 rooms with bathroom, phone, fan. Restaurant, bar, pool. (SL).

Bagana Ranch Motel, Yukarı Karaman Köyü (village), Antalya, tel: (242) 425 2270; fax: 425 2444. 10 rooms with bathroom, TV, radio, refrigerator, air conditioning, balcony. Restaurant, bar, swimming pool, garden. Riding, trekking, mountain biking, table tennis.

Altun Pension, Marina, Kaleiçi (Old Quarter), tel: (242) 241 6624. Bed & breakfast.

Dedekonak Pension, Kılıçarslan Mahallesi, Hıdırlık Sokak 13, Kaleiçi (Old Quarter), tel/fax: (242) 247 5170. Bed & breakfast.

Doğan Pension, Kılıçarslan Mahallesi, Mermerli Banyo Sokak 5, Kaleiçi (Old Quarter), tel: (242) 241 8842; fax: (242) 247 4006. Bed & breakfast.

Hadriyanus Pension, Kılıçarslan Mahallesi, Zeytin Çıkmazı, Kaleiçi (Old Quarter), tel: (242) 241 2313. Bed & breakfast.

Ninova Pension, Barbaros Mahallesi, Hamit Efendi Sokak 9, Kaleiçi (Old Quarter), tel: (242) 248 6114; fax: (242) 352 0479. Bed & breakfast.

Sabah Pension, Kılıçarslan Mahallesi, Hesapçı Sokak 60, Marina, Kaleiçi (Old Quarter), tel: (242) 247 5345; fax: (242) 247 5347. Bed & breakfast.

Dalyan

Antik, Dalyan, tel: (252) 284 2136; fax: (252) 284 2138. 43 rooms with toilet and shower, phone, air conditioning, balcony, central heating. Restaurant, bar, swimming pool, garden, playground. ☆☆☆

Binlik, Sulungur Sokak 16, Dalyan, tel: (252) 284 2148; fax: (252) 284 2149. 80 rooms with toilet and shower, phone, minibar, balcony. Restaurant, bars, swimming pool, garden. ☆☆☆

Asur, Dalyan, tel: (252) 284 3232; fax: (252) 284 3244. 34 rooms with bathroom, phone, TV, air conditioning, minibar. Restaurant, bar, swimming pool, garden, health cabin, river and sea sports. (SL).

Fethiye-Ölüdeniz

Lykia Botanik Holiday Village, Kargı, Yanıklar Köyü, Fethiye, tel: (252) 633 6151; fax: (252) 633 6142. Inside a 2.2 hectar botanical garden, beach, swimming pool.

Montana Pine Resort, Ovacık Köyü, Ölüdeniz, tel: (252) 616 6252; fax: (252) 616 6451. 90 rooms with toilet and shower, phone, air conditioning, balcony. Restaurant, bars, swimming pool, garden, shop. ☆☆☆

St Nicholas Park, Hisarönü, Fethiye, tel: (252) 616 6353; fax: (252) 616 6356. 48 rooms with toilet and shower, phone, central heating. Restaurant, bars, swimming pool, Turkish bath, gym, shop, sports. ☆☆☆

Meri, Ölüdeniz, tel: (252) 616 6060; fax: (252) 616 6456. 75 rooms with toilet and shower, phone, TV, baclony, air conditioning, central heating. Restaurant, bar, garden, beach, TV room, meeting room. ☆☆

Prenses, Iskele Meydanı 7, Fethiye, tel: (252) 614 1305; fax: (252) 614 4479. 65 rooms with toilet and shower, phone, TV, balcony, air conditioning, central heating. Restaurant, bar, TV room, meeting room. In city centre. ☆☆

Belcekız Beach Holiday Village, Ölüdeniz, tel: (252) 616 6009; fax: (252) 616 6448. 119 rooms with toilet and shower, phone, balcony. Restaurants, bars, swimming pool, disco, sports.

Club Tuana Vista Holiday Village, Yanıklar Köyü, Fethiye, tel: (252) 633 6316; fax: (252) 633 6324. 244 rooms with bathroom, phone, TV, air conditioning, balcony. Restaurants, bars, swimming pool, beach, garden, Turkish bath, gym, shop, disco, sports.

Hillside Beach Club, Kalemya Koyu, Fethiye, tel: (252) 614 8360; fax: (252) 614 1470. 330 rooms with bathroom, phone, air conditioning, minibar, balcony. Restaurants, bars, night club, swimming pool, beach, Turkish bath, fitness centre, sports.

Ocakköy Holiday Village, Ocakköy, Ovacık, Fethiye, tel: (252) 616 6155; fax: (252) 616 6158. 8 rooms, 30 villas, 8 rooms for handicapped, with toilet and shower, fan, minibar, balcony. Restaurant, bar, swimming pool, garden, shop, sports.

Telmessos, Hisarönü, Ölüdeniz, tel/fax: (252) 616 6888. 85 rooms with toilet and shower, phone, balcony. Restaurant, bars, swimming pool, garden, sports.

Anıl Pension, Barbaros Sokak 13, Çalış Yolu, Fethiye, tel: (252) 613 1192; fax: (252) 613 1711. 17 rooms with toilet and shower, balcony. Restaurant, bar, swimming pool.

König Pension, Barbaros Sokak 113, Çalış Yolu, Fethiye, tel: (252) 613 1904; fax: (252) 613 1299. 18 rooms with toilet and shower, balcony. Restaurant, bar, swimming pool.

Villa Doffodil, Karagözler, Fevzi Çakmak Caddesi 115, Fethiye, tel: (252) 614 9595; fax: (252) 612 2223. Pension with 15 rooms with toilet and bathroom, phone. Restaurant, bar, swimming pool.

Finike

Anadolu Hotel, Sahil Yolu, Finike, tel: (242) 855 3804; fax: (242) 855 3805. 25 rooms with toilet and shower, phone, balcony. Restaurant.

Gökova Bay

Dedegil, Akyaka Beldesi, Gökova, Muğla, tel: (252) 243 5054, fax: (252) 243 5301. 51 rooms with toilet and shower, phone, balcony. Restaurant, bar, swimming pool, garden. ☆☆☆

Yücelen, Akyaka Beldesi, Gökova, Muğla, tel: (252) 243 5108; fax: (252) 243 5435. 75 rooms with toilet and shower, phone, balcony, central heating. Restaurant, bar, swimming pool, garden, shop, sports. ☆☆☆

Kalkan

Club Xanthos, Kalamar Koyu, Kalkan, tel: (242) 844 2388; fax: (242) 844 2359. 52 rooms with bathroom, phone, TV, air conditioning, minibar, balcony. Restaurant, bars, swimming pool, garden, disco, Turkish bath, fitness room, beach. ☆☆☆

Enerhan, Kalamar Yolu, Kalkan, tel: (242) 844 3162; fax: (242) 844 3449. 21 rooms with bathroom, phone, air conditioning, balcony. Restaurant, bar, swimming pool. ☆☆☆

Pirat, Marina, Kalkan, tel: (242) 844 3178; fax: (242) 844 3183. 126 rooms with bathroom, phone, air conditioning. Restaurant, bar, shop, swimming pool, diving centre. ☆☆☆

Kelebek, Mentefleoğlu Mahallesi, Kalkan, tel: (242) 844 3770; fax: (242) 844 3771. 20 rooms with toilet and shower, phone, air conditioning. Restaurant, bar, garden, pool. ☆☆

Dionysia, Cumhuriyet Caddesi, Kalkan, tel: (242) 844 3681; fax: (242) 844 3139. 23 rooms with toilet and shower, phone, fan, balcony. Restaurant, bar, swimming pool. ☆

Diva, Cumhuriyet Caddesi, Kalkan, tel: (242) 844 3175; fax: (242) 844 3139. 15 rooms with toilet and shower, phone, fan, balcony. Restaurant, bar, swimming pool. ☆

Kalkan Han Pension, Köyiçi, Kalkan (village centre), tel: (242) 844 3151; fax: (242) 844 2048. 16 rooms with toilet and shower, ceiling fan. Restaurant, bar, terrace.

Tekin Berk Pension, Yalıboyu Mahallesi, Kalamar Yolu, Kalkan, tel: (242) 844 3090; fax: 844 3398.

Kas

Aquapark, Çukurbağ Peninsula, Kaş, tel: (242) 836 1901; fax: (242) 836 1992. 124 rooms with bathroom, phone, air conditioning, balcony. Restaurants, bars, swimming pool, beach, garden, disco, shop. ☆☆☆☆

Club Antiphellos, Çukurbağ Peninsula, Gazeteciler Sitesi, Kaş, tel: (242) 836 2651; fax: (242) 836 2654. 16 rooms with bathroom, phone, TV, air conditioning, minibar, balcony. Restaurant, bar, swimming pool, sports. ☆☆☆

Club Phellos, Doğruyol Sokak 4, Kaş, tel: (242) 836 1953; fax: (242) 836 1890. 81 rooms with bathroom, air conditioning, balcony. Restaurant, pool, garden. In city centre. ☆☆☆

Ekici, Arısan Sokak 1, Kaş, tel: (242) 836 1417; fax: (242) 836 1823. 75 rooms with bathroom, phone, air conditioning, balcony. Restaurant, bars, swimming pool, Turkish bath, disco. In city centre. ☆☆☆

Mimosa, Elmalı Caddesi, Kaş., tel: (242) 836 1272; fax: (242) 836 1368. 24 rooms with toilet and shower, phone, fan. Restaurant, bar, disco. ☆☆

Golden Pension, Ilkokul Caddesi, Kaş, tel: (242) 836 1736.

Hamarat Pension, Çukurbağ Peninsula, Kaş, tel: (242) 836 1547. 8 rooms. Kitchen.

Puya Pension, Meltem Sokak 6, Kaş, tel/fax: (242) 836 2163. 12 rooms with toilet and shower, phone. Restaurant, bar.

Talay Pension, Küçükçakıl Mahallesi, Kaş, tel: (242) 836 1101. 12 rooms.

Uzun Pension, Yeniyol Mahallesi, Kaş, tel: (242) 836 1721; fax: (242) 836 1697. 17 rooms. Breakfast room, bar.

Yalı Pension, Hastane Caddesi 11, Kaş, tel: (242) 836 1132.

Kemer

Around the Mediterranean coast west of Antalya City, including Kemer, Çamyuva, Göynük, Beldibi and Tekirova, accommodation facilities mostly consist of holiday villages, club/resorts and large hotels. These have, almost invariably, extensive gardens, large swimming pools, many types of sea and land sports, nightclubs, fitness centre, Turkish baths, children's clubs, etc. The rooms have air conditioning and minibars.

To save space, we are listing only addresses, phone and fax, and number of rooms. For smaller hotels and pensions, facilities will be stated for each place.

Favori Aqua Resort, Çamyuva, Kemer, tel: (242) 824 6214; fax: (242) 824 6210. 133 rooms. ☆☆☆☆☆

Kiriş World Magic, Kemer, tel: (242) 824 6800; fax: (242) 824 6820. 410 rooms, 60 villas. ☆☆☆☆☆

Phaselis Princess, Tekirova, Kemer, tel: (242) 821 4070; fax: (242) 821 4069. 341 rooms. ☆☆☆☆☆

Club Alda, Beldibi, Kemer, tel: (242) 824 8151; fax: (242) 824 8159. Holiday village with 364 rooms.

Club Aldiana Milta, Göynük, Kemer, tel: (242) 815 1650; fax: (242) 815 1680. Holiday village with 394 rooms.

Club Mediterranee, Kemer, tel: (242) 814 1009; fax: (242) 814 1018. Holiday village with 462 rooms.

Club Phasells, Kemer, tel: (242) 815 1631; fax: (242) 815 1637. Holiday village with 296 rooms.

Club Turtle's Marco Polo, Çamyuva, Kemer, tel: (242) 824 6336; fax: (242) 824 6346. Holiday village with 404 rooms.

Kemer Holiday Village, Göynük, Kemer, tel: (242) 815 1450; fax: 815 1465. 277 rooms.

Martı Myra Holiday Village, Tekirova, Kemer, tel: (242) 821 4030; fax: (242) 821 4352. 351 rooms.

Park Kimeros Holiday Village, Göynük, Kemer, tel: (242) 815 1663; fax: (242) 815 1671. 244 rooms.

Pirate's Beach Club, Tekirova, Kemer, tel: (242) 821 4001; fax: (242) 821 4003. Holiday village with 256 rooms.

Grand Hotel Kemer Vista, Göynük Beldesi, Kemer, tel: (242) 815 1700; fax: (242) 815 1697. 318 rooms. ☆☆☆☆

Phaselis Rose, Tekirova, Kemer, tel: (242) 821 4780; fax: (242) 821 4792. 300 rooms. ☆☆☆☆☆

Tekirova Corinthia, Tekirova, Kemer, tel: (242) 821 4750; fax: (242) 821 4758. 402 rooms. ☆☆☆☆☆

Club Hotel Şato-Montana, Beldibi, Kemer, tel: (242) 824 8460; fax: (242) 824 8462. 90 rooms with toilet and shower, phone, air conditioning, balcony. Restaurant, bar, swimming pool, garden, health cabin, disco, sports. ☆☆☆

Gelidonya Club, Atatürk Bulvarı, Kemer, tel: (242) 814 5041; fax: (242) 814 5045. 51 rooms with toilet and shower, phone, air conditioning, minibar, balcony. Restaurant, bars, swimming pool, garden, beach, TV room. ☆☆☆

Seagull, Çifte Çeşmeler Mevkii, Beldibi, Kemer, tel: (242) 824 8465; fax: (242) 824 8466. 50 rooms with toilet and shower, phone, air conditioning, balcony. Restaurant, bars, swimming pool, beach, sports. ☆☆☆

Belhan, Çifte Çeşmeler, Beldibi, Kemer, tel: (242) 824 8054; fax: (242) 824 8733. 21 rooms with toilet and shower, phone, air conditioning. Restaurant, bar, swimming pool, garden, beach, sports. ☆☆☆

Dragos, Deniz Caddesi 37, Kemer, tel: (242) 814 2489; fax: (242) 814 3241. 58 rooms with toilet and

shower, phone, air conditioning, balcony. Restaurant, bars, health cabin, swimming pool, health cabin. ☆☆

Elit Hotel, Çifte Çeşmeler Mevkii, Beldibi, Kemer, tel: (242) 824 8629; fax: (242) 824 8453. 43 rooms with toilet and shower, phone, TV, air conditioning, minibar, balcony. Restaurant, bar, swimming pool, disco, garden, helth cabin, beach, sports.

Ambassador Plaza Apart Hotel, Kavaklı Caddesi 14, Kemer, tel: (242) 814 5030; fax: (242) 814 5035. 67 flats with bathroom, phone, air conditioning, kitchen, refrigerator, balcony. Restaurant, bar, babysitting, swimming pool, beach, garden, Turkish bath, fitness centre, shops.

Nona Hotel, Deniz Caddesi, Kemer, tel: (242) 814 3170; fax: (242) 814 1389. 63 rooms with bathroom, phone, air conditioning, TV, central heating. Restaurant, bar, game room, swimming pool, beach, garden.

Köycegiz

Kaunos, Cengiz Topel Caddesi, Köyceğiz, tel: (252) 262 4288; fax: (252) 262 4836. 40 rooms with toilet and shower, phone, balcony. Restaurant, bar, swimming pool, lake sailing, disco. ☆☆

Özay, Kordon Boyu 11, Köyceğiz, tel: (252) 262 4300; fax: 262 2000. 32 rooms with toilet and shower, phone, balcony, central heating. Restaurant, bar, swimming pool, garden, lake sailing, disco. ☆☆

Panorama Plaza, Cengiz Topel Caddesi 69, Köyceğiz, tel: (252) 262 3773; fax: (252) 262 3633. 28 rooms with toilet and shower, phone, TV, balcony. Restaurant, bars, swimming pool, garden, health cabin, sports.

Patara

Beyhan Patara Hotel, Gelemiş Köyü, Patara, Kalkan, tel: (242) 843 5096; fax: (252) 843 5097. 132 rooms with bathroom, phone, air conditioning, TV, minibar. Restaurants, bar, swimming pool, garden, Turkish bath, gym, disco, sports. ☆☆☆

Hotel Merhaba, Patara, Kalkan, tel: (242) 843 5113; fax: (242) 843 5133. 14 rooms.

Golden Pension, Patara, Kalkan, tel: (242) 843 5162.

Hotel Mehmet, Patara, Kalkan, tel: (242) 843 5032; fax: (242) 843 5078. Pension.

Patara View Point, Patara, Kalkan, tel: (242) 843 5184; fax: (242) 843 5022. Pension.

Side-Manavgat

Asteria, Kumköy, Side, tel/fax: (242) 753 1830. 310 rooms with air conditioning, minibar. Facilities include swimming pools, beach, conference centre, disco, shops, fitness centre, sports. ☆☆☆☆☆

Ceasars Resort, Kumköy, Side, tel: (242) 753 2480; fax: (242) 753 1852. 175 rooms with air conditioning, minibar. Facilities include, swimming pools, beach, beauty and fitness centres, Turkish bath, conference centre, casino, disco, sports. ☆☆☆☆☆

Novotel Turquoise, Acısu Mevkii, Sorgun, Side, tel: (242) 756 9330; fax: (242) 756 9345. 272 rooms with air conditioning, minibar. Facilities include swimming pools, beach, Turkish bath disco, gym, shops, sports. ☆☆☆☆☆

Club Aldiana Holiday Village, Titreyengöl Mevkii, Sorgun, Manavgat, tel: (242) 756 9260; fax: (242) 756 9268. 300 rooms with air conditioning. Pool, beach, fitness centre, mini club, disco, shops, sports.

Dedeman Club Blue Waters Holiday Village, Sorgun, Manavgat, tel: (242) 756 9464; fax: (242) 756 9556. 312 rooms with air conditioning. Swimming pool, beach, disco, Turkish bath, health cabin, shop, sports.

Paradise Apart Hotel, Titreyengöl Mevkii, Sorgun, Manavgat, tel: (242) 756 9210; fax: (242) 756 9269. Holiday village with 285 aparts, 50 studios with kitchen, air conditioning. Swimming pool, beach, nightclub, fitness centre, shops, sauna, sports.

Robinson Club Pamşlya Holiday Village, Sorgun, Side, tel: (242) 756 9350; fax: (242) 756 9358. 331 rooms with air conditioning, central heating. Facilities include disco, Turkish bath, sports.

Turtel Sorgun Holiday Village, Titreyengöl Mevkii, Sorgun, Manavgat, tel: (242) 756 9300; fax: (242) 756 9309. 362 rooms with air conditioning. Swimming pool, beach, disco, Turkish bath, fitness centre, animation, shops, mini club, sports.

Defne Star, Side, tel: (242) 475 rooms with air conditioning, minibar. Swimming pools, beach, Turkish bath, gym, sports. ☆☆☆☆

Excelsior Corinthia, Titreyengöl Mevkii, Sorgun, Manavgat, tel: (242) 756 9110; fax: 756 9114. 151 rooms all with air conditioning. Swimming pools, beach, disco, Turkish bath, fitness centre, shops, sports. ☆☆☆☆

Linda, Titreyengöl Mevkii, Sorgun, Manavgat, tel: (242) 756 9130; fax: 756 9133. 150 rooms with air conditioning. Swimming pool, disco, Turkish bath, sports. ☆☆☆☆

Sunrise Golf Hotel, Kızılağaç Mevkii, Manavgat, tel: (242) 748 2610; fax: (242) 748 2635. 501 rooms with air conditioning, minibar. Swimming pools, beach, Turkish bath, gym, disco, sports, golf. ☆☆☆☆

Emirhan, Manavgat, tel: (242) 753 3090; fax: (242) 753 3093. 265 rooms with air conditioning, minibar. Swimming pools, beach, disco, health cabin, sports. ☆☆☆

Sidelya, Çolaklı Beldesi, Manavgat, tel: (242) 763 6370; fax: (242) 763 6114. 271 rooms with balcony. Swimming pool, beach, shop, sports. ☆☆☆

Kleopatra, Manavgat, tel: (0-242) 753 10 33; fax: (0-242) 753 3738. 42 rooms with bathroom, phone. Restaurant, bar. ☆☆

Apollo Pension, near the Temple of Apollo, Side, tel: (242) 753 1941. Bungalows.

Morning Star Pension, Barbaros Sokak, Side, tel: (242) 753 1134; fax: (242) 753 1389. 6 rooms.

Yıldırım Pension, Tiyatro Arkası (behind the ancient theatre), Side, tel: (242) 753 2398. 6 rooms.

Büyük Sürmeli, Özler Caddesi 175, Kuruköprü, Adana, tel: (322) 352 3600; fax: (322) 352 1945. 166 rooms with air conditioning, minibar. Facilities include swimming pool, casino, night club, Turkish bath, gym. ☆☆☆☆☆

Seyhan, Turhan Cemal Beriker Bulvarı 30, Adana, tel: (322) 457 5810; fax: (322) 454 2834. 140 rooms with air conditioning, minibar. Facilities include swimming pool, casino, night club, Turkish bath, gym. ☆☆☆☆☆

Zaimoğlu, Özler Caddesi 72, Kuruköprü, Adana, tel: (322) 351 3400; fax: (322) 351 6811. 77 rooms with air conditioning, minibar. Facilities include night club. ☆☆☆☆

Reşit Ener Tesisleri Mocamp, Girne Bulvarı 138, Adana, tel: (322) 321 2758; fax: (322) 321 2775. 16 rooms with toilet & shower, phone, air conditioning, minibar. Restaurant, garden, swimming pool, camping.

Anamur

Vivanco, Kaledibi Mevkii, Bozyazı, Anamur, tel: (324) 851 4200; fax: (324) 851 2291. 66 rooms with air conditioning, minibar. Facilities include swimming pool, beach, disco, sports. ☆☆☆☆

Hermes, Iskele Civarı Mevkii, Anamur, tel: (324) 814 3950; fax: (324) 814 39 95. 70 rooms with air conditioning. Restaurant, bars, swimming pool, beach, disco, sauna. ☆☆☆

Yan, Anamur Iskele Mahallesi, Yalı Evleri, Anamur, tel: (324) 814 2123; fax: (324) 816 4888. 24 rooms with bathroom. Restaurant, bar, swimming pool. ☆

Antakya

Büyük Antakya, Atatürk Caddesi 8, Antakya, tel: (326) 213 5860; fax: (326) 213 5869. 72 rooms with air conditioning, minibar, phone. Restaurant, bars, disco, shops, games room. ☆☆☆☆

Orontes, Istiklal Caddesi 58, Antakya, tel: (326) 214 5931; fax: (326) 214 5933. 35 rooms all with air conditioning, minibar. Restaurant, TV room. ☆☆

Sara Antiochia, Ürgen Caddesi, Harbiye, Antakya, tel: (326) 231 3380; fax: (326) 231 3381. 20 rooms with bathroom, phone. Breakfast room, bar, central heating.

Iskenderun

Grand Hotel Ontur, Muammer Aksoy Caddesi 8, Iskenderun, tel: (326) 616 2400; fax: (326) 616 2410. 95 rooms with air conditioning, minibar. Restaurant, bars, disco. ☆☆☆☆

Arsuz, Arsuz (Uluçınar), Iskenderun, tel: (326) 643 2444; fax: (326) 643 2448. 104 rooms with bathroom, phone, central heating. Restaurant, bars, beach, sports. ☆☆☆

Kızkalesi

Club Barbarossa, Kızkalesi, Erdemli, tel: (324) 523 2364; fax: (324) 523 2090. 103 rooms with air conditioning, TV. Restaurant, bars, swimming pool, beach, sports. ☆☆☆

Kilikya, Kızkalesi, Erdemli, tel: (324) 523 2116; fax: (324) 523 2084. 63 rooms with air conditioning, minibar. Restaurant, bars, swimming pool, beach, sports. ☆☆☆

Yaka, Kızkalesi, Erdemli, tel: (324) 523 2041; fax: (324) 523 2448. 17 rooms with bathroom. Restaurant, bar. ☆☆

Mersin

Hilton Sa, Adnan Menderes Bulvarı, Mersin, tel: (324) 326 5000; fax: (324) 326 5050. 189 rooms with air conditioning, minibar. Facilities include, swimming pool, casino, disco, fitness centre, conference hall. ☆☆☆☆☆

Merit, Kuvayı Milliye Caddesi 165, Mersin, tel: (324) 336 1010; fax: (324) 336 0722. 247 rooms with air conditioning, minibar. Facilities include swimming pool, casino, disco, conference hall, gym. ☆☆☆☆☆

Gondol, Gazi Mustafa Kemal Bulvarı 20, Mersin, tel: (324) 234 1200; fax: (324) 234 1207. 78 rooms with air conditioning, minibar. Facilities include swimming pool, gym, disco. ☆☆☆☆

Sahil Martı, Silifke Caddesi, Mezitli, Mersin, tel: (324) 358 3700; fax: (324) 358 1716. 61 rooms with air conditioning, minibar. Restaurant, bar, swimming pool, beach, disco, gym. ☆☆☆

Silifke

Altınorfoz Banana, Atakent, Silifke, tel: (324) 722 4211; fax: (324) 722 4215. 112 rooms with air conditioning. Facilities include pool, beach, Turkish bath, disco, sports. ☆☆☆☆

Where to Eat

Restaurants

Antalya

Ahtapot, Kaleiçi, Yacht Marina, 38, tel: (242) 247 1141. A fish restaurant right on the harbour.

Club 29, Kaleiçi, Yacht Marina, Antalya, tel: (242) 241 6260. Housed inside a restored warehouse with a superb view overlooking the harbour, this restaurant serves gourmet international and Turkish dishes. Complete with a terrace swimming pool, 29 turns into a disco after midnight.

Develi, Konyaaltı, Birinci Arap Suyu, tel: (242) 229 1200. The Antalya branch of one of Turkey's foremost meat restaurant chains. It serves the kebabs of southeastern Turkey, accompanied by such regional dishes as *houmus, içli köfte,* and other *mezes. Develi Kebab* is the house speciality.

Deniz, Karaalioğlu Parkı, 1311 Sokak 7, tel: (242) 241 5799. Hidden away on a side street, this restaurant has exceptional sea views and equally good Turkish dishes. It regularly features Turkish dancing and floor show later in the evening.

El Toro, Atatürk Caddesi 50/A, tel: (242) 247 1024. Italian pizzas and ice creams, steak dishes, fresh vegetables and salads in a warm, attractive atmosphere.

Gaziantep, Konyaaltı Sahil Şeridi 6, tel: (242) 242 4250; and Balbey Mahallesi, 410 Sokak 4, (in the Old Bazaar, opposite the Clock Tower). Turkish grilled meat specialities, *mezes* (starters) and seafood dishes, served attentively.

Hisar Turistik Tesisi, Cumhuriyet Meydanı, Tophanealtı, tel: (242) 241 5281.This restaurant, set inside the historic fortress walls, boasts magnificent sea views over the harbour. Good food and entertainment.

Kırk Merdiven, Musalla Sokak 2, Kaleiçi, tel: (242) 242 9686. Set in a cosy corner inside the fortress walls in the Old Quarter of Kaleiçi, this is an excellent restaurant serving fish and meat dishes, accompanied by traditional Turkish *mezes* in a homely atmosphere, made warmer in winter with a fireplace and piped classical Turkish music.

Koru, Yacht Marina, Kaleiçi, tel: (242) 248 1914. Serves fish, grilled steaks and chicken dishes on the harbour front. *Mantı* is the house speciality.

Kral Sofrası (King's Table): Yacht Marina, Kaleiçi, tel: (242) 241 2198. Housed in a charming old building, Kral Sofrası is one of the long-established and very popular restaurants of Antalya. It serves delicious regional *mezes,* fish and meat dishes in a traditional and cosy decor. Not much sea view, but friendly and comfortable ambience inside to compensate.

La Notte, Mermerli Sokak 1, Kaleiçi, tel: (242) 243 2751. This is one of the most ambitious and classy restaurants in Antalya, set in the charming Kaleiçi Quarter in the Old Town. La Notte offers two beautiful terraces overlooking the harbour, excellent Italian and international dishes and pleasing live music, fit for special, candlelit occasions.

La Trattoria, Fevzi Çakmak Caddesi 3/C (opposite Belediye), tel: (242) 243 3931. Excellent Italian cuisine in a friendly, intimate atmosphere is offered in this restaurant run by a Turkish-Italian couple.

Maritime Bar and Restaurant, Sheraton Voyager Hotel, 100 Yıl Bulvarı, tel: (242) 243 2432. Gourmet international dishes and seafood are accompanied by live guitar music in the luxurious, lush green atmosphere of this largest five-star hotel in Antalya city centre.

McDonald's, Atatürk Caddesi 38, Üçkapılar, tel: (242) 248 9073. Famous for its beefburgers.

Mermerli, Banyo Sokak 25, Kaleiçi, tel: (242) 248 5484. Established more than 50 years ago, the Mermerli Restaurant overlooks the Antalya Harbour and serves tasty food that has been popular with locals and visitors alike, at reasonable prices.

Met Fish, Lara Yolu, tel: (242) 321 1828/322 5879. Serving tasty and inexpensive seafood and sea views, Met is popular with Antalya's local families.

Müze (Museum) Restaurant: Teomanpaşa Caddesi, Falez Apt., 124/1, (near Falez and Sheraton hotels), tel: (242) 242 7013.

Parlak, Behind Yapı Kredi Bankası, Clock Tower end of Kazım Özalp Caddesi, No: 7, tel: (242) 241 9160. A typical Turkish *lokanta* (traditional restaurant) and tavern, Parlak serves tasty *mezes* and barbecued chicken in a welcoming ambience.

Pasta Villa, Akdeniz Bulvarı, Mobil Istasyonu, Konyaaltı, tel: (242) 229 1700. Italian-Turkish food, in a chain restaurant, located near the Konyaaltı Beach.

Sıla, Iskele Caddesi 25, Kaleiçi, tel: (242) 244 1910. Housed inside another restored old building, with traditional decoration and cool interiors, this restaurant serves a large menu of Turkish dishes.

Sini, Hükümet Caddesi 34, tel: (242) 241 1912. Turkish dishes, including a refreshing soup, served 24-hours a day.

Sırrı, Selçuk Mahallesi, Uzunçarşı Sokak 25, Kaleiçi, tel: (242) 241 7239. This original 19-century wooden building with 14 rooms and a courtyard now serves as a restaurant and family home.

Tropic Terrace, Sheraton Voyager Hotel, 100 Yıl Bulvarı, tel: (242) 243 2432. The terrace restaurant of the Sheraton serves a wide menu of light food in a luxurious atmosphere.

Yat, Yacht Marina, Kaleiçi, tel: (242) 242 4855. Turkish and international dishes served in a lively atmosphere.

Yedi Memet, Konyaaltı Plajı, tel: (242) 241 1641. A long-established, traditional Turkish meat restaurant, Yedi Memet is very popular with the locals and always crowded.

Yelken, Yacht Marina 6, tel: (242) 242 9789. Another seafront restaurant serving well prepared Turkish dishes.

Yörükoğlu, Yenikapı (opposite Belediye), tel: (242) 247 5171. A traditional and popular Turkish restaurant with a pleasant garden.

Bodrum

Alarga, Türkbükü Village, Bodrum Peninsula, tel: (252) 377 5006. A gourmet fish restaurant, popular with Turkish holidaymakers for its food as well as its spectacular sea view. Booking is essential.

Amphora, Neyzen Tevfik Caddesi 172, tel: (252) 316 2868. Housed in an atmospheric old olive press building, Amphora serves Turkish dishes including seafood.

Bar-B-Q House, Bitez Village, Bodrum Peninsula, tel: (252) 343 1724. A stylish restaurant serving grilled dishes in a charming garden with citrus trees.

Batı, Gümüflük Village, Bodrum Peninsula, tel: (252) 394 3079. Delicious Turkish *mezes*, casserole and fish dishes are offered at this restaurant which boasts an impressive sunset view.

Buğday, Türkkuyusu Caddesi 72, tel (252) 316 2969. A friendly, vegetarian-only restaurant.

Han, Kale Caddesi 23, tel: (252) 316 7951. Housed in an old *caravanserai* with an inner courtyard, Han is one of the oldest restaurants of Bodrum. It features Turkish music and belly dancing, too.

Ibo's, Meyhaneler Sokak, off Dr Alimbey Caddesi. Locally known as the *Street of Taverns*, this alleyway is lined with many small restaurants and bars offering a jovial ambience, Turkish music, *meze* and fish dishes. Ibo's is one of the older and most popular eating and drinking spots on this street.

Kortan, Cumhuriyet Caddesi 32, tel: (252) 316 2141. Great fresh seafood and a lovely view of the castle are offered at this terrace restaurant.

Ladda's, Neyzen Tevfik Caddesi, tel: (252) 313 1504. One of Bodrum's several oriental cuisine restaurants, Ladda's is owned by a Thai lady and the food is prepared by chefs from Bangkok.

Mausolus, Neyzen Tevfik Caddesi, tel: (252) 316 4176. This downtown restaurant offers fish and *meze* dishes, and a castle view.

MB, Gereflaltı 101, Yalıkavak Village, Bodrum Peninsula, tel: (252) 385 4959. This is an upmarket, chic restaurant which serves good food in a comfortable atmosphere. Reservation is essential.

Mey, Türkbükü Village, Bodrum Peninsula, tel: (252) 377 5118. A gourmet restaurant popular with high-heeled Turkish visitors, Mey serves a set fish menu and has its own jetty. Reservation is essential.

Nur, Cumhuriyet Caddesi, tel: (252) 313 1065. Good food served in a romantic old courtyard and accompanied by soft music.

Pancho's, Cumhuriyet Caddesi, opposite Halikarnas Disco, tel: (252) 316 0893. Pancho's serves Argentinian-style steaks and tasty salads.

Picante, Külcü Sokak 8, tel: (252) 316 0270. A stylish restaurant in a cool environment, Picante serves Mexican food and excellent margaritas. Reservation recommended.

Sakız Ana, Yahfli Köyü (village), Ortakent, Bodrum Peninsula, tel: (252) 348 3703. Run by a female proprietor, Sakız Ana serves delicious homemade Turkish dishes.

Salmakis, Cumhuriyet Caddesi, Bodrum Town, and at Bitez Village. Authentic Chinese cuisine.

Şamdan, Yalıkavak Village, Bodrum Peninsula, tel: (252) 364 4424. The Bodrum branch of the elegant, gourmet restaurant chain, serving international cuisine. Popular with the jet set, reservations are essential.

Sapa, Türkkuyusu Caddesi, Külcü Sokak 10, tel: (252) 316 7093. A highly popular restaurant and bar, Sapa offers excellent buffet meals and an amusing ambience.

Ship Ahoy, Türkbükü Village, Bodrum Peninsula, tel: (252) 377 5070. Set on a private jetty, Ship Ahoy is popular with the trendy set for people-watching and listening to good music at the bar.

Sunny's, Cumhuriyet Caddesi, tel: (252) 316 0716. Sunny's serves British-style dishes, as well as some unusual Turkish *mezes*.

Çesme

Körfez, Yalı Caddesi, tel: (232) 712 6718. A long-established, dependable restaurant on the waterfront, Körfez serves fish and *meze* dishes at reasonable prices. Other dependable restaurants on the same street are **Meydan, Sahil** and **Yalı.**

Fethiye

Amfora, Paspatur Hamam Sokak 5, tel: (252) 612 1282. A good seafood restaurant, Amfora specialises in fish baked in salt.

Fedir, Tutum Sokak 3, tel: (252) 614 1095. Good Turkish dishes offered at reasonable prices at this restaurant.

Meğri, Likya Sokak 8-9, tel: (252) 614 4046. An excellent fish restaurant.

Pizza Villa, Çarflı Caddesi 36, tel: (252) 614 6451. Offers tasty and inexpensive fare including hot chicken wings.

Pizza 74, Atatürk Caddesi 4, tel: (252) 614 1869. A good Italian restaurant.

Rafet, Kordonboyu, tel: (252) 614 1106. A long-established, friendly restaurant serving delicious fish dishes.

Yacht, Yat Limanı Karşısı (opposite the yacht marina), tel: (252) 614 7014. Yacht offers pleasant sea views, fish dishes and occasional belly dancing.

Yaka Park, Yaka Köyü (village), tel: (252) 638 2011. Fresh fish served right from their own trout farm.

Kas

Blue House, Ilkokul Caddesi, tel: (242) 836 2171. Traditional Turkish food is served from a small menu in this restaurant with a wonderful harbour view.

Chez Evy, Terzi Sokak 2, tel: (242) 836 1253. Country-style French cuisine, prepared by a French lady, is served in the charming garden of this restaurant. Reservation is essential.

Çınar, Ibrahim Serin Sokak, tel: (242) 836 1735. A long-established Turkish restaurant with outdoor seating and inexpensive prices.

Eriş, Uzun Çarşı Caddesi, Orta Sokak 13, tel: (242) 836 1057. Another well-established Turkish restaurant offering grilled meat and fish dishes and *mezes.*

J.P. Spaghetti House, Öztürk Sokak (next to Orman Çay Bahçesi), tel: (242) 836 1733. Tasty spaghetti, ravioli, lasagne and *tiramisu* are offered in this friendly restaurant.

Mercan, Yacht Marina, tel: (242) 836 1209. Right on the seafront, Mercan serves delicious *mezes,* fish and spit-roasted lamb.

Oba Ev Yemekleri, Çukurbağlı Caddesi 28, tel: (242) 836 1687. Homemade traditional dishes are served in a pretty terrace under fig trees.

Smiley's, Uzun Çarşı Sokak 11, tel: (242) 836 2812. An attractive restaurant which, besides seafood dishes, offers garlic and cheese on pide bread.

Marmaris

Birtat, Barbaros Caddesi, near the marina, tel: (252) 412 1076. Grilled meats, shish kebabs and fish are offered at moderate prices, with a view of the harbour.

Napoli, Barbaros Caddesi, Barlar Sokak 70, tel: (252) 412 6555. Napoli serves a variety of good pizzas.

Pineapple, Netsel Marina, tel: (252) 412 4999. A stylish restaurant for good meat and fish dishes, and to watch the yachting crowd.

Yakamoz, Kemeraltı Caddesi, opposite Selen Otel, tel: (252) 412 5160. A well-established fish restaurant serving delicious food.

Attractions

The Turkish coast is an open-air museum with the ruins of several hundred ancient Hittite, Carian, Lycian, Greek and Roman cities. And there are scores of museums, operated by the Ministry of Culture, where excavated artifacts from ancient sites are on display. Here is a series of museums, grouped by province.

The Northern Aegean

Edirne

The Edirne Museum
The Museum of Turkish and Islamic Arts

Çanakkale

The Morto Bay 1915 Dardanelles Campaign Museum (under the Mehemetçik War Memorial).
Archaeological Museum
Sultaniye Castle War Museum
Kabatepe War Museum
Alçıtepe War Museum (Private)
Museum of Troy
Ruins of Troy
Ruins of Alexandria Troas
Ruins of Assos

The Southern Aegean

Izmir

Ruins of Pergamum (Bergama)
Pergamum Museum (Bergama)
Archaeological Museum (Izmir)
Atatürk Museum (Izmir)
Agora Sites
Ethnographical Museum
Çeşme Museum
Ephesus Museum
Ruins of Ephesus
Church of St John Monument
House of Virgin Mary
Ödemiş Museum

Aydin

Ruins of Priene
Ruins of Miletus
Miletus Museum
Ruins of Didyma
Aydın Museum
Ruins of Nysa
Ruins of Alinda
Aphrodisias Museum
Ruins of Aphrodisias

Denizli

Ruins of Pamukkale/Hieropolis
Laodiceia

Mugla

Ruins of Heracleia Under Latmus
Ruins of Euromos
Ruins of Iassus
Ruins of Labraynda
Milâs Museum
Beçin Kale
Bodrum Museum of Underwater Archaeology
Mausoleum of Halicarnassus
Ruins of Cedrae
Ruins of Ceramus
Ruins of Datça
Ruins of Loryma
Marmaris Museum
Ruins of Caunos
Fethiye Museum
Ruins of Letton
Ruins of Pinara
Ruins of Tilos

Antalya

Ruins of Xanthus
Ruins of Patara
Ruins of Kekova Island
Ruins of Kaleköy
Ruins of Myra
St Nicholas Church
Ruins of Olympus
Ruins of Phaselis
Antalya Museum
Ruins of Termessos
Karain Caves
Ruins of Perge
Ruins of Aspendos
Ruins of Sillyum
Ruins of Side
Castle of Alanya
Red Tower (Alanya)
House of Atatürk

İçel

Heaven and Hell
Alahan Monastery
Kanlıdivane
Pompeiopolis
Kızkalesi

Adana

Archaeological Museum
Atatürk Museum
Ethnographical Museum
Karatepe Museum
Misis Mosaic Museum
Ruins of Anavarza
Ruins of Castabala
Ruins of Şar

Hatay

Antakya Archaeological Museum
Grove of Daphne

Sports & Leisure

Yachting

Arranging a Blue Voyage: Many European and some American travel agencies specializing in trips to Turkey organize yachting holidays to the Turquoise Coast – the area from Bodrum to Antalya.

However, chartering through a local agency in Bodrum, Marmaris, Fethiye and Antalya not only cuts down costs but also enables a wider selection of yachts and fares. These agencies also arrange transfers from airport to hotels in Turkey. Any travel agent in Bodrum or Marmaris can make reservations for a Blue Voyage, a cruise along the Turquoise Coast.

As a rule, one third to half of the boat's charge is taken in advance, at the time of reservation. But if you are already on the Turquoise Coast, you can always bypass the agency and rent a yacht yourself. This is even cheaper, but you must be sure of what you are choosing.

Bodrum Cup

If you wish to cruise in a *gulet*, you must consider participating in the Bodrum Cup, a regatta held at the Gulf of Gökova. The Cup is held in last two weeks of October. This is not only a race in which you can crew, but it is also a chance to get acquainted with Turkish wooden-framed yachts and Turkey's magnificent sailing grounds. The programme includes stops in Gökova, Knidos, Datça, Bencik, Serçe and Ekincik; a sampling of anchorages as good as any express tour allows. For reservations, contact Era Yachting in Bodrum.

Major bareboat agencies are usually connected with foreign agencies and are mostly sold out in the summer. So, do not leave it to chance, and reserve early.

Rental Prices

Bareboat prices change according to the size of the yacht and the season. In March or November, a 47-foot (14-metre) *Sun Kiss 47* is priced at $1,200 to $1,500 per week. The highest price is in July or August, when a one-week rental of the same nine-berth yacht is $2,400-$2,700. A small, 26-foot (eight-metre), four-passenger *Gib Sea 27* in March or November costs $400-450 per week and in July and August the same boat costs $1,000.

Bodrum-built *gulets* (the name derives from the French *goelette*, meaning schooner) are priced on a per diem basis. A 39-48 foot (12-15 metre) boat with two or three cabins sells for around $225-275 a day in May and October. In July, prices soar to $300 and in August climb to $400. A more luxurious 63-66 foot (19-20 metre) *gulet* can be rented for $600-800 a day in August or as low as $300 in October. Maximum-size luxury yachts over 66 feet (20 metres) go for as high as $1,250-$1,300 in August and $600-800 in the lower season.

Quayside Bargaining

Just call any travel agency in Bodrum or Marmaris to find out about prices. During the low season quayside bargaining can lower prices by as much as half. Certain agencies market the Blue Voyage on a per cabin basis as well. That means if you can't find enough friends to share a boat, you can join a group on the same boat. You will have your own cabin, probably with a bathroom. The passengers eat together and conform to the program of the boat. Depending on which season one takes the one-week Blue Voyage, it would cost $275 to $400 per person.

Flotilla Cruise

Though it somewhat dampens the sense of adventure and individuality that is the essence of being at sea, a middle-of-the-road solution for those who want to steer their own ship but lack the skill and/or the courage to go it alone is chartering a bareboat in a "flotilla cruise". In a flotilla cruise, three to 12 yachts will form a group, headed by a guide who leads the way and attempts to solve problems, ranging from broken transmission gear to

bee stings, as they come up. Turkish bareboat operators favour French-made yachts. The majority of the fleet consists of Jeanneaus and Benettaux with occasional Moodys and a few German and Scandinavian models. The yachts are fairly new and kept in above average condition. The better known companies change the bulk of their yachts every five years or so.

Bareboat Cruise

For all practical purposes, a bareboat is the charterer's own yacht, a vehicle of freedom. The boat is easy to sail shorthanded. Inside, it is apt to be cosy and comfortable. One does not have to contend with a crew, who, no matter how friendly, are strangers. A bareboat leaves the charterer free to explore and experiment, and match his skills against the elements.

All about Gulets

Yachts are classified according to their rigs in the tradition of seamanship: schooners, sloops, ketches and others. A *gulet* was actually a schooner with a rounded stern. Turkish yachting agencies applied the term to any boat whose rounded rump resembled a *gulet*. In the last few years, owners began building yachts with transom sterns, *aynakıç* (mirror ass), which gave them more room below decks to squeeze more cabins into. The term *gulet* then expanded to describe yachts of any shape, except the smaller, double-ended triandils. A *gulet* in the strict sense is considered superior to the *aynakıç* because it has to have more overall length per cabin. Secondly – and perhaps this is the most important – in the farthest astern of the deck, there is a small aftcastle embellished with soft mattresses and cushions in the shade of the awnings, known as a "pigeon nest." To many connoisseurs, the essence of a Blue Voyage is enjoying the journey lying on the pigeon's nest. Since almost all meals are taken in the open air, too, a *gulet's* wide deckspace is a welcome comfort.

Chartering with Crew

Wooden charter yachts with crew vary in size from 33 feet (10 metres) to 83 feet (25 metres). They have from a single to eight, even ten, double cabins, sometimes with upper bunks. The interiors are generally decorated with massive wood and make a pleasant bedroom. Lockers and drawers solve the problem of storage in the cabins. Lighting is usually natural with sunlight flowing in from the portholes. A proper wooden yacht carries no less than 2.5 tons of freshwater, at least five times more than a bareboat. That means the voyagers can often have two showers a day – a blessing in hot weather and salty seas – virtually impossible to have on a bareboat. Heated pressurized water is almost a standard item on *gulets*.

Crews, according to the size of the boat, vary from two to four. They do all the work, including preparing the meals. However, many captains are willing to allow an eager guest to play with the ropes and lines, steer the boat or enter the galley and mess it up in the name of cooking a "special."

Pastimes in an anchored *gulet* include skin diving, fishing, windsurfing, rowing, or motoring in a dinghy; at additional cost possibly water skiing or waterbiking – though the agency should be well forewarned to provide these. A *tavla* (backgammon) tournament is a must on a *gulet*. Consumption of food and beverages increases by half during a Blue Voyage, but with hardly any effect on dieting ladies.

Blue Voyagers must hike. Taking to the densely vegetated hilltops to discover invariably some ruin in every anchorage is a joy. The backdrop of an embroidered coastline, the azure sea, the clear blue sky, make it a perfect setting for photography. Afterwards, it is possible to lie in the back of the *gulet*, eating sandwiches and drinking tea from tulip-shaped glasses. The Blue Voyage is the ultimate experience in relaxation that the visitor to the Turkish Coast should take at least once.

Yacht Chartering

The following travel agencies specialize in yacht chartering on the Turkish Coast. The single asterisk denotes that the company is a major bareboat agency:

ANTALYA

Air Tour, Kızılsaray Mahallesi, 79 Sokak, Emin Apart. 9/A, tel: (242) 248 3422.
Akay Travel, Cumhuriyet Caddesi 54, tel: (242) 243 1700.

Fantazi Marine Centre, Esentepe, Göynük (between Kemer and Beldibi on the main road), tel: (242) 815 1833.
Maki Tur, Tuzcular Mahallesi, Uzun Çarşı Caddesi 16/B, Kaleiçi, tel: (242) 243 1402.
Pamfilya, 30 (Otuz) Ağustos Caddesi 57/B, tel: (242) 243 1500.
Rosemary's Yacht Charter, Kemer Marina, Kemer, tel: (242) 814 3404.
Setur, Fevzi Çakmar Caddesi 12/5, tel: (242) 241 6938.
Tantur, Atatürk Caddesi 31, Ulusoy Işhanı, tel: (242) 426 2530.

BODRUM

Aegean Yacht Services, Paşatarlası Caddesi 21, tel: (252) 316 1517.
Bodrum Pruva Yachting, Neyzen Tevfik Caddesi 48/B, tel: (252) 316 0443.
Era Tour, Neyzen Tevfik Caddesi 160/A, tel: (252) 316 2054.
Fora Yachting, Neyzen Tevfik Caddesi 220, tel: (252) 316 3046.
Giz Yacht Services, Neyzen Tevfik Caddesi 230/A, tel: (252) 316 8799.
Nautilus, Neyzen Tevfik Caddesi 224/A, tel: (252) 316 6835.
Pupa Yachting, Firkateyn Sokak 19, tel: (252) 316 2398.
Uncle Sun, Ondört Evler Sitesi 4, Sanayi Sitesi Yanı, tel: (252) 316 2659/316 5501.

MARMARIS

Ekin Tour, Iskele Meydanı (at the Harbour Square), tel: (252) 412 2552.
Gino Tour, Netsel Marina, tel: (252) 412 0676/412 5220.
Mengi Yachting, Hacı Sabri Sokak 7/A, tel: (252) 412 1307.
Setur, Barbaros Caddesi 87, tel: (252) 412 4608.
Venüs Yachting, Talatpaşa Sokak, Demirtaş Apt. 24, tel: (252) 412 8535.
Yeşil Marmaris Tourism, Barbaros Caddesi 11, tel: (252) 412 2290.
Yüksel Yachting, Netsel Marina, tel: (252) 412 1016.

FETHIYE

Alesta Yachting and Travel Agency, across from the Marina, Korbey Apartment 21, tel: (252) 612 2367.
Lama Tours, Hamam Sokak 3/A, tel: (252) 614 4964.
Light Tours, Atatürk Caddesi 104, tel: (252) 614 4757.

Simena Travel, Atatürk Caddesi, PTT Santral Sokak, Urantaş Sitesi, tel: (252) 614 4957.

Yacht Maintenance

ANTALYA

Setur Marina, Commercial Dockyard, Free Trade Zone, tel: (242) 229 1494.
Turban Marina, Kaleiçi, Customs Building, Yacht Harbour, tel: (242) 243 4750.

BODRUM

Agantur, Içmeler Mevkii, tel: (252) 316 1708.
Canel Ticaret, Cevat Şakir Caddesi 48/A, tel: (252) 316 1650.
Nautilus, Neyzen Tevfik Caddesi 224/A, tel: (252) 316 6835.
Yat Lift, Içmeler Mevkii, tel: (252) 316 7842.

MARMARIS

Netsel Marina, Harbour, tel: (252) 412 2708.

Watersports

In addition to yachting and sailing, windsurfing, scuba diving, sea biking, para-sailing and banana boat riding are extremely popular all along the Turkish Coast. Bodrum's Gümbet Beach is already renowned as one of the world's leading windsurf centres, competing with places like Maui of the Hawaiian Islands.

Below is a list of Turkish companies involved in watersports along the Bodrum-Fethiye region:

BODRUM

Ayaz Watersports, Gümbet Beach.
Bitez Surf School, Bitez Village, about 6 miles (10kms) from Bodrum Town.
Club Ersan, Içmeler.
Zulu Turizm, Güvercinlik Village, about 12 miles (20kms) from Bodrum Town.

Scuba Diving

Scuba diving is becoming popular all along the Turkish Coast, where numerous sunken cities and marine life abound. But Bodrum has always been the centre of Turkey's scuba diving because of its sponge divers and underwater archaeologists. Scuba diving schools exist in Bodrum, Marmaris, Fethiye and Çeşme. An authorized local diving guide must accompany foreign divers at all times. Diving is permitted only in certain areas. It is strictly forbidden to dive where there are ancient shipwrecks, which are protected by as national treasures. Anyone diving in these areas without a permit may land himself in jail. Local diving guides must be either PADI or CMAS certified and have a Turkish diving licence (*Balık Adamı Belgesi*). Following is a list of scuba diving centres.

BODRUM

Aegean Pro Dive Centre, Neyzen Tevfik Caddesi 174/C, tel: (252) 316 0737.
Aquamarine, Neyzen Tevfik Caddesi 214, tel: (252) 313 5933.
Aşkın Diving, Paşa Tarlası Caddesi 11, tel: (252) 316 4247/316 9703.
Motif, Neyzen Tevfik Caddesi 48, tel: (252) 316 6252.

MARMARIS

Aquavision, Ulusal Egemenlik Caddesi 36/2, tel: (252) 413 4811.
European Diving Centre, Marina, Içmeler, near Marmaris, tel: (252) 455 4733.
Fey Diving Centre, Kenan Evren Bulvarı, next door to Turban Holiday Village, tel: (252) 412 5681.
Professional Diving Centre, Sarıalan Mahallesi, Dördüncü Sokak 19/12, tel: (252) 412 9989.
Scuba Diving Centre, tel: (252) 455 3781.

FETHIYE

Diver's Delight, Atatürk Caddesi 38, tel: (252) 612 1099.
European Diving Centre, the Harbour, tel: (252) 614 9771.
German Diving Centre, Çalış Beach, near Fethiye city, tel: (252) 613 3113.
Marin Diving Centre, Atatürk Caddesi 36, 2nd floor, tel: (252) 614 9788.

ALANYA

Active Divers, Iskele Caddesi 80, tel: (242) 512 8811.

KAS

Barracuda, based at Hotel La Villa, tel: (242) 836 2144.
Lykia Diving Club, based at Hotel Lykia, tel: (242) 836 1270.

Between August and March one can hunt ibex, bear, roe deer, wolf, coyote and wild boar on the Turkish Coast.

The ibex, an agile, wild mountain goat with stupendous upturned horns, is found in Antalya in the Cevizli Gidengelmez Mountains, in the Pozantı-Karafil and Demirkazık Mountains in Adana, in Cehenemderesi around Mersin and Tarsus, and in the Mut-Mersin Kestel Mountains. Ibex and roe deer are also found in Arsuz, in the Hatay area.

All animals must be hunted in designated hunting areas determined by the Forestry Management Department (*Orman Isletme Müdürlügü*).

Wild boar, wolf and coyote may be hunted all year round in specific areas.

Obtain a hunting permit (*Özel Avlandırma Izin Belgesi*) from a travel agency before coming to Turkey.

A fee of $50 is charged for each day of hunting. It is illegal to kill animals that one can't carry. It is also illegal to hunt by means of traps, lights or poisons.

The hunting season for henna partridges, sand partridges, sand grouses and rabbits is between October 7 and December 31. In order to guarantee a standard level of hunting, all hunters are required to be members of internationally-recognized hunting organizations.

A list of travel agents organizing hunting tours can be obtained from the Union of Turkish Travel Agencies (TURSAB):
TURSAB Antalya, Barbaros Mahellesi, Kandiller Geçidi Sokak 8, Kaleiçi, Antalya, tel: (242) 243 1996.
TURSAB Izmir, Maraton Turizm, 1462 Sokak 48, Alsancak, Izmir, tel: (232) 464 0347.
Pamfilya is one of the well-known tourism companies which organizes hunting tours:
Pamfilya Tourism, 30 (Otuz) Ağustos Caddesi 57/B, Antalya, tel: (242) 243 1500.
Also contact: **Avcılar Derneği** (Hunter's Association), Ismetpafla Caddesi, Kilit Işhanı, Antalya, tel: (242) 241 7626.

Off-road driving is becoming more and more popular in Turkey. Various vehicles can be hired throughout the area, particuarly in Bodrum:

Bodrum

Botur, Cevat Şakir Caddesi, opposite Shell Station, tel: (252) 316 8815. Motorbike and moped rentals.
Highland Jeep Adventures, tel: (252) 316 8924.
Minimoke, Neyzen Tevfik Caddesi 236/A, tel: (252) 316 8074. Jeep rentals.

Language

Travellers to the Turkish Coast will find many English, German and French speakers. Nevertheless some basics of the Turkish language may be needed. Turkish is a phonetic language. All words and letters are pronounced as they are written. There are several vowels and consonants in Turkish, such as c, that are pronounced differently than in English.

These are given in a list below, as well as their pronouncities.

c is pronounced like j as in jam.
ç (c cedilla) is pronounced like ch as in chicken.
ğ (soft g) is silent and lengthens the preceeding vowel.
ı (undotted i) is pronounced like a short e as in open.
i is pronounced like a long e as the first e in evening or i in ink.
ö (o umlaut) is pronounced like o umlaut in Köln in German or œu in French as in bœuf.
ş (s cedilla) is pronounced like sh as in shell.
u is pronounced like a double o (oo) as in book or rook.
ü (u umlaut) is pronounced like a round u as in the French word unite or für in German.

Useful Phrases

hello	merhaba
help	imdat
thank you	sağol
cheap	ucuz
expensive	pahalı
good night	iyi geceler
just a minute	bir dakika
good morning	merhaba
far	uzak
near	yakın
please	lütfen

Numbers

one	bir
two	iki
three	üç
four	dört
five	beş
six	altı
seven	yedi
eight	sekiz
nine	dokuz
10	on
11	on bir
12	on iki
13	on üç
14	on dört
15	on beş
16	on altı
17	on yedi
18	on sekiz
19	on dokuz
20	yirmi
21	yirmi bir
30	otuz
40	kırk
50	elli
60	altmış
70	yetmiş
80	seksen
90	doksan
100	yüz
101	yüz bir
200	iki yüz
1,000	bin
1,000,000	milyon

Hotel Terms

hotel	otel
room	oda
room price	oda fiyatı
bed	yatak
single bed	tek yatak
double bed	çift yataklı
bathroom	tuvalet
shower	duş
breakfast	kahvaltı
lunch	oğle yemeği
dinner	akşam yemeği

Further Reading

General

Antiquities Smuggling

Pearson, Kenneth, and Connor Patrica. *The Dorak Affair*, Michael Joseph, London, 1967.

Archaeology

Akurgal, Ekrem. *Ancient Civilizations and Ruins of Turkey*, Haşet Kitabevi, Istanbul, 1985.

Alkım, U. Bahadır. *Anatolia I*, Nagel Publishers, Geneva, 1968.

Aşkın, Mustafa. *Guide Book of Troy*, Galeri Troya, Çanakkale, 1981.

Bayhan, Suzan. *Priene, Miletus and Didyma*, trans. Anita Gillett, Keskin Color, Istanbul, 1989.

Bean, George E. *Aegean Turkey*, Ernest Benn Limited, London, 1979.

Bean, George E. *Lycian Turkey*, John Murray, London, 1989.

Bean, George E. *Turkey Beyond the Maeander*, Ernest Benn, London, 1980.

Bean, George E. *Turkey's Southern Shore*, Ernest Benn, London, 1979.

Blake, Everett C. & Edmonds, Anna G. *Biblical Sights in Turkey*, Redhouse Press, Istanbul, 4th ed., 1990.

Danışman, H.H. Günhan. *Archaeological Perspectives: Anatolian Archaeology in 1980's*, Redhouse Press, Istanbul, 1983.

Garsting, John. *Prehistoric Mersin: Yümüktepe in Southern Turkey*, Oxford, 1953.

Lloyd, Seton. *Early Highland Peoples of Anatolia*, Thames and Hudson, London, 1967.

Mellaart, James. *Earliest Civilizations of the Near East*, Thames and Hudson, London, 1965.

Metzger, Henri. *Anatolia II*, Nagel Publishers, Geneva, 1969.

Muller, Herbert. *The Uses of the Past*, Oxford University Press, Oxford, 1952.

Pamukkale (Hierapolis), Net Turistik Yayınları A.Ş, 1986.

Schliemann, Heinrich. *Ilios, The City and Country of the Trojans*, Harper & Brothers, New York, 1881.

Seyfert, Oskar. *Dictionary of Classical Antiquities*, Meridian Library, New York, 1956.

Toksöz, Cemil. *Ancient Cities of Lycia*, Toksöz Publications, Istanbul, 1988.

Umar, Bilge. *Trakya*, Akbank Kültür Yayını, Istanbul, 1978.

Biography

Kinross, Lord. *Atatürk: The Rebirth of a Nation*, K. Rustem & Brother, Nicosia, Northern Cyprus, 1981.

Tanju, Sadun. *Hacı Ömer Sabancı: The Turkish Village Boy who Built an Industrial Empire*, trans. Geoffrey Lewis, World of Information, Saffron, Walden, 1988.

The Crusades

Atiya, Aziz Suryal. *The Crusades in the Later Middle Ages*, Methuen & Co. Ltd., London, 1938.

Fedden, Robin and John Thomson. *Crusader Castles*, John Murray, London, 1957.

Gibbon, Edward. *History of the Decline and Fall of the Roman Empire*, Vol. 6; Phillips, Sampson and Co., Boston, 1851.

Krey, August C. *The First Crusade*, Princeton University Press, 1921.

Lamb, Harold. *The Crusades: Iron Men and Saints*, Thornton Butterworth Limited, London, 1931.

Lamb, Harold. *The Crusades: The Flame of Islam*, Thornton Butterworth Limited, London, 1931.

Müller-Wiener, Wolfgang. *Castles of the Crusaders*, McGraw-Hill Book Company, New York, 1966.

Art

Altun, A., Carswell, J., Öney, G. *Turkish Tiles and Ceramics*, Sadberk Hanım Museum Publications, Istanbul, 1991.

Bektaş, Cengiz. *Turkish Style*, London, 1992. (A finely illustrated book on Turkish architecture and decorative arts.)

Belge, Murat & Yerasimos, Stephane. *Turkey from the Air*, photos by Ara Güler, Thames & Hudson, London, 1993.

Ertuğ, Ahmet & Grabar, Prof. Oleg. *In Pursuit of Excellence: Works of Art from the Museum of Turkish and Islamic Arts*, 1993.

Freely, John. *Classical Turkey*, Penguin Books, London, 1991.

Güler, Ara. *Memories of Old Istanbul* (*Eski Istanbul Anıları*), Dünya Press, Istanbul, 1994. (A volume of moving black-white pictures of mid-20th century Turkish society by a master photographer.)

Küçükerman, Prof. Önder. *The Industrial Heritage of Costume Design in Turkey*, Istanbul, 1997.

Food

Arsel, Semahat. *Timeless Tastes: Turkish Culinary Culture*, Istanbul, 1996.

Ramazanoğlu, Gülseren. *Turkish Cooking*, Istanbul 1990.

Turkish Language

Lewis, Geoffrey. *Teach Yourself Turkish*, Hodder & Stoughton, London.

Fiction & Autobiography

Devrim, Shirin. *A Turkish Tapestry*, Quartet, London, 1994. (The story of the Shakir Pasha family, autobiography.)

Kemal, Yashar. *The Undying Grass*, Collins Harvill, London, 1989.

Kemal, Yashar. *The Sea-crossed Fisherman*, Collins Harvill, London, 1986.

Pamuk, Orhan. *The White Castle*, Faber & Faber, London, 1991.

Tekin, Latife. *Berji Kristin: Tales from the Garbare Hills*, Marion Boyers, London, 1996.

Classic Literature & Mythology

Aeschylus. "Agamemnon" in *The Complete Drama*, vol. 1, trans. Morshead, Random House, New York, 1938.

Bulfinch's Mythology, The Modern Library, New York, 1971.

Butcher, S.H. and Lang. A. *The Odyssey of Homer*, The Macmillan Company, London, 1911.

Euripides. "The Trojan Women" in *The Complete Greek Drama Vol. 1*, trans. Gilbert Murray, Random House, New York, 1938.

Hamilton, Edith. *Mythology*, Little Brown and Co., Boston, 1940.

Homer. *The Odyssey*, trans. E.V. Rieu, Penguin Books, Baltimore, 1946.

Kitto, H.D.F. *The Greeks*, Penguin Books, Harmondsworth, 1967.

Lang, Andrew. *The Iliad of Homer*, The Macmillan Company, London, 1911.

Lattimore, Richmond. *The Iliad of Homer*, University of Chicago Press, 1971.

Reinhold, Meyer. *Essentials of Greek and Roman Classics*, Barrons Educational Series Inc., 1946.

Virgil's Works, trans. J.W. Mackail, Modern Library, New York, 1934.

Sailing & Yachting

Heikell, Rod. *The Turquoise Coast of Turkey*, Net Turistik Yayınları A.Ş, Istanbul, 1988.

Reis, Piri. *Kitab-ı Bahriye: Volume I*, The Historical Research Foundation, Istanbul Research Centre, Istanbul, 1988.

Travels of St Paul

Blake, E.C. and A.G. Edmonds. *Biblical Sites in Turkey*, Redhouse Press, Istanbul, 1986.

Ramsay, W.M. *The Cities of St. Paul*, Baker Book House, Grand Rapdis, 1963.

Schillebeeckx, Edward. *Paul the Apostle*, Crossroad, New York, 1983.

The New English Bible, Oxford, 1970.

Turkish Carpets

Akatay & Schwartz. *Turkish Flat Weaves*, Scorpion, London, 1979.

Ayıldız, Uğur. *Contemporary Handmade Turkish Carpets*, Net Turizm Ticaret ve Sanayi A.Ş., Istanbul, 1982.

Thompson, David. *Magic of Carpets*, London, 1990.

Yetkin, Şerare. *Historical Turkish Carpets*, Türkiye Iş Bankası Cultural Publications, 1981.

Turkish History

Cook, M.A., ed. *A History of the Ottoman Empire to 1730*, Cambridge University Press, Cambridge, 1976.

Davison, Roderic. *Turkey: A Short History*, Huntington (UK), 2nd ed., 1988.

Lloyd, Seton. *Ancient Turkey: A Traveller's History*, British Museum Press, London, 1992.

Moorehead, Alan. *Gallipoli*, Harper and Brothers Publishers, New York, 1956.

Price, M. Phillips. *A History of Turkey from Empire to Republic*, George Allen and Unwin Ltd., London, 1968.

Shaw, Stanford J. *History of the Ottoman Empire*, Volume I, Cambridge University Press, Cambridge, 1987.

Shaw, Stanford J. and Ezel Kural Shaw. *History of the Ottoman Empire and Modern Turkey*, *Volume II*, Cambridge University Press. Cambridge, 1987.

Yasar Kemal's Novels

Anatolian Tales, trans. Thilda Kemal, Collins and Harvill Press, London.

Iron Earth, Copper Sky, Trans. Thilda Kemal, Collins and Harvill Press, London, 1989.

Memed, my Hawk, trans. Thilda Kemal, New York, 1961.

The Legend of the Thousand Bulls, trans. Thilda Kemal, Collins and Harvill Press, London, 1976.

They Burn the Thistles, trans. Margaret E. Platon, Collins and Harvill Press, London.

Other Insight Guides

Three distinctive series from Apa Publications are designed to meet your varying travel needs.

The 194-strong **Insight Guides** series, companions to this title, includes titles on *Turkey, Istanbul, Crete* and *The Greek Islands*.

The **Insight Compact Guide** series, which packs easily accessible information into a small format, together with carefully referenced pictures and maps, includes titles on *Turkey, The Turkish Coast and Rhodes* and *Crete*.

The **Insight Pocket Guides** series contain personal recommendations from local hosts and includes an invaluable full-size, fold-out map. Titles in this range include: *Istanbul, The Turkish Coast, Crete, Rhodes* and *Athens*.

347

Index

349

354

357